# FAITH AND MODERN THOUGHT

# FAITH AND MODERN THOUGHT

*The Modern Philosophers for Understanding Modern Theology*

Timothy Hull

CASCADE *Books* · Eugene, Oregon

FAITH AND MODERN THOUGHT
The Modern Philosophers for Understanding Modern Theology



Cascade Books
An Imprint of Wipf and Stock Publishers
199 W. 8th Ave., Suite 3
Eugene, OR 97401

www.wipfandstock.com

PAPERBACK ISBN: 978-1-4982-3675-1
HARDCOVER ISBN: 978-1-4982-3677-5
EBOOK ISBN: 978-1-4982-3676-8

*Cataloguing-in-Publication data:*

Names: Hull, Timothy, author.

Title: Faith and modern thought : the modern philosophers for understanding modern theology / Timothy Hull.

Description: Eugene, OR: Cascade Books, 2020 | Includes bibliographical references and index.

Identifiers: ISBN 978-1-4982-3675-1 (paperback) | ISBN 978-1-4982-3677-5 (hardcover) | ISBN 978-1-4982-3676-8 (ebook)

Subjects: LCSH: Christianity—Philosophy. | Faith and reason. | Philosophy and religion. | Kant, Immanuel, 1724–1804—Criticism and interpretation. | Hegel, Georg Wilhelm Friedrich, 1770–1831—Criticism and interpretation. | Theology, Doctrinal—History.

Classification: BR100 NUMBER 2020 (print) | BR100 (ebook)

Manufactured in the U.S.A. October 26, 2020

For Michelle
All you could wish for in a partner and friend

CONTENTS

# PREFACE

INITIALLY GETTING THIS BOOK written did not look hopeful. Having left school at sixteen with no academic qualifications to speak of, and crippled by dyslexia, writing a book was not the first thing that sprung to mind. Even after gaining the requisite academic qualifications and teaching theology for many years, this project was still going to be a major uphill struggle. Then add to those educational challenges a recent mental breakdown and the accompanying years of clinical depression, I wouldn't have put much money on the completion of this project. So what made the seemingly impossible possible? I have no doubt that the answer has been the gracious and very generous help and assistance of others.

Primarily this came from family. From my two daughters (and greatest friends) Rowan and Katy, and from a very supportive family of siblings, brother Martin (and his regular and encouraging phone calls of support even through the darkest of times) and sisters Rosemary, Alison, and Miriam.

The first person to read a chapter of this work and comment on it was my daughter Rowan, a model of critical honesty, encouragement, and good advice. The whole manuscript was then worked through by my friend Ian Dunn, with numerous corrections suggested and made. My son-in-law Gilly then worked hard on the chapter dealing with Hegel's philosophy, and showed what a polished document could look like. My sister Rosemary took on the mammoth job of working through the whole document again making numerous editorial suggestions that moved the manuscript from a spoken document (yes, it had all been dictated in voice recognition software) to one that resembled written prose. She also thankfully shortened the document greatly by getting rid of the hundreds of times I had said "as we have seen." I refer to this process as "Rose's magic!" Finally my sister Miriam and her husband Philip proofread and edited the parts on Immanuel Kant and Karl Barth. They are partly to blame for this whole project and my many years of teaching for it was largely their intellectual stimulation that got me thinking about theology and philosophy originally. It was almost worth writing the manuscript to get positive feedback from my brother-in-law Philip, one of the brightest people I know.

This is also a good opportunity to thank Doctor Graham Bell for getting me on the road to recovery so I could work again, and to Anthony Thistleton for his encouragement, support, and friendship which has meant so much to me over recent years. For the reading group that met at Christina Baxter's home and for all her prayers and support over the years and the reading group that met at Peter Cansfield home and for their fellowship.

I am also very thankful for all the encouragement and patience of the publishers, particularly that of Caleb Shupe and Robin Parry. In working on this project I clearly had no idea how long it would take to complete.

I have wrestled in this book long and hard trying to express clearly the thoughts of some of the greatest minds of the modern world. But the greatest challenge has been to think how I could fully and adequately express what my wife Michelle has meant to me through this whole process. I would probably need to compile another volume listing all the ways in which she has been appreciated. But without her selfless, sacrificial love, care, and companionship, this book (and I for that matter) would have never seen the light of day. "Love you lots."

# INTRODUCTION

## *Why You Are Utterly Lost without This Book*

### Answers without the Questions

It is impossible to understand modern theology without understanding modern thought. That's a bold statement, but thinking about it, it's an obvious one too. For the modern theologian the questions that need to be addressed are of course (in order to be modern) questions raised by modern thought. In my mathematics class at school I often felt like asking the teacher, "Miss, why don't you just give us the answers?" Why do we have to spend time understanding these difficult questions? It would make class so much shorter if you just gave us the answers and we can get back to our game of football and not spend the time having to understand the questions.

The teacher would, of course, have pointed out to me, "Tim, you would have no idea what the answers I gave you meant unless you understood the questions. In fact, knowing you, Tim, you would not even know which answer went with which question. For even to do that you need some understanding of the questions first."

It is just like that with modern theology. Unless you understand the questions that are raised by modern thought you will not understand the answers suggested by the modern theologians.

Now, I imagine most people will be happy with the logic so far, but it's the next step that can be uncomfortable. Almost by definition, or shall we say nine times out of ten, when exploring any aspect of modern thought, you will end up encountering some modern philosopher or some modern philosophy. So, without some idea of what has been going on in modern philosophy, modern theology may well feel like reading a lot of answers to questions you don't understand. (Which, however hard I tried, was always my experience in a maths class.)

## The Next Few Problems

For at least three reasons most books I have encountered are of little help here.

### *Irrelevant*

If, like most books written about philosophy, they are written by people who have little if any interest in faith, the author more often than not will not bother mentioning how the philosophers' ideas are of relevance to theology or to faith.

### *Incomprehensible*

When I first started theology and asked tutors what to read in order to understand the philosophy that the theologians had been referring to, or often just presupposing, the two books I was advised to read were honestly more trouble than they were worth.

They were so difficult to understand you needed another more basic introduction to understand the introduction you had been given to read (and that was not just my experience as I know other people far brighter then I will ever be who felt the same about the same books).

### *Too Much, Too Many, Too Briefly*

That might sound like a very strange thing to complain about. How can there be too much information in a book? Well, if you're trying to find your way around somewhere or something for the first time, too much detail can be just as annoying as too little. You need to know about the main landmarks to get some basic orientation about where you are and what's going on. You don't need huge amounts of detail.

To say something about every thinker who said anything of significance over the last three hundred years is very impressive, but when approaching any of this for the first time it is of little help for at least two reasons. Firstly, it means the big names only get one or two pages, which is of little use when understanding such significant thinkers. Secondly, with so much detail listing so many people, it is difficult to get a clear picture of what's going on, you just get a thumping headache.

## The Solution

### *Relevant for Theology*

If you're interested in understanding theology, then you are in the right place as there is often as much in this book about the relevant theologians as there is about the relevant philosophers. As soon as you have been introduced to the key ideas in a philosophy, we will explore how these become of such great importance in theology. We will also note how often religious concerns lie at the heart of so much modern (particularly continental) philosophy.

### *Comprehensible and Accessible*

I have constantly tried to illustrate philosophical ideas with the use of metaphors, stories, examples, and illustration. Interestingly many major works in modern philosophy are laced with metaphor and peppered with illustration. As one scholar has observed, "Evidently, Kant cannot make any of his key points without the help of metaphors,"[1] but for some odd reason these are rarely developed by introductory texts. I have made the very most of the philosopher's own metaphors, developing them for all their worth.[2] I have avoided whenever possible unnecessary technical language. I have sometimes introduced a philosopher's ideas over a longer narrative, to take the opportunity to see the relevance for theology of each idea before discussing the next. I will then often quote from the philosopher's own text or someone's expert analysis (so that you get to encounter the real thing). But my hope is that by then, with the help of illustration, example and metaphor, you will be able to grasp adequately what is quoted.

So, as the twentieth-century philosopher Ludwig Wittgenstein once said, I am wanting to make ideas *"as simple as possible but no simpler than that."*

1. Michalson, *Kant and the Problem of God*, 86.

2. Following Friedrich Schelling (1775–1854) and early romanticism metaphor was not mere ornamentation or illustration but might express what was inexpressible in purely conceptual or philosophical terms.

### *Only Big Names and Major Themes*

Rather than endless lists of different names and movements (and the accompanying bewilderment) we will look at only a few major names and key themes in modern philosophy. But these will be the names and themes that transformed modern thought (and therefore made it modern). I have then used these as an entry point to discuss some contrasting or related thinkers.

The philosophies discussed will not be read uncritically. There will be questions raised that have concerned theology about each philosophy.

### *A Focus on Faith*

The introduction to the key philosophers and philosophies has a purpose. The hope is that the introduction to these dominant philosophies will be a means to understand the essence of modern theology. So, the philosophers will be used as an interpretive key for unlocking theology. In order to demonstrate this we will engage in some fairly detailed study of the relevant theologies and theologians, so there will be three chapters on the most famous of modern theologians, Karl Barth, followed at the end by the most famous of contemporary theologians Jürgen Moltmann and his one-time colleague Wolfhart Pannenberg (and a number of other historical representatives).

If you are at all familiar with theology you will immediately ask the question, "Why just Protestant theologians?" Well, some Catholic thinkers will be mentioned, but to do justice to their thought would have involved another volume, so some difficult choices had to be made. Because I am more familiar with Protestant theology and because modern Protestant theology probably exemplifies what is modern (and the influence of modern philosophy) in a way that I think is easier to demonstrate than with Catholic theologians, Protestants were selected.

### *More Than an Introduction*

I would like to think that what follows is more than just an introduction. I'd like to think that it develops an interesting reading of some of the philosophers in question in their theological and historical context, that it might also introduce those familiar with this topic to some illuminating secondary material, and most of all that it develops some neglected metaphors in a fresh way.

## Where to Begin

We will begin with the origins of the modern world in the Enlightenment (and Scientific Revolution), examining its theological origins and implications. We will then concentrate particularly on the two colossi of continental philosophy, Immanuel Kant and Hegel.

We will see how their philosophies tried to hold together, on the one hand modernity with its new learning and values and on the other, Christian faith and its morality. We will explore something of the theological debate surrounding them in their own day and then how transformative their new philosophies become for theology over the last 200 years.

## What It's All About

When reading the introductory chapters of this book you might well lose the wood for the trees. For example, there is the risk that the stories I tell, and the key actors in those stories, might distract from getting an overall sense of an argument. Therefore, even though it is rather formal I am going to lay out the argument of the first few chapters in the next few pages. So, if you start getting lost in the detail of what follows, you can always return to this brief summary as a means of orientation.

### Two Cultural Crises

In order to understand the distinctive character of so much modern theology, we will be exploring the debate that has revolved around two philosophies, philosophies that can be traced back to the eighteenth century. The first to Immanuel Kant, the other to Hegel. (For some strange reason, in philosophical texts Hegel's first name is not used.)

In order to do this, we first need to understand at least two crises that European culture endured and were pivotal for the making of modernity. The first crisis resulted from the sixteenth-century European Reformation. The second from the eighteenth-century Enlightenment. Both crises were completely unintended.

The sixteenth-century reformers (Luther, Calvin, and co.) did not intend to leave Europe in tatters. They did not intend to fragment religion, politics, and culture, leading to interminable conflict. After the Reformation and the cultural crisis it caused, the age of reason which we call the Enlightenment (late seventeenth to early eighteenth) was originally intended to heal the first crisis and did not intend to create a second. Those concerned hoped it might resolve the cultural fragmentation caused by the Reformation. In fact, the age of reason itself (the Enlightenment) was to produce its own unintended conflicts and casualties.

Now why will we in the first few chapters be exploring these two unintended crises? The reason is that I am going to argue that Kant and Hegel's philosophy in two contrasting ways try to resolve the second predicament resulting from the Enlightenment.

### Healing the Wounds of Enlightenment

It is important to understand that we will not be seeing this second crisis (left by the Enlightenment) purely in terms of the normal suspects: the so-called conflict between faith and reason or religion and science. Rather, what was of particular concern for Kant and Hegel was another unintended consequence of the age of reason: that the mechanistic outlook of cause and effect that dominated scientific explanation in the eighteenth century (science at the time was called natural philosophy) was in turn threatening the Enlightenment's own ethical ideals and political aspirations.

Ironically the age of reason also betrayed its most successful child. That critical philosophy was beginning to call into question the underlying rationality and logic of science itself. So, when introducing the philosophy of Kant and Hegel we will see the ways in which they were seeking to heal these wounds left by the Enlightenment. Why do we need all this to understand modern theology? Because this reconciliation (by Kant and Hegel) was to largely define modern theology.

Now in this compressed form you might be struggling to follow the twists and turns, but at least you will know that the first two chapters are going somewhere (and are setting the stage for understanding modern theology). Therefore, if in doubt you can remind yourself of that direction by referring back to this scintillating introduction.

## The Content of Section 1

### *Motivation and Meaning*

Section 1 of Part 1 is all about motivation and meaning. I am going to argue against a ubiquitous misconception, that the Enlightenment was primarily about defining, defending, and reforming the faith and to begin with was not in any sense a secular assault upon it.

### *Method*

Section 2 of Part 1 starts by exploring method. What made the Enlightenment revolutionary was not its rejection of religion, but the method that was used in defining and defending it. Yet, as we will see, it was a method that may have held within it the seeds of its own demise and could be seen as ill-suited to defending the faith.

### *Material Content*

Section 2 of Part 1 ends by exploring the kind of world this new philosophy created. How this new world did not only prove problematic for faith but for the future of the Enlightenment itself. All of this will lead to outlining Kant and Hegel's solution to the problem bequeathed by the Enlightenment for philosophy and faith, which are explored in Part 2 and 3.

## Definitions before Diving In

It probably goes without saying that philosophy is infamous for its impenetrable terminology. Once we have become engaged in discussing the details of Immanuel Kant or Hegel's philosophy you may not believe what I'm about to say. However I say this with my hand on my heart that whenever possible I have gone out of my way to avoid technical terminology and when I have felt obliged to use it I've tried my best to explain it in words of one syllable.

There are, however, two philosophical terms that are almost impossible to avoid. Firstly, there is the word "metaphysics."

Metaphysics is literally what is *beyond physics*, in other words, something that transcends the physical world. Therefore, religious beliefs (like the existence of God or the existence of an eternal soul) are often seen as metaphysical beliefs.

Like many philosophical terms, examples for me are more helpful than concise definitions. So, here is an example: Possibly the most famous piece of classical metaphysics would be a belief that is associated with Plato's philosophy. Plato's metaphysical idea is that lying behind the physical world that we perceive through our senses is an everlasting blueprint (of super sensible forms or eternal ideas) that the physical world is based and modelled on. Because this eternal blueprint is the very basis of the physical world it is therefore not directly perceivable within the physical world of our senses and consequently this belief (in a heavenly blueprint) would be seen as a classic example of a metaphysical belief.

The other philosophical term that is very difficult to avoid is the word "epistemology." The best concise definition that is often used is that epistemology is the study of "How we know what we know." In other words, it is the study of how we come to have true beliefs about anything at all. So, a book on epistemology will discuss the different theories of how we acquire any form of knowledge. Therefore, epistemology refers to the discussion and debate about the origins, limits, and nature of human knowing.

# Part 1

# AN AGE OF REASON

*Its Dawn and Twilight*

# Section 1

## The Dawn of Enlightenment

# 1

# REFORMATION TO THE ENLIGHTENMENT

## Alien Reason

WHAT IS THE MOST far-fetched theory proposed by a modern scientist? In my opinion, it is the suggestion that life on Earth had come from outer space and therefore had alien origins. For me, this theory is so far-fetched that when I first encountered it I was convinced the person telling me was joking. The theory proposed by the astronomer Fred Hoyle is based on the idea that it was inconceivable for life to have evolved during the history of our planet and therefore life's origins must have been extraterrestrial, supposedly hitching a ride on an asteroid (it sounds to me like a perfect Disney World attraction).

The suggestion that life is alien to this planet and appeared as a bolt from the blue might not be a particularly popular theory, appearing too far-fetched for many. But there is a theory that appears to be very popular and that I for one just accepted during my education, which now strikes me as just as implausible as life appearing from beyond our terrestrial sphere. This is a belief about the appearance of something just as crucial, just as vital for life on planet Earth, just as transformative, but again, according to this theory, seemingly from out of nowhere. Something in fact that transformed our benighted hemisphere from a planet wrapped in deepest darkness to a world of illumination and liberty. For this is an account of the origins of our modern world, a world now teeming with technology and science, graced with every form of cultural and social liberation and every kind of political freedom and human self-expression.

The story goes that at some propitious point near the end of the seventeenth century (no one knows for sure exactly when) something completely new appeared. This was to produce a great cultural, social, and intellectual Enlightenment; the vanguard of modernity that took humanity from endless night into glorious day. Then the story continues to explain how everything great and good that we have experienced over the last three hundred years can be traced to that unique event. But if that wasn't incredible enough, on the standard account of this story, it all seems to have appeared from out of the blue. Indeed, it might as well have been from a different planet.

What was it that arrived in the midst of human history that began such a radical transformation? Well, it has been given different names: Enlightenment reason, freedom of thought, scientific rationality, critical judgement. There is even still to this day some debate about who exactly discovered it and applied it, producing such change in the human condition. Was it a Jewish lens grinder living in Amsterdam (Baruch Spinoza, 1632–77) or was it an English esoteric who failed to dodge some falling fruit (Sir Isaac Newton, 1642–1727). Even though there is some debate about when it was discovered and who discovered it, there is no doubt that what was discovered was to transform an unenlightened world into a new, fully illuminated one, banishing the darkness of prejudice and oppression.

It's difficult to find anything that the self-confessed secular humanist and the religious fundamentalist have in common. What is interesting, however, is that both the fundamentalist and the secularist adhere fervently to this common theory, that in the Enlightenment and the birth of the age of reason we are dealing with something never seen before, something novel, something discontinuous with and alien to what preceded it; our intellectual bolt from the celestial blue, making for the most unlikely of co-conspirators.

But why should the Enlightenment, the age of reason, and the origins of our modern world be seen in these terms? Probably because both the secular humanist and the religious fundamentalist are convinced that what we find in the Enlightenment's age of reason is a total antithesis to what had been there before. For what was there before was the dominance of the church, the prevalence of faith and its theological systems of thought, the very opposite of an age of reason, its veritable antithesis. There has to be a radical break from that to explain the dawning of our modern world. For what was to come was so different, so alien, when compared to what it preceded.

## Nothing Comes from Nothing

As common as this story is, and even though it is propagated by both the intellectual right and left, it's historically highly implausible. Historians abhor a lack of explanatory antecedent almost as much as nature abhors a vacuum.

Historians do not believe in creation *ex nihilo* (out of nothing). Historians understandably believe that what's happening now can be explained by what happened before. If they didn't they would be out of a job. But the only explanatory antecedent prior to an age of reason was an age of faith.

Apart from being in principle implausible, our common theory also makes little sense of the facts. We are therefore left with an interesting dilemma. If the Enlightenment was not a creation out of nothing, an alien visitation, a bolt from the intellectual blue, it means that the secular must have come from the sacred, that humanism came from divinity, that an age of reason was born from an age of faith, that critical reason came from the very religious culture we are told it eventually threatened. And I assure you that there are no end of studies that are making this very point and we are going to examine a few prime examples.

In fact, if you get nothing else from this volume, it's worth remembering the simple fact that our modern world had its roots in a religious one (there was little else before that it could have had its roots in).

However, this raises many questions: How can religious faith be seen as the origins of the Enlightenment? Why would the church be advocating an age of reason? How could the sacred give birth to the secular? Why would religion want to elevate reason? Why would faith want to promote science? How could faith have given birth to our modern world?

## Erase All Tradition: Martin Luther

I believe the Enlightenment had its theological origins in the actions of an Augustinian monk teaching biblical studies at the beginning of the sixteenth century. The simple action for which he was responsible shook Christendom to its core. It can be seen quite clearly, in a request which this teacher, Martin Luther, made to the printer of student resources at Wittenberg University, where Luther taught.

Up to that point the biblical text that the students studied had been printed in the middle of a page taking up surprisingly little space. Around it, surrounding it on all sides, enveloping the biblical text right up to the margins, was tradition. These notes explained how to interpret the text, as traditionally understood by the church, and the authorities of the past (a basic Internet search will give you many fascinating examples of this; they are worth looking at because they make the point quite powerfully). It was therefore impossible to encounter the biblical text alone, without the interpretive tradition to guide you. Luther's simple request to the printer was for these traditions to be erased, to be wiped away, for the text not to be mediated in these terms but left for the students to decide the meaning for themselves.[1] As the philosopher Nicholas Wolterstorff explains, "For about a thousand years Western intellectuals had been schooled to consult the texts bequeathed them, when they found themselves in quandaries as to what to believe on matters of morality and religion, and more besides."[2] At the heart of tradition were the Christian Scriptures, but all the ancient authorities of the past were of use in terms of interpretation:

> If one assigned the proper priorities among the texts (with the Bible being preeminent), selected the right senses, used the appropriate strategies of interpretation, and made the right distinctions, a richly articulated body of truth would come to light. St.. Paul and Virgil, Aristotle and Augustine, would all be seen to fit together. Where once texts had appeared contradictory now, they would be seen as getting at different facets of the complex truth.[3]

I think it's fair to say that in that simple request and the simple act that followed, Luther was wiping away the intellectual and cultural unity of Christendom, eroding and erasing what held Europe together and had given it a basis for religious and political unity. Of course, Luther did not realize this at the time. That such a modest act could have such momentous repercussions. That such a simple act within a generation would leave Western Europe in tatters. That this would not only generate a radical diversity of religious interpretation but in the process facilitate the fragmentation of Western Christendom, culturally, intellectually, and then politically, fuelling religious conflict and being a significant factor in the so-called European wars of religion that tore Christendom apart. For where the word of God had been mediated through the church and its traditions surrounding the text, now, without that mediating structure and interpretive key, anyone was free to make up their own mind on how to interpret God's word, God's law.

It might seem obvious that there could be a conflict between what the text means and how the surrounding tradition interprets it, but that is because we are post-Luther, Luther's children, living in the wake of the Reformation. That is why we immediately think in those terms. Prior to the Reformation the church tradition surrounding the word of God and mediating it was simply seen as the amplification of the text, an outworking of it, something growing organically from it. For Scripture was seen as the first wave of church tradition and surrounding it was the second wave, but both waves were produced by the same body of Christ.

1. Harrison, *Bible, Protestantism*, 93.
2. Wolterstorff, *John Locke*, 2.
3. Wolterstorff, *John Locke*, 2.

So, prior to the Reformation, the established traditions of the church that had been built up over the centuries were seen as at one with its Scriptures. But the Reformation that Martin Luther set in motion would see a clear distinction between the two, Scripture and tradition, and rather than seeing them as one unified and unifying authority, they would be seen as competing authorities. (This of course was helped by the fact that Luther was drawing on the Renaissance Humanist study of the original biblical languages rather than the translation Jerome [347–420] had made into Latin.) Therefore, the reformers were wanting to peel back the layers of church tradition that had grown up round the Scriptures to reveal the original revelation and often demonstrating a conflict between the two.

## Critical Questions, Critical Judgments[4]

The emergence of competing authorities called for critical judgments to be made. Why follow one authority rather than another, which is genuine and authentic, which supersede? If the authority of the church and its traditions are no longer decisive, how should any of these disputed questions be adjudicated and how should any remaining authority be interpreted?

As the theologian Hyman sums up the situation, "The phenomenon of the pluralization of legitimacy gave rise to a situation in which the Western mind was awash with uncertainty. . . . Some common source of authority and procedure would have to be found that would not rest upon Catholic or Protestant criteria (in order to mediate between the Reformation divide). . . . Such a procedure, if it could be found, would thus appeal to Protestants, Catholics . . . alike, cutting across these disagreements and resulting in a universal assent."[5]

## "The . . . Light, which Lighted Every Man"

At this stage, it's worth examining a couple of examples of how this argument has been developed. Examples that firmly root the origins of the Enlightenment within the Christian theology of a post-Reformation Church. Firstly, the church of mainland Europe, then the church in England. In a remarkable volume entitled the *Soul of Doubt*, Erdozain Dominic argues that the beginning of a critical rationality (the roots of the age of reason) was

4. To explore the radical implications of the Reformation, see Gregory, *Unintended Reformation*.

5. Hyman, *Short History of Atheism*, 24.

forged in this context of controversy following Luther and the Reformation. On this account, the rationalism of the Enlightenment was not something that developed as an external assault on religious belief but can be seen as emerging from the heart of religious conviction, from the soul of faith.

It can be heard primarily as a Christian outcry at the deeply un-Christian nature of persecution that was practised by all sides after the Reformation. As Erdozain Dominic argues, "The foundations of the Enlightenment . . . were established by men of intense but bruised Christian convictions."[6] He therefore claims that modernity can be "characterized by the internalization of religious ideas, not their disintegration" and that this began with what he calls a "kind of spiritual rationalism."[7] He traces this to the radical theology of Sebastian Franck (1499–1543) and Sebastian Castellio (1515–63), two members of what has become known as the radical Reformation. This radical Reformation being a "third force" in the "struggle between Catholic and Protestant that slowly moved from theology to an independent . . . doctrine of reason, grounded in . . . conscience."[8]

Both Franck and Castellio had originally worked closely with Luther and Calvin respectively. The story of Castellio and his lifelong abhorrence of religious persecution is particularly relevant in terms of the roots of Enlightenment rationalism. Castellio had been appalled by the persecution the Catholic Church had inflicted on Protestants in his native France and as a consequence converted to the Protestant Evangelical faith, moving then to John Calvin's (1509–64) Geneva. Castellio so impressed Calvin that he appointed Castellio to be rector of a college for training pastors. But it was not long before Castellio became disillusioned with what he experienced in Calvin's Geneva, voluntarily leaving his post and then Geneva itself.

What confirmed Castellios misgivings was the news he then received from Geneva that Calvin had handed someone over to the civil authorities for execution on the charge of heresy. It was therefore this experience of persecution that was to move Castellio to reconsider his theology. As Erdozain Dominic explains, "The role of the high priest of biblical scholarship (Calvin) in the cruel demise of a fellow Protestant raised grave questions about religious knowledge.[9] So for Castellio, "The need for a firmer criterion of truth was increasingly apparent."[10] This was to move Castellio from a "piercing plea for toleration to a cautious appeal for doubt, reason,

6. Erdozain, *Soul of Doubt*, 7.

7. Erdozain, *Soul of Doubt*, 6.

8. Erdozain, *Soul of Doubt*, 34.

9. Erdozain, *Soul of Doubt*, 58.

10. Erdozain, *Soul of Doubt*, 62.

and undogmatic faith."[11] In this process, "Castellio retained a fervent faith in God and an undying esteem for the Bible, but the axis of his piety broke away from any kind of dogmatic orthodoxy."[12]

Castellio began one of his works with a poignant analogy of the predicament the church was facing after Luther's Reformation. Not knowing with certainty which authority to follow and on what to build the faith, "Castellio humbly stepped forward with a solution. Reason would provide a line of rescue, but only for those willing to lay down the weapons of combat . . . the explicit conviction that only an untainted, pre-theological force could stand up to the violence of dogma."[13] So, "Reason pressed its case not as intellectual presumption but as shelter."[14]

For Castellio this was not an appeal to the secular to settle a sacred dispute. Neither was it a move away from his faith to something distinctly alien. Castellio believed this was the reorientation of Faith back to a fundamental. For Castellio this was an appeal to the "logos" of God (this Greek word used in the Bible has a number of meanings including that of "reason") which according to the Gospel of John had been there since the dawn of creation and "was the true Light, which lighted every man that cometh into the world . . . full of grace and truth."[15]

Castellio penned what has become known as his "Hymn to Reason" and in it suggested the incarnation of the Logos "was no interruption of this ancient fabric of divine rationality. Christ embodied what was already there."[16]

In his article "A Heavenly Poise: Radical Religion and the Making of the Enlightenment," Dominic explains that "reason," Castellio concluded, "is a sort of eternal word of God, much older and surer than letters and ceremonies."[17] So Castellio's rationalism was a " profoundly spiritual rationalism."[18]

Starting with Luther's Reformation, Dominic documents the case that the elevation of reason in adjudicating religious disputes was a precursor to Enlightenment rationalism. "To engage the Christian underworld of the radical Reformation is to discover striking prototypes of ideas considered

11. Erdozain, *Soul of Doubt*, 62.
12. Erdozain, *Soul of Doubt*, 63.
13. Erdozain, *Soul of Doubt*, 64, 48.
14. Erdozain, *Soul of Doubt*, 4.
15. John 1:9 (KJV).
16. Erdozain, *Soul of Doubt*, 65.
17. See Castellio, *Concerning Heretics*, in Erdozain, "Heavenly Poise," 78.
18. Erdozain, *Soul of Doubt*, 66.

'fully secular' and resolutely 'natural' in [philosophers associated with the origins of the European Enlightenment like] Spinoza and Bayle."[19]

## The Sovereignty of Reason

In an equally fascinating study, *The Sovereignty of Reason: The Defence of Rationality in the Early English Enlightenment*, the intellectual historian and philosopher Frederick C. Beiser makes a very similar case for the prioritizing of reason in the seventeenth-century church in England. The appeal to rationality, Beiser argues, was again due to the problem of competing authorities within the turbulent life of a post Reformation Church. "Luther's break with the Roman Catholic Church raised the general question of the criterion of religious knowledge. How, amid all the conflicting claims of the competing sects and churches, do I know the true faith? Should I defer to Church tradition, as the Roman Catholics demand? Should I rely upon Scripture alone, as the Protestants insist? Or should I follow the inspiration of the Spirit?"[20]

It was within this context of post-Reformation debate that Anglican theologians would begin prioritizing reason as a means of coping with its many challengers.

> If we wish to understand the origins of the rationalism of the English Church, then we have to look closely at its early debates with its rivals, the radical Puritans, the Roman Catholics, and the enthusiasts. A large part of the explanation for the Church's rationalism is simply the pressure of polemics. Reason proved to be the most effective weapon for the Church to establish its authority and Legitimacy against its many enemies. It was reason that undermined the apostolic tradition of the Roman Catholics, that exposed the pretensions to inspiration of the enthusiasts, and that undercut the biblicism of the radical Puritans.[21]

The case again is not that a critical rationality (say in the form of philosophy or science) was putting external pressure on the church and its beliefs. Rather reason was seen as a constructive resource for theology and had always been there within the Christian tradition. This was not a critical invasion of the secular into the sacred; the appeal to reason was coming very naturally from within theology itself.

19. Erdozain, *Soul of Doubt*, 77.
20. Beiser, *Sovereignty of Reason*, 5.
21. Beiser, *Sovereignty of Reason*, 10

> Rationalism did not arise from the new natural philosophy extending its domain into the sacred sphere, or from the spread of freethinking and materialism. Rather, the authority of reason grew because it combated the Church's many enemies, justified its constitution, and provided a guide to salvation. Indeed, most of the leading seventeenth-century rationalists were clerics. . . . The English rationalists of the seventeenth century were anything but "secular priests" or "religious pagans." Rather, most of them were zealous clerics, faithful divines of the Church of England. Although they affirmed the principle of the sovereignty of reason, they did so not to attack but to defend their faith and Church. They did not use reason to transform their Christian legacy because they never broke with it in the first place.[22]

Beiser sees the beginnings of this tendency within the Church of England in the English theologian Richard Hooker (1554–1600). He then charts this increasing prioritizing of rationality within the church and its theology in the seventeenth century. Many of the examples Beiser reviews are not famous names in the pantheon of Western thought but were important to the life of the Anglican Church.

## Richard Hooker

Hooker is considered by many as the most significant English theologian of the sixteenth century. When Hooker took up a post at what was the old St. Paul's Cathedral in London, he found himself mired in controversy, particularly disagreeing with a number of Puritans in London.

These Puritans not only saw the Scriptures as dictating the nature of faith but also the ordering of church and society. Hooker believed in contrast that reason had an important part to play in these debates. Hooker was to write about the ordering of the church in terms of Scripture, tradition, and reason in his landmark work "Of the Lawes of Ecclesiastical Politie." In his study of the rise of reason in seventeenth-century theology Beiser goes so far as to say,

> If there is any single point that must be chosen as the beginning of the English Enlightenment, as the first glimmering of its dawn, then that would have to be the publication in 1593 of the first four books of Richard Hooker's *Of the Lawes of Ecclesiastical Politie*. The importance of the Lawes for the development of the early Enlightenment consists in its defense of the powers

22. Beiser, *Sovereignty of Reason*, 14.

> of reason. . . . If Hooker's Lawes marks the birth of the English Enlightenment, then his dispute with the Puritans represents its birth pangs, its first battle and proving ground. There was no more fateful controversy for the inception of the English Enlightenment. For it was during this dispute that Hooker made his influential defense of reason against the biblicism of the more radical Puritans. Reason thus received its credentials, its imprimatur, from the Church itself.[23]

Even though Beiser might be getting somewhat carried away in making this point, there is little doubt that the theologians and philosophers who followed Hooker, would appeal to Hooker's theology as justifying their turn to reason in defining and defending the faith. For example, the Enlightenment philosopher John Locke quotes Richard Hooker repeatedly to theologically justify his own prioritizing of reason in theology. Reason is not seen by Hooker as contrary to faith or as some opposing secular force, as is so common today. Reason for Hooker is the logos (word) of God:

> It is just false that Scripture is the only source of God's laws. There are other kinds of laws by which God makes his will known to us, and among these is the law of reason. Hence in acting according to our reason we obey God no less than if we were to follow Scripture (Hooker I, xvi, 5; II, ii, 2). Here again it is apparent how much of Hooker's defence of reason rests upon his belief in its divine origin and status. Only if reason has divine authority does Hooker think that it deserves to stand on a par with the revealed law of Scripture.[24]

The argument of "The sovereignty of reason" that started with Hooker's theology, is then developed and extended further in a number of forms of Anglican theology throughout the seventeenth century. These are not thinkers that are normally discussed in introductions to modern philosophy but the point I wish to emphasize is that the prioritizing of rationality came from *within the church itself* and that the Enlightenment did not have origins that were completely alien to it.

23. Beiser, *Sovereignty of Reason*, 46, 48.

24. Beiser, *Sovereignty of Reason*, 70.

# 2

# REASON RESCUES RELIGION

THE FIRST GROUP OF theologians that stressed the importance of reason for defining and defending the faith is a group that became known from the name of the location where they gathered. That being a manor house in the village of Great Tew in the Cotswolds hills of Oxfordshire.

As Beiser points out when comparing the theology of the Great Tew Circle with what we have seen of Richard Hooker's,

> their rationalism was much more explicit, emphatic, and general than his. They made the principle that we should examine all beliefs according to reason into a religious duty, indeed into the characteristic obligation of the Protestant. The liberty of the Christian to examine the Church according to Scripture became with them the liberty to examine all beliefs according to reason. They were therefore especially responsible for the later association of Protestantism with rationalism.[1]

Their main aim was not to undermine what had been revealed by God in the Christian Scriptures, rather they believed one needed to rely on a God-given reason to interpret, explain, order, and defend what is found in Scripture.

> Although all necessary articles of the faith had been laid down in Scripture, it was the task of reason to determine which of these articles are fundamental, and to make them simple, plain, and evident. The broad-Church policy of the Great Tew circle therefore made some very bold claims about the powers of

1. Beiser, *Sovereignty of Reason*, 86.

> reason: that it could determine the fundamental principles of the Church, and make them clear and credible to everyone.[2]

But why did they see reason as so important in defining and defending the faith? They believed that whatever you looked to as the authoritative source of your beliefs, reason will have been involved in that choice. So, if you are asked "Why did you choose that authority rather than another, as the basis of faith?" you will most likely give reasons for the preference. Therefore, reason, whether you like it or not, has become a deciding factor. This, they believed, was true for the Roman Catholic preference for tradition, the Protestant prioritizing of Scripture, and even those who would want to rely solely on religious experience.

> One of their main arguments on behalf of the sovereignty of reason is that we cannot avoid it, that we inevitably presuppose it. In other words, we ought to give supreme authority to reason for the simple reason that we must do so. The attempt to justify any kind of authority, they argue, will ultimately involve an appeal to reason. Thus the papist gives supremacy to the pope because he thinks that he has good reasons to give him more authority than Scripture or inspiration; and the enthusiast bestows sovereignty upon inspiration because he believes that he has better reasons to trust personal experience than the dictates of Scripture or the Church. So, whether they acknowledge it or not, the papist and the enthusiast covertly give more authority to reason than to the church or inspiration.[3]

## Reason and Moral Responsibility

As well as the growing sovereignty of reason was the corollary, that we are not bound by any authority but in the process of reasoning come to our own mind on important matters.

For the Enlightenment, one is intrinsically tied up with the other. Coming to your own mind on the basis of your own reasoning presupposes the freedom to do so. So according to the rise of reason, if you are determined in any way that is against your will, to make a decision or act in a particular way, then you have not made up your own mind. So, the bid for moral, religious, and intellectual freedom goes hand in hand with the rise of rationality.

2. Beiser, *Sovereignty of Reason*, 116.
3. Beiser, *Sovereignty of Reason*, 124.

> Hooker, the Great Tew men, [and a number of other seventeenth-century examples that are discussed] all insisted that to cease to inquire into the reasons for our beliefs is to forfeit our responsibility as moral agents. It is to allow someone else to think for us and so to govern us, when we should think for and govern ourselves. The great value of reason, then, is that it guarantees and indeed exercises, our moral responsibility.[4]

## The Captain of Your Soul

The ethicist and theologian Helmut Thielicke uses the example of steering a vessel at sea. Where prior to the Enlightenment we might be happy to sit within the boat of tradition and let those in authority stand at the helm, with the rise of the Enlightenment everyone will want to captain their own soul, navigate their own destiny. The implications of taking the helm are of course still with us today:

> To continue to condemn those who commit crimes simply in the name of authority, because we believe that they have somehow forfeited the moral responsibility to reflect upon the basis of their own actions. In this regard, then, we are still the heirs of the Enlightenment, and we have our debts to the early liberal divines of seventeenth century England. With justice, their portraits still adorn the dining halls of Cambridge and Oxford.[5]

## Making of the Modern Mind: The New Philosophy

Now the story we have been telling is, I believe, the context in which to best understand the philosophy of René Descartes (1596–1650) and John Locke (1632–1704), the two philosophers most famously associated with the dawn of the European Enlightenment and the beginnings of modern philosophy. For both develop their philosophies as a response to the intellectual and social crisis that appeared in the wake of the Reformation. Both used reason to defend, define, and reform the faith.

It is worth remembering that before Descartes dedicated himself to developing a philosophy of pure reason (in what are known as his *Philosophical Meditations*), he had witnessed firsthand the religious conflict that

4. Beiser, *Sovereignty of Reason*, 327.
5. Beiser, *Sovereignty of Reason*, 327.

was devastating continental Europe. For Descartes had played his part as a mercenary for hire between the warring parties on both sides. As the philosopher Gavin Hyman explains:

> When Descartes' Meditations were written, Europe was in a state of religious and political upheaval. The Reformation was less than a century old, and Christendom had not yet recovered from the resulting fracture. . . . In any attempt to find a peaceful way forward, the solution was not to be found in appeal to revelation, scriptures, and creeds. For these were the very things in dispute. . . . The challenge, therefore, was to develop a universal . . . method that would yield universal assent. Descartes' rationalist . . . [approach] . . . was an attempt to do precisely this.[6]

In this respect Descartes was so sure of what he could achieve with his new philosophy, that he could write with such modesty, "I say to you also that I do not fear that anything against the faith would be found in my [physics and metaphysics] for on the country I dare boast that faith has never been so strongly supported by human reason as it maybe if one follows my principles."[7] Additionally, he can conclude, "It is at least as certain that God, who is this perfect being, is or exists, as any demonstration of geometry can possibly be."[8]

> His meditations [on first Philosophy] were famously dedicated to the Faculty of Theology in Paris and, in his summary of its contents, Descartes gave the impression that it was a profoundly theological work, whose primary purpose was to ground belief in God and immortality of the soul on indubitable foundations, so that not even unbelievers would have any further grounds for their doubt. Descartes thus presented himself as a champion of theological orthodoxy and he would no doubt have been accepted as such by most of his contemporaries. Far from conceiving himself as inaugurating atheism, Descartes presents himself as its archenemy, upon which he will inflict a terminal defeat.[9]

The theologian Michael Buckley points out that this new rationalist philosophy that Descartes was to develop was not written in opposition to traditional theology but was *sanctioned* by it.

6. Hyman, *Atheism in Modern History*, 34.
7. Ariew, *Descartes and the Last Scholastics*, 148.
8. Hackett, *Resurrection of Theism*, 186.
9. Hyman, *Short History of Atheism*, 19.

> Theology itself has indicated that this is the way it should be. Philosophy did not come to this task simply on its own. Catholic theologians have assured the philosophers that the existence of God can be demonstrated from natural reason, and they founded this assertion on the Wisdom of Solomon and the first chapter of Romans. The thirteenth chapter of the Wisdom of Solomon offers not only an encouragement, but a pattern which the arguments of Descartes followed. . . . In the Epistle to the Romans he discovers confirmation of this conviction.[10]

As Descartes himself says "We seem to be instructed that all of those things which can be known about God, can be shown by reasons which we do not need to look for from any other source than our own mind."[11]

## The Closed Book

As far as Descartes is concerned, if he was to bequeath a logo for the age of Enlightenment, it would not be an image of an open book but of a closed one. One might imagine that, to symbolise the Enlightenment's fascination for human knowledge, an open book would be the obvious image for an age of reason. But for Descartes you first needed to close the book of tradition and start your thinking again from scratch.

Whereas up till then tradition had played an important part in coming to the truth of the matter, for Descartes his philosophy was to be an explicit rejection of the value of tradition. He would come to a basis for belief through a process of reasoning, predicated on doubting all you did not know with certainty. In the words that begin the first of Descartes's philosophical meditations, "Some years ago I was struck by the large number of falsehoods that I had accepted as true in my childhood, and by the highly doubtful nature of the whole edifice that I had subsequently based on them. I realized that it was necessary, once in the course of my life, to demolish everything completely and start again right from the foundations if I wanted to establish anything at all in the sciences that was stable and likely to last."[12]

There is much that is still very conventional and even classical in the nature of Descartes's philosophy, but in closing the book of tradition, Descartes is very modern. Where the unifying factor for the intellectual culture of the West had been its inherited tradition, both Christian and classical, reminiscent of Luther, Descartes is wanting to wipe the slate clean in order

10. Buckley. *At the Origins of Modern Atheism*, 76.
11. Buckley. *At the Origins of Modern Atheism*, 76.
12. Descartes, "Meditations on First Philosophy," sec. 17.

to start afresh. The whole process of wiping away received tradition was not a way of removing religious faith, it was a means of defending it and establishing it on better foundations that were more certain and secure. For as Descartes said, "I profess completely that there is nothing which pertains to religion which could not equally or ever with greater ease be explained through my principles rather than through those commonly received."[13]

In the light of this reading of Descartes's theological ambitions, it is not surprising that the theologian Michael Buckley, who has surveyed this period in some detail, can conclude. "It would be false to tax the Enlightenment with indifference to religion. It would be more discerning to say that it was obsessed with it. . . . [B]y and large the enlightenment . . . did not countenance atheism; it rejected it."[14]

But the main point Buckley wants to make is that "The Enlightenment gradually took over the discussion of the meaning and existence of God."[15]

## The Modern Mind: John Locke

In a contemporary study of our final example of this rise of reason, that being the philosophy of John Locke, its author, Nicholas Wolterstorff, states that in studying Locke's most significant philosophical work, *An Essay Concerning Human Understanding*, we are witnessing the making of the modern mind. "Locke was the great genius behind our modern ways of thinking of rationality and responsibility in beliefs. And Locke's vision became classic: for many, compelling; for some, contested; by no one, ignored. Locke, *on this issue*, is the father of modernity."[16]

This father of the English Enlightenment makes it abundantly clear why he began to work on his most important philosophical project. In an epistle to the reader that begins John Locke's *Essay Concerning Human Understanding*, he lets us into the reason he has been so concerned to pursue this project. It was not because of some disinterested curiosity into the extent of human knowing, rather he begins the work on this essay as a response to a particular theological crisis he was trying to resolve. Locke explains that he had met up with half a dozen of his friends in his rooms one day and they had become thoroughly entangled in a debate they had been unable to resolve. It also seemed to Locke as if frustratingly they were not making

13. Descartes, "Letter to Dinet," 7:581, in Buckley, *At the Origins of Modern Atheism*, 76.

14. Buckley, *At the Origins of Modern Atheism*, 37, 38.

15. Buckley, *At the Origins of Modern Atheism*, 67.

16. Wolterstorff, *John Locke and the Ethics of Belief*, xiv; emphasis original.

any real headway in addressing the questions, particularly in the terms they had been discussing them. Locke eventually comes to the realization that in order to make any real progress on these questions he needed to work on a more fundamental task. First, he needed to ask the more basic question: *given our human faculties, what kind of knowledge can we ever be expected to obtain?*

As Locke explains, "After we had a while puzzled ourselves, without coming any nearer a resolution of those doubts which perplexed us, it came into my thoughts that we took a wrong course; and that, before we set ourselves upon inquiries of that nature, it was necessary to examine our own abilities, and see what objects our understandings were, or were not, fitted to deal with."[17]

Now of course, it might help in understanding John Locke's major philosophical work, to know what the questions were that Locke and his friends were debating and which Locke's philosophical project was hoping to resolve. There is a way of finding out about this as we have another account of this famous meeting and also a clear recollection of what was being discussed. As a contemporary editor of Locke's essay explains, Locke's friend James Tyrrell was at the meeting in Locke's chamber; he reports that the topic was "the principles of morality and revealed religion."[18] So, "As Locke suggests . . . his aim in the Essay is to prepare his readers to conduct, with some hope of success . . . [this] . . . kind of ambitious inquiry that brought Locke and his friends to a standstill."[19]

So—what a surprise—the reason Locke is writing a philosophy that will be the making of the modern mind is largely to resolve a *theological* dispute. Its aim is to establish some firm philosophical parameters in order to rightly construct theology. But why does theology in Locke's day need this preparatory work to be done? We now know very well what had happened, for, as far as Locke and his contemporaries were concerned in their post-Reformation context, the old moorings of the faith had been found wanting. They had been experiencing in seventeenth-century England the same post-Reformation diversity and discord that Descartes had faced on the Continent.

The philosopher Nicholas Wolterstorff in his book *John Locke and the Ethics of Belief* sets the stage for John Locke's philosophy in terms that should be very familiar to us by now:

17. Locke, *Essay Concerning Human Understanding*, "Epistle to the Reader."
18. Winkler in Locke, *Essay Concerning Human Understanding*, 235.
19. Winkler in Locke, *Essay Concerning Human Understanding*, 235.

> For centuries European humanity had resolved its moral and religious quandaries by appealing to its intellectual inheritance—its tradition. By Locke's day and in Locke's place this tradition had split into warring fragments. Thus, on the cultural agenda there was the question: How should we form our beliefs on fundamental matters of religion and morality so as to live together in social harmony, when we can no longer appeal to a shared and unified tradition?[20]

## Religious Enlightenment

So, the great Enlightenment philosophies of Descartes and John Locke, at the dawn of our modern epoch, were both motivated by theological anxiety and were a response to addressing theological debate and doubt. The mother and father of the age of reason is therefore *religion*. This is not sounding very much like secular enlightenment to me, much more like a religious one.

Locke consequently developed a method, which he believed to be far more trustworthy than any authority from the past: rather than looking to tradition, we might be guided by a common human rationality. What is so distinctive and so modern about Locke's approach, however, is that this rationality is to be evidence-based and will be firmly rooted in experience.

## Militant Consequences

John Locke's modern philosophy not only arises from the context, of post-Reformation debate, it is also concerned with correcting unexamined, militant faith. A faith that he had encountered far too frequently:

> If anyone should a little catechize the greatest part of the partisans of most of the sects of the world, he would not find, concerning those matters they are so zealous for, that they have any opinions of their own: much less would he have reason to think, that they took them upon the examination of arguments, and appearance of probability. They are resolved to stick to a party that education or interest has engaged them in; and there, like the common soldiers of an army, show their courage and warmth, as their leaders direct, without ever examining, or so much as knowing the cause they contend for.[21]

20. Wolterstorff, *John Locke and the Ethics of Belief*, xiv.
21. Locke, *Essay Concerning Human Understanding*, 4.20.18.

As Wolterstorff explains,

> We can specify more precisely the crisis which Locke addressed. It, was not merely that the grand textual tradition was no longer perceived as presenting a unified body of wisdom on moral and religious matters. In their situation of fractured tradition, people were being schooled into becoming unreflective partisans of their own party and its particular tradition. They were being schooled into uncritical acceptance on the say so of the deliverances of the leaders of their own faction. Traditions had replaced tradition; the religious wars were a consequence.[22]

## Ending as He Began

What is so often unacknowledged, is the fact that John Locke's major philosophical work is in one sense just a very long prolegomena to what he was really wanting to settle, which was a lively theological debate with his friends. So, at the conclusion of his work, he returns to the question that fired his philosophical interest in the first place, that being the nature of revealed religion and morality, the focus interestingly being very much on the former. As Wolterstorff concludes,

> I remarked at the beginning of my exposition that the genesis of the Essay was a resolution Locke formed after perplexities that arose in a discussion among some friends and himself "about the principles of morality and revealed religion." Having described the . . . practice he recommends, Locke did not neglect to go back and indicate how it applied in these two areas; it was these areas which Locke always regarded as properly of the greatest "concernment" of every human being.[23]

If in this seminal philosophical text, we see the forging of the modern mind, and the foundry is an explicitly theological one. Here again we are not seeing the incursion of secular modernity into the sacred, we are seeing the birth of modernity from theological origins. In fact, if we put this most significant of philosophical texts in the setting of Locke's abiding interest as an author, the theological point is only reinforced.

His first published works were a number of pamphlets defending Anglican orthodoxy. One of his last published works before retirement was a text with a title that says it all, "The Reasonableness of Christianity." In

22. Wolterstorff, *John Locke and the Ethics of Belief*, 4.

23. Wolterstorff, *John Locke and the Ethics of Belief*, 118.

retirement he wrote commentaries on the apostle Paul's New Testament epistles and as he lay dying, he asked a friend to read to him Psalms from the Hebrew Scriptures.

Now I am not suggesting for one moment, that the father of the English Enlightenment and the maker of the modern mind was some kind of Christian fundamentalist; his sympathies were rather with a party in the Church of England known by the pithy title of Latitudinarians; an inclusive party in favor of a broad Church of England. What I am suggesting is that here again, reason is not understood in any of John Locke's works as some secularizing power or corrosive acid, intrinsically opposed to religious belief. Reason is being employed by the most influential of all English philosophers at the dawning of modernity as a means of demonstrating, in his words, the reasonableness of Christianity.

So, it does, in fact, seem to be possible to sing the praises of rationality without of necessity being opposed to faith; and that advocating reason might come from religious conviction; and finally, that Enlightenment philosophy may well be motivated by theological concerns. So hopefully this introduction has made it clear that just because the authors we have looked at are advocating the virtues of rationality it does not make them secular humanists and definitely not atheists of any stripe.

As Beiser again sums up our conclusion:

> Seventeenth-century rationalism was almost entirely religious. Rationalism did not arise from the new natural philosophy extending its domain into the sacred sphere, or from the spread of freethinking and materialism. Rather, the authority of reason grew because it combated the Church's many enemies, justified its constitution, and provided a guide to salvation. Indeed, most of the leading seventeenth-century rationalists were clerics, and even the dissenters . . . had religious motives for their rationalism.[24]

## Another Story

Even though I have repeatedly made the point (ad infinitum) that the age of Enlightenment reason was not an encroachment into Christendom, an invasion of secular science and rationality on to holy ground, that it was primarily advocated by the religious faithful in order to help resolve theological disputes, there is also another side of this story to tell.

24. Beiser, *Sovereignty of Reason*, 16.

It may be true that, as the seventeenth century drew to a close, reason was being heralded as savior of the faith, its ultimate definer and defender, amidst sectarian strife. But the philosophers who left the greatest impression on modern theology (our examples will largely be that of Kant [1724–1804] and Hegel [1770–1831]) were writing nearly a century later and saw things somewhat differently. For much had happened since the sovereignty of reason had been promoted for broadly theological reasons.

It is not as if Kant and Hegel were about to deny the story we have told so far. For them the rise of reason in the midst of sectarian conflict was undeniably a positive development. The aims of the Enlightenment inspired them, and it was in the wake of this age of reason that their philosophies were formulated. But they were also both very well aware that there was another side to this story that needed to be addressed. And as I will argue, an all-important way to understand their philosophies is in terms of the way they responded to this other story, which I will call the twilight of the Enlightenment.

# Section 2

## Twilight of Enlightenment

# 3

# TRUTH FROM ABOVE

## Philosophical Tourist

It is only after you have spent some time in a culture that is very different than your own that what is distinctive about your own culture is likely to fully strike you. It's at times like that when you will declare, "I had no idea how unusual that aspect of my culture was." I now want to attempt that in historical terms. I want us to build up a picture (it will take a few pages so please bear with me) of how classical philosophy largely thought about the process of acquiring knowledge and truth. That is before our modern world and its eighteenth-century Enlightenment. It is only then that what is distinctive about our modern view of knowledge and its acquisition is likely to hit home.

The founder of the modern mind John Locke wrote in the seventeenth century as if his readers were perfectly familiar with these premodern ideas. He often compared and contrasted his modern revolutionary proposal and the illustrative metaphors he used against this premodern understanding. But it's not just in order to put the modern mind in context that we are going to do some philosophical time travel. It will also help to see how narrow the modern mind became during the Enlightenment and how Kant and Hegel in very different ways sought to broaden it again until it resembled in some ways its premodern condition. It is this broadening of the modern mind by Kant and Hegel that will be so attractive to theology and then define its character as modern theology. So, let us enter the premodern mind for a few pages before we return to the making of the modern.

## It Just Dawned on Me

What is it like for something to dawn on you for the first time? You've gone through the frustrating period of trying to understand it for days now, but not getting anywhere. You don't know which way to turn. It feels as if you have been wandering aimlessly in the dark. It doesn't matter how often you think about it or how much you research it; you're still feeling none the wiser for all your efforts.

One morning you're lying in bed delaying as long as you can the effort of getting up, and your mind starts to think about it again and suddenly it dawns on you. There's a real breakthrough, what you haven't been able to understand for days now falls into place. All of a sudden, you're making sense of it, and in one leap you have moved from the darkness of not understanding to the light of knowing.

I'm sure I'm not alone in having this experience. I am keen on reading detective books and I am assured by their authors that detectives trying to solve a crime can, after weeks of thinking about a case, suddenly see, in a flash, what's going on and who's responsible. Some of the great discoveries of the past have also dawned on research scientists in that way. It even has a name: it's the Eureka moment. It mainly happens to me when thinking about something I've been reading (a book on philosophy or theology like this one) that I cannot make sense of, and then I suddenly get the picture of what's going on. I gather it even happens to artists, musicians, and authors who are looking for inspiration.

But the experience of something dawning on you is not the only thing that happens. I can then get caught up in what I've understood in the breakthrough I have experienced. I can get so engrossed in thinking about what it means and its implications and working out the idea fully and getting it down on paper that I can lose track of time. I can forget about things that are normally uppermost in my mind. I forget about, for example, food. Professors, scientists, composers, detectives, mathematicians, whoever is having the breakthrough can forget to eat, to comb their hair, to go to bed, or to contact their family. The revelation has become all consuming. It is as if the life of the mind, the intellectual breakthrough you have had suddenly becomes more important than the physical world around. (I must admit it never gets that extreme for me, the smell of what's cooking normally wins, but I gather it can be like that if you're a genius.)

## In Good Classical Company

Now if you have had that experience, firstly that something has dawned on you, and secondly, that you have been so absorbed by it and forgotten your next meal, you're in very good company. Two of the greatest minds in the past reflected philosophically and theologically about exactly that experience, Plato and Augustine.

The most famous analogy found in Plato's dialogues describes the experience of education or illumination as leaving a dark cave in which you live and coming out and being dazzled by the full light of day.

And the experience of working through lunch in order to fully grasp the insight you have had and the truth you have discovered always reminds me of Plato's words: "It isn't surprising that the ones who get to this point are unwilling to occupy themselves with human affairs and that their souls are always pressing upwards, eager to spend their time above, for, after all, this is surely what we'd expect, if indeed things fit the image I described."[1]

The life of the mind has transcended the carnal appetites and at that moment seems much more real, meaningful, and worthwhile. And that our sensual existence would feel pretty thin without it. I think Plato would have fully empathized with the scene depicted at the end of the film *The Imitation Game* (2014), where Alan Turing, the genius mathematician who has cracked the German enigma code, shortening the war by several years, is forced to take mind-numbing drugs because of his sexual orientation. When he realizes that he is no longer able to think straight, his bodily existence without the life of the mind and his beloved, math feels empty, pointless, worthless.

The example of mathematics works particularly well with Plato's philosophy. It may sound strange, but Plato believed that the world of mathematical equations (Plato also believed this was true of geometry and a number of other things) was in a way more permanent and stable than the world around us.

For example, 2 + 2 seem to equal 4 whatever happens in the world and however things change. It does not matter how many objects there are in the world and whatever they are, our arithmetic does not seem to be altered. There is a sense in which even if the world passed away 2 + 2 would still mathematically make 4. I'm not a mathematician, but I'm sure you can get the point. Plato may have been happier with ideas taken from geometry. For example, even if every triangular object disappeared and there was nothing resembling a triangle left anywhere in space and time, the eternal geometry

1. Plato, *Rep.* 7.100.1135.

of a true triangle would not be affected. The point is the same: there seems to be something permanent about these ideas that does not depend on the world around us for their existence in the mind.

If you want to get metaphysical (or ontological) about this—and I'm sure Plato did—in contemplating these things, you are, it seems, contemplating something everlasting, even eternal, something beyond change and decay, beyond time and space, a different dimension to reality than the one we experience with our senses

Plato did not only talk about this when it came to ultimate truths about reality (like math and geometry), he also believed that a similar idea was at work when we talk about the ideals of beauty and goodness. We seem to have a perfect ideal in mind when we say one thing is more beautiful than another and as ugly as things might get that ideal doesn't disappear, we can still recognize the beautiful. When we experience what is beautiful, whether it be music or art it's interesting that we can have a remarkably similar experience to the Eureka moment we began with. We can get so caught up in what is beautiful (music, art, poetry) that our carnal appetites seem insignificant and the beauty of what we are listening to, or contemplating, becomes of all importance and lo and behold we've missed lunch again.

## A Marriage Made in Heaven: Theology's Perfect Partner

To the first Christians who encountered Plato's philosophy, all of this sounded rather promising and something they felt they could work with, for these Platonists believe there was an eternal world compared to the change and decay we experience in the body, and part of us that can commune with what is everlasting.

I think in reading this next passage it is quite possible you might credit it to Plato. As you will see it talks about being freed from a cave and moving from darkness to light and fleeing "From things of sense."

> There is only one prescription I can give you. I know no other. You must entirely flee from things of sense. So long as we bear this body, we must beware lest our wings are hindered. . . . We need sound and perfect wings if we are to fly from this darkness to yonder light, which does not deign to manifest itself to men shut up in a cave unless they can escape, leaving sensible things broken and dissolved. When you achieve the condition of finding no delight at all in earthly things, in that moment, believe me, at that point of time, you will see what you desire.[2]

2. Augustine, *Solil.* 1.13.23, 38.

But in fact, this is just a sample of how Plato's philosophy was deeply resonate with Christianity. For this quote is from the other great mind who, along with Plato, probably shaped the nature of Western thought more than any other. These are the words of the fifth-century Christian theologian Saint Augustine (354–430).

There are many ways in which Saint Augustine as a theologian would question the Platonism that made such an impression on him, but there was still an underlying Platonism there for Augustine always ready to surface. For example, the vision of God that Saint Augustine glimpsed on a number of occasions clearly echoes Plato's illustration of leaving the material cave of sense experience and glimpsing the light of eternal truth. For example, in his vision of God, in Book 7 of his confessions, he writes, "Having been admonished by the Platonists' books to return into myself, I entered into my innermost self with you [God] as my guide. . . . I entered and with whatever sort of eye it is that my soul possesses, I saw above with that same eye of my soul an immutable light. . . . And shining intensely on me you shocked the weakness of my sight, and I trembled with love and awe . . . and there was absolutely no room left for doubt."[3]

As church historian Owen Chadwick explains, "Augustine cannot be understood at all if he is treated as some timeless figure out of relation to his age. . . .The intellectual climate of his time is dominated in philosophy by the . . . Platonism taught by Plotinus [205–70] at Rome in the middle years of the third century A.D. . . . At a crucial stage of his quest . . . Neoplatonic philosophy came to have a permanent lodging in his mind."[4] Therefore, in Peter Brown's words, "For Augustine . . . [the Platonists] . . . are grafted almost imperceptibly into his writings as the ever-present basis of his thought."[5]

For Saint Augustine, coming to know the truth was not primarily focused on our bodily senses, but was about the divine illumination of our minds; something that Augustine recognized Platonic philosophers had glimpsed. To this extent theology and philosophy seem to be on the same page; the highest form of knowledge for the philosopher and the theologian in this tradition look remarkably similar. For the Augustinian tradition faith is seeking this kind of understanding and is not at odds with it. The kind of opposition we hear about today with regard to faith and reason is quite foreign to this classical Christianity. As Thomas Williams, the scholar of medieval thought, writes, "The great medieval Christian thinkers would all have been bewildered by the idea, widespread in contemporary culture,

3. Augustine, *Conf.* 7.10.16, 123.

4. Chadwick, *Augustine of Hippo*, 3.

5. Brown, *Augustine of Hippo*, 86.

that faith and reason are fundamentally at odds. Though their philosophical outlooks varied widely, they were in general agreement that philosophical reasoning could and should be used to defend and elucidate the doctrines of the Christian faith."[6]

## The Mechanics of Illumination

Different stories are told about the origins of this rational illumination that we can experience. Plato seems to suggest that the way to explain our access to such truths of reason is that at some point we must have communed in the transcendent realm (perhaps in a previous heavenly existence that we should be doing all we can to return to). Therefore, for Plato, the innate reason and knowledge we seem to possess comes from recalling or remembering that prior learning. Augustine in contrast believed that this rational Illumination was something God supplied on a continual basis. As Saint Augustine writes in his confessions, "The mind needs to be enlightened by light from outside itself, so that it can participate in truth, because it is not itself the nature of truth. You will light my lamp, Lord."[7] The medieval theologian Thomas Aquinas also believed that our rationality had divine origins but that we were endowed with access to this resource from birth. The contrast between them has been illustrated in terms of the different ways we might access a water supply. Whereas Aquinas thinks that from birth we have been given a deep well of heavenly enlightenment we can draw on throughout our lives, for Augustine, we appear to experience a continual rain of illumination, a constant shower of enlightenment, in order for us to reason and understand rightly. However, within all these classical models we can see that intellectual enlightenment comes from above and is not seen in purely naturalistic terms.

As Robert Pasnau states plainly, "Divine illumination is the oldest and most influential alternative to naturalism in the areas of mind and knowledge. The doctrine holds that human beings require a special divine assistance in their ordinary cognitive activities."[8]

6. Williams, *Reason and Faith*, 4.
7. Augustine, *Confessions*, 4.15.25, 68.
8. Pasnau, "Divine Illumination," 1.

## Where Is All This Going

But how is this helping us to understand the eighteenth-century European Enlightenment and the origins of modern thought? Within the classical model of understanding we have been looking at, truth seems to be revealed from above, the very reason we can come to know anything is as a gift from above. A top-down approach to knowledge, revelation from above to below. This is reasoning and knowing as transcendent illumination.

This is a vision of knowledge that fits particularly well with faith, the idea that knowledge is the opening up of an eternal realm, a revealing of what's beyond. In these terms, theology and Platonism could be seen literally as a marriage made in heaven.

In knowing this other world we are given as Augustine said "wings . . . to fly from this darkness to yonder light."[9] In this way the heavens are open to us, we can see the light breaking through; we are taken out of our dark cave into heavenly day.

Even though much had changed in theology and philosophy since Augustine's Platonic vision of divine illumination, we can still find influential advocates of this basic Augustine/Platonic approach to knowledge immediately prior to the eighteenth-century Enlightenment in the aptly named Cambridge Platonists. A school of philosophy and theology active in Cambridge from about 1630 to 1680, its key representatives were fellows of Emmanuel and Christ's colleges in Cambridge. True to what we have said so far, they saw the highest kind of knowledge we can ever gain this side of eternity as a divine illumination. On the basis of this Platonic approach to knowledge they could see philosophy and theology as naturally enriching each other and faith and reason in heavenly harmony. "It was indeed the greatest attempt to reconcile the realms of reason and faith, philosophy and religion, in seventeenth-century England, . . . [for] . . . Cambridge Platonism laid the foundation for that 'holy alliance' between reason and faith, philosophy and religion, which dominated so much of English thought in the last half of the seventeenth century."[10]

## Explaining the Fundamental Mystery

Hopefully, what we've been looking at might explain a mystery. For us thinking of how faith and reason might mix can be like contemplating the blending of oil and water. For us faith and reason can seem to be intrinsically

9. Augustine, *Solil.* 1.13.23, 38.

10. Beiser, *Sovereignty of Reason*, 138.

different things. The modern mind seems to work with a fundamental divide with science and reason on one side, faith and belief on the other. But hopefully our rather lengthy discussion of Plato and Augustine will have clearly demonstrated that before the eighteenth century it was not at all uncommon to see faith and reason in harmony. If reason was primarily divine illumination no wonder theology could enthusiastically embrace reason and see it fit hand in glove with faith. But what we will eventually explore is the modern world's redefinition of reason, with its very different understanding of what reasoning is all about. But just a little excursion before then.

# 4

# BETWEEN TWO WORLDS

## How Modern Was Descartes's Modern Philosophy?

THERE IS CONTINUING DEBATE about how modern Descartes's modern philosophy really was. He makes much of the fact that he is wanting to philosophize afresh, without inheriting anything from the past in terms of preconceived ideas or beliefs. He talks in terms of demolishing the great building of inherited tradition and constructing everything completely from scratch on new foundations.

He goes through a tortured and drawn-out process of doubting in order to demonstrate what cannot be doubted. His final resting place, it has often been pointed out, is not God or divine revelation but *the human knowing subject* itself. For the only thing he believes he cannot doubt is that there must have been some cognitive subject that has been asking all these skeptical questions. In other words, he cannot doubt that something must have been doing all this doubting. So, at rock bottom he cannot doubt the existence of the doubter. In doing all this questioning he must have been thinking. Therefore, he knows at the very least he as a thinking thing must exist.

## The New Science

Descartes also saw his mission as incorporating the new natural philosophy (natural science) of the seventeenth century into his system of philosophy. The new science of the seventeenth century was turning away from classical interpretations of the natural order (an approach that could be traced back to Plato and Aristotle, and had been prevalent through much of the Middle Ages) and in stark contrast was developing a material science of nature, that as we know has since come to dominate our modern world.

For Plato, true knowledge was to be found in finding what was eternal and unchanging behind the transient, material, and sensory. It is about finding the fundamental blueprint, the eternal essence of every object of experience—what Plato calls the universal form or idea of all the particulars we experience.

Aristotle, in contrast to his teacher Plato, wanted to bring together what Plato had kept apart—that being the heavenly forms (the blueprint or essence of each thing) and the particulars of our experience. Rather than follow Plato and see knowledge in terms of contemplating the heavenly blueprint that the material world was modelled on, Aristotle would not separate the objects of our experience from their universal forms. The abiding essence we seek in every object we study could not be separated from the individual instance. But for Aristotle it's still the essential essence of any object of experience that interested him, not its transient qualities (and in that sense there's still plenty of Plato there).

As Robert Pasnan explains:

> from its very start [what it is to truly know something ] fell under the sway of the Platonic ambition to grasp the essences of things. . . . Although Aristotle brought the Forms down to earth, he still assumed that the aim of . . . inquiry is the necessary and eternal. That assumption dominated scholastic thought [the philosophy of the high middle ages]. . . . As a result, it is only in the seventeenth century, when philosophers finally overthrew the Aristotelian doctrine of essences, that they were able to rethink . . . in a way that gave a central role to contingent particulars as worthy objects of knowledge.[1]

## Should Science Be Deep or Precise?

In Robert Pasnan's study of these seventeenth-century changes, in how knowledge and science were to be newly perceived, he uses the helpful contrast between depth and precision to clarify the change. Those following Plato and Aristotle's lead were looking for a depth of philosophical insight in seeking to discover the essential core of things. In contrast, the new physical sciences of the seventeenth century raised doubts whether this

1. Pasnau, *After Certainty*, 39.

classical approach was really needed. They argued that you could see and predict how things worked without having to plumb those philosophical depths. So for those in the classical tradition, as Robert Pasnan explains, "The governing program . . . was to understand a thing's inner nature—its essential qualities and, above all, the substantial form that gave a substance its coherence and enduring character. . . .Those who investigate these are rightly said to be searching deep into the secrets of nature."[2]

Pasnan argues that "What in fact happened . . . is that the great seventeenth-century figures whom we now think of as scientists . . . articulated a new, post-Aristotelian conception of the . . . ideal, one that relinquished the goal . . . [of an] . . . understanding grounded in a grasp of essences."[3]

Now Descartes (yes, we are still talking about Descartes), inspired by the new natural science, believed we could not plum such philosophical depths of understanding as Aristotle and Plato had hoped for—even if they existed. We had to content ourselves in analyzing only the properties we immediately experienced. So, turning away from the pretensions of classical philosophy, the new science was to concentrate on observing, analyzing, and precisely measuring the sensory reality we all know.

A contemporary of Descartes's had been leading the way.

> A key transitional figure is Galileo. In his third letter on sunspots (1612), he writes that "in our speculating we either seek to penetrate the true and internal essence of natural substances, or content ourselves with a knowledge of some of their properties . . . ." He goes on to set aside the ideal of grasping essences, judging it impossible for us to have such knowledge, and in its plaice he extols inquiry into the mere properties of both earthly and celestial phenomena: 'location, motion, shape, size, opacity, mutability.'[4]

So Pasnan argues Galileo turned his back on what the classical philosophies of Plato and Aristotle wanted to achieve.

> Philosophy is damaged, Galileo thinks, by demanding a goal that, often, cannot be achieved. Instead of pushing ourselves into speculation over causes we cannot understand, we should celebrate our ability to grasp the "properties" of bodies and the rules that govern them. . . . It would be hard to overstate the

2. Pasnau, *After Certainty*, 14.
3. Pasnau, *After Certainty*, 14.
4. Pasnau, *After Certainty*, 14.

> dramatic shift that this method represents, when contrasted with the prevailing approach of the Aristotelians.[5]

With this change we have the beginnings of natural science as we now know it.

> As the story goes, modern science is born. We rightly celebrate this development for the way it saved science from the limitations of speculative metaphysics, and we rightly see Galileo and Newton as its founding figures . . . [for] . . . . In place of armchair speculation, there is a striking emphasis on observation grounded in experiment.[6]

The new natural sciences might not have been able to offer the depths of philosophical insight that Plato and Aristotle were wanting to fathom, but they could offer remarkable precision and with its impressive prediction. Under a subheading, "Trading Depths for Precision," Pasnan sums up this change:

> Scholastic philosophers went deep into identifying the substantial forms and elemental qualities that ground the natural world but in so doing they made precision impossible, because they had postulated the existence of entities they were unable to characterize in any sort of accurate detail. In this respect one might say that their method in natural philosophy recapitulated their theology. . . . Inevitably, there is a trade-off here. We can seek precision about what lies close to the surface; or we can aspire, inchoately, to the murky depths. . . . When it comes to the sort of ideal that might have normative force for our . . . practices, we have to make a choice between the competing ideals of depth and precision.[7]

Surely therefore in turning his back on the classical tradition in the form of Plato and Aristotle's philosophy of nature and by enthusiastically embracing the new science, with its detailed analysis of our physical environment (something Descartes contributed to in no small measure himself), Descartes must be the perfect candidate for the grand title of "first modern philosopher." This connection between the new sciences and Descartes's philosophy is probably the best chance Descartes has of gaining that title. As the philosopher Nick Wolterstorff concludes, "The philosophical

5. Pasnau, *After Certainty*, 15.
6. Pasnau, *After Certainty*, 17.
7. Pasnau, *After Certainty*, 17.

career of Descartes was intimately interwoven with the emergence of the new science. That's what makes him a modern philosopher."[8]

## Descartes the Classical Philosopher

In terms of being a practitioner of and enthusiast for, the new natural science Descartes' project is novel and seemingly modern. On the other hand, as the Cartesian (pertaining to Descartes) specialist John Cottingham, has argued, there is much in Descartes' thought that still sounds remarkably like medieval theology. For example, we have already seen in the last section Descartes wanting to be seen by the church as a stalwart defender of the Catholic faith. Also, still prominent in Descartes' philosophy is a good deal of classical Metaphysics. For example, central to Descartes' approach is the conviction that humanity is in the possession of an incorporeal mind or soul and this for Descartes is the basis of belief in immortality.

## The Almighty Foundation

In addition, what every secular reading of Descartes seems to be so quick to gloss over (perhaps hoping the reader might not notice), is the fact that Descartes has to presuppose the existence of God to ensure that we are not being deceived about the most basic of beliefs (that there is a material world as well as thinking things).

For Descartes's process of doubting all he cannot be certain of has painted him into a rather precarious philosophical corner. The only thing he thinks he can be certain about is that something is doing the doubting, that there is a thinking thing that is doubting.

That's a pretty isolated and lonely place to end up. What about the rest of the world, all the other things and all the other people? How can he now be certain any of that exists? Descartes believes that without the existence of God he cannot be certain about the existence of any of these other things. The only way he knows about them is through the witness of his senses which in turn was one of the things he said he could not be sure about when he first began the persistent doubting.

Descartes reasons that if there is a good and faithful God he would not fool or trick us about such fundamental beliefs or cause our senses to deceive us. Descartes writes: "in order to remove this . . . reason for doubt . . . I must examine whether there is a God, and, if there is, whether he can be

8. Wolterstorff, *John Locke*, 245.

a deceiver."[9] In other words, if we have clear and distinct perceptions about the world God would not fool us about the truth of what we perceive.

As Descartes concludes, "Hence you see that once we have become aware that God exists it is necessary for us to imagine that he is a deceiver if we wish to cast doubt on what we clearly and distinctly perceive. And since it is impossible to imagine that he is a deceiver, whatever we clearly and distinctly perceive must be completely accepted as true or certain."[10]

Strangely then, for "The first modern philosopher," Descartes, the existence of God becomes more fundamental and believable than our sense perceptions and the world they witness to. Therefore, for Descartes, belief in God's existence is more certain and secure than belief in the objective world around us. As Cottingham further concludes,

> In his Synopsis to the Meditations, Descartes, far from insisting on the absolute primacy of the thinking subject, emphasizes not one but two equally ranked items that enjoy the utmost certainty and self-evidence: the mind's awareness of itself and its awareness of God. The point of my procedure, says Descartes, is not to prove that, for example, there is an external world (something no sane man has doubted) but to help us to realize "that these reasonings . . . are not as solid and transparent as those whereby we reach awareness [cognition] of our own minds and of God."[11]

## I Always Knew It!

Crucially Descartes affirmed something that we have seen, and we can trace, in one form or another, back to Plato, and that is belief in innate ideas. The theory of innate ideas argues that as rational beings we are clearly in possession of cognitive principles and maxims that we have not acquired from experience. As John Cottingham observes,

> In Descartes's Third Meditation, the meditator makes an inventory of the ideas he finds within him, and observes that some seem to be innate. . . . [For example,] the idea we have of ourselves as thinking things, the idea of God, and basic mathematical concepts . . . also included are certain fundamental truths of logic. . . . Since Plato, innatists [philosophers who believe in innate ideas] had commonly pointed to the fact that our

9. Descartes, "Meditations on First Philosophy," sec. 35.

10. Descartes, "Meditations on First Philosophy," sec. 144.

11. Cottingham, "Desecularization of Descartes," 25.

> mathematical knowledge does not seem to be, in any obvious way a function of empirical observation. . . . The philosophical task according to Descartes . . . is to "direct reason aright," so that we can free ourselves from the obstructions to truth, and make use of the God-given knowledge which is implanted within each of us.[12]

## More Divine Illumination

Perhaps most telling of all is the explicit religious context in which Descartes frames his philosophy, one that should be very familiar to us by now. For he sets all his philosophizing in a context that should immediately remind us of Augustine's theology. As John Cottingham explains,

> in a passage in the Meditations, whose style and tone is such that it could easily have come from Augustine . . . Descartes expresses the longing "to gaze with wonder and adoration on the beauty of this immense light, so far as the eye of my darkened self can bear it." This is hardly the tone of the dispassionate analytic philosopher, engaged for purely instrumental reasons on the . . . project of validating the edifice of science. Rather, it is the voice of the worshipper, one for whom philosophy and science would make no sense without the divine source of truth and goodness that irradiates it from start to finish.[13]

In this way John Cottingham argues,

> the idea of God as the source of truth is no mere cautious concession to prying theologians; it is the very centre of gravity of Cartesian thought, exerting a decisive pull throughout the reasoning of the Meditations. God, glimpsed at the outset of the inquiry, and never effectively eclipsed by the extremity of doubt, is recognized and adored as the "immense light" in the Third Meditation, declared in the Fourth to be the fountain of "wisdom and the sciences," upheld in the Fifth as the perfect bestower of all we need to avoid error, and finally, in the Sixth, vindicated as the creative power of "immeasurable goodness," who secures our human well-beings.[14]

12. Cottingham, *Rationalists*, 70, 71.
13. Cottingham, "Desecularization of Descartes," 26.
14. Cottingham, "Desecularization of Descartes," 25.

So, Cottingham concludes his article looking at Descartes's sacred credentials with these words.

> Descartes is often called a "rationalist"— . . . one whose philosophy is founded on a fundamental belief in the power of reason—the ability of the human mind to discern the truth without any help from received wisdom or established authority and to distinguish what is clear and coherent from what is obscure and confused. But it is vital to add that for Descartes, the true, desecularized Descartes, we are not the authors of truth or the creators of value. Reason is our greatest human gift, but it is a gift we did not construct ourselves, and it is an instrument we must learn to use properly by directing it toward the "immense light" of truth and goodness, which we did not create. That kind of rationalism still has much to teach us.[15]

Therefore, "At the very centre of Descartes' thinking is a kind of submission to the higher and the greater, an implicit withdrawal from the claim to self-sufficiency and autonomy that is the hallmark of the modern secular mind."[16]

15. Cottingham, "Desecularization of Descartes," 28.
16. Cottingham, "Desecularization of Descartes," 28.

# 5

# THE TRUTH FROM BELOW

## DIY Illumination

I AM NOT SUGGESTING for one moment that divine illumination was the only game in town when it comes to a knowledge of the truth. But what struck me when I first read the writings of John Locke was the fact that he employs a number of key metaphors that are the very antithesis of divine illumination; pictures which express so clearly what is distinctively new and modern about his philosophy; metaphors that you would have very little chance of understanding if you did not know anything about the influential idea they were opposing. As we have heard repeatedly, it is John Locke who is responsible for the making of the modern mind. By looking at these image's employed by Locke we will see that there could hardly be more of a contrast between what Locke is suggesting in terms of understanding and reasoning and the vision of divine illumination which had been so influential from Plato right up to and including Descartes.

## The Kindling of Candles

Firstly, Locke makes the stark contrast between the light of a candle and the broad light of day. If for Plato and Augustine and even Descartes, in order to see the truth, we need divine illumination from beyond and above ourselves, in Augustine's terms being given heavenly wings to fly out of the darkness into the divine light of day, Locke's humble image that knowledge is really all about the lighting of candles could hardly be a greater contrast. As Locke says, "It will be no excuse to an idle and untoward servant, who would not attend his business by candlelight, to plead that he had not broad sunshine. The Candle that is set up in us shines bright enough for all our purposes. The discoveries we can make with this ought to satisfy us; and we shall then use our understandings right, when we entertain all objects in that way."[1]

As the philosopher Nicholas Wolterstorff explains,

> Over and over in the Essay, when Locke wants to draw our attention to the main features of his picture of our place as knowers . . . in the world, he uses three terms as a metaphor cluster: day light, darkness, and twilight. The sort of "half-light" he has in mind when he speaks of twilight is not only the half-light produced by the sun just below the horizon but also the half-light produced by the glow of candles.[2]

The light of a candle appears to symbolise for Locke what is happening all around him in the new natural philosophy (in what became known as the Scientific Revolution). He depicts the experimental method of the natural philosophers as generating its own light. He sees around him in the Scientific Revolution, a host of little lights, not a heavenly host but rather a very human one which nonetheless creates genuine illumination. Every time the natural philosopher makes a detailed observation or carries out an experimental process, he sees them lighting another wick, dispelling a little more of the dark unknown. The natural philosopher (scientist) does not sit there meditatively contemplating eternal truths and hoping for the dawning of a heavenly light. The aim is to generate their own illumination, not waiting for a celestial dawn. It may be modest compared to a heavenly light, but the important point that Locke wants to make is that this empirical knowledge (based on experience and experiment) may not seem that impressive but at least it is tangible, real, and not specious speculation. As Locke explains,

> God has made the intellectual world harmonious and beautiful without us; but it will never come into our heads all at once; we must bring it home piece-meal, and there set it up by our own industry, or else we shall have nothing but darkness and a chaos within, whatever order and light there be in things without us . . . Locke regarded the new natural philosophy coming to birth in his day as a concrete paradigm of how we should conduct our understandings; there one saw, already in place, the practice which bore the promise of resolving our anxiety.[3]

1. Locke, *Essay Concerning Human Understanding*, 1.1.5.
2. Wolterstorff, *John Locke*, 120–21.
3. Locke, *Conduct of the Understanding*, in Wolterstorff, *John Locke*, 1.

According to Locke we cannot leave the cave and experience the light of day; the best we can do is light our own candles in the hope of dispelling a little of the darkness. Not divine illumination but DIY illumination.

## Coming to Your Senses

In contrast to what we heard from Augustine, Plato, and Descartes, rather than leaving our sense experience behind, in pursuing a knowledge of the truth, genuine knowledge, in fact all knowledge for Locke is based on what the senses can tell us, primarily through experimentation.

> Knowledge for Locke is awareness of some fact . . . To know is to be directly acquainted with some fact, to be directly aware of it, to "perceive" it, as Locke was fond of saying . . . Our knowledge, therefore is real, only so far as there is a conformity between our ideas and the reality of things. . . . Wherever we perceive the agreement or disagreement of any of our ideas there is certain knowledge: and wherever we are sure those ideas agree with the reality of things, there is certain real knowledge.[4]

## Legs, Not Wings: Using Your Own Two Feet

The second contrasting metaphor John Locke uses is that between being given wings to fly into the light and our natural ability to walk around in whatever twilight we can kindle. We can forget about flying off with Augustine on angelic wings into the heavens. We need to walk around on our own two feet and investigate the world for ourselves as the finite embodied creatures we are. Locke's logic then is that we should not refuse to get up and walk just because our legs are so limited in what they can achieve when compared to what wings can. As Locke explains, "it will be unpardonable, as well as childish peevishness, if we undervalue the advantages of our knowledge, and neglect to improve it to the ends for which it was given us, because there are some things that are set out of the reach of it . . . [we would be like] he, who would not use his legs, but sit still and perish, because he had no wings to fly."[5]

In employing these DIY metaphors, Locke is expressing what philosophers call empiricism in stark contrast to the Platonic and Cartesian high-flying rationalism we surveyed above. Empiricism is "the doctrine that there

4. Wolterstorff, *John Locke*, 13, 26.

5. Wolterstorff, *John Locke*, 9.

is no knowledge that is not dependent in some way upon experience." So to sum up "Locke's . . . project in the Essay was to replace an account of human knowledge based on the doctrine of divinely instituted innate ideas and principles by one which sees human knowledge as the product of individual Experimental processes, originating in sensory perception."[6]

## Narrowing the Modern Mind

What is not often observed is that, according to John Locke, what is being suggested is the narrowing of the mind, not the broadening of the mind. We don't normally associate the Enlightenment and its age of reason with narrowing the mind. If as one scholarly account of Locke's work has suggested, in Locke's philosophy we see the making of the modern mind, it is, according to its maker, a far narrower mind than the medieval one ever was. As Locke writes, "We shall not have much reason to complain of the narrowness of our minds, if we will but employ them about what may be of use to us; for of that they are very capable."[7]

## Emancipated Knowing

What should not be overlooked is the fact that this new philosophy was not being developed in a social or political vacuum but can be seen as a bid for emancipation. Emancipation, that is, from the clericalism and authoritarianism Locke saw was still prevalent in church and state. So not only did Locke want to see his philosophy as working alongside the new natural philosophy (physics and biology) but also as a way of refuting the idea that some beliefs are God given in terms of divine illumination and therefore are not to be questioned.

> Locke held that all of the "materials"—as he put it—of human knowledge and understanding arise from experience. In maintaining this, he aligned himself with some of the leading experimental scientists of his day and firmly against a dominant philosophical doctrine of the time, the doctrine of innate ideas. According to this doctrine, certain fundamental components of human knowledge are inborn rather than acquired by processes of observation, learning and reasoning—inborn because they are of the very frame of the human mind as God designed it.

6. Lowe, *Locke*, 57.
7. Locke, *Essay Concerning Human Understanding*, 1.1.5.

> In virtue of their supposedly divine source, these components of human knowledge were not to be questioned or doubted, in the view of upholders of the doctrine—many of whom had vested interests of a religious or political character which could, by this device, be placed beyond the scope of publicly acceptable criticism.[8]

As we have stressed all along, this does not make Locke a secular humanist. Although Locke may well have been in sympathy with some representatives of the Radical Reformation known as Socinians, secular humanists do not write books about the reasonableness of Christianity. I've used Plato, Augustine, Aquinas, and Descartes as a contrast to John Locke, in order to see the dramatic difference between a classical view of what constitutes human knowing and the new Enlightenment understanding of how we know what we know (this is most clearly the case when it comes to the English Enlightenment) that has largely dominated modern thought since John Locke.

As the contemporary philosopher E. J. Lowe explains,

> His [John Locke's] writings . . . have been of lasting significance, changing the course of European thought and justly earning him the title of England's greatest philosopher. He was the first Western philosopher in modern times to focus his inquiries on the structure and formation of the human mind in order to gain insight into the objects and extent of human knowledge. The subsequent projects of David Hume . . . and Kant . . . would, very arguably, have been unthinkable without the precedent set by . . . [the] . . . great masterpiece, *An Essay Concerning Human Understanding*."[9]

## Can Theology Start from Below

In terms of working well with theology, a philosophy that aimed to contemplate the perfect form of the true, the good, and the beautiful, and in doing so sought divine illumination, seemed like a marriage made in heaven. As one scholar of Platonism has argued, Platonism was probably much more spiritual than most religions of the ancient world. Indeed, it could be argued that Christianity's incorporeal God owes a good deal to a form of Platonism. That certainly seemed to be the case for Augustine. For in his *Confessions*

8. Lowe, *Locke*, 22.

9. Lowe, *Locke*, 20–21.

he tells us that he came to understand that God must be fundamentally nonmaterial and incorporeal (spiritual) through reading the books of the Platonists.[10]

If, in terms of coming to know the truth, what makes John Locke's philosophy so modern is his outright rejection of the Platonic idea of heavenly illumination, this raises the difficult question of whether theology could work with his new philosophy. How could theology survive this making of the modern mind? Platonism and Christianity might have been a heavenly marriage, but this is looking like a down-to-earth divorce. How can a philosophy that believes that the only light that can be kindled is that of a modest candle be of any help to theology? If we can never get beyond tentatively moving around in semi-darkness, how could that help affirm the things of God?

The fact that Locke was trying to account for what was happening in the Scientific Revolution was not the problem; it was rather the fact that Locke believed this form of knowledge was the only kind there was. Consequently, much of classical metaphysics (like Platonism) was to Locke a momentous flight of fancy based on the delusion that you can indeed have angelic wings rather than your pedestrian feet, the Platonic delusion that we can be granted a heavenly knowledge of what transcends this dark domain.

## The Test-Tube God

For example, if like Locke you came to believe that all knowledge must be based on what is received from our senses, why would you, on that basis, be led to believe that anything could exist that transcends those senses? In terms of experimental science, it's akin to trying to get God into a test tube, in order to confirm the Almighty's existence. If in order for anything to be believed, it has to become experimentally observable, it doesn't bode well for the future of theology. As the theologian Hyman explains,

> if God exceeds the bounds of the rational, even more so does God exceed the bounds of the empirical (experimentally observable). Indeed, according to theological discourse, God not only exceeds the empirical, but is precisely that which is non-empirical. . . . It appears that these rationalist and empiricist methodologies were almost pre-determined to secure an atheistic outcome from the outset.[11]

10. Augustine, *Conf.* 7.111.

11. Hyman, *Short History of Atheism*, 30.

The greatest challenge, then, that theology faced from this new modern mind was not the sovereignty of reason, but rather that rationality had had its wings clipped (by empiricism) and had been well and truly grounded. Theology could cope with reason; it had done a remarkably good job of that in the Middle Ages. It was this new definition of what reason could and could not do that was the problem. The problem for theology was the *narrowing* of the modern mind, its narrow-mindnedness when it came to what could be countenanced and what could not.

One of the ways to approach and understand Kant and Hegel's work is as an attempt to broaden the modern mind, to discover again the expansive and multifarious nature of human rationality and to demonstrate that human reason cannot be confined to the dimensions of a test tube.

## The Radical Reformer

It has often been claimed that it was the Scottish philosopher David Hume who first pursued the radical implications of Locke's empiricism. But after studying the work of one of John Locke's acquaintances, John Toland, the philosopher and intellectual historian Frederick C. Beiser comes to a very different conclusion.

Toland became infamous for publishing in 1696 a work entitled *Christianity Not Mysterious*. According to Beiser, he was the first person to pursue what he saw as the critical implications of Locke's empiricism for religious faith. "Toland strips reason of any substantive content—the innate ideas or common notions of the Platonic tradition—and avows a straightforward empiricism. He maintains that all the materials of reason are derived ultimately from our experience . . . from the senses."[12]

Although Toland rejected the need for innate ideas, he insisted upon clear and distinct ones. He held that to believe something we must be able to describe it in clear and simple terms. He then put a further restriction upon these clear and distinct ideas: they must be derived from experience.

## Positivism

Beiser believes we have here the origins of a principle that dominated large swathes of Western philosophy at the beginning of the twentieth century: that any statement you care to make will only make sense if based either in logical reasoning or can be verified by some form of sense experience.

12. Beiser, *Sovereignty of Reason*, 225.

If it cannot meet those criteria, then you are just talking nonsense. This so-called logical positivism did make an exception for theology, calling it "a special kind of nonsense."

> Toland's criterion of belief is therefore akin to the empiricist's verifiability criterion of meaning. What we cannot verify in any possible experience is meaningless and therefore unbelievable. It was this radical demand for verifiability a step that Locke did not dare to take—that so shocked Toland's contemporaries. It seemed to them as if Toland were ready to sweep away all religion simply because it transcends the bounds of ordinary experience. The horror of the seventeenth-century public becomes a little more understandable when we compare it with the indignation of twentieth-century reactions to logical positivism.[13]

The key issue to stress here is not that reason has become sovereign and is ruling out faith, rather the point is that this is a very different vision of rationality, a very different picture of what reasoning is all about. We've moved from top-down to bottom-up. We've moved from Platonism to empiricism. We've moved from a reason that was transcendent to one that is strictly imminent. We have shifted from a philosophy that can be seen as hospitable to theology to one that can make little if any sense of it.

> The new critical role of reason . . . was based upon a new conception of reason itself. The grand synthesis of reason and faith . . . rested upon a Platonic conception of reason, according to which reason is an intuitive . . . non-natural power. Toland undercut this synthesis by questioning this conception. His view of reason is based upon . . . Locke's . . . *Essays Concerning Human Understanding*.[14]

I am not suggesting for one moment that a theology in the spirit of John Locke's philosophy is impossible (Locke himself clearly did not think so). I am merely suggesting that in comparison to the Platonic or Aristotelian outlook that had been theology's intellectual home since antiquity (with the exception of nominalism), the idea of finding a home for theology in eighteenth-century empiricism seemed implausible to say the least.

13. Beiser, *Sovereignty of Reason*, 251. For a statement to make any sense, it needs to be in principle verifiable in terms of sense experience.

14. Beiser, *Sovereignty of Reason*, 225.

## Not Humanism

Beiser also argues that we should not see Toland's published work as an early form of secular humanism, but rather as a philosophy for religious reformation.

> For all his rationalism and naturalism, it would be wrong to consider Toland as a purely secular or antireligious writer. . . . The aim of his rationalism and naturalism was not to undermine religion but to support a new kind of religion. . . . For all his criticisms of Protestant orthodoxy, then, Toland remained a self-conscious adherent of Protestantism. Time and again he reaffirmed his allegiance to the Spirit of the Reformation, and he associated the right to examine all beliefs according to reason with Luther's principle of Christian liberty. He is another striking illustration of how rationalism ultimately grew from the Reformation.[15]

15 Beiser, *Sovereignty of Reason*, 229.

# 6

# FIRST CRISIS

## *No Reason for Science*

### David Hume

ALTHOUGH IT WAS TOLAND who pressed home what he saw as the radical implications of Locke's empiricism for theology, in many introductions to modern philosophy this radical application of Locke's empiricism is more often than not associated with the Scottish philosopher David Hume.

This is expressed most clearly in what has become known as Hume's Fork. Here Hume envisages someone sorting through a library and working out which books are worth keeping and reading and which are vacuous and are to be rejected or even burnt. The person comes across some books of Christian theology and also books of the kind of classical metaphysical philosophy we have seen associated with Plato. According to Hume, because it doesn't use the kind of empirical, experimental reasoning that the sciences employ and which Locke advocated, they can be thrown, in Hume's words, "committed to the flames." As Hume put it, "If we take in our hand any volume—of divinity or school metaphysics, for instance—let us ask, Does it contain any abstract reasoning concerning quantity or number? No. Does it contain any experimental reasoning concerning matter of fact and existence? No. Commit it then to the flames for it can contain nothing but sophistry and illusion."[1]

The problem is that the natural sciences that so inspired Locke and Hume's philosophy can be seen today in its contemporary form as often

1. Hume, *Enquiry Concerning Human Understanding*, 12.3.25.

going well beyond anything that resembles Locke and Hume's strict empiricism. Think for example of any of the big questions occupying contemporary physics and it is difficult to see how these questions could be settled by the method Locke or Hume advocated. In fact, contemporary cosmology seems to be pushing at the boundaries of what might constitute science all the time. For instance, one of the most interesting BBC documentaries I have seen asked the question, "What happened before the big bang?" The programme featured half-a-dozen well-respected physicists, each passionately committed to different theories about the origins of the big bang, finally the documentary drew a parallel between the commitment of the physicists to their amazing theories and religious belief. I wonder what Hume would have made of these speculative theories expounded by scientists. I don't think Locke or Hume's empiricism could have easily settled that question. The theories that these scientists were advocating were far too speculative to be adjudicated in strictly empirical terms. Perhaps Hume would have committed the whole debate and all its scientific theories to the flames? (But hopefully not the participants.) As philosopher of religion Keith Ward comments,

> Quantum physicists speak of electrons as probability-waves in Hilbert space. Particle physicists speak of a ten-dimensional curved space-time in which most of the energy ("dark energy") is completely unobservable. Cosmologists speak of a multiverse, in which different space-times can all exist. . . . Stephen Hawking suggests that the universe could be finite in imaginary time but without boundaries or singularities. What sense could Hume make of what he is saying? . . . If you concede so much, it is hard to rule out the postulate of God as quite different in kind from the most general postulates of physics.[2]

## Science Self-Destructs

It is not just the outer reaches of speculative cosmology that make this point. A major theme in Hume's own philosophical reflections was to argue that there is something that is assumed by the natural sciences, but that goes well beyond what can be established on the grounds of experience. Perhaps a home-spun illustration might make Hume's basic point. Hume starts by pointing out that so much of what we call scientific explanation is based on the simple idea of cause and effect. The natural philosopher or scientist is

2. Ward, *God Conclusion*, 61–62.

faced with some or other phenomenon in the world and comes up with an explanation about what caused it and then in turn what effect is produced by it.

For example, a horticulturist comes across a sapling and recognizes it as a fruit tree. She then says confidently, this sapling will one day grow to produce red fruit and this sapling itself was produced from the seeds of a red fruit. From looking at the sapling in front of her she has worked out a whole chain of cause and effect, from the past to the future. But what she confidently says caused the sapling to grow in the first place and what it will produce are not there in front of her at that moment, they are not something that at present she is experiencing. All she sees in front of her is the sapling. She has come to a conclusion about what comes before it and what will follow based on something other than what is before her. Her knowledge is based, I imagine she would say, on the accumulation of all her previous experience as a horticulturist. But not only is she not directly experiencing what she says caused the sapling and what effect it will have, according to Hume, but if she works purely on the basis of experience, she cannot establish beyond doubt any of the conclusions she has reached.

This is where you have to follow things closely because the philosopher is like the annoying, difficult child who will never stop asking why you believe what you believe. Hume would say to her, "You may have seen hundreds of saplings that looked like this one eventually producing red fruit (past experience), but you cannot know beyond all possible doubt that this example in front of you is going to be the same as all the others. This may be the exception to the rule." To be ever more awkward, it could feasibly be argued that she might have experienced a hundred exceptions in the past and the rule is that saplings that look like this don't normally produce red fruit (given the fact that there are many millions of saplings that look like this one throughout the world the hundred examples she has experienced in the past are to be honest just a very small sample and it is possible that her sample might not have been that representative).

## Belief, the Basis of Science

Underlying all this reasoning from cause to effect (and I promise this is the main point now), Hume argues, is a fundamental belief, the belief that things in the future will always behave as they have in the past. In fact, the idea of cause and effect relies on the fundamental premise that there is conformity and uniformity in nature. "If reason determined us, it would proceed upon that principle, that instances, of which we have had no experience, must resemble those, of which we have had experience, and that the course of nature continues always uniformly the same."[3]

But crucially Hume argues that this basic belief in the uniformity of nature is not something our horticulturist can establish *on the basis of any experience*. It is rather, he suggests, something she must just *presuppose*; it is not, as Hume says, "determined by reason."

As Hume writes, "We suppose, but are never able to prove, that there must be a resemblance betwixt those objects, of which we have had experience, and those which lie beyond the reach of our discovery. When the mind, therefore, passes from the idea or impression of one object to the idea or belief of another, it is not determined by reason."[4]

Let's hear a specialist in Hume's philosophy explain where we have got to with Hume's argument so far. To the question,

> "What is the nature of all of our reasonings concerning matters of fact?" Hume answers that they are all "founded on cause and effect." For whenever the mind forms a belief about some never-or-not-yet-observed matter of fact—whether past, present, or future—it always reaches that belief by inference from something that it treats as related to that matter of fact by cause and effect. . . . Hume then poses a deeper question: "What is the foundation of all of our reasonings and conclusions concerning the relation of cause and effect?" in a word, "experience"—specifically, experience of constant conjunctions of like objects or events, in which something of one kind is regularly and immediately followed by something of a second kind. . . . Hume then poses the deepest question of all, one that, he thinks, no one has ever thought to ask before: "What is the foundation of all conclusions from experience?" . . . He variously describes this . . . as "supposing the uniformity of nature."[5]

Let's say you wanted to establish this belief in the uniformity of nature, that everything will behave in the future as it has in the past (which is the basis of any belief in cause and effect). How would you go about establishing this? Well you might say, I would study all past experience and see how things have behaved and assure myself that things have always been predictable and uniform. But how does that assure you about the nature of the future, that you have not experienced yet? To move from the past to the future with any assurance that things will always behave in the same way,

3. Hume, "Treatise of Human Nature," 3.6.4.

4. Hume, "Treatise of Human Nature," 3.6.11.

5. Garrett, *Hume*, 176.

you will have to have presupposed the very thing you are wanting to prove, the uniformity of nature. (You may say this is a typically stupid philosophical puzzle that has no basis in reality. But we do find things that behave in ways that we could not have predicted based on our prior experience. Take the puzzling nature of quantum physics, for example.) I would suggest that you would need to experience nature at all times and in all places to know that nature always behaved in a predictable manner. In other words, only the Almighty could be sure about the basis of cause and effect, that the totality of reality is predictable and acts in a uniform way. (But of course, if you had such knowledge as the Almighty has, you would not need to rely on the idea of cause and effect in order to know what has happened in the past and what is going to happen in the future, since reasoning on the basis of cause and effect more often than not, is trying to give you some idea about what you cannot experience.)

## At Long Last, a Conclusion!

Hume argues that the very basis of natural science, which is cause and effect, is not something you can establish purely on the basis of experience. Often the cause or the effect is not something you are experiencing at that moment our experience being so limited (being finite creatures it's always limited). You also cannot be certain that all the examples of what you are studying in the past or the future have or will behave in the same way (the uniformity of nature).

If it is true that the scientist's belief in cause and effect cannot be established on the basis of experience alone (purely empirically) therefore, rather worryingly, according to Hume, *empiricism cannot even support the natural sciences* that Hume and his contemporaries so admired and was in many respects the inspiration for the philosophy of empiricism in the first place. Was Hume's philosophy therefore sawing off the branch the Enlightenment was sitting on?

If according to Hume, in all this reasoning from cause to effect, we are in fact working with a fundamental presumption or belief that we have not established on the basis of experience—the belief in the uniformity of nature—and if, as we have seen, we also cannot prove the validity of that presupposed belief on the basis of experience, where then do we get such a fundamental faith from? Hume suggests controversially that such a basic belief as the uniformity of cause and effect in nature is based not in any kind of logical reasoning from experience but on *custom and habit*. Hume sums up where we have got to so far thus.

> It follows, then, that all reasonings concerning cause and effect are founded on experience, and that all reasonings from experience are founded on the supposition that the course of nature will continue uniformly the same. All probable arguments are built on the supposition that there is this conformity betwixt the future and the past, and therefore can never prove it. But our experience in the past can be a proof of nothing for the future, but upon a supposition that there is a resemblance betwixt them. This, therefore, is a point which can admit of no proof at all, and which we take for granted without any proof. We are determined by custom alone to suppose the future conformable to the past.[6]

Hume concludes that it is in fact on the basis of habit and custom that we believe these fundamental things about nature. Should an Enlightenment philosopher be telling us that the very basis of science is a received tradition from the past? Talk of a crisis of Enlightenment confidence. As the philosopher Gavin Hayman sums things up,

> All reasonings concerning cause and effect, are founded on experience, and . . . all reasonings from experience are founded on the supposition, that the course of nature will continue uniformly the same. But the uniformity of nature is a point, which can admit of no proof at all, and which we take for granted without any proof. We are determined by Custom alone to suppose the future conformable to the past. . . 'Tis not, therefore, reason, which is the guide of life, but custom.[7]

Gavin Hayman also gives a helpful summary of the overall thrust of Hume's analysis and in the process anticipates what we will see when we get to Kant and Hegel's critique of empiricism and of Hume's philosophy.

> The brilliance of Hume lay in the fact that he was willing to confront, unflinchingly, the implications of a thoroughgoing empiricist epistemology. He saw that if empiricism were adopted consistently, this would mean reasoning "merely from the known phenomena, and [dropping] every arbitrary supposition or conjecture." The result was that one could have knowledge of nothing that was not derived from sense experience. . . . As soon as the mind begins to organise these impressions and to make claims on the basis of them, then we are immediately in the arena of psychological activity.

6. Hume, "Treatise of Human Nature," 562.
7. Hyman, *Short History of Atheism*, 34.

> That which the mind adds to the empirical experience is merely a "belief" or construction, described by Hume as "nothing but a peculiar sentiment, or lively conception produced by habit." The error of so much historical philosophy has been to imagine that this activity of psychological "construction" is the articulation of objective "truths." On the contrary, such activity may tell us something of the operation of the human mind, but it is a folly to suppose that they can tell us anything of the structure of the external world.[8]

The crisis we will observe is not just philosophy undermining the logic of science (in Hume), we will next see science undermining the Enlightenment's philosophy.

8. Hyman, *Short History of Atheism*, 32.

# 7

# SECOND CRISIS

## *The Dark Side of Enlightenment*

### Satanic Mills

John Locke may have forged the modern mind, but as we all know it was Isaac Newton who was responsible for reimagining the world. John Locke may have reconceived the workings of the modern mind in terms of what we can know, and how we can know it, but it is to Newton that we look for reconceiving how the world works.

If Locke's new modern mind was just inhospitable to divinity and its classical metaphysics, with Newton's new physics we are frequently told how entirely incompatible that was for theology. On this account, by mapping out the universal laws of the physical world with mathematical precision and mechanistic determinacy we are told Newton left no room for God.

As one author concludes, "The hand of God, which once kept the heavenly bodies in their orbits, had been replaced by universal gravitation. Miracles had no more place in the system whose workings were automatic and unvarying. Governed by precise mathematical mechanical laws, Newton's universe seemed capable of running itself."[1]

In this account Newton's role was to introduce a mechanistic vision of the world, a clockwork universe where God's role is reduced to that of the mechanic who might be involved in terms of construction but is from then on redundant. God as this distant first cause is not about to and also not allowed to tinker with the works. As one writer sums things up, "The story

1. Greer, *Brief History of the Western World*, 597.

of the clockwork universe as applied to Newton has several components. . . . These include the idea that the universe is like a machine or clockwork mechanism, that God created the cosmos and set it in motion but now no longer intervenes in it or governs it; that the cosmos follows deterministic laws . . . that Newton thought his physics either unwillingly or even willingly excluded God from the universe."[2]

This dramatic and ubiquitous story about Newton making the Almighty redundant has only one rather annoying problem with it, and that is the simple fact that it is completely mistaken. We cannot examine this Newtonian myth in detail, but we can note in passing that with regard to the metaphor of the universe being seen as a great machine, this metaphor had been extensively employed well before Newton's day. For example, "Descartes, while not advocating a cogged machine per se . . . does describe the World as a machine and is fond of describing animals as clocks and humans as clocks with souls."[3]

In terms of Newton's use of the metaphor, "To date, not a single example of Newton unambiguously referring to the universe as a clockwork system has surfaced."[4] Newton may have avoided the mechanistic metaphor for the very reasons we have noted above. That it seems to suggest an autonomous nature that could run itself, without the need of any Almighty assistance, and that this mechanistic clockwork would also preclude intervention, all this therefore leading to heavenly unemployment.

In fact, Newton's friend and defender Samuel Clarke saw only too clearly that this clockwork metaphor may have negative implications for theology and consequently went out of his way to avoid the thought. "Clarke offers a direct, forceful, and unambiguous repudiation of the clockwork analogy. The Notion of the World's being a great Machine, without the Interposition of God, as a Clock continues to go without the Assistance of a Clockmaker; is the Notion of Materialism and Fate, and tends to exclude Providence and God's Government in reality out of the World." Thus Clarke does not merely reject the clockwork analogy but, without hesitation, associates it with materialism and fate and, what is more, is at pains to emphasize the deleterious theological consequences of such a view of the cosmos for the sovereignty of God."[5]

The irony is that even though Newton avoided the metaphor and his chief defender (Samuel Clarke) vehemently rejected it (for theological

2. Firestone and Jacobs, *Persistence of the Sacred in Modern Thought*, 150.

3. Firestone and Jacobs, *Persistence of the Sacred in Modern Thought*, 153.

4. Firestone and Jacobs, *Persistence of the Sacred in Modern Thought*, 153.

5. Firestone and Jacobs, *Persistence of the Sacred in Modern Thought*, 166.

reasons), it is this clockwork vision of how the world works that captured the imagination of the eighteenth century and became forever associated with the new physics pioneered by Newton. In fact, we have to travel to eighteenth-century France for a clear example of a materialistic and naturalistic interpretation of Newton's physics.

Before we make that journey across the channel it's worth noting in passing what Newton says himself about his new system of physics and divinity. "When I wrote my treatise, I had an eye upon such Principles as might work with considering men for the belief of a Deity and nothing can rejoice me more then to see it useful for that purpose."[6] This does not sound like someone who thinks their science is antithetical to theology: "the link between the system of the world and the theological interests of Newton had been established from the very beginning."[7] In fact, Newton wrote far more about theology than he ever did about physics, being particularly (possibly fanatically) interested in the interpretation of the biblical book of Revelation.

## Channel Crossing

Denis Diderot was best known as the main editor of the eighteenth-century encyclopaedia that proudly showcased the Enlightenment's new learning. Diderot, in the encyclopaedia, takes Newton and Descartes's now famous natural philosophy and strips it of any supporting theology. For Diderot, God was not needed to explain anything that could not be accounted for in his now autonomous natural philosophy. Everything according to Diderot can now be understood in purely naturalistic terms without the addition of any divine assistance.

Descartes's God, who had got the world up and running, and Newton's God, who had ensured its continued smooth running, was now an unnecessary hypothesis that Diderot believed science could at last do without. Matter, he believed, could move and maintain itself. The Almighty hadn't just been put out to pasture but had been put out of its misery.

> Descartes had . . . established God as the guarantor of nature. Newton had begun with the phenomena of nature and had established God as a force by which phenomena were structured . . . In both systems, God entered as a causal necessity. . . . In both physics, God gave movement or designed to nature. Diderot . . . eliminated this inferred necessity by positing movement not as

6. Buckley, *At the Origins of Modern Atheism*, 102.

7. Buckley, *At the Origins of Modern Atheism*, 124.

> an effect upon matter, but as an effect of matter. Matter was . . . responsible for its own movement. . . . Toland . . . opened up this possibility . . . and Diderot seized upon it to exclude any divine intervention in the movement of things. For Diderot, matter moved itself and possessed this self-movement inherently.[8]

For Diderot and the other contributors to the encyclopaedia the scientific means of explanation was complete. As we have seen David Hume argue, the inescapable logic of scientific explanation for those who contributed to this encyclopaedia of Enlightenment learning was of course cause and effect. Whatever we encounter as we explore our natural environment is to be understood in terms of preceding explanatory conditions that fully determined the following effect. "Nature is but an immense chain of causes and effects, which unceasingly flow. . . . Anything else is . . . a denial of our experience, and a negation of . . . natural philosophy."[9]

"If a Universal Mechanics were ever to be realized, it would be only by admitting no other than mechanical hypotheses, more specifically hypotheses of matter in movement. . . . Matter now emerges as the ceaseless cause of all things, and in its causality Diderot fathers a revolution. The stone that the builders so long rejected has become the cornerstone."[10] Where Diderot pioneered a mechanistic and causally deterministic Science of Nature it was not long before this form of explanation would be applied to humanity.

## *Man a Machine*

It was the French physician and philosopher La Mettrie who in 1747 published a work entitled *Man a Machine*. For La Mettrie the "The human body is a watch, a large watch constructed with . . . skill and ingenuity."[11] Descartes in the seventeenth century had used mechanistic explanations for understanding the workings of the body, both animal and human. But Descartes had not in any sense been a materialist. Descartes believed that humanity had been endowed with an immaterial mind or soul, the seat of the human intellect and the basis of immortality. In this sense Descartes resembled the classical tradition going back to Plato and kept alive in Christian theology. But La Mettrie challenged Descartes's fundamental mind/body distinction: "all the faculties of the soul depend to such a degree on

8. Buckley, *At the Origins of Modern Atheism*, 277, 279.
9. Buckley, *At the Origins of Modern Atheism*, 283.
10. Buckley, *At the Origins of Modern Atheism*, 232, 249.
11. Buckley, *At the Origins of Modern Atheism*, 266.

the proper organization of the brain and of the whole body, that apparently they are but this organization itself, The soul is clearly an enlightened machine. . . . That mysterious word soul should only be used for that part of the machine which thinks."[12]

But once humanity has been reduced to this form of explanation, and conceived of in materialistic mechanistic terms, has not the individual become just one more cog in a machine, one more component in a cosmic clock? Therefore, even humanity at its most noble, most creative, most elevated and ideal, becomes as mindlessly predetermined as the rest of the physical environment, part of nature's dark satanic mill. "The fact of the matter is, however, that the laws that govern the movement of human beings are as unvarying and the constraints that govern all bodies, and their laws not only dictate how they move, but that they move necessarily."[13]

"The more the sciences progress the more they discover the causes of life, human action, and the origin of the universe; but the more they find these causes, the more they support materialism, determinism, and atheism . . . not a few people in the late eighteenth century believed the sciences were heading in just this direction."[14]

It not surprising that behind the grinning mask of Enlightenment self-emancipation could not be hidden for long the dark mill of materialism."It seemed to many that if the mechanistic principles of the new natural philosophy were only extended and universalized, then they would not leave any room in the world for spirit, freewill, or God himself."[15]

Historian of philosophy Beiser points out that if, in this model, whatever you care to contemplate can be explained in terms of some prior sufficient cause or reason, there will consequently be little in the way of room left for freedom, divine or human.

> If we believe in the existence of God, then we must assume that God is the cause of his own existence and everything else that exists. Similarly, if we believe in freedom, then we must suppose that the will is spontaneous, acting as a cause without any prior cause to compel it into action, In both cases, then, it is necessary to assume the existence of some unconditional or spontaneous cause, that is, a cause that acts without any prior cause to compel it into action. But this is of course just the assumption that we cannot make if we universally apply the principle of sufficient

12. Buckley, *At the Origins of Modern Atheism*, 265.
13. Buckley, *At the Origins of Modern Atheism*, 279.
14. Beiser, *Fate of Reason*, 85.
15. Beiser, *Sovereignty of Reason*, 283.

> reason. If universally applied, this principle states that for every cause there is some cause that compels it into action.[16]

"Universal nature is now an iron sequence of necessity."[17] So "the progress of the sciences is leading to the destruction of our essential moral and religious beliefs."[18]

## Paradox of Enlightenment

The threat posed by mechanistic causation and naturalistic explanation was not merely restricted to traditional forms of morality and religion it could also be seen as challenging and ultimately undermining the Enlightenment's own aims and ideals. The philosophers contributing to the great Enlightenment encyclopaedia could on the same page preach a gospel of emancipation and argue a science of determinism. One paragraph might be passionate about breaking the chains that bind us, the next arguing just as convincingly for the iron grip of cause and effect in everything we seek to understand. It wasn't long before it was realized you couldn't have it both ways, either we are fundamentally determined as everything else in nature is and therefore could not know genuine freedom or had to believe that there was some aspect of humanity that could not be fully accounted for. As nature abhors a vacuum, the new learning in the encyclopaedia of Enlightenment thought abhorred a mystery.

> The philosophers urged the gospel of unhampered human Liberty, a gospel that should have had a telling effect on private morality and on social structures. At the same time often within the same exhortations, they formulated a rigorously mechanical doctrine of nature and of human beings enclosed within this nature. Every form of nature, each of its movements and its resultant organisation, emerged necessarily, completely determined by the interaction of its particles and by the iron rule of their invariant laws. The rhetoric of human freedom registered a sharp, if unnoticed, dissonance with . . . causal determinacy.[19]

Science appeared more tyrannical and soul-destroying than any authoritarian regime ever did, regimes that Enlightenment philosophers had fought to be free from. It threatened human self-determination and moral

16. Beiser, *Fate of Reason*, 84.
17. Buckley, *At the Origins of Modern Atheism*, 279.
18. Beiser, *Fate of Reason*, 85.
19. Buckley, *At the Origins of Modern Atheism*, 274.

freedom more thoroughly than any libertarian objector to Calvin's pernicious doctrine of predestination to damnation could have imagined. The Enlightenment again seemed to be cutting off the branch it now precariously perched on. As we saw with David Hume, its philosophy was not only undermining its science but now its science is undermining its libertarian philosophy. The philosophy of human emancipation, the need to be masters of our own destiny, in throwing off the shackles of tyranny were being undermined by deterministic materialism. No longer were we free spirits captaining the soul, we were now lifeless cogs. What might have been seen at the dawn of the Enlightenment (late seventeenth century) as mutually supportive (science and philosophy) by the middle of the eighteenth century were seen as reciprocally threatening. "The central paradox of the Enlightenment gradually assumed its ironic shape; . . . [it] . . . effectively reduced culture to nature, leaving the age with as strong and eternal contradiction as any civilization had borne."[20] As the encyclopedist Baron d'Holbach explained, "Man is a work of Nature: he exists in Nature: he is submitted to her laws: he cannot deliver himself from them nor can he step beyond them even in thought."[21] In his engaging work *The Theological Origin of Modernity* Michael Gillespie put this crisis in theological terms.

> The hopes of the Enlightenment were: deeply shaken by the realization of the contradiction of its essential goals. . . . Humanity was caught in a nest of contradictions. . . . Freedom, for example, could only be attained by the use of a science that at its core denied the very possibility of freedom. Similarly, if humans were natural beings, they could not be free because they would be subject to the laws governing the motion of all matter, and if they were free they could not be natural beings. Humans were thus either mere matter in motion or they were gods, or to put the matter more clearly they constantly lived the contradiction of being both mere matter in motion and gods.[22]

We looked at Toland's reforming philosophy in the last section, but the paradox we are now facing had already been there, hiding in plain sight. The motivation for Toland and his peers'

> campaign against the supernatural was the belief that it poses a grave threat to human autonomy. Rather than asserting their power to direct and control their lives, people see the state, society, and religion as the product of supernatural forces beyond

20. Buckley, *At the Origins of Modern Atheism*, 274.
21. Buckley, *At the Origins of Modern Atheism*, 276.
22. Gillespie, *Theological Origins of Modernity*, 277.

> their control. The great attraction, of the naturalistic worldview for Toland . . . is that it will give human beings greater self-awareness of their powers, and thus the courage to use them. There was, however, a deep irony to their campaign: the attempt to eliminate the supernatural in the name of freedom seems to deprive people of their freedom. For, if all actions are determined by the natural order are we really free to direct society as we wish?[23]

What added insult to injury was that the situation the Enlightenment philosopher found himself in (and the fact that it was more than often a "he" was too true to be good) was little better than the predicament that had perplexed medieval theologians. As the theologian Michael Buckley explains, "The Enlightenment had forged as severe an internal inconsistency as previous generations had found between faith and reason, grace and nature, or predestination and freedom."[24]

It is precisely in response to this deeply conflicted climate that Kant and Hegel's philosophy is written. What we have surveyed in terms of this looming crisis is to my mind an (if not *the*) interpretive key to Kant and Hegel's thought. As Frederick C. Beiser states, "Kant was determined that the fundamental . . . principle of freedom—had to be saved at all costs against the encroachments of a scientific method."[25] It is these modern philosophers who are also largely responsible for the genesis of modern theology, a theology that also addresses with the help of Kant and Hegel the crises left by the Enlightenment. As we said in the introduction if you don't understand the question you will have no hope in understanding the answer.

## Some Questions Just Don't Go Away

It is interesting to note that this dissonance between the experience we have of human freedom and the explanatory method that governs the natural sciences (that so concerned Kant and Hegel) is still with us today. This is illustrated perfectly in Richard Dawkins's answer to a question from the audience in a live debate. The question he was asked was "Is there a scientific basis for the concept of freedom?" Richard Dawkins replies,

> It's a question that I dread actually because I don't have a very well-thought-out view about it. I think that I mean I have a

23. Beiser, *Sovereignty of Reason*, 229.
24. Buckley, *At the Origins of Modern Atheism*, 274.
25. Guyer, *Cambridge Companion to Kant*, 52.

> materialist view of the world. I think that things are determined in a rational way by antecedent events and so that commits me to the view that when I think I have free will, when I think that I'm exercising free choice, I am deluding myself, . . . that my brain states are determined by physical events and yet that seems to contradict, to go against the very powerful subjective impression that we all have, that we do have free will.[26]

Before we explore Immanuel Kant's response to the crisis of the Enlightenment it is worth hearing a final example of how this question is posed. As the philosopher Robert Pasnau concludes his chapter on the new natural philosophy of the eighteenth-century scientific revolution.

> If we suppose that all there is is particles in motion, subject to forces of various sorts, then the great task of . . . inquiry must be to measure those forces as accurately as possible. But what if there is more to the world than this? What if we live in a world with beings whose agency runs beyond anything hitherto imagined by science? What if these beings are sensitive to values that cannot be weighed in any laboratory? Who, then, will measure these things, and how much precision may we demand? Of course, these glimmers of transcendence are perhaps just illusions, destined to be assimilated to the ever-growing reductive empire of science. Yet who will decide when that reduction has succeeded? How will we know?[27]

26. See ShirleyFilms, "FREE WILL."

27. Pasnau, *After Certainty: A History of Our Epistemic Ideals and Illusions*, 20.

# Part Two

## THE GREAT DIVIDE

*Radical Freedom—Human and Divine:*
*From Kant to Barth via Schleiermacher, Fries, and Otto*

# 8

# KANT

## *Defender of the Faith*

### Your Husband Knows Immanuel Kant

I WANT YOU TO imagine that your husband Albert knows Immanuel Kant. Now I realize that's going to take a bit more imagination for some of us than others. In fact, your husband's family lived in the same part of Konigsberg where Kant grew up. Konigsberg was a Baltic Prussian port that is now Kaliningrad in Russia and a place that Kant never left. Kant's grave is the nearest thing Kaliningrad has to a saint's shrine, that as we will see would have appalled Kant. Where Kant's family lived was the part of town you went to if you wanted to buy some good reins for your new horse or an excellent saddle (leatherwork was Immanuel's father's trade). Your husband often pointed out that in this regard Immanuel could not have been more different. His family's business as far as we know had always been working as artisans, so you could hardly predict that Immanuel Kant was going to become the best known of modern philosophers.

Today your husband's memories of Immanuel are at the front of his mind. For today you are calling on one of your husband's wealthier clients. This well-to-do client has a home adjacent to some university buildings near Konigsberg's Cathedral (the university library at the time being in the cathedral cloisters). So today more than ever he's reminiscing about having known Immanuel the saddlemaker's son who became the famous professor.

Your husband didn't only know Kant's family through their similar work, but he also knew them through church. You see for both his family and Kant's their faith was so much more than just Sunday attendance, rather their brand of Protestant Christianity permeated every aspect of their lives. During weekday evenings members of the congregation would meet for bible study and prayer and each day there would be family devotions. Also, in the way they lived and ran their business they would try to put their faith into practise. You see, your husband's family and Kant's family were part of a spiritual revivalist movement within the Lutheran Church known as Pietism. Even though Kant was thankful for the stable home his parents and their Christian faith had provided, in later life Kant found it difficult to say anything positive about the Pietism that had nurtured him. Possibly the least damning thing Kant was able to say was that "a 'pietist' is someone who 'tastelessly makes the idea of religion dominant in all conversation and discourse.'"[1]

As you begin walking past the university buildings your husband comments, "Immanuel was probably never cut out for our line of work anyway, he really didn't have the physique for it. He could not endure much in the way of physical exertion and always seemed to have difficulties with breathing when played any game where he needed to run." (So, you will recognize him when we meet him, as Kant is only 5 feet, 2 inches of slight build and his chest is somewhat sunken.)

Even though your husband could talk about Immanuel with sympathy when telling you about Kant's poor physique, you could at other times hear a note of envy. Because of his obvious intellect and potential academic ability both at church and at school, Kant was a child who was noticed and shown favor in a way Albert never was. For Albert recalls that when a new pastor Franz Schulz arrived to lead the pietistic fellowship it was not long before he noticed Immanuel's promise. Franz Schulz was also rector of the newly founded Collegium Fredericianum, a Pietist private school, and Albert recalls how Franz Schulz arranged for Immanuel to be educated there, which was rare for a boy of Immanuel's social class. With this education sixteen-year-old Immanuel was enabled to enter Konigsberg University. It was at this point that your husband had largely lost contact with him. Albert certainly wasn't going to meet Immanuel among the Pietists in Konigsberg as Kant now had no time for organized religion in terms of ritual or outward displays of devotion. Even though the University was close to the cathedral and had regular services there, Kant would often peel off from the faculty procession leading from the university to the cathedral and sneak back to his study.

1. Wood, *Kant*, 157.

Albert still knew some of Kant's relatives. But Immanuel's mother had passed away in tragic circumstances when Immanuel was a boy of thirteen and his father had not that long ago also died.

You have now seen the client near the university, and it was time to find some lunch, you didn't normally frequent taverns but there were few other places to eat around here. As you walk in you see that there is a large group congregated around one of the tables at the back of the tavern. There seems to be a lively debate in progress. At the center of it your husband spots a familiar face. (Kant may not have been an imposing physical presence, but his dry wit and quick mind always meant he was popular company.) Looking across to where you were entering the room, Kant immediately recognizes your husband and insists that you both joined him and his friends at their table. You are very aware of how proud your husband is of this immediate recognition and you must say you are impressed by being recognized and welcomed by a professor. From the brief introductions it becomes clear to you that most of those surrounding Kant at the table are his university colleagues.

Kant says, "I'm sorry, Albert. You've joined us in the middle of something of a debate. One of my young colleagues Andreas," pointing to a rather handsome spectacled young man sitting near you, "insists that there is no such thing as freedom of the will. That we are not free in the actions we take, that whatever action we might take they are all in fact determined in advance." It was occasions like this you had come to dread. You knew from bitter experience that Albert could never keep his opinions to himself and would always voice what he was thinking. "Why Kant," your husband says very confidently, "is your young friend here a Calvinist, believing that everything is an outworking of God's will?" Much to your embarrassment they all find this comment highly amusing. And Kant explains that Calvinism could not be further from Andreas's mind. Kant then went on to explain that his young friend Andreas was more of a materialist than a Calvinist and might if he were pressed deny the reality of God as vehemently as denying the existence of free will. You are immediately taken back, you have heard that there are people who deny God's existence, but you've never met such a radical free thinker before.

Kant, turning to Andreas says, "Come on, Andreas. Explain your ideas to my friends and don't try blinding them with technical terms."

Andreas says, "Well, thanks to Newton—I'm sure even you have heard of Newton," Andreas says somewhat patronizingly, "We know now how much of the material world works. And the fundamental thing we observe, as I am sure you know, is the regularity of cause and effect. That the nature and state of everything around us can be explained by what preceded it. For example, your friend Kant is fond of playing billiards. Well, of course the balls on the billiard table do not move themselves; they only ever move if something causes them to do so. For example, if a ball that Kant has queued strikes another, that second ball only moves because of the movement of the one Kant first set in motion."

Kant intervenes. "Andreas, you're not talking to children. Even though my friends might not have your university education, I think they understand well enough what you're saying."

Andreas continues unperturbed. "You see what science has clearly demonstrated is that it's not just the balls on the billiard table that work like that, everything we know works like that. What happens, without exception, is always determined buy a prior material cause."

By this time the two of you are catching on. Your husband turns to Andreas and says, "I see what you're suggesting, Andreas, is that the world is deterministic. What happens is always determined by what precedes it."

Andreas then concludes, "Therefore there can be no choice in what we do. For what we do is always determined by a prior cause. Because we are all part of the material world that operates in that way this must apply to us as much as anything else. Consequently, all that we do must be determined and therefore we can never have free will."

Unbelievably, without a moment's consideration, your husband disagrees (as everybody looks around at your husband astonished at such a quick and abrupt reaction). "That may be true of material objects, Andreas, but as everyone knows we are more than just material objects, so what you are saying does not apply when it comes to humanity. For we have a spiritual nature as well as a physical one. The Bible is clear about this, Andreas, for in Genesis, Moses writes that we are all made in God's image. You see, we unlike the rest of creation have a soul as well as a body, a mind as well as a brain, and furthermore, do not the Scriptures at many points make it plain that we are all answerable to God for the decisions we make in this life?" (As you can see, Pietism in Konigsberg at this time was not Calvinistic.)

The way Kant's friends were reacting was not looking favorable, if frowns and the shaking of heads is anything to go by. So, you felt it was your duty to say something in your husband's defence, but what comes out even surprises you. "I'm astonished that such learned men have to be told this, I was told about such basic Christian truths on my mother's knee. I didn't need to go to university to learn that we will one day be judged for what we have done in this world. You should be ashamed of yourselves not knowing such things."

At that moment it does dawn on you that you might have gone a bit far, you have stood up to make the point and everybody else is still sitting down.

Your Albert is looking up at you with approval and is clearly impressed, but Andreas is definitely not impressed and again in his patronising tone says, "You may not have fully understood or grasped what I'm saying, dear. I'm a man of science, not of faith. Consequently, I only believe in the things I can confirm and verify through the use of my senses. And as I'm sure you know this is the very basis on which science has developed its understanding of the world. So, all our scientific understandings of the world are based on such empirical observations and experiments. And science through this method has established the material nature of things and that this material nature is governed by the deterministic laws of cause and effect. What science has definitely not observed is this spiritual world of yours, that we are all supposed to have learnt about, as you so eloquently put it, on our mother's knee.

"Put simply, we can prove beyond all possible doubt the things that science investigates, but you cannot do the same for your spirituality. It seems to me just the product of years of blind indoctrination. You see, scientific investigation is stripping away all that religious mythology and is showing us for the first time the way the world really is in itself, getting beyond your illusions or delusions and showing us the facts of the matter. And in doing this, I am sorry to say, science has not discovered your spiritual realm populated by divine beings and everlasting souls or your final judgment and all that other stuff you Pietists bang on about." And looking at you with some sympathy, he concludes, "Now I know this might seem rather harsh and hard to stomach and not the way you would like things to be, but at least it's honest and not just wishful thinking. At least I am not in a dream world of my own making but facing things as they really are."

By now you realize all of this was a mistake, not just standing up and saying what you believe, but coming over to join this table in the first place and meeting your husband's famous friend. You are wishing you'd gone straight home, as you are beginning to feel very out of your depth and very alone.

To make it worse, Kant has stood up as well and is looking in your direction. You know very well from what your husband has said that Kant is unlikely to be on your side in any of this. Much to your surprise, he is not addressing you but Andreas. And he says to Andreas, "Of course, Andreas, it could be the other way around."

Andreas looks astonished. "What do you mean, Immanuel, it could be the other way around?"

"That the way my friends are describing things maybe the way things really are 'in themselves,' to use your interesting phrase, Andreas."

Andreas says mockingly, "You mean that we are all really spiritual beings with immaterial souls responsible before an almighty God. Surely not. Come on, Kant, you cannot be serious. You're just playing games with me, you don't believe in all that otherworldly Pietistic nonsense. I know you're a man of science Kant as I am."[2]

"No, Andreas, I'm serious. I might not believe in the detailed description my friends seem to be able to give about such a spiritual world but in principle there is the possibility they could be right. For it is logically possible that things could be that way around. You see it is conceivable that your scientific description of how things are maybe just the way things appear to us, and not in fact the way things really are in themselves."

Let's hear this next point in Kant's own words (from the end of his most influential work and his first book to propose this approach), as what Kant suggests may seem rather surprising and may not fit with what we have heard so far about Kant. If we quote him directly there can be no doubt that he really makes such an unexpected point, though I must admit it is a passage I have never seen quoted or commented on before. "You see, against what you say, Andreas [and from the context in the book Kant clearly has this kind of debate with a free-thinking materialist in mind] one

> could propose a . . . hypothesis: That all life is really only intelligible [non-material], . . . not subject to temporal alterations at all, and has neither begun at birth nor will be ended through death; that this [earthly] life is nothing but a mere appearance, sensible representation of the purely spiritual life, and the entire world of the senses is a mere image, which hovers before our present kind of cognition and, like a dream, has no objective reality in itself that if we could intuit the things and ourselves as they are we would see ourselves in a world of spiritual natures with which our only true community had not begun with birth nor would not cease with bodily death (as mere appearances).[3]

Andreas, for a moment, is dumbstruck with astonishment, and so was most of the rest of the table; for that matter, so were you and Albert (and I was somewhat surprised when I found such hypothetical hyperbole near the end of Kant's critic of pure reason).

You and Albert were definitely not expecting Kant to turn the tables on Andreas and science in that way, in suggesting that Andreas the scientist

2. Immanuel Kant's first published work was a scientific text on physics and cosmology.

3. Kant, *Critique of Pure Reason*, The Transcendental Doctrine of Method 1.3, A780/B808.

and not the religious believer are in a "dream" and what Andreas was saying about the scientific truth of things "has no objective reality." That it is not *religion* that is a subjective human construction, as Andreas had suggested (and so many materialists have done since), but *science!* What a turn up for the books.

Andreas says, "So Kant, let's get this right. Are you saying that I may be the one who is deluded, who is not really in touch with reality, with the way things really are, and that the scientific picture may be 'nothing but a mere appearance, a sensible representation of the purely spiritual life, and the entire world of the senses is a mere image, which hovers before our present kind of cognition and, like a dream, has no objective reality in itself'?"[4]

Says Kant, "Well-remembered, Andreas. All right, I concede that there may be a good deal of hypothetical hyperbole in what I said, but I was using it because I want to get over an important point that I don't want to be missed. The point is, and I stand by this Andreas, the way the sciences see things may be just the way things have to appear to us as sentient beings. It may be overdoing it somewhat to call the way we experience things an illusion or delusion or dream. But nonetheless the regular way we see things, that the sciences work with so successfully, may be just the way we have to order and construct the world in order to make sense of reality at all.

"So rather than the world being mechanistic, deterministic, and materialistic, as you suggest, Andreas, leaving no place for the spiritual or ethical in our outlook, it may be just that our minds can only work with such categories. And that the way things are in themselves, before our minds get to work on them, may be very different from the way you describe the world in your scientific categories.

"So, Andreas. If hypothetically, very hypothetically, we could totally strip away all that mental processing and see things before all that conditioning happens, things may be very different from your scientific picture of the world. In fact, the world in itself could be more like the spiritual place that my friends have been describing."

Now this may sound like a very strange way of thinking about nature, the idea that it conforms to our subjective understanding. But if what we are talking about is just the appearance of things and not as they are in themselves this contrast could make perfect sense.

Again, to quote Kant's own words, "That nature should direct itself according to our subjective ground of apperception, indeed in regard to its lawfulness even depend on this, may well sound quite contradictory and

4. Kant, *Critique of Pure Reason*, The Transcendental Doctrine of Method 1.3, A780/B808.

strange. But if one considers that this nature is nothing in itself but a sum of appearances, hence not a thing in itself but merely a multitude of representations of the mind, then one will not be astonished to see . . . nature, solely in the radical faculty of all our cognition."[5]

So, to put it simply, the machine and its mechanistic determinism might be in our heads and not in the world at all.

## "I Have Denied Reason to Make Room for Faith"

Hopefully from the dialogue we have rehearsed so far, and Kant's own words, taken from his most famous book (*Critique of Pure Reason*), you can see straight away that Kant had something of major significance to say about religion and spirituality. In fact, probably the most quoted words from that book come from the second preface where Kant concludes, "I have denied reason to make room for faith."[6]

And of course, the dialogue we have started with is a perfect example of Kant doing this. He has suggested that there are limits to scientific reasoning and has consequently suggested that there may be room for faith in what is beyond the scientific picture.

Now the argument we have seen Kant make in the dialogue above is not some aberration that Kant slips into towards the end of writing six hundred pages: out of fatigue. Rather, what Kant is doing here in depriving reason of all "damaging detrimental influence." For "it is the first and most important occupation of philosophy to deprive reason once and for all of all disadvantageous influence, by blocking off the source of the errors."[7]

## The Eighteenth-Century Socrates

In questioning what it is possible to know, Kant sees himself as a modern equivalent of the great Athenian, Socrates. But why Socrates? Well, Socrates became infamous (leading eventually to his execution) for exposing those in Athens who felt they knew what was, what and believed they had a sure knowledge of how things were and could instruct others accordingly. Socrates as in our hypothetical dialogue above between Kant and Andreas would demonstrate that the "know-it-all" could never be that cocksure about what he prided himself in understanding. And often when they realized that

5. Kant, *Critique of Pure Reason*, Doctrine of Elements 2.1.1.11, A114.
6. Kant, *Critique of Pure Reason*, Preface to second edition, Bxxx.
7. Kant, *Critique of Pure Reason*, Preface to second edition, Bxxx.

Socrates was publicly exposing their folly, they suddenly remembered they had to catch a train (or the Athenian equivalent) and departed red-faced saying, "it all sounds very interesting but perhaps another time, Socrates." So, Kant in the hypothetical dialogue above is playing that Socratic role in questioning our man of science in his desire to educate our unenlightened believer. He does so, as Kant puts it, "in the service of Morality and religion . . . we see it above all when we take account of the way criticism puts an end for all future time to objections against morality and religion in a Socratic way, namely by the clearest proof of the ignorance of the opponent."[8]

How does Kant think he is doing this? Well, in the preface to *Critique of Pure Reason* he argues that, for the materialist to deny the reality of God, freedom, and immortality, reason would have to apply rational principles that only apply to appearances, to "objects of possible experience," and not to things in themselves beyond those appearances.

"Reason would have to help itself to principles that in fact reach only to objects of possible experience and which, if they were to be applied to what cannot be objects of experience, then they would always actually transform it into an appearance."[9] Which of course is the very argument we saw Kant using in our imaginary dialogue above.

This way of arguing against his opponent appears again and again at a number of places throughout the book before we get to our hypothetical example we dramatized at the beginning. So in this way Kant says, "much is . . . won if . . . I can nevertheless repel the dogmatic attacks of a speculative opponent, and show him that he can never know more in which to deny my expectations about the nature of my subject than I can in order to hold to them. . . . Through criticism alone can we sever the very root of materialism, fatalism, atheism, of freethinking unbelief."[10] In fact, some have argued that the whole six-hundred-page book has this aim of denying knowledge in order to make room for faith at its center. As one Kant scholar says, "That is the purpose of the whole project of the First Critique . . . that we have 'to deny knowledge in order to make room for faith.'"[11] Twentieth-century philosopher of religion Rudolph Otto gave clear expression to what Kant's philosophy means for faith: "the conviction gains ground that nature and natural processes are inadequate appearances, an incomplete picture of true things, . . . [an] inadequate image of the true world, which is a world free

8. Kant, *Critique of Pure Reason*, Preface to second edition, Bxxxi.

9. Kant, *Critique of Pure Reason*, Preface to second edition, Bxxxi.

10. Kant, *Critique of Pure Reason*, Preface to second edition, Bxxvi.

11. McCormack, *Karl Barth and American Evangelicalism*, 79.

from natural law, from mathematics and mechanics. . . . a 'realm of grace,' a world of God."[12]

## Kant: The Philosophical Cop

Now Kant is very well aware that some might say to him at this point, "big deal. You may have stopped the religious sceptic in his tracks which at first sight is quite impressive, by saying that their scientific rationality can only go so far and may not be telling us how things really are. But you haven't actually given us any positive arguments for the faith; you have just shown the critic the error of his ways."

Kant was always ready to provide some helpful illustration. For Kant argues that to say what he has done is not that significant is like saying to the police, "the only thing you've ever done is save us from being molested by thieves and brigands; you never do anything positive for us, you just prevent other people from attacking us so we can live in peace."

Kant's point is that the police are doing a pretty worthwhile job, in defending and protecting you. So why would you complain when I also defend you against those who would attack your faith? "To deny that this service of criticism is of any positive utility would be as much as to say that the police are of no positive utility because their chief business is to put a stop to the violence that citizens have to fear from other citizens, so that each can carry on his own affairs in peace and safety."[13]

## The Factory of the Mind

Now in trying to describe how Kant, in his most famous book (*Critique of Pure Reason*), does this most important critical job, there is the suggestion of a promising metaphor. He talks about what we receive through the senses with respect to our knowledge of the world as "raw material."

In the introduction I said we would make the most of Kant's suggested metaphors, so here goes. We are very familiar (in a way Kant would not be) with the idea of something going through a radical process of transformation before it reaches us. For example, we are used to seeing how thoroughly a modern-day factory can process raw materials. That it can take in at the start some raw material and process it in such a thorough way that you would be hard-pressed at the end to recognize what it was originally. So,

12. Quoted in Chapman, *Ernst Troeltsch and Liberal Theology*, 122–23.

13. Kant, *Critique of Pure Reason*, Doctrine of Elements 1.2, B60.

when you see the gleaming electric vehicle driving out at one end of the factory, to the uninitiated it is difficult to conceive how this car is related to the crude iron ore that was mined before ever being processed.

One way then to understand what Kant is saying (and I say this knowing that any one metaphor will have its limitations when it comes to Kant) is that he thinks that the mental categories that we use to process our experience of the world are similar to the processing that happens to raw material in a factory. So, our minds might start by receiving some stimulus (from the world around us) that is unprocessed and unconditioned, but in order for us to make any sense of that raw material the mental processing has to do a lot of work. The importance of this conditioning in order to gain any coherent knowledge of the world is expressed well by the philosopher Ronald Green: "It is the active process of synthesizing information by means of concepts. Without this synthetic activity, says Kant, we would not have knowledge at all but a 'rhapsody of perceptions' that would not form a completely connected consciousness."[14]

Kant sometimes uses the terms "form" and "content," that the things in themselves supply the content, and our mental categories of understanding give that content some form.

## Your Shiny New SUV

As we have seen the formation can be so significant that even if you could see the content without the form you might never connect the two. To stretch the factory illustration further, it's like going to a quarry and seeing an excavator dig up a huge shovel of iron ore, and then asking the foreman, "What is that?" and being told that is your new shiny Land Rover SUV. Well, of course its most of the content, but very little of the form.

The crucial point here for Kant, and it's a point that will be made much of, is that the end product in terms of our fully conditioned understanding will not be able to tell us anything much about the nature of the raw material before it entered the human factory of mental processing. For what we know is "nothing but the representation of appearance" and not the unconditioned raw material. Kant has an interesting term for what is there before the processing has happened; he calls this "the thing in itself." So if you could strip away all the mental conditioning and get back to the raw material of our senses, that would be for Kant getting back to "the thing in itself." As Kant explains with little in the way of metaphorical amusement,

14. Green, *Hidden Debt: Kierkegaard and Kant*, 37.

> We have therefore wanted to say that all our intuition [perception/awareness] is nothing but the representation of appearance; that the things that we intuit [perceive] are not in themselves what we intuit [perceive] them to be, nor are their relations so constituted in themselves as they appear to us; and that if we remove our own subject or even only the subjective constitution [structure] of the senses in general, then all the constitution [structure], . . . would disappear. . . . [15]

> We have nothing to do with anything except appearances anywhere (in the world of sense), even in the deepest research into its objects.[16]. . . .

> All (outer and inner) experience is merely subjective conditions of all our intuition, in relation to which therefore all objects are mere appearances and not things given for themselves in this way; about these appearances much may be said, but nothing whatsoever about the things in themselves that may ground them.[17]

Kant's point to our doubting Andreas, then, is that it is possible that in the natural sciences that Andreas so admires, he is not witnessing the raw material, the things in themselves before the processing has happened, but rather the end product that has been through the mental factory's transformative procedure. Therefore, the things in themselves that science can never know may be of a totally different nature, and may in fact resemble the way faith sees the world.

## An Anthropocentric Revolution

Kant's own illustration for what is going on here, and an illustration that appears in most of the secondary literature, is I think a little confusing. It compares Kant's revolution in the way we understand our knowledge of the world to that of the Copernican revolution in astronomy.

> Up till now it has been assumed that all our cognition must conform to the objects; . . . let us once try whether we do not get farther . . . by assuming that objects must conform to our cognition . . . before they are given to us. This would be just like

15. Kant, *Critique of Pure Reason*, Doctrine of Elements 1.2, B60.
16. Kant, *Critique of Pure Reason*, Doctrine of Elements 1.2, B63.
17. Kant, *Critique of Pure Reason*, Doctrine of Elements 1.2, B49.

> the first thoughts of Copernicus, who when he did not make good progress in the explanation of the celestial motions of the Planets assumed that the entire celestial host revolves around the observer, and tried to see if he might not have greater success if he made the observer revolve and left the stars at rest.[18]

But ironically what Kant is suggesting in his new approach to how we should think of knowledge is surely the opposite to the Copernican revolution. Copernicus moved from a solar system centred on us to a solar system centred on something external to us, that being the Sun. But for Kant, as we have seen, we are now at the center of the process of knowing. Perhaps another allusion to the Copernican revolution in a footnote more naturally fits: "Copernicus . . . ventured, in a manner contradictory to the senses yet true, to seek for the observed movements not in the objects of the heaven but in their observer."[19] Whatever we make of Kant's example in expressing his new perspective in philosophy his *Critique of Pure Reason* has become known as the Copernican revolution of modern philosophy.

## Just Crazy

I think, one of the main reasons why students struggled to understand Kant's philosophy, is that they cannot believe that anyone could countenance such a radically counterintuitive and frankly outlandish idea. When I first read about Kant, and after a number of self-inflicted headaches, I think the penny eventually dropped. But because what Kant was suggesting seemed such a crazy, strange, and counterintuitive idea, I then read as much as I could on Kant, just to reassure myself that I had come to the right conclusion.

Kant clearly recognizes this reaction and describes his new idea as exaggerated, quite contradictory and strange.

> Thus, as exaggerated and contradictory as it may sound to say that the understanding is itself the source of the laws of nature, and thus of the formal unity of nature, such an assertion is nevertheless correct and appropriate to the object, namely experience.[20]

Kant expands this point further:

18. Kant, *Critique of Pure Reason*, Preface to the second edition, Bxvi.
19. Kant, *Critique of Pure Reason*, Preface to the second edition, Bxxii.
20. Kant, *Critique of Pure Reason*, Doctrine of Elements 2.1.1.2, A128.

> That nature should direct itself according to our subjective ground of apperception . . . may well sound quite contradictory and strange. But if one considers that this nature is nothing in itself but a sum of appearances, hence not a thing in itself but merely a multitude of representations of the mind, then one will not be astonished.[21]

A few pages on, Kant continues:

> Thus, we ourselves bring into the appearances that order and regularity in them that we call nature, and moreover we would not be able to find it there if . . . our mind had not originally put it there.[22]

## Space and Time

Kant does not just have in mind (get the pun!) categories like cause and effect, which are so important to the natural sciences. He sees what he is suggesting as also true of space and time itself. In fact, the first two major sections of *Critique of Pure Reason* put forward the case that space and time are also not to be found in the things in themselves, but again are a product of the way our minds perceive things. As Kant explains,

> The . . . concept of appearances in space . . . is a critical reminder that absolutely nothing that is intuited in space is a thing in itself, and that space is not a form that is proper to anything in itself, but rather that objects in themselves are not known to us at all, and that what we call outer objects are nothing other than mere representations of our sensibility, whose form is space, but whose true correlate, i.e., the thing in itself, is not and cannot be cognized through them . . . and . . . time is therefore merely a subjective condition of our [human] intuition . . . and in itself, outside the subject, is nothing. Nonetheless it is necessarily objective in regard to all appearances, thus also in regard to all things that can come before us in experience . . . .
>
> It is therefore indubitably certain, and not merely possible or even probable, that space and time, as the necessary conditions of all [outer and inner] experience, are merely subjective conditions of all our intuition, in relation to which therefore all

21. Kant, *Critique of Pure Reason*, Doctrine of Elements 2.1.1.2, A114.
22. Kant, *Critique of Pure Reason*, Doctrine of Elements 2.1.1.2, A126.

> objects are mere appearances and not things given for themselves in this way.[23]

For my own benefit, let alone for yours, I have always been keen to try and find authors who explain Kant's philosophy accurately but clearly, and Frederick C. Beiser is possibly the best example of this I have found:

> It was Kant's central thesis . . . that space and time . . . are the universal and necessary manner in which the human mind perceives the matter given to it by sensation. In other words, the human mind, by the necessary laws of its operation, must perceive things in some space and at some time. These forms, Kant argued, cannot be abstracted from experience because they are necessary conditions of experience; before we abstract anything from experience, they must already be in operation. Since these forms are therefore subjective, arising from our own mental activity, Kant concluded that they are valid only for how we perceive things, that is, only for appearances and not things-in-themselves.[24]

## Virtual Reality, But Not as We Know It, Jim

Some people try to use examples from science fiction (for example, living inside the Matrix) or computer technology to illustrate what Kant is saying. Yet as I hope we will see, I don't think these illustrations fully grasp the nature of Kant's radical proposal.

Yes, it's right that we now have within computer technology the idea of virtual reality. And I must admit it was very disorienting the first time I put on a virtual reality headset, for what I then saw after putting on the headset bore no relationship to the way things really were in the room at the time. But there are some major differences here from what Kant is getting at. For example, I can always take the headset off and compare it to how the room is in itself. For Kant, we could never do that as it is inconceivable that we could step outside of our own minds, our own subjectivity, and look at how things really are without the categories of space or time, cause and effect, and all our other forms of comprehension. For these categories are the necessary conditions for us to be able to apprehend and perceive anything at all.

Moreover, with virtual reality your surroundings are not related in any way to the room in which you are situated. For example, the first time I

23. Kant, *Critique of Pure Reason*, Doctrine of Elements 2.1.1.2, A126.

24. Beiser, *Genesis of Neo-Kantianism*, 212.

experienced a virtual reality simulator, one moment I was in my next-door neighbor's front room and the next in the Wild West in the midst of a shoot-out, trying unsuccessfully to save my life. By contrast, for Kant, the things in themselves are the "cause" (be it ever so indirectly) of what we perceive, even though we don't perceive their "true" nature as they are in themselves.

## Entirely Unknown to Us

Now it's worth pausing here to explore a point we are going to observe repeatedly when it comes to the theological use of Kant's philosophy. For Kant, in order to limit reason and make room for faith, it's crucial that the things in themselves could be radically different from the processed reality we experience. In fact, in Kant's words they are "entirely unknown to us." As Kant makes clear, "What may be the case with objects in themselves and abstracted from all this receptivity of our sensibility remains entirely unknown to us. We are acquainted with nothing except our way of perceiving them, which is peculiar to us."[25] The fact that they remain entirely unknown to us is stated at least four times in his *Critique of Pure Reason*. Even though the thing in itself may be the cause of what appears to us, again in his words it remains "worlds apart from the appearances we experience."[26] For "The representation . . . contains nothing at all that could pertain to an object in itself, but merely the appearance of something and the way in which we are affected by it; and this receptivity . . . remains worlds apart from the cognition of the object in itself even if one might see through to the very bottom of it [the appearance]."[27]

## To Impress the Reader

Some of the technical philosophical terms that Kant uses may be there as much to impress the reader as anything else, and I have never been that sure how necessary they are. But when talking about "things in themselves" and "things as they appear to us" the philosophical terms Kant uses save a sentence or three in any discussion of his philosophy (not that this made his books any shorter). So here goes: Kant calls "things in themselves," "noumena"; and "the way things appear to us," "phenomena." (Now there's something to impress your tutor within your next assignment.) It's not too

25. Kant, *Critique of Pure Reason*, Doctrine of Elements 1.2, A49.
26. Kant, *Critique of Pure Reason*, Doctrine of Elements 1.2, B60.
27. Kant, *Critique of Pure Reason*, Doctrine of Elements 1.2, A44.

difficult to remember the distinction because the word "phenomena" is sometimes used more generally to describe "things as they appear to us," so "noumena" is therefore the opposite of that. And to stress yet again (as this distinction is crucial to Kant's whole scheme), even if our experience of the phenomena (as things appear to us) are understood in the categories that the natural sciences work with, it does not mean that noumena (things in themselves) need to be seen in those terms, for they "may remain worlds apart" from how things appear to us.

## Two Worlds Clash

This distinction is central to a major dilemma that Kant is keen to resolve. Recall that we began with the heated debate concerning human freedom. This belief was challenged by "Andreas" our man of science and his mechanistic worldview. As we will see, this all-important distinction between phenomena (the way things appear to us) and noumena (things in themselves, without our forms of understanding) is the way Kant addresses this big burning question.

We saw in part 1 that what was expressed in our imaginary dialogue between Albert and Andreas had also become a crisis point for the Enlightenment in the eighteenth century. As Beiser reminds us,

> Throughout the first three-quarters of the eighteenth-century philosophers of the mind were caught in the grip of a dilemma. . . . "Is the mind part of nature because it is explicable according to physical laws?" "Or is the mind outside nature because it is inexplicable according to physical Laws?"[28] It seemed . . . as if . . . [one]. . . had to choose between materialism or dualism—a materialism that explained the mind by reducing it to a machine, or a dualism that put the mind in a supernatural realm inaccessible to scientific study.[29]

Therefore, Kant's division between phenomena (the way things appear to us) and noumena (the world in itself, beyond our forms of understanding) is the way Kant will try to escape this crisis. For in the world of phenomena we seem to be determined by the cause and effect of scientific explanation, but Kant wants to argue that at the level of noumena that may not be the case. As Beiser explains "Through the distinction between appearances and things-in-themselves, [Kant] upholds the possibility of freedom, because

28. Beiser, *Fate of Reason*, 128.

29. Beiser, *Fate of Reason*, 128.

even though everything in the realm of appearances is determined according to the principle of sufficient reason, the world of things-in-themselves is not subject to this law."[30]

It is in this all-important distinction between appearances (phenomena) and things-in-themselves (noumena) that Kant is limiting what reason can tell us about the world and thereby making room for faith. "The only escape from these evils [materialism or dualism] is then to curtail the power of reason and to postulate: a supernatural mental realm. . . . [So] Kant [and a number of his contemporaries] . . . felt compelled 'to deny knowledge in order to make room for faith'; hence they postulated an unknowable supernatural realm to preserve freedom and immortality from encroachments of natural science."[31] As Kant explains this solution (I am sure it's easy to follow in the German),

> Now if we were to assume that the distinction between things as objects of experience and the very same things as things in themselves, which our critique has made necessary, were not made at all, then the principle of causality, and hence the mechanism of nature in determining causality, would be valid of all things in general. . . . I would not be able to say of one and the same thing, e.g., the human soul, that its will is free and yet that it is simultaneously subject to natural necessity, i.e., that it is not free, without falling into an obvious contradiction; because in both propositions I would have taken the soul in just the same meaning namely as a thing in general . . . and without prior critique, I could not have taken it otherwise. But if the critique has not erred in teaching that the object should be taken in a twofold meaning, namely as appearance or as thing in itself; if its deduction of the pure concepts of the understanding is correct, and hence the principle of causality applies only to things taken in the first sense, namely insofar as they are objects of experience, while things in the second meaning are not subject to it; then just the same will is thought of in the appearance (in visible actions) as necessarily subject to the law of nature and to this extent not free, while yet on the other hand it is thought of as belonging to a thing in itself as not subject to that law, and hence free, without any contradiction hereby.[32]

The Kant scholar Paul Guyer puts all this succinctly: "But precisely because the most fundamental laws of nature are in fact only our own

30. Beiser, *German Idealism*, 261.

31. Beiser, *Fate of Reason*, 128.

32. Kant, *Critique of Pure Reason*, Doctrine of Elements 1.2, A44.

impositions on the appearance of reality, we can also believe that our own choices, contrary to their appearance, are not governed by the deterministic laws of nature, but can be freely made in accordance with and for the sake of the moral law."[33] Which would allow for thoroughgoing determinism at the level of appearance while postulating the complete spontaneity of action at the level of reality.[34]

## Factories Don't Do Their Own Thing?

I once sat in on a class with students where the lecturer was introducing the philosophy of Kant, and much to my surprise Kant's philosophy was being explained to the students as if Kant was advocating a kind of individual subjectivism or even a subjective relativism. The lecture went on to suggest that Kant's philosophy was at the root of the kind of subjectivism and relativism many associate with postmodern philosophy.

So, to return to our cognitive factory illustration, it was being suggested that each factory did its own thing. Each factory had declared its independence and each production line was making whatever it fancied, that universal truths were not being produced and that individual preference determined what was made. Therefore, there was no common world that we all shared, but it was for each of us an illusion of our own making.

As congenial and polite as Kant may have been, I think if he was in the class at that point he would have walked out in a Kantian huff and slammed the door on the way out. And I'm sorry to say it wasn't that long before I interrupted, I think at the point when the lecturer associated Kant with postmodern philosophy, I really couldn't stand it any longer.

This lecturer (who will remain nameless) was not alone in his view of where Kant's philosophy was leading. What he was suggesting was a common interpretation of Kant's *Critique of Pure Reason*, when it first appeared. As Frederick C. Beiser has pointed out, in the first few years after Kant's *Critique of Pure Reason* was published, "this subjectivist criticism of Kant . . . was virtually universally shared by philosophers of every school. . . . To all these critics, it seemed as if Kant had trapped us inside the circle of our own consciousness, so that the entire world appeared to be a dream or illusion."[35] Beiser then asks, "But was Kant really guilty of subjectivism?"[36]

33. Guyer, *Kant*, 2–3.
34. Guyer, *Kant*, 21.
35. Beiser, *German Idealism*, 48.
36. Beiser, *German Idealism*, 48.

As the subtitle of Beiser's study makes clear, "The Struggle against Subjectivism," subjectivism had never been Kant's intention, and from the start Kant was deeply concerned about this interpretation of his new philosophy. It can in fact be argued that in the second edition of his *Critique of Pure Reason* Kant goes out of his way to try to correct this misunderstanding.[37]

If all our knowledge of the world is as indirect, as Kant suggests, and we never get to see things as they are in themselves, and if Kant himself can constantly talk about us knowing nothing but the "representation of appearances," why you may ask is this philosophy of Kant's not a form of subjectivism or even relativism? Well, for Kant there are a number of reasons why he believes that his philosophy does not lead to subjectivism and relativism.

## It Has To Be That Way.

Kant repeatedly argues that for us to perceive or understand anything at all, the processing that the raw material goes through is a necessary one. These are the necessary conditions for the possibility of having any knowledge at all; without them we would know nothing. This is not something that can be individually determined or negotiated. Paradoxically this is a subjectivity that delivers objectivity. If the world is going to be objectively known to us, that is in time and space and causally related, then this subjective processing is a necessary condition for any of that objectivity to take place. It would be hard for example to think of having experience of anything not in time and space. In that sense there is no relativism here.

> Taking the example of the category of space, Beiser explains: Kant stresses the . . . necessary condition of experience, and more specifically the necessary condition under which anything appears to the external senses, sight or touch. To say that space is a necessary condition of the external senses means that if we see or touch anything, we must perceive it as somewhere in space. According to this explanation, then, the empirical reality of space means that appearing in space is a universal and necessary property of all objects of the external senses. . . . If . . . universally and necessarily true, then what appears in space cannot be an arbitrary or private perception, still less an illusion of the

37. The way German academics think nothing of producing an almost completely different book but retaining the title of an earlier work, is something that Anglo-American scholars find very difficult to comprehend. So, it is far more important when dealing with German literature to know what edition of a book you are reading as it may bear little if any resemblance to other editions.

imagination. Rather, these appearances will be real in virtue of their universal and necessary structure.[38]

## Tedious Technicalities

Now for the next technical term you cannot get away from when reading Kant. Kant calls these universal and necessary structures, these categories of understanding "transcendental." These transcendental structures of understanding are not something we can verify experimentally like a scientific hypothesis; they are far more basic than that. Rather, they are for Kant *the very preconditions of any possible understanding*, for they must be in place for us to have any objective knowledge of the world whatsoever. Science could not verify them, but science *presupposes* them.

If you think we have moved a long way from what Kant was debating with Andreas at the beginning of the chapter that is not at all the case. For the argument Kant used when debating with Andreas he introduces in his *Critique of Pure Reason* as a transcendental argument. As he says, "[I] could propose a transcendental hypothesis: that all life in reality is not material and cannot be reached by our senses, is really only intelligible (nonmaterial), not subject to temporal alterations at all, and has neither begun at birth nor will be ended through death'; . . . that this life is nothing but a mere appearance, sensible representation of the purely spiritual life."[39]

38. Beiser, *German Idealism*, 57.

39. Kant, *Critique of Pure Reason*, Preface to second edition, Bxxvii–xxviii.

# 9

# DEFENDING SCIENCE AND FAITH

## Back to Andreas

ANDREAS, IS VERY KEEN to make another point as he is not at all happy with the direction Kant has been taking (and is also rather concerned we might have forgotten about him).

Andreas says, "Now, hold all your philosophical horses, Kant. What you are suggesting sounds very ingenious and highly imaginative and quite entertaining, but let's be fair—you're getting a little carried away with your hypothetical hypothesis. At the end of the day I'm not interested in philosophical flights of fancy, I'm interested in what can be proved, what can be verified through our senses, what we can be certain about. And as far as I can see we can only find such solid and indisputable grounds in science.

"Modern science has proved on the basis of experimental observations, I think you philosophers call this 'empirically,' that the world does in fact work in these causal deterministic terms." (My wife has never read a theological or philosophical book, but when I told hear about this chapter on Kant's philosophy this was precisely the point she made, so Andreas you're in good company!) "So scientific observations have established beyond all possible doubt that that is the way the world works. We experience such cause and effect constantly and nothing could be better established than that.

"So, my argument against Albert and his charming wife, that we are all part of a cosmic machine, is well-founded, founded on universal experience. And even religious pietists need to face this reality if they are not to delude themselves. And at this point, Kant, you're just confusing things with your philosophical gymnastics, and like your friends not facing the facts of the matter."

Kant says, "But Andreas, this is exactly what I would want to question. Has science in fact proved beyond all doubt on the basis of empirical evidence your mechanistic outlook? Have such fundamental ideas as cause and effect been universally established beyond all possible doubt? Take my favorite example, that of the Scottish philosopher David Hume. It was he who woke me up and made me realize that your scientific outlook is not as well-established as I once thought it was. I was once half asleep like you, Andreas, and accepted such unexamined dogmas on faith."[1]

Says Andreas: "Before you go any further, Kant, you can't suggest that David Hume is going to support your wacky philosophy. There is no doubt that David Hume is well and truly on my side of this debate. It was he who said we can only know anything about the world on the basis of experience.[2] There is no doubt, Kant, that his whole approach to knowledge was modelled on what he saw happening in the scientific revolution."

Kant replies, "Andreas, that's exactly the problem. Hume, as any philosopher will do (they sometimes even get paid for it), started to examine this approach and pursue it to its logical conclusion. When he did this, he saw there was in fact little of any significance that you could establish through an appeal to our sense experience of the world. Take, for example, the very basis of your scientific outlook. As a scientist you don't just want to make lots of separate observations about the world around you. As a scientist you want to come up with universal statements, principles, or laws that apply to every instance of what you are examining. It is these laws about how things universally and necessarily behave the makes science so influential and so significant and so dependable. But Andreas, David Hume realized that no scientist could collect enough data to justify making such universal claims or establish such laws."

Andreas says, "But Kant, scientists are doing this all the time. They are discovering laws of nature that govern the material universe, that's what they do, so what are you on about? And they clearly prove all this on the basis of what they have observed."

1. In *The Prolegomena to Any Future Metaphysics*, published in 1783, Kant, wanting to make more popular his philosophy of the *Critique of Pure Reason* that had appeared two years earlier, famously wrote "I freely admit that the philosophy of David Hume was the very thing that many years ago first interrupted my dogmatic slumber and gave my investigations in the field of speculative philosophy a completely different direction" (*Prolegomena*, 4.260).

2. This became known as Hume's fork, which was discussed in chapter 6.

Says Kant: "But that's the problem, Andreas. David Hume, being the astute philosopher he was, realized that is exactly what they cannot do! Take a simple example. We know that all swans are white. How have we established this basic piece of knowledge about our material world?"

Andreas replies, "Well we have gone around looking at swans and after seeing a good number on the basis of that evidence we have concluded that all swans are white."

Kant says, "Andreas, what constitutes a good number? How many do we have to observe before we can establish the fact that all swans are white? A hundred swans? A thousand swans? A million swans? When should we stop and draw our conclusion? Would it just be swans in this country or should we go to other countries as well before we make our universal claim that all swans are white. How do you know that the next swan you see might not be black? I suggest to you that before you could establish that universal claim or law you would have to observe every swan on the planet.

"But of course, Andreas, that's still nowhere near universal. A universal statement does not just apply to swans today. To be truly universal it needs to be all swans at all times and in all places. So, we would need to observe all future swans and all past swans as well. So, I submit to you, Andreas, that not even you with all your experimental enthusiasm are able to manage that. I suggest to you that only the almighty could manage it" (and I imagine he may have smiled when Europeans, being so sure of this fact, first came across black swans on a voyage in 1697).

"Now this is a particularly trivial example, I admit. A less trivial one is the basis for your scientific outlook, namely, the belief that everything operates in terms of cause and effect. But as with my trivial example of swans, what would we have to do to establish that universal claim? We would have to do the same thing. Examine every possible instance throughout the cosmos, throughout history, and throughout time. So, David Hume concluded that our confidence in the universal law that is at the heart of any science, may not be as well-established as we might have imagined. And it was David Hume's analysis of this problem of scientific induction that woke me up from my dogmatic slumbers" (there is a good chance that a number of other things helped wake Kant up, but this is the one Kant examines a number of times).

"I am in fact writing about this in my new book. If I remember rightly I put the point something like this: 'Experience never provides true or strict . . . universality (through induction) for its judgments, so that one must properly say: So far as we have observed until now no exception is found for this or that rule. Empirical universality is thus only an optional . . .

augmentation of validity from that which holds in most cases to that which holds in all.'[3]

"Of no event could one say: something must have preceded it, upon which it necessarily followed, that is, it must have a cause; and thus, however frequent the cases one knew of in which there was such an antecedent, so that a rule could be derived from them, one could still not, on account of this, assume it as always and necessarily happened in this way . . . and this firmly grounds and makes irrefutable scepticism with respect to inferences rising from effects to causes."[4]

In his chapter on Kant's approach to this question entitled "Causal Laws and the Foundations of Natural Science," Michael Friedman explains: "For, according to Kant, such merely inductive considerations can never ground the strictly universal judgment that all events A are followed by events of type B: What we are entitled to say here, strictly speaking, is only that all events of type A observed have been followed by events of type B. Hence, neither the necessity nor the true or strict universality involved in the causal relation can be grounded empirically."[5] And as Kant explains (and here we hear the echoes of David Hume again) "Therefore the concept of a cause is itself fraudulent and deceptive and, to speak of it in the mildest way, an illusion to be excused insofar as a custom, . . . thus the concept of a cause is acquired surreptitiously and not rightfully—indeed, it can never be acquired or certified."[6]

I think we may have wandered away from the debate somewhat and there are still some final points that Andreas and Kant want to make. Kant says, "So David Hume's conviction that everything we know can only be based on experience (which has become known as empiricism) in fact led Hume to scepticism with respect to the sciences. As I have written, 'So, with respect to all cognition having to do with the existence of things . . . empiricism was first introduced as the sole source of principles, but along with it the most rigorous scepticism with respect to the whole of natural science.'"[7]

Andreas replies, "Kant, I cannot believe David Hume left things there. He must have come up with some good explanation of why we believe in cause and effect even if it cannot be wholly based on experience."

Kant says, "Well, Hume put such beliefs down to custom and habit of mind, things we just become used to. But you may, like me, feel that Hume's

3. Kant, *Critique of Pure Reason*, Introduction, 1.2 B4.

4. Kant, *Critique of Practical Reason*, 1.1.2.5.52.

5. Guyer, *Cambridge Companion to Kant*, 163.

6. Kant, *Critique of Practical Reason*, 1.2.5.50.

7. Kant, *Critique of Practical Reason*, 3.2.5.51.

solution is not sufficient. As I explain in what I am writing, 'Hume . . . as is well known . . . asked nothing more than that a merely subjective meaning of necessity, namely custom, be assumed in place of any objective meaning of necessity in the concept of cause'[8] and 'that science, so highly esteemed for its apodictic certainty, must also succumb to empiricism in principles on the same ground on which Hume put custom in the place of objective necessity in the concept of cause; despite all its pride, it must consent to lower its bold claims.'"[9]

Kant's philosophy, as we have seen, has a way out of this very dilemma. He has a way of returning universality and necessity to such scientific claims. For according to Kant, in order for us to have any experience of the world at all, that experience has to be presented in a particular way, and one of those ways is in terms of cause and effect. This then gives universality to our experience and in this way, science can be grounded on what is always the case. For if the cognitive factory has no choice but to process our experience in terms of cause and effect, then that will be universally true and necessarily so.

## Saving Science and Faith

Kant therefore not only wants to be seen as a defender of the faith (demonstrating that science does not give us the whole picture with regard to reality but just how it appears to us), but also as establishing universal and necessary foundations for science. In this way he sees his philosophy as liberating faith from scientific materialism and determinism, and also giving science what it craves in terms of universality and necessity.

As Kant explains, but not perhaps in the clearest of terms:

> I was able not only to prove the objective reality of the concept of cause with respect to objects of experience but also to deduce it as an a priori concept because of the necessity of the connection that it brings with it, that is, to show its possibility from pure understanding without empirical sources; and thus, after removing empiricism from its origin, I was able to overthrow the unavoidable consequence of empiricism, namely skepticism . . . with respect . . . to natural science.[10]

8. Kant, *Critique of Practical Reason*, Preface, 5.12.
9. Kant, *Critique of Practical Reason*, 1.2.5.52.
10. Kant, *Critique of Practical Reason*, 1.2.5.53.

In this way a peaceful resolution was to be established between faith and science, each with its own sphere of influence and activity.

## More Technicalities: The Synthetic *a Priori*

This is not, I believe, essential for getting the gist of what Kant was getting at, but Kant clearly saw this as important and of course there will be a test at the end to make sure you know all the technical stuff.

Kant believed that he had established in his theory of knowledge what he calls a "synthetic a priori" account of our understanding. (He must have been "well chuffed," as we say in England, as it is not often you come across a "synthetic a priori," it must have made his philosophical day.) Any philosopher reading Kant for the first time was, I am sure, meant to be impressed, in fact amazed, at how Kant could possibly manage to do this, as bringing together the "synthetic" and "a priori" is like mixing philosophical oil and water. But to the average punter it can feel like one more bit of elitist jargon to trip you up.

To try to explain this, Kant contrasts what he calls *a posteriori* knowledge with *a priori* knowledge. A posteriori knowledge is the knowledge I have of the guitar standing next to me and tempting me to pick it up. I see that it is a glorious deep red, I did not tell my wife that was the main reason I wanted it. This is a knowledge based on my experience of seeing it. A priori knowledge by comparison is not based on the experience of a particular object, but is independent of any experience, or prior to any experience. For example, it is common to see the knowledge acquired in logical or mathematical equations in such terms. And what is characteristic of such knowledge is that it is again necessary and universally valid.

The next distinction Kant makes is between "analytic" and "synthetic." An analytic judgment is one where what we are claiming is already contained by definition in the initial terms; for example, "all bachelors are unmarried." Saying that they are unmarried is not that surprising as that is what "bachelor" means. In contrast to this, "synthetic" knowledge is the kind of knowledge that cannot be derived by definition but offers us something we could not know in that way.

So, Kant, always wanting to amaze us, is bringing two very different types of knowledge together: "synthetic," which is normally not universal or necessary, but which is likely to be based on our experience; and "a priori," knowledge which is not normally based on experience but is by definition universal and necessary. (If you don't understand it, blame it on the fact that the author clearly hasn't explained it very well; I normally blame the author too.)

As one of the most meticulous and trustworthy contemporary commentators on Kant's philosophy put it:

> Kant argues, if we assume that the basic forms of our intuitions and concepts of objects, that is, of their sensory representations and conceptual organization, are derived from our experience of given objects, then our knowledge of them will never be more than a posteriori, thus contingent and limited, but if we can discover fundamental forms, for the sensory representation and conceptual organization of objects within the structure of our own minds, then we can also know that nothing can ever become an object of knowledge for us except by means of these forms, and thus that these forms necessarily and universally apply to the objects of our knowledge—that is, that they are synthetic a priori.[11]

Why one needs to know that Kant believes that our knowledge of the world can be referred to as technically both "synthetic" and "a priori" is somewhat beyond me. Surely all you need to be aware of is the fact that Kant believes that there are universal and necessary categories that shape, determine, condition, and process all we know and experience of the world. And I think we know that by now.

## The Philosopher of Protestantism Par Excellence

Now if Kant's basic intention in the *Critique of Pure Reason* (as stated in the preface) is to "deny knowledge in order to make room for faith," Kant's new philosophy was surely to be celebrated, for was he not single-handedly rescuing an embattled faith from the rising tide of secular thought? Should Kant not be seen as a philosophical saint, an intellectual savior, the providential answer to the threatening specter of scientific materialism, saving the faithful from determinism's iron cage?

So understandably Kant was heralded as the "philosopher of Protestantism" by modern theology, a phrase first used by Friedrich Paulsen in an influential study of Kant philosophy of 1899. Therefore, the modern theologian Ernst Troeltsch 1865–1923 put Kant's philosophical revolution on a par with Luther's Reformation: "Kant did for philosophy what Luther did

11. Guyer, *Kant*, 50.

for religion."[12] So, Friedrich Troeltsch's successor in Heidelberg saw Kant's philosophy "as the most significant event since the reformation . . . which made him the philosopher of Protestantism par excellence."[13]

What exactly did theology see in Kant's new philosophy that was worthy of such praise? Well, historian of theology and modern thought Helmut Thielicke underlines the point we have emphasized from the very beginning which started with the debate between the pietist and the skeptic: "[Kant] has rendered theology a service by establishing the philosophical basis for the possibility of faith. He had made it impossible for philosophers . . . to enter into competition with religion. . . . He has made a place for faith by excluding knowledge . . . from the sphere of transcendence. Hence knowledge can no longer compete with faith. He has made it impossible that an atheistic metaphysics should disturb the certainties of faith with the weapons of thought."[14]

In fact, Kant's new philosophy can be seen as the defining factor for a whole new era of theology. For example, the theologian Bruce McCormack argues that with the acceptance of Kant's philosophical revolution, in other words, the "limitation of what may be known by . . . theoretical reason to phenomenal reality,"[15] is key to answering the question "what is the meaning of 'modernity' in the realm of Christian theology? What is it that makes any theology modern rather than ancient?"[16]

## The Conversion Experience

From the time Kant wrote *Critique of Pure Reason* up to the present day Kant's novel approach to the question of faith and knowledge has engendered what can only be described as dramatic conversions. This was true of the philosopher Karl Leonhard Reinhold, who was the most influential publicist of Kant's philosophy in the eighteenth century; "there can be no doubt that Karl Leonhard Reinhold's 'Letters on the Kantian Philosophy' which first appeared during 1786 and 1787 in the [German Mercury] . . . played a significant role in changing the philosophical climate, and that after 1787 Kant's philosophy became all the rage among the younger students of philosophy."[17]

12. Chapman, *Ernst Troeltsch and Liberal Theology*, 85.
13. Chapman, *Ernst Troeltsch and Liberal Theology*, 85.
14. Thielicke, *Modern Faith and Thought*, 310.
15. McCormack, *Orthodox and Modern*, 11.
16. McCormack, *Orthodox and Modern*, 11.
17. Guyer, *Cambridge Companion to Kant and Modern Philosophy*, 631.

Originally critical of Kant's innovative approach Reinhold tells how an in-depth study of Kant's *Critique of Pure Reason* changed his view of this new philosophy entirely. As Beiser tells the story "The effect of Reinhold's study of the Kritik [*Critique of Pure Reason*] could not have been more dramatic: a complete conversion to the critical philosophy. The sharp critic of Kant had become his ardent disciple. Such indeed was the ardor of Reinhold's conversion that he felt called upon "to become a voice in the wilderness to prepare the way for the second Immanuel."[18]

> What brought about Reinhold's sudden conversion to the critical philosophy? Why this abrupt volte-face, so that an antagonist of Kant became a protagonist almost overnight? In a short essay and in a letter to Kant Reinhold himself explained the reasons for his conversion. In that gloomy Autumn of 1785 he was suffering from a severe intellectual crisis, which he was desperate to resolve at any price. His head and heart were in conflict. His heart led him to faith in the existence of God, immortality, and providence; but his head forced him to doubt these cherished beliefs.[19]

But as Beiser goes on to argue the acute existential conflict that Reinhold had personally experienced and was desperate to find some relief from was in fact just the personal expression of a spiritual crisis that was gripping the intellectual culture of his time. "The two sides of this dilemma, Reinhold argues, can be seen in the conflict between the pietism and rationalism of the day, appealing to his heart and head respectively. What he sees in Kant's new philosophy was a way to resolve this dilemma by drawing the limits to what reason could know in order to leave room for faith."[20]

> What Reinhold was looking for was some middle path between rational disbelief and irrational belief. Only a critique of pure reason is in a position to resolve the dispute between rationalists and pietists, Reinhold contends. To prove his point, he shows that the dispute has reached a stalemate the rationalist cannot convince the pietist, since the pietist can always pick holes in his most elaborate and subtle demonstrations. Conversely, the pietist cannot persuade the rationalist, because the rationalist will always be able to question the authority of revelation and scripture through the latest philological and historical research. This deadlock has now made the fundamental issue plain to see,

18. Beiser, *Fate of Reason*, 232.
19. Beiser, *Fate of Reason*, 232.
20. Beiser, *Fate of Reason*, 234.

> Reinhold thinks. The pietist accuses the rationalist of expecting too much of reason, and the rationalist charges the pietist of expecting too little of it. Because each side maintains that the other fails to understand the true nature of reason, the whole dispute turns into the question, what are the limits of reason. The only way to settle the dispute, then, is through an investigation into the faculty of reason itself such an inquiry is the only step forward in the dispute.[21]

Then Reinhold explains to those reading his published letters that such an analysis of the limits of reason had been published by Immanuel Kant five years previous, but had not received the acclaim that it had warranted. Reinhold then goes on to call the *Critique of Pure Reason* "the greatest masterpiece of the philosophical spirit" and that it had resolved the crisis between head and heart.[22]

## A Contemporary Conversion

But I need to warn you such a conversion experience can occur in studying his philosophy today. For example, a lecturer in New Testament studies at the university department near to a college where I was teaching was keen to come and lead a seminar for college faculty and research students. When I found out what he would be talking to us about I was somewhat surprised. I imagined he would be leading us in studying some area of Paul's theology as I had heard that was his specialism, but then I found out that he wanted to lead a seminar on the philosophy of Immanuel Kant. When we heard his passionate presentation of Kant's philosophy and its significance for faith today, it was clear he had also experienced a dramatic conversion. He had originally studied physics before he studied theology and clearly Kant's philosophy was a way of bringing these two worlds into some kind of harmony. Why he had not already encountered Kant's ideas when a student at Oxford I would not like to say.

## Kant and Popular Culture

Helmut Thielicke is, I think, right when he takes the importance of Kant's influence a stage further. He sees Kant's influence in terms of the way modern culture in the West conceives of religious faith. As he states, "it is due to

21. Beiser, *Fate of Reason*, 234.
22. Beiser, *Fate of Reason*, 234.

Kant's influence that religion occupies in the general consciousness today a completely different place from the one it occupied in previous epochs."[23] What Thielicke has in mind here is that where for the medieval theologian or even for most philosophers at the beginning of the Enlightenment, a synthesis between faith and reason was conceivable, after Kant such a synthesis was plainly inconceivable. After Kant religion and reason, faith and science, spirituality and rationality were to occupy different hemispheres, different biospheres, different states of the mind and heart, and become oil and water's epistemological (how we know what we know) equivalent.

## Taking Stock

In what we have surveyed we have seen that Kant may be considered savior of the Protestant faith. But does Kant's salvific act have implications for the nature of that faith? In other words, do Kant's philosophical services come at a price? This question is the theological storm center in any understanding of the implications of Kant's philosophy for religious faith. It is therefore into these stormy seas we now enter.

23. Thielicke, *Modern Faith and Thought*, 292.

# 10

# BAD NEWS IN DISGUISE

## *The Other Side to the Story*

*God is being increasingly pushed out of a world that has come of age, out of the spheres of our knowledge and life, and that since Kant he has been relegated to a realm beyond the world of experience.*

—DIETRICH BONHOEFFER

IF KANT CAN HOLD the head and the heart apart in such a satisfactory way, halting the conflict between piety and rationalism; if he can single-handily defend the faith against the ravages of reason, in his own words "denying reason to make room for faith"; if he can liberate us from the iron cage of materialism and determinism and restore to us our spiritual nature and everlasting soul; if Kant became "the philosopher of Protestantism par excellence," how can such a philosophical wonderworker on behalf of religion also be an atheist? How can he be described by the Jewish philosopher Moses Mendelssohn, one of Kant's contemporaries, as the "all-crushing . . . destroyer?" For Mendelssohn was convinced that Kant was a skeptic and a nihilist, and that his philosophy constituted a major threat to morality and religion.

We first get one of the most influential summaries of the significance of Kant's life and thought in the German Jewish poet and literary critic, Heinrich Heine's *History of Religion and Philosophy in Germany* (1834). He can write about the consequence of Kant's philosophy in these terms: "Immanuel Kant, the great destroyer in the realms of thought, far surpassed

Maximilian Robespierre in terrorism, yet he had certain points of resemblance to the latter that invite a comparison of the two men."[1]

He draws a sharp distinction between the quiet and orderly life of Immanuel Kant the parochial citizen of Konigsberg and the devastating significance of his thought:

> What a remarkable contrast between the external life of this man and his destructive, world-crushing thought! Indeed, had the citizens of Konigsberg sensed the true meaning of his thought, they would have been in much greater dread of him than of the executioner, who only kills people. But the good citizens saw in him only a professor of philosophy, and when he walked by at the proper time, they gave him friendly greetings, and set their watches.[2]

So, as Peter Byrne sums up Heinrich Heine's conclusion, "Thus Kant's message to humanity on the front of his great work should have echoed those of Dante's, 'abandon all hope,'"[3] an assessment that Peter Byrne finds convincing. As he makes clear, "It will come down closer to Heine as this study proceeds."[4] So, this negative assessment is not some outdated and irrelevant misunderstanding, but also a contemporary scholarly assessment.[5] As the theologian Hans Küng concludes,

> Kant became known at an early date as the *Alleszermalmer* ("the man who crushes everything"), a judgment that has pursued him even up to the present time; . . . the philosopher from Konigsberg has continually been suspected of agnosticism and disguised atheism, . . . although it was he in particular, . . . at a time of rising atheism, who protected belief in God against a "devouring" reason and tried to tie down the latter in its own chains.[6]

How than can we get such completely contradictory assessments of Immanuel Kant's philosophy from his own day up to the present: on the one hand, "the philosopher of Protestantism par excellence" and on the other, the dramatic "crusher of everything."

1. Heine, *On the History of Religion and Philosophy in Germany*, 79.
2. Heine, *On the History of Religion and Philosophy in Germany*, 79.
3. Byrne, *Kant on God*, 3
4. Byrne, *Kant on God*, 3.
5. Rumor has it that after some time the inhabitants of Königsberg caught on to the radical nature of Kant's philosophy and were known to name their vicious dogs "the destroyer" in honor of Immanuel.
6. Küng, *Does God Exist?*, 537–38.

The answer is surprisingly simple, being a consequence of what we have been exploring since the beginning of this chapter, and perfectly illustrated in an extended metaphor Kant uses to sum up his critique of reason.

## An Island of Knowledge and Sea of Faith

Kant explains in an extended metaphor in the second addition of his *Critique of Pure Reason* that so far, we have been exploring a land, the domain of phenomenon (things as they appear to us) where rationality rules and all our scientific categories work perfectly. In this metaphorical land everything of course works in terms of cause and effect within space and time. Everything can be explained by the natural sciences in those familiar materialistic and deterministic terms we have looked at. As Kant writes at the beginning of this major metaphor, "We have now . . . travelled through the land of pure understanding, and carefully inspected each part of it."[7]

But then Kant makes a now familiar point, the one he made at the beginning of this chapter when debating with Andreas. Namely, that the land that the materialist thinks is the totality of existence, all there is to reality, is not at all what it seems. That this land we have been investigating with our pure rationality is not all that there is, that we have not been aware of the whole picture. So in Hollywood terms, as the camera pans back (I'm sure Kant would have used this cinematic technique if he knew about it), much to our surprise what we have been investigating up until now is just a small island. In Kant's words, "This land, however, is an island, and enclosed in unalterable boundaries by nature itself."[8]

We know enough about Kant's philosophy by now for this not to be too much of a surprise, because we have investigated his arguments concerning the limitations of pure rationality. The rational categories of understanding so important to us in our scientific endeavours will only work in the limited area of phenomena (things as they appear to us) and not with things as they are in themselves. So, it is little wonder that Kant can call the realm of phenomena an island.

But this is not the major point of Kant's metaphor; the main point, as we will see, is considering what lies beyond, what surrounds the island, our island (the kind of nail-biting drama I bet you never thought you would find in philosophy). But it's when Kant does the big reveal that we begin to understand why his thought has generated such conflicting interpretations.

7. Kant, *Critique of Pure Reason*, Doctrine of Elements 2.1.2, A235/B294.
8. Kant, *Critique of Pure Reason*, Doctrine of Elements 2.1.2, B295/A236.

You would imagine that Kant would at this point go on to contrast the difference between the land and the sea in negative and positive terms respectively. For the land is surely where faith is threatened, threatened by our now-familiar mechanistic materialism from which Kant has sought to save us. By contrast, we should find liberation beyond the Island. It should hold all that we have been deprived of on the materialistic island. For are we not expecting a realm of freedom, everlasting spirit, of faith and hope?

When they get to the edge of oppressive materialism would not the faithful expect their beatific vision? The shining crystal sea, the seraphic ocean of eternal life, caressing a golden beach of faith hope and love. (One could get wonderfully carried away with this kind of thing.) For was not Immanuel's aim to restrict reason to the limited land of appearance (phenomena) to make room for religious faith in the way things really are the unconditioned spiritual and everlasting noumenon.

Yet in stark contrast to the faithful's expectations, the open sea that Kant's philosophy reveals is not presented in positive terms at all. It is surprisingly uninviting and extremely problematic. As Kant explains, starting from the very beginning:

> We have now not only travelled through the land of pure understanding and carefully inspected each part of it, but we have also surveyed It, and determined the place for each thing in it. This land, however, is an island, and enclosed in unalterable boundaries by nature itself. It is the land of truth (a charming name), surrounded by a broad and stormy ocean, the true seat of illusion, where many a fog bank and rapidly melting iceberg pretend to be new lands and, ceaselessly deceiving with empty hopes the voyager looking around for new discoveries, entwine him in adventures from which he can never escape and yet also never bring to an end. [9]

Once Kant has thought of a metaphor, he certainly likes to make the most of it (I know the feeling). In fact, this is not the first time that Kant has used a nautical metaphor to describe the metaphysical voyage into the unknown. In 1762 he published an essay entitled "The Only Possible Basis for a Demonstration of the Existence of God." In the preface to it he also gives us a wayfarers warning about venturing on metaphysical speculation concerning the existence of God, and note the obvious parallels to the passage we have just examined in his *Critique of Pure Reason*.

9. Kant, *Critique of Pure Reason*, Doctrine of Elements 2.2.2, A235/B294, B295/A236.

> Achievement of this goal [proof of the existence of God], however, requires that one venture into the fathomless abyss of metaphysics. This is a dark ocean without coasts and without lighthouses where one must begin like a mariner on a deserted ocean who, as soon as he steps on land somewhere, must test his passage and investigate whether perhaps unnoticed currents have confused his course despite all the care which the art of navigation can command.[10]

## The Inside-Out Cave: Platonism, But Not as We Know It

One way to see why Kant's philosophy has been open to such contradictory interpretation is to notice the fact that Kant in this most developed of metaphors seems to be reversing the most famous of philosophical analogies. It seems to me that it is a reversal of the most memorable of analogies that Plato left us with (that we discussed in part 1). For Plato's subterranean simile of people trapped in a cave, needing to find their way out in order to find some kind of illumination and enlightenment, also involves the dramatic contrast between two forms of knowledge or understanding. But even though Kant's analogy is looking at the same contrast in understanding that Plato's metaphor was representing, Kant is coming to a very different conclusion than that in Plato's story. Let's look at the precise similarities first.

### Similarities: The Material World and Empirical Knowledge

The first kind of knowledge that Plato talks about is one that resides in the cave, and for Plato amounts to no more than fleeting shadows. This is a form of understanding that can only deal with the material world around us. Kant has almost an exact equivalent here in terms of his island analogy. Again, the kind of knowledge that is considered here is likewise our engagement with the material world around us.

### Similarities: The Material World Is Not All There Is

Here again we have almost an exact parallel in the fact that we're told that this knowledge of the world around us is not all there is, for it is not giving us the whole picture of reality. So, in both metaphors we have the big reveal. In Plato's it is the fact of realizing that all along we have been inside the cave

10. Kant, *One Possible Basis for a Demonstration of the Existence of God*, 43.

and that there is something consequently beyond. With Kant we have the obvious parallel that what we have been exploring in terms of the world around us hasn't been land at all as we thought it was, it has been an island, and consequently again there is something beyond the island as there was beyond the cave. The parallels are so clear that some of both Kant's most faithful disciples and his most severe critics were convinced that in this way Kant was seeking to reinstate his own form of Platonism.

## Differences: The Reversal

But this is where the similarities stop, and a strange reversal seems to take place. This reversal is not a denial of Plato's philosophical analogy; a denial of his metaphor would be materialism. That would not accept that we are in a cave or on an island at all. For a denial would say there is nothing outside or beyond to consider. Rather than a denial of Plato's analogy, it in fact looks as if we have a strange reversal of the simile. And it is this I think that explains why Kant's philosophy can be seen in such contrasting terms.

The reversal comes in the way Kant contrasts the nature of the island and what goes on there, with the nature of the sea and what happens on the ocean. For Plato at this point we move from the negative to the positive, from the unenlightened to the enlightened, one might say from uncertain faith to definite knowledge. But for Kant strangely it seems to be almost the opposite.

So, where Plato has nothing positive to say about what happens in the cave, for because it's happening within a cave it is dark and it deals only in shadows, therefore anything purporting to be knowledge is based on illusion or delusion. Whereas what's beyond the cave is in contrast in bright daylight, everything is revealed, and true knowledge found. But this is exactly where the reversal is so apparent in Kant's philosophy and his island analogy. For Kant (in stark contrast to Plato), the dark shadowy illusions and delusions are not on the land (the equivalent to the cave) but are out at sea (the equivalent to what lies beyond the cave). When Kant leads us to the edge of the island as we have seen, we do not then survey a bright and shining sea but rather we look out on a dark,[11] stormy, fogbound, and rather foreboding berg-infested ocean.

But this is not the only reversal, the way the island is presented is also the reverse of what we have in Plato. It may be an island indicating that it's limited and that's not all there is, that yes there is something beyond, but

11. I'm surmising dark, as in my experience when it is stormy it is pretty dark, but of course we cannot make universal and necessary statements about such things.

unlike Plato this is not the island of shadows and illusion (as with the cave) but it has Kant's rather charming name "the land of truth."

The contrast at this point could not be greater; it would never cross Plato's mind to call the cave "the cave of truth" for it is the very reverse of that. So, for Kant, the inside and outside of his metaphor is the reverse of Plato's. It's the reverse because it is largely dealing with the same contrast but reversing the way it's described.

Even though I am unaware of the suggestion being made anywhere else that Kant reverses Plato's analogy of the cave, some comments have got fairly close. "The bright day of the phenomena that Kant's thought opens up is thus surrounded by an impenetrable night. The thing-in-itself which constitutes the true reality remains merely a dark, unknown x. Kant warns us not to enter this night. . . . He suggests that the noumenal night may in fact be the true world and the day in which we dwell only a representation of this nocturnal."[12]

## Immanuel's Mixed Message

We need to note also that this is not just a reversal of what the religious believer might have been expecting and certainly a reversal of Plato's parallel analogy about the limits of empirical knowledge. It's also (just to confuse things) almost a reversal of what we've seen Kant say so far. We started for example with the hypothetical hyperbole that Kant suggests we might use against a materialist and as you read it again note that it is pure Platonism.

> You could propose a transcendental hypothesis: that all life is really only intelligible, not subject to temporal alterations at all, and has neither begun at birth nor will be ended through death; that this life is nothing but a mere appearance, i.e., a sensible representation of the purely spiritual life, and the entire world of the senses is a mere image, which hovers before our present kind of cognition and, like a dream, has no objective reality in itself; that if we could intuit the things and ourselves as they are we would see ourselves in a world of spiritual natures with which our only true community had not begun with birth nor would not cease with bodily death (as mere appearances), etc.[13]

Would not the reader of this passage find it strange that in the same book Kant calls this dreamlike understanding "of mere appearance . . . that

12. Gillespie, *Nihilism before Nietzsche*, 74.

13. Kant, *Critique of Pure Reason*, The Transcendental Doctrine of Method 1.3, A780/B808.

has no objective reality," the sure and stable "island of truth," in contrast to a dark sea of the metaphysical unknown? No wonder Kant can be seen in such contradictory terms as the philosopher of modern "Protestantism par excellence" and also the "destroyer of all religious hope and faith." The reason is that we seem to be receiving a mixed message from Kant and as we will see possibly a conflicted one. For me, it's Kant's metaphors that are in fact most helpful in bringing these contrasting elements together.

Kant's land, in this most developed of Kant's allegories, may be an island, which suggests "that it is limited," it is not the totality of reality, and that something greater lies beyond. It may be the island of truth, but it's not the *whole* truth and nothing but the truth, being as it is an island. But even though the island constitutes a limited perspective on things, it is still the sum total of what's true about our experience of the world. And even though limited, it is a knowledge we can be sure of. So, when it comes to this knowledge, we are not all at sea. It is right to call it a land of truth, specifically an island of scientific truth. In this way, Kant can rightly see himself as a defender of the truth of natural science.

But as we've seen Kant also wants to be seen as a defender of the faith. The island simile expresses that well, for saying it's an island preconceives that it sits *within a greater reality*, that of the ocean surrounding it. But this is where things get tricky, and this is the key point that we are going to spend much of what follows exploring. Because Kant has restricted reason—that is, any form of pure rationality—to this island, to claim to have knowledge about what lies beyond the island is going to consequently become deeply problematic. This is where Kant's cautionary maritime metaphors come into play. For when it comes to any form of knowledge or faith, once we move beyond the island of well-substantiated truth, in Kant's terms we are literally all at sea. This is where Kant warns us about the treacherous nature of what is beyond our land of truth: "a broad and stormy ocean, the true seat of illusion, where many a fog bank and rapidly melting iceberg pretend to be new lands and, ceaselessly deceiving with empty hopes the voyager looking around for new discoveries."[14]

In time we will explore the idea that Kant's maritime allegory may not have fully captured how difficult things have become for theology, given Kant's account of what constitutes knowledge. That for metaphysics and religion things might in fact be bleaker than even this cautionary simile suggests.

14. Kant, *Critique of Pure Reason*, Doctrine of Elements 2.1.2, A235/B294.

## Two Accounts of Knowledge and of Faith

As this is such an important point for understanding what follows, I want to look at this by examining the two contrasting sides of Kant's analysis of human knowledge and religious faith.

On the one hand, Kant has provided human knowledge (as exemplified in the natural sciences) with a necessary and universal "transcendental framework." This provides the necessary categories of our human understanding that Kant believes his philosophy has extracted and exposed in a way no philosophy had done before. But, as we have seen, there is another side to his analysis, for this universal and necessary way in which we process the world does not present things as they are in themselves. The way things are in themselves could be very different than the way things look after they have been processed by the ubiquitous categories of our understanding.

But as there are two contrasting sides to Kant's approach to knowledge there are equally two very different sides to Kant's approach to faith. On the one hand, Kant makes the things of faith a possibility because he claims that the rational knowledge exemplified by the natural sciences does not tell us the whole story or give us access to how things are in themselves; this opens up the possibility for a form of faith in what lies beyond. But, and here is the stinger, because Kant consigns all rationality to the world of appearances, this promising sea of faith, beyond pure reason, becomes unfathomable and seemingly impossible to navigate. And that is why, when Kant develops his sea-of-faith simile, it is so cautionary and bleak. In fact, when Kant alludes to this vivid picture elsewhere in his *Critique of Pure Reason* things are not any more promising: "that the voyage of our reason may proceed only as far as the continuous coastline of experience reaches, a coastline that we cannot leave without venturing out into a shoreless ocean, which, among always deceptive prospects, forces us in the end to abandon as hopeless all our troublesome and tedious efforts."[15]

To summarize in a (long) sentence: Kant uses his critical philosophy to restrict reason and knowledge in order to make room for faith; ironically, these very restrictions makes the content of the faith he was hoping to defend very difficult to establish with any certainty.

15. Kant, *Critique of Pure Reason*, Doctrine of Elements 2.2.2.1, A396.

# 11

# NO PROOF OF GOD, A VERY MODERN MYTH

## Beyond the Coastline of Experience

When Kant voiced concern about the "voyage of reason going beyond the coastline of experience," he no doubt has in mind a particular kind of theology that he once pursued, but now castigates: what was known as natural theology, which tries to establish the existence and nature of God without the aid of any special revelation. To use a phrase that we will be exploring later, this is the very epitome of a theology "from below" in contrast to one "from above." It starts from nature rather than grace, it starts from what we already know, rather than what has been revealed; it starts from the world, and then argues from that to God's existence and nature. The most famous example of this prior to the Enlightenment became known as the "five ways," taken from Thomas Aquinas's *Summa Theologiae* (1265–74). But where these proofs take up only a few pages in Thomas's major work, the arguments for God's existence and nature during the Enlightenment and the scientific revolution take center stage.

Where theology prior to the Enlightenment had been developed in the context of the church's rich tradition, and in the light of revelation, these were the very motifs that the Enlightenment criticized. For the Enlightenment's raison d'être was to promote a new learning, exemplified by the burgeoning sciences, not based on the authority of past tradition or revelation. It was therefore argued that if theology was to survive in this new age, it needed to adopt new ways. In fact, in line with this, natural theology argued that the wonders of the world that science was revealing could lead quite naturally to a belief in its divine designer. Natural philosophers (later called scientists) were generally not opposed to this use of their work, and often made these connections themselves as it was a good way of demonstrating to the public that their work was also of religious value. (How strange that science once used religion to legitimate itself.)

This rational theology of the Enlightenment was pioneered in England by philosophers such as John Locke and Samuel Clark (he was a household name at the time), but could also be found on the Continent in the work of the German philosopher Gottfried Wilhelm Leibniz (1646–1716). When Kant was a student, the author that was most famous or infamous in Germany for this rationalist approach to religious faith was Christian Wolff (1679–1754). It was largely Wolff's rationalist approach to religion that brought the Enlightenment to Germany. And his theology was based on a key argument of natural theology that became known, thanks to Kant, as the cosmological argument for the existence of God. As Paul Guyer explains:

> [a] current that fed the Enlightenment (in Germany) was rationalism, deriving from the philosophy of Christian Wolff (1679–1754). Under the influence of Leibniz, Wolff combined traditional scholasticism with the new science, producing a comprehensive philosophical system. In theology he argued that scriptural revelation was distinct from rational theology, but wholly consistent with it. Wolff's rational theology was founded on the cosmological argument that the contingent world must depend for its existence on a necessarily existent and supremely perfect being. . . . Wolff's philosophy was the medium in which the German Enlightenment grew.

The philosopher Lewis Beck points out, "At the time of his death in 1754 [Christian Wolff] . . . was certainly the best-known thinker in Germany, fully deserving the honorific tile of Preaseptor Germaniae [teacher of Germany]."[1] The full title of Christian Wolff's most influential book commonly known as the "German metaphysics" gives us a good idea of Wolff's modest ambitions, *Rational Thoughts on God, the World, and the Soul of Man, and on All Things in General.*[2] Even though in addressing these questions Wolff was hoping for mathematical precision and certainty, I don't think the answer was forty-two.

Because of his strictly rational approach to religion Christian Wolff's philosophy and theology was vigorously opposed by professors in many university faculties in Germany who at the time were sympathetic to Pietism. Because of their complaints Frederick William the First, King of

1. Beck, "From Leibniz to Kant," 8.
2. Beck, "From Leibniz to Kant," 8.

Prussia, once gave Christian Wolff forty-eight hours to leave his jurisdiction under threat of hanging. Although Kant was never an uncritical follower of Wolff's philosophy, before his Copernican revolution Kant defended a form of Christian Wolff's natural theology in his *The One Possible Basis for a Demonstration of the Existence of God.*

In his landmark study of *Kant's Rational Theology* Allen Wood sees the significance of Kant's attack on natural theology in its broadest terms:

> Kant's immediate target, of course, is the rationalism of eighteenth-century Germans such as Christian Wolff. . . . But in a broader sense, the tradition he attacks is one which goes back many centuries to the religious ideas derived from Hebrew monotheism and found expression and defence in a metaphysics derived from the Greeks. This tradition, moreover, not only survived but actually drew strength from the modern scientific revolution. (In this connection, it should not be forgotten that the three principal theistic arguments, as Kant knew them, were closely associated with the names of Descartes, Leibniz, and Newton.) It is certainly understandable that Kant's attack on traditional theology should have been experienced by his contemporaries . . . as something profoundly disturbing. In this sense, perhaps . . . it was no exaggeration for Heine to speak of Kant as the Weltzermalmender, "the great destroyer in the kingdom of thought."[3]

Kant's wholehearted critique of any proof of God was one reason Kant was to be feared as a dangerous exponent of atheism. As Peter Byrne explains:

> Kant's critique of the arguments of natural theology is justly famous. It is one of the crucial steps in establishing the point that knowledge of God lies beyond the boundary set for reason by the Critical Philosophy and is therefore impossible. It helped Kant earn the reputation of the philosopher who attempted to assassinate God. The critique has been much discussed and reactions to it have varied from warm endorsement to rejection. Endorsement is shown in those many thinkers who take it that, along with Hume, Kant dealt the deathblow to natural theology.[4]

3. Wood, *Kant's Rational Theology*, 10.
4. Byrne, *Kant on God*, 19.

## Seeking the Unconditioned Is the Human Condition

As critical as Kant is of these rationalistic arguments for God's existence, he sees their pursuit as a perfectly natural part of the human condition. "For Kant, the pseudosciences of rationalist metaphysics all have their foundation in a natural tendency of human reason to transcend its limits and to seek a completeness in its knowledge which it will be forever beyond the finite nature of humanity to achieve."[5]

The cosmological argument is a perfect example of this.[6] When I have heard this argument defended in public debate, those who have employed it, have often made much of the fact that it is driven by a principal at the heart of the scientific revolution and universally confirmed by the natural sciences. For it works from the fact that every effect we see in the world around us can be explained by something prior to it. That nothing in the world we observe is self-explanatory; we can always seek for what caused it to be the way it is, or why it exists at all. But the further back we go in asking this question, the more fundamental the questions becomes, until we end up asking the ultimate question, "What explains the fact that there is anything at all?" As the German philosopher Gottfried Leibniz (whom Christian Wolff was following here) put it, the ultimate question is "Why is there something rather than nothing?"

Clearly nothing within the world can answer that question since that's what you are seeking to explain, so you need to seek an explanation that transcends the material world. But when you start talking about what transcends the material universe things naturally enough get pretty metaphysical, perhaps postulating an ultimate divine explanation a cosmic cause of the something rather than the nothing.

As I am sure you have realized by now, any such causal reasoning leading to an ultimate theological explanation will hit philosophical buffers when it comes to Kant's Copernican revolution, for in Kant's new philosophy, we can only be certain that cause and effect work in the world of appearances. Cause and effect are a necessary condition for our experience of things, but such necessary conditions do not apply beyond the world of our experience to things in themselves. So, we cannot use these essential but limited categories when talking about something that transcends the world of our experience.

5. Wood, *Kant's Rational Theology*, 17.

6. The terms in which the different arguments for God's existence have been designated have largely come from the way Kant refers to them in his *Critique of Pure Reason*; for example, the "ontological" and "cosmological" arguments.

To go back to our factory illustration, Kant makes the obvious point that our mental factory will only work if you give it raw materials to process, it cannot process thin air. It can apply the categories of cause and effect to the raw material of sensory content but to ask it to process supersensory questions about ultimate origins gives it nothing in the way of sensory content to work on. As Kant argues:

> A short time ago, I said that in this cosmological argument an entire nest of dialectical presumptions is hidden, which transcendental criticism can easily discover and destroy. . . . For example: . . .The transcendental principle of inferring from the contingent to a cause, which has significance only in the world of sense, but which outside it does not even have a sense. . . . The principle of causality has no significance at all and no mark of its use except in the world of sense; however, it is supposed to serve precisely to get beyond the world of sense.[7]

So as Peter Byrne says, Kant "accuses the [cosmological] argument of misusing the principle that every contingent thing has a cause, an accusation grounded on the assertion that the principle 'has no meaning at all and no criterion for its use, except in the sensible world.'"[8] As Kant sums up the situation, "But if . . . to infer from this to a cause that is entirely distinct from the world, then this once again would be a judgment of merely speculative reason, because the object here is not any object of a possible experience. But then the principle of causality, which holds only within that of possible experience and outside it is without any use or indeed without any meaning would be completely diverted from its vocation."[9] For Kant the cosmological argument is a perfect example of wanting to pursue our reasoning beyond its limits.

## Kant's Aeronautical Metaphor: The Dizzy Dove

We have seen Kant develop an extended metaphor warning us about the perils of leaving the island of truth for speculative seas. But Kant uses other vivid similes to make a similar point. In fact, most of Kant's powerful metaphors give vivid expression to the limits of reason. A favorite metaphor of Kant's here is not this time nautical but aeronautical. "Encouraged by . . . the

7. Kant, *Critique of Pure Reason*, Doctrine of Elements 2.2.2.3, A609/B637, A610/B638.

8. Byrne, *Kant on God*, 32.

9. Kant, *Critique of Pure Reason*, Doctrine of Elements 2.2.2.3 A636/B664.

power of reason, the drive for expansion sees no bounds. The light dove, in free flight cutting through the air the resistance of which it feels, could get the idea that it could do even better in airless space."[10]

For Kant the wings of the dove are, of course, the elevating powers of rationality and the air that the wings beat against is the experience of our senses. Trying to fly beyond the sensory into the supersensory, beyond that earthly atmosphere, are the speculations of metaphysics where reason has nothing to work on, no content to process, and as Kant says, "beats its wings to no effect." Kant also uses this metaphor in his book entitled *Fundamental Principles of the Metaphysics of Morals.* Talking about speculation that goes beyond possible experience he writes that reason "may . . . impotently flap its wings without being able to move in the . . . empty space of transcendent concepts . . . and so lose itself amidst chimeras."[11]

This analogy should be familiar by now for we saw it used by Augustine and John Locke in terms of Plato's metaphysical speculations. The classical example for Kant is also that of Plato and his speculations about the supersensible. "Likewise, Plato abandoned the world of the senses because it posed so many hindrances for the understanding, and dared to go beyond it on the wings of the ideas, in the empty space of pure understanding not noticing that he made no headway by his efforts, he had no resistance, no support, as it were, by which he could stiffen himself, and to which he could apply his powers in order to get his understanding off the ground."[12]

Kant's philosophical argument against moving "ever higher to more remote conditions" should be familiar to us by now but Kant never tires in reminding us of its perils.

> Human reason has the peculiar fate . . . that it is burdened with questions . . . which it also cannot answer, since they transcend every capacity of human reason. . . . It begins from principles whose use is unavoidable in the course of experience and at the same time sufficiently warranted by it. With these principles it rises . . . ever higher, to more remote conditions. But since it becomes aware in this way that its business must always remain incomplete because the questions never cease, reason sees itself necessitated to take refuge in principles that overstep all possible use in experience.[13]

10. Kant, *Critique of Pure Reason*, Introduction, A5/B9.
11. Kant, *Fundamental Principles of the Metaphysics of Morals*, 50.
12. Kant, *Critique of Pure Reason*, Introduction, A5/B9.
13. Kant, *Critique of Pure Reason*, Preface, Aviii.

Trying to reach such heights is also a dizzying experience for our Icarus of a dove. "But if we depart from this restriction of the idea to a merely regulative use, then reason will be misled in several ways, by forsaking the ground of experience, which has to contain the markers for its course, and by venturing beyond experience into the incomprehensible and inscrutable, in whose heights it necessarily becomes dizzy because from this standpoint it sees itself entirely cut off from every use attuned to experience."[14]

In surveying the collection of metaphors Kant uses to warn us against any speculations that venture beyond sensory experience into the supersensible, beyond the phenomenal realm into the noumenal, one is obviously struck by similarities, but I am keen for us to notice something of a contrast as well. As we look at these parallel metaphors I will repeatedly highlight this contrast. This difference is not only in the pictures that Kant is painting but also in the moral that Kant draws from them.

Let's look at the picture first before we look at the moral. The first story we looked at was a nautical one. It concerned leaving the island of truth, the world of phenomena, and sailing into the noumenal. In this first story, moving beyond the island of truth, was not impossible it was just treacherous. But the aeronautical metaphor that Kant now employs is not a metaphor for what is difficult to navigate, it's a metaphor for what is impossible to achieve.

In Kant's day the possibility of flying above the earth's atmosphere is not just treacherous it's inconceivable. The nautical parallel would not be a perilous voyage. Rather, it would be attempting to do what cannot be done. If you want a maritime equivalent of flapping your wings where there is no atmosphere, it's trying to walk where there is no dry land. It's walking on water! It's not just navigationally treacherous; it's downright impossible. And that's the moral he draws from the aeronautical simile. For beyond any air resistance, beyond any atmosphere Kant tells us that the dove "impotently flaps its wings without being able to move."[15] The dove is not finding flying that high purely disorienting, it's finding it impossible.

When discussing this example Kant says of the Platonic dove of speculative reason "in the empty space of pure understanding . . . he made no headway by his efforts, he had no resistance, no support, as it were, by which he could stiffen himself, and to which he could apply his powers in order to get his understanding off the ground."[16] So not only is the metaphor an example of trying to achieve what in principle cannot be achieved, this is also precisely the moral Kant draws from it. The understanding doesn't get "off

14. Kant, *Critique of Pure Reason*, Critique of All Speculative Theology, A689.

15. Kant, *Fundamental Principles of the Metaphysics of Morals*, 463.

16. Kant, *Critique of Pure Reason*, Introduction, A5/B9.

the ground," "it makes no headway," "it flaps its wings impotently without being able to move."

Metaphysical reasoning here is not just difficult to navigate; rather, in principle, it cannot get off the ground. We're not just faced with a stormy sea and banks of fog, we are faced with the fact that we don't have a boat and can't walk on water. I would suggest that this is quite a contrast. To mix our metaphors, we're not just talking about a difficult road ahead; we're talking about a dead end.

In a moment we will find a similar contrast to Kant's maritime metaphor when it comes to another simile Kant employs, this time Kant asks the question "How high are we able to build rather than how high are we able to fly?"

## The Conflict Thesis

An accompanying point that Kant makes repeatedly also employs a metaphor, this time that of a battlefield, a battlefield of conflicting metaphysical conclusions.

> But since it becomes aware in this way that its business must always remain incomplete because the questions never cease, reason sees itself necessitated to take refuge in principles that overstep all possible use in experience. . . . But it thereby falls into obscurity and contradictions, from which it can indeed surmise that it must somewhere be proceeding on the ground of hidden errors; but it cannot discover them, for the principles on which it is proceeding, since they surpass the bounds of all experience, no longer recognize any touchstone of experience. The battlefield of these endless controversies is called metaphysics.[17]

Kant spends a good deal of time visiting these philosophical battlefields and exploring what he calls their metaphysical "antinomies." These "antinomies" are created for Kant when two philosophical lines of reasoning that are addressing the same question come to very different conclusions. Kant argues that this is exactly what you are going to get when pursuing any form of reasoning beyond its natural limit.

17. Kant, *Critique of Pure Reason*, Preface, Aviii.

## High as the Heavens Above

There is yet another allegorical story on this theme. Towards the end of the *Critique of Pure Reason* Kant tells us about a towering structure that reason has always dreamt of erecting.

> If I regard the sum total of all cognition of pure and speculative reason as an edifice for which we have in ourselves at least the idea, then I say that . . . [up to this point in the *Critique*] . . . we have made estimate of the building materials and determined for what sort of edifice, with what height and strength, they would suffice. It turned out, of course, that although we had in mind a tower that would reach the heavens, the supply of materials sufficed only for a dwelling that was just roomy enough for our business on the plane of experience and high enough to survey it; however, that bold undertaking had to fail from lack of material, not to mention the confusion of language that unavoidably divided the workers over the plane and dispersed them throughout the world.[18]

Again, we have a story of limitations following high aspiration. That reason is limited to "the plane of experience and high enough to survey it" in contrast to "a tower that would reach the heavens."[19]

We also have a story of human hubris. For anyone who is familiar with the Hebrew Scriptures immediately recognizes that Kant is alluding to Genesis 11. The tower that the people of the nations hope to build in Genesis is "a tower whose top may reach unto heaven"[20] and Kant says in his story that our human rational ambitions also "had in mind a tower that would reach the heavens."[21] The consequence of their hubris is also mirrored. In Genesis 11 when God thwarts their ambitions he confounds "their language, that they may not understand one another's speech. So, the Lord scattered them abroad from thence upon the face of all the earth."[22] The parallel in Kant's story is "the confusion of language that unavoidably divided the workers over the plane and dispersed them throughout the world."[23]

18. Kant, *Critique of Pure Reason*, Transcendental Doctrine of Method 2, A707/B735.

19. Kant, *Critique of Pure Reason*, Transcendental Doctrine of Method 2, A707/B735.

20. Gen 11:4 (ESV).

21. Kant, *Critique of Pure Reason*, Transcendental Doctrine of Method 2, A707/B735.

22. Gen 11:8 (KJV).

23. Kant, *Critique of Pure Reason*, Transcendental Doctrine of Method 2, A707/

## Sailing without a Sea

But again I want to point out some contrasts, particularly the way this story (like the space dove) is different to the island of truth analogy. Again this is not a story of what is difficult to navigate (as with the nautical metaphor). It's another story like the aeronautical one of what is impossible to achieve. For the story is about making an "estimate of the building materials and determined for what sort of edifice, with what height and strength, they would suffice." And it comes to the disappointing realization that "although we had in mind a tower that would reach the heavens, the supply of materials sufficed only for a dwelling that was just roomy enough for our business on the plane."[24]

Kant is facing us with the fact that the building materials we have could build us a house, but not a skyscraper. Kant is not saying it would be difficult to build a skyscraper; he's saying it would be impossible given the materials we have. If all you have are standard house bricks, building a humble dwelling in which to comfortably live is definitely a possibility, but you cannot construct Manhattan. You need more than house bricks for skyscrapers. It's not that it's difficult, treacherous, or perilous, it's plainly not possible.

But isn't building a skyscraper for Kant allegorically equivalent to leaving the island of truth and going to sea? Both are about going beyond the world of phenomena and moving into the noumenal. But the prognosis is quite a contrast. In one metaphor we are faced with the difficulties of navigation, with the other the impossibility of ever getting off the ground. This is not only what the metaphor would imply but again it's the moral that Kant draws from it. As the story of construction continues, he describes our metaphysical ambition to reach the heavens as "arbitrary and blind projects that might entirely exceed our entire capacity."[25] It would be difficult for our polite and genial Kant to be more damning than that. The philosophical voyages into the supersensible Kant described in the first metaphor were perilous and problematic, yes, but not "arbitrary and blind, entirely exceeding our entire capacity." This now sounds less of a cautionary tale and more like an intellectual dead end.

Above we saw a real contrast between Kant's nautical analogy and his aeronautical one and we seem to have a similar contrast here. The nautical one warning us about the perils of navigating any metaphysical voyage, the

B735.

24. Kant, *Critique of Pure Reason*, Transcendental Doctrine of Method 2, A707/B735.

25. Kant, *Critique of Pure Reason*, Transcendental Doctrine of Method 2, A707/B735.

others telling us plainly it will never even get off the ground. Not that the flight or our building will be difficult to complete but rather that it is impossible to countenance. As impossible as birds flying without air or builders trying to build without the materials. The allegorical equivalent of these two metaphors would be the impossibility of boats trying to sail without a sea, not, I would suggest, just the difficulties of navigation. To mix our metaphors yet again, the first analogy is warning us of a difficult and treacherous road ahead, the others that there is no road at all, just a complete dead end. If his analogies are anything to go by (and the morals he draws from them) Kant appears to be wavering when assessing the consequences of his Copernican revolution.

## Kant's Very Modern Myth

If you were to ask a theologian what is different between modern theology and the theology in the centuries that proceeded it, one of the major differences is that in modern theology you do not see the classical proofs of God's existence in evidence. The most obvious examples here being the father of modern theology, Friedrich Schleiermacher, or the most famous names of the twentieth century, Karl Barth, Rudolf Bultmann, and Paul Tillich. But why did these arguments, which became so very popular at the dawn of the Enlightenment and that accompanied the Scientific Revolution, disappear from modern theology in the nineteenth and twentieth century? At one moment historically they are being commonly employed by philosophers and theologians as the basis of belief, and the next they have vanished from view. Why?

Well this fact is in large part just vivid validation of Kant's critical philosophy setting the stage for modern theology. For this dramatic change in how theology makes its case is testimony to how Kant's Copernican revolution became the norm for modern theology. For when Kant's critique of reason is taken seriously, such arguments are obsolete. I would suggest though that something very peculiar may have happened here. For even though this change occurred, there are a number of specialists in Kant's philosophy of religion that are not at all convinced by Kant's era-defining critique of theistic proofs.

For example, at the end of Allen Wood's *Kant's Rational Theology* he says,

> Kant's criticisms of the received proofs for God's existence have frequently been lauded as epoch-making . . . [but] I have been arguing toward a different conclusion. It seems to me . . . that the

> Kantian critique of the traditional theistic proofs is on the whole unsuccessful. No serious defender of any of the proofs need give them up as a result of Kant's criticisms.... If, as a matter of intellectual history, Kant's attack succeeded in bringing those proofs into disrepute, then we must conclude that it did not do so on its philosophical merits.[26]

Wood concludes that "A good deal of attention, it is true, has been devoted to Kant's famous attacks on the three brands of theistic proof. Even so, it seems to me that there is widespread misunderstanding of Kant's ideas in this area . . . and . . . the philosophical force of Kant's critique of these proofs has often been greatly overestimated."[27]

In order to see what is going on here it is worth recalling the key critique that Kant employs against the cosmological argument for God's existence. In brief, Kant complained that such an argument transgressed the boundary between phenomena and noumena; that it takes a category like cause and effect that only works in the world of sensible appearances, and tries to apply it to a supersensible world of things in themselves; that it takes the categories that can be used for what has been produced in our cognitive processing, and tries to apply them to the raw material that has not been conditioned. Wood puts this very concisely: "In the . . . first critique, Kant argues that the human faculty of knowledge is limited to the world of sense; and in the . . . same work, he systematically criticizes the attempts of rationalist metaphysics to overcome this limitation."[28] It is this that appears to be distinctive and decisive in Kant's argument, developed on the basis of his new philosophy and not seen before. Apart from this argument it is difficult to see anything particularly new in Kant's dismantling of the classical proofs of God's existence. So, one can only imagine that it was this concern that stopped natural theology in its tracks; that it was keeping this clear distinction between phenomena and noumena that led to modern theology's abandonment of all theistic proof.

The problem is that Kant's epoch-making argument is only properly effective in the context of Kant's overall philosophy. For the argument to have any real purchase, do you not have to accept the distinction between phenomena and noumena in the first place? Do you not need to go along with Kant's idea that there is a real difference between things as they appear to us and things as they are in themselves? You need first to be convinced of this critical distinction at the heart of his *Critique of Pure Reason* before

26. Wood, *Kant's Rational Theology*, 149.

27. Wood, *Kant's Rational Theology*, 10.

28. Wood, *Kant's Rational Theology*, 10.

Kant's distinctive argument against the theistic proofs become irresistible. If for some reason you are not convinced about the strict limitations Kant puts on human reason and knowledge, it is difficult to see how his argument remains decisive. If you don't think that there is an epistemological firewall between our human knowledge of the world and what might lie beyond, then Kant's decisive point against the classical arguments for God's existence is not that decisive after all. Peter Byrne in his *Kant on God* could not be any clearer about this.

> An initial problem with Kant's attempted refutation of the proofs of natural theology arises out of the extent to which they depend on the main tenets of the Critical philosophy, particularly on embracing the Copernican Revolution in philosophy. . . . It is evident that elements of the refutation do so depend. Dependence is shown, for example, in the critical comment on the cosmological proof that castigates it for employing the principle that everything must have a cause beyond the world of sense. Kant's claim that "the principle of causality has no meaning at all and no criterion for its use, except in the sensible world" seems to depend on the previous pages of the *Critique of Pure Reason* and is likely to be seen as question-begging by a proponent of traditional natural theology.[29]

This is also a point reiterated in Paul Guyer's standard introduction to Kant. "Now since Kant's criticisms of the metaphysical arguments for the existence of God depend on the central assumptions of his own epistemology, rather than on self-contradictions or other flaws internal to those arguments themselves, it is possible to maintain that they are not knock-down criticisms."[30] So it is not surprising that after a book-length study of Kant's argument against the traditional proofs of God, Alan Wood can conclude "that the philosophical force of Kant's critique of these proofs has often been greatly overestimated."[31] Rather ironically it seems as if the way Kant's *Critique of Pure Reason* has appeared to us is more convincing than the thing in itself.[32]

29. Byrne, *Kant on God*, 19.

30. Guyer, *Kant*, 152.

31. Wood, *Kant's Rational Theology*, 10.

32. It is only fair to note that after Paul Guyer says "it is possible to maintain that they [Kant's criticism of the proofs of God] are not knock-down criticisms," he adds, "By the same token, however, Kant's criticisms have the weight of his whole theory of knowledge behind them" (Guyer, *Kant*, 152).

# 12

# KANT'S THEOLOGICAL CUL-DE-SAC

As we have seen, Kant's *Critique of Pure Reason* questions whether it is possible to have any knowledge of God based on the philosophical reasoning of natural theology. But on the basis of what we have already explored in Kant's philosophical revolution, the question concerning a knowledge of God can be taken much further. It has in fact been asked whether on the basis of Kant's new philosophy, it is possible to have any knowledge of God whatsoever. This of course questions the possibility of theology at all, not just natural theology. If human knowing is only possible because of the processing that takes place in our minds, it would seem impossible to know anything that is unprocessed. For if our human apparatus for knowing, as Kant insists, resides in our categories of understanding, anything beyond those categories is unknowable. So, for Kant knowledge of any kind whatsoever can only reside on the island of truth, and cannot be there in any form out at sea. Because Kant defended the things of faith by placing them beyond the realm of phenomena, beyond our human knowing apparatus and therefore beyond all human categories of knowing, it is difficult to see how we could ever claim to have any knowledge of such unconditioned noumena. Kant at times seems clear about this agnostic tendency:

> Now I assert that all attempts of a merely speculative use of reason in regard to theology are entirely fruitless and by their internal constitution null and nugatory [worthless] . . . that the principles of reason's natural use do not lead at all to any theology; and consequently . . . there could be no theology of reason at all. For all . . . principles of understanding are of immanent use; but for the cognition of a highest being a transcendent use

> of them would be required, for which our understanding is not equipped at all.[1]

To use Kant's metaphor again, our human knowledge can only find traction within its earthly atmosphere and cannot reach the heavens above.

## The Unknown God

The two most famous American philosophers of religion in the twenty-first century have become rather concerned about where this Kantian embargo on the knowledge of God has been leading modern theology. As Alvin Plantinga explains in his book *Knowledge and Christian Belief*:

> According to this line of argument, we human beings can't have any beliefs about God; God is beyond all of our concepts; our minds are too limited to have any grasp at all of him and his being . . . .
>
> Here those who think this way follow the great Prussian philosopher Immanuel Kant (1724–1804) in his monumental *Critique of Pure Reason*. As these people understand him, Kant teaches that there are really two worlds. On the one hand there is the world of things in themselves, things as they are apart from any intellectual activity on our part; on the other hand, there is the world of things for us. The latter is the familiar world of experience, the world of houses and people and oceans and mountains. The former, however, is the world of things as they are apart from us, "in themselves"; this world is entirely inaccessible to us.[2]

Then Plantinga, as we have been doing, draws out the implication of this distinction for religious belief.

> Therefore, there is the world of things in themselves, the world as it is in itself, and also the world of appearance, the world as it is for us. We are at home in the world of appearance, at least in part because we ourselves have constituted it, conferred on it, somehow, the basic structure it displays. But we have no grasp at all of the world of things in themselves. We can't think about these things; our concepts don't reach to them; they are in that regard wholly beyond us.

1. Kant, *Critique of Pure Reason*, Doctrine of Elements 2.2.2.3, A636/B664.
2. Plantinga, *Knowledge and Christian Belief*, 2 .

> Now God, of course, would certainly be among the things in themselves. This strand of Kant's thought, therefore, would imply that human beings can't think about God. We don't have any concepts that apply to God. . . . Our minds, and our thought, and our language simply have no purchase on God. So some people who understand Kant this way, and think that Kant is fundamentally right about these things, conclude that we can't think about God. And of course, if we can't think about God, we also can't talk about him.[3]

To put this in Kant's now familiar terminology, "therefore, our concepts surely wouldn't apply to God, if there were such a person. For God would be a noumenon. God would not be something we have constructed by applying concepts to the manifold of experience (God has created us; we have not constructed him).[*sic*] So . . . we can't refer to, think about, or predicate properties of God."[4]

Plantinga then goes on to spell out the obvious implications that Kant's basic distinction will have for theology and religion:

> Of course, this Kantian way of thinking can wreak considerable havoc with religious belief and with theology. One thinks of theology as telling us about God: what he is like and what he has done. One thinks the subject matter of theology is God himself, but if we can't think or talk about God, then nobody can tell us what God is like and what he has done. If we can't think or talk about God, then of course we can't think the thought that he has created the world or is the Father of our Lord and Savior Jesus Christ . . . or whatever. If Kant (thus interpreted) is right, theology can't be about God; no one, not even theologians, can think about God, and if they can't think about God, they can't write about him. As the philosopher P. Ramsey once said, "What can't be said, can't be said; and it can't be whistled either."[5]

In the journal *Modern Theology*, the philosopher Nicholas Wolterstorff spends the best part of an article examining this radical dilemma that Kant's philosophy appears to leave us with. Like Plantinga, for Wolterstorff the problem lies in the distinction between appearances and things in themselves, the first being knowable to us, the second being unknowable. "The . . . employment of the categories determines the boundary between the humanly knowable and the human unknowable, between the phenomenal

3. Plantinga, *Knowledge and Christian Belief*, 2–3.
4. Plantinga, *Warranted Christian Belief*, 20.
5. Plantinga, *Knowledge and Christian Belief*, 4.

and the noumenal, between reality as it puts in its appearance to us and reality as it is in itself."[6] But again Wolterstorff sees here the radical implications for any claim to a knowledge of God: For this means in Kant's terms that "Knowledge of the transcendent . . . is unavailable to us, since the bounds of the . . . employment of the categories define the bounds of human knowledge."[7] For as Kant puts it, "it would be absurd for us to hope that we can know more of any object than belongs to the possible experience of it."[8] If therefore the categories of our knowing constitute the bounds of all possible experience it makes no sense that we could know anything beyond that possible experience. So Wolterstorff suggests that on Kant's account of what constitutes the limits of all human knowing, things are not looking very promising for theology. As he says plainly, "Theology on Kantian premises, looks impossible."[9]

Understandably then, Wolterstorff sees Kant's philosophy as a major turning point for theology. "Kant is a watershed in the history of theology—ever since Kant, the anxious questions, 'Can we? How can we?' have haunted theologians, insisting on being addressed before any others."[10]

Wolterstorff not only see this as a problem of academic theology but for religious faith more generally: "In Kant, it is . . . our supposed inability to gain knowledge of God that is menacing to the religious life and to the understanding of God embedded therein; more menacing yet is the fact that it is not the least bit clear that even faith is possible, for it's not clear that we can get God well enough in mind even to believe things about God."[11]

In conclusion, as one writer commenting on Wolterstorff's interpretation of Kant can say,

> According to Wolterstorff, the Kantian strictures on human knowledge and experience set forth in the first Critique appear to make theological discourse that is actually about God impossible. . . . Therefore, while Kant may have "[denied] knowledge in order to make room for faith," Wolterstorff submits that the only examples of faith that seem to fit Kant's philosophical paradigm are those that shade off into agnosticism, non-realism, or perhaps radical fideism.[12]

6. Wolterstorff, "Is It Possible and Desirable," 11.
7. Wolterstorff, "Is It Possible and Desirable," 12.
8. Wolterstorff, "Is It Possible and Desirable," 11.
9. Wolterstorff, "Is It Possible and Desirable," 13.
10. Wolterstorff, "Is It Possible and Desirable," 15.
11. Wolterstorff, "Is It Possible and Desirable," 16.
12. Firestone and Jacobs, *In Defense of Kant's Religion*, 56.

## Apophatic Theology

We are not though saying that it has only ever been Kant and those who follow his lead who have insisted on the limits of human knowledge when it comes to God talk. There are no lack of voices in the Christian tradition who have questioned and human claims to an unqualified knowledge of God. Possibly the most important example being the mysterious (as we know very little about who he or she was) theologian with the wonderful name Pseudo-Dionysius the Areopagite (fifth to sixth century AD). The tradition most often associated with Pseudo-Dionysius is that of apophatic theology or negative theology (being able to say only what God is not).

Although I think it is right with Peter Byrne in his book *Kant on God* to suggest that even though Kant's strictures on a knowledge of God can be seen as part of a long Christian tradition Kant has raised this to a new level of philosophical intensity, and that Kant sees this now not as a consequence of theological reflection but rather out of philosophical necessity. Kant "stands in a long tradition of Western thinkers who have denied that there can be direct, univocal property ascriptions to God. Many thinkers have reached the same conclusion as Kant: direct talk about God, as opposed to talk about God's acts or his relations to the world, comes up against a boundary of sense. Kant's own, unique way of drawing the boundary of sense is dependent on the precise claims of his critique of reason. . . . Kant's boundary is in part built on these same foundations, but as we have seen, rises still higher on the building blocks provided by transcendental Idealism."[13]

After completing his review of Kant's philosophical restrictions on knowledge of God, Wolterstorff then asks a fundamental question, "Do we have to take this philosophical context in which these boundaries function as a given or could this distinction be questioned? Kantian questions arise out of the Kantian context. So, the issue is whether that context is like a fact of nature to be coped with, or a human artefact to be questioned."[14]

Wolterstorff is ready, as is Plantinga, to offer an alternative to Kant's approach and their suggestions are well worth exploring. But at present we are still examining why Kant can be seen as both the savior of theology (the Protestant philosopher par excellence) but also its destroyer.

For some it can feel hip or heroic to follow the apophatic impulse, wherever it may lead. But as the philosopher of religion Plantinga points out, this move can have practical as well as theoretical consequences. "If the Real has no positive properties of which we have a grasp, how could we

13. Byrne, *Kant on God*, 70, 72.

14. Wolterstorff, "Is It Possible and Desirable," 16.

possibly know or have grounds for believing that some ways of behaving with respect to it are more appropriate than others? . . . If the Real has no positive properties of which we have a grasp, what is the reason for thinking we live in relation to it?"[15]

## Taking Leave of God

It is worth noting that this understanding of the implications of Kant's critical philosophy for faith can for some theologians lead to "Taking leave of God" entirely; this was true for the Cambridge theologian and philosopher Don Cupitt.

As the Kant scholar Chris Firestone explains in a chapter subtitled "Kant and Theological Nonrealism":[16]

> Cupitt wrote three pieces laying out his understanding of Kant's philosophy and constituting in very clear terms the philosophical grounds for his turn to theological nonrealism. Setting the stage for this period, Cupitt wrote "God and the World in Post-Kantian Thought" (1972), and then, soon after his "coming-out" contribution to the *Myth of God Incarnate*, *The Nature of Man* (1979) and "Kant and the Negative Theology" (published in 1982 but written in 1978). . . . They constitute the Kantian pivot point in Cupitt's career toward theological nonrealism. Much of Cupitt's work from this point . . . is a frontal assault on the theological realism of classical Christian thought. In this regard, Cupitt calls *Taking Leave of God*, and *The World to Come* (1982) his "breakout" books and all else that follows them an elaboration of these positions.[17]

Cupitt sees the basic dilemma Kant's philosophy left theology with in terms that are only to familiar to us by now. As Firestone quoting Cupitt explains,

> . . . Kant argued that ways of thinking which apply within the realm of experience cannot be used in any attempt to go beyond the range of possible experience.
>
> There is a strict boundary line between the phenomenal and noumenal realms, making phenomenally based language ineffective in reference to noumenal realities.[18]

15. Plantinga, *Warranted Christian Belief*, 57.
16. Firestone and Jacobs, *Persistence of the Sacred in Modern Thought*, 273.
17. Firestone and Jacobs, *Persistence of the Sacred in Modern Thought*, 277–78.
18. Firestone and Jacobs, *Persistence of the Sacred in Modern Thought*, 278.

So the very distinction we have been exploring and its implications for faith, we are told, was the very thing that led the Cambridge theologian and philosopher Don Cupitt from Christian faith to *Taking Leave of God*.

I think we are beginning to see why even contemporary scholarship on Kant is still sympathetic to Heinrich Heine conclusion of Kant as "that arch-destroyer in the realms of thought":

> The fundamental concepts, the categories, only yield cognition of things insofar as things are taken as objects of possible experience . . . and thus "Our sensible and empirical intuition can alone give them sense and meaning." . . .
>
> Kant's principle of significance looks as if it must culminate in making him the all-destroying Robespierre of the world of thought that Heine accuses him of being. . . . We simply cannot have knowledge of objects that cannot be given in a possible experience . . . it follows that we cannot have knowledge that there is a God, that we have free will, that there is an eternal life. Thus, there arises the part of the first Critique which so struck Heine: . . . all the false metaphysical proofs of these ideas of pure reason are exposed as resting on illusion.[19]

## Now It's Your Turn

I wonder if you could help me with an experiment. We have seen that Kant is rather partial to a philosophical parable or allegorical story. But rather than just Kant creating them for us I wonder if you could try your hand at one. What they had in common was that the conclusion they all reached was fairly stark, even bleak. The reason for this became obvious, it is the fact that according to Kant we can only have knowledge of the sensible world around (of phenomena) and not of any supersensible world beyond (that of noumena). And of course any knowledge of God would imply a knowledge of the supersensible that Kant's philosophy denies.

I want your imaginary metaphor therefore to illustrate the distinction between those two worlds, the knowledge we can have of them, and of course by implication what this means for a knowledge of God.

Before you do your imaginative work, you might want to be reminded of the conclusion reached by the philosophers of religion we looked at regarding knowledge of any super-sensible world and the implication for a knowledge of God.

19. Byrne, *Kant on God*, 58, 14.

To repeat Plantinga's conclusion:

> [As that] world is entirely inaccessible to us . . . we have no grasp at all of the world of things in themselves. We can't think about these things, . . . they are in that regard wholly beyond us. . . . This strand of Kant's thought, therefore, would imply that human beings can't think about God. . . . Our minds, and our thought, and our language simply have no purchase on God. . . . And of course if we can't think about God, we also can't talk about him. . . . As the philosopher P. Ramsey once said, "What can't be said, can't be said; and it can't be whistled either."[20]

Wolterstorff argued, "It is not the least bit clear that even faith is possible, for it's not clear that we can get God well enough in mind even to believe things about God,"[21] and as Byrne points out, "We simply cannot have knowledge of objects that cannot be given in a possible experience . . . it follows that we cannot have knowledge that there is a God."[22]

It's now over to you! So think how you might illustrate this distinction between the world of phenomena and the world of noumena and its implications for a knowledge of God. I won't bore you with some of the examples that I've been contemplating, but they are pretty radical and depressing, involving, for example, being ejected into the deep darkness of outer space, or variations on that kind of theme.

I know Kant did not have the sci-fi options available to him as a metaphor, but I bet none of you, when trying to express such a radical contrast between the known and the completely unknown, came up with the distinction between land and sea. For however you present the difference between land and sea, that hardly captures the fundamental contrast being expressed by the philosophers of religion we have looked at. For the sea and what lies out at sea is not "entirely inaccessible to us," "wholly beyond us," "shading off into agnosticism, non-realism or perhaps radical fideism." When people go to sea, they do not generally drop off the face of the earth into a realm "wholly beyond us" (not since the Middle Ages). What is particularly interesting is that as Kant's nautical metaphor develops we get the distinct impression that Kant is wanting to take us all on such a voyage out to sea: "But before we venture out on this sea, to search through all its breadth and become certain of whether there is anything to hope for in it." So in no way is Kant's metaphor about what is wholly beyond "us" and "entirely inaccessible to us" an expression of agnosticism. The agnostic cannot be "certain of

20. Plantinga, *Knowledge and Christian Belief*, 2, 4.

21. Wolterstorff, "Is It Possible and Desirable," 16.

22. Byrne, *Kant on God*, 14.

whether there is anything to hope for" but that is Kant's stated aim at the end of his sea of faith analogy.[23]

So why has Kant come up with such an inadequate metaphor? Well, I imagine there are four basic possibilities:

1. That Kant, in using this homely metaphor of nautical exploration, is in fact just sugaring the epistemological pill big-time and not really telling us how it is.
2. That the use of this metaphor clearly demonstrates that Kant is in fundamental disagreement with the eminent philosophers of religion we have quoted, and perhaps has some other possibilities "up his sleeves" (to quote Gollum), yet to be revealed. (At the very least, the philosophers of religion we quoted should note that this detailed picture that Kant develops concerning what kind of knowledge we can have beyond the land of truth does not fit that well with their conclusion.)[24]
3. That the use of this mild metaphor shows that Kant himself is deeply conflicted and therefore ends up saying contradictory things about any possible knowledge of God.
4. That the use of this metaphor is a clear demonstration that Kant may not himself have fully grasped the devastating implications of his own philosophy for religious belief.

By the end of our discussion hopefully you may have your own ideas. (My own hunch is that it may be a rather untidy mixture of all four. So much for the Enlightenment's clear and distinct ideas.)

## In the Same Boat: Materialist and Believer

At the very least, Kant seems a little one-sided and consequently inconsistent in his reasoning when it comes to speculating beyond our finite experience.

23. If you have read about Kant before, at this point you might be saying, "but what about his appeal to practical reason, rather than pure reason, in terms of a knowledge of God?" We will discuss that later, but there is a basic reason why I do not mention it here, and that is the fact that the modern theologians we will be surveying were not sympathetic when it came to Kant's appeal to practical reason. Consequently they had to face the stark implications of Kant's Copernican revolution for any knowledge of God, without Kant's safety net of practical reason.

24. It should be noted that there is a significant move in contemporary philosophy of religion that questions the conclusion we have seen Plantinga, Wolterstorff, and Byrne came to with regard to the implications of Kant's philosophy for a knowledge of God. See for example, Firestone and Palmquist, *Kant and the New Philosophy of Religion*. And Firestone and Jacobs, *In Defense of Kant's Religions*.

I think this is seen in the fact that when he uses his new big idea to counter the materialistic freethinking and rational skeptic (in other words, our Andreas), he lays it on with a trowel. For he argues that the reasoning employed by the freethinker to deny the existence of God is of no use. As Kant can say with the skeptic in mind, "for we already know before and with complete certainty that all their allegations, while perhaps honestly meant, had to be absolutely null and void, because they dealt with information which no human being can ever get."[25]

If though on the basis of Kant's philosophy the freethinker cannot say anything for certain about the nature of ultimate reality (and therefore cannot rule out religious beliefs) why are not these same restrictions applicable to the theologian? For when with the nautical metaphor Kant has the religious believer in mind, we are not told that such religious exploration is "absolutely null and void" dealing "with information which no human being can ever get." Yet according to Kant, aren't they in exactly the same epistemological boat (pun intended), and consequently face exactly the same problem? For Kant is using the same philosophical technique, exactly the same logic and argument to shoot down the atheist as he is in cautioning the believer. But one is shot down in flames, the other just cautioned. If our skeptic Andreas is not allowed to make negative metaphysical pronouncements (his reasoning being "absolutely null and void") because he can only have knowledge of appearances and cannot make pronouncements about how things really are, why is this not as equally true for the believer when she makes positive metaphysical pronouncements? Why be so rough with the skeptic but develop a story of possible voyages for the believer? Strictly speaking, are they not in the same boat philosophically (or epistemologically) according to Kant?

## Why Believe in an Island or a Sea?

One could also see some inconsistency in why Kant thinks that there is a mysterious sea of things in themselves out there at all, and that consequently we inhabit an island. I think Kant would say (and sometimes does say) the sea of things in themselves must be there to explain what we experience in the world of phenomena. That there must be things in themselves as an explanation of the phenomenal world that we all experience. That to explain the car coming off the very end of the production line we need to postulate raw material being received at the beginning.

25. Kant, *Critique of Pure Reason*, 2.2.2.3 A703/B731.

Did not Kant castigate natural theology for employing exactly that logic? Was not that Kant's key argument against the classical proof of God? That had argued we must believe in a supersensible reality to explain our experience of sensible reality. In other words, we must believe in a God beyond nature to explain the existence of nature. But if the idea of seeking explanations or finding a cause for this world by looking beyond it was not legitimate for the natural theologian (because that logic only works within the world of appearances and not beyond it) why is it acceptable for Kant to use the same logic in postulating his mysterious sea of things in themselves?

The problem Kant has in substantiating his claims that we are on an island surrounded by a sea of things in themselves is not just an issue for the theologian who wants to work with Kant's Copernican revolution, it also became a concern from day one for anyone who wanted to employ Kant's philosophical distinctions. As Beiser expresses the concern, "The problem is that Kant's own critical limits gave him no grounds to claim knowledge of the existence of the thing-in-itself. Given that knowledge is limited to possible experience, and given that the thing-in-itself cannot be given in possible experience, how is it possible to know that things-in-themselves exist? But if they cannot be known to exist, how is it possible to say that we know appearances of things-in-themselves?"[26]

Obviously one of the main reasons Kant wants to keep the thing in itself is to refute the accusation of pure subjectivism. To use our well-worn rough-and-ready metaphor, Kant wants to continue affirming that our factory is processing the raw material of reality. If Kant were saying that the factory could produce things without these raw materials, he would be rightly called a subjectivist as there would be no reference to a reality independent of us. But even though Kant wants to affirm that raw material is needed, on the basis of the fully processed objects of our experience, he is not able to tell us much if anything about that unprocessed material.

> Kant insists that appearances have objects, or that they are appearances of something namely things-in-themselves. . . . [So] it appears as if Kant does not adhere to the subjectivist principle that the immediate objects of perception are only ideas. For what we now perceive are things that exist independent of us; its just that we do not perceive them as they are in themselves but only as they appear to us.[27]

26. Beiser, *German Idealism*, 49–50.

27. Beiser, *German Idealism*, 49.

## Desertion in the Ranks

This concern about being able to continue believing in the thing in itself has never gone away. This was not just an issue that the critics of Kant's philosophy were keen to highlight, it was also a concern for many of Kant's would-be loyal followers. Now it is tempting to ask what has this endless debate about the elusive thing in itself got to do with theology and religion. Well, for theology after Kant, I would suggest everything. For is that not the sphere according to Kant where the things of faith reside? So every time a Kant scholar comes to the conclusion on the basis of Kant's own logic that it is nonsense to talk about "the thing in itself" they also must be saying that on the basis of Kant's philosophy it is nonsense in principle to talk about the things of God. For as Plantinga states. "Now God, of course, would certainly be among the things in themselves."[28]

28. Plantinga, *Knowledge and Christian Belief*, 2–3.

# 13

# THE ORIGINS OF MODERN THEOLOGY

## What a Surprise

WHETHER WE THINK KANT'S cautionary maritime metaphor had gone far enough in its warnings about going beyond the island of truth, or whether we think the philosophers of religion we looked at, who suggested we are more likely facing a dead end to any faith or belief, are correct, things on either scenario are not looking that promising for theology. So, whether surrounding our island is a dark stormy sea populated by icebergs, fog banks, and similar navigational perils, or whether with our philosophers of religion things are even worse than that, being faced by impenetrable night, and oceans of agnosticism, it must be said that it is looking pretty grim for the prospect of doing theology after Kant.

In the light of these challenges for a theology that works with Kant's Copernican revolution, one may be rightly surprised that Kantian philosophy became the default position for so much theology at the end of the nineteenth century and the beginning of the twentieth. To understand this wholesale adoption of Kant's perspective one needs to be aware of the cultural crisis of the time. For Kant's critical philosophy reached its peak of influence at a time of cultural crisis towards the end of the nineteenth century and the beginning of the twentieth, and not as you might have expected at the end of the eighteenth. And it was also at this critical point culturally, that theology most clearly saw the value of Kant's critique of reason.

## The Materialism Controversy

This turning point in German intellectual culture was precipitated by the most important philosophical debate of the late nineteenth century. This controversy sounds as contemporary and relevant today as it's ever been, as it raised the ongoing modern dilemma of whether the advance of science would end in materialism, whether the scientific method and all it has achieved would be the end of metaphysics and religion.

> The most important intellectual dispute of the 19th century—one can declare with complete confidence—was the materialism controversy, which began in the 1850s, and whose shockwaves reverberated until the end of the century. No philosopher of that epoch could ignore it, and every philosopher had to stake his position with reference to it. The controversy raised the troubling question whether modern science, whose authority and prestige were now beyond question, necessarily leads to materialism.[1]

This of course is familiar territory as the intellectual background to Kant's first critique. This materialism with its mechanical view of reality, not only sees religious beliefs as superfluous but also questioned the existence of human freedom and morality. "Materialism was generally understood to be the doctrine that only matter exists and that everything in nature obeys only mechanical laws." If such a doctrine were true, it seemed there could be no God, no free will, no soul, and hence no immortality. These beliefs, however, seemed vital to morality and religion. So the controversy posed a drastic dilemma: either a scientific materialism or a moral and religious "leap of faith." It was the latest version of the old conflict between "reason and faith."[2]

For those who were concerned about where this rampant materialism might lead, it is fascinating to note that a work written in 1780 was seen as the most promising response to a crisis of the 1860s. For it was to Kant and his critic of pure reason (1780) that they almost unanimously turned, for the cry went up "Back to Kant." We started with our story of Andreas's materialism of the eighteenth century and Kant's response to it, but we now see the same thing happening at the end of the nineteenth century.

1. Beiser, *Genesis of Neo-Kantianism*, 183.
2. Beiser, *After Hegel: German Philosophy*, 53.

## Kant's Resurrection

In a chapter entitled the "The Resurrection of Immanuel Kant" Frederick C. Beiser in his study of the origins of late nineteenth century neo-Kantianism explains that "The 1860s was . . . the breakthrough decade for neo-Kantianism. The calls for a return to Kant now became more vocal and frequent. . . . Some of the most dynamic young philosophers in Germany wrote articles, manifestos, essays, and even whole books, championing the cause of Kant's philosophy. No longer seen as obsolete or dated, Kant's philosophy was now deemed not only worthy of study in its own right but the best solution to the crises and controversies of the day . . . Kant's spirit was rising from his grave."[3]

It was this neo-Kantian revival that formed the intellectual setting and philosophical stage for twentieth-century theology. If the neo-Kantians were building and manning the barricade against militant materialism, it was natural for the theologians to join them. As theologian Mark Chapman explains,

> The theological appropriation of . . . Kantianism, by . . . theologians from all schools was spurred on, at least in part, by the task of countering the widespread popularity of materialism . . . at the turn of the twentieth century. Theologians were forced to tackle the pressing question of how the human spirit and the domain of freedom could survive the assault from naturalistic determinism.[4]

As Chapman concludes, "This meant that to the younger generation, the scientific justification of Christianity over and against the all-pervasive materialism of popular culture appeared to be more important than anything else."[5]

So in Germany, at the end of the nineteenth century and early twentieth century, theology was to work within this predominately Kantian philosophical position. So theologians where to presuppose the fundamentals of Kant's critic of reason, that we have spent our time exploring above. In other words, they all thought Kant was right to deny the extent of scientific knowledge to make room for faith. "Instead of seeing the materialistic view of science as the 'true' reality . . . [they] insisted that the 'scientific and the faithful world-views' were to be pursued 'alongside one another, without disturbing or destroying one another'. In this way Christianity was removed

3. Beiser, *Genesis of Neo-Kantianism*, 207–8.
4. Chapman, *Ernst Troeltsch and Liberal Theology*, 85.
5. Chapman, *Ernst Troeltsch and Liberal Theology*, 85.

from the sphere of theoretical understanding altogether . . . 'quite distinct from that of science.'"[6]

## What Kind of Faith?

Where these theologians differed from Kant is in what to make of faith. They were happy to follow Kant's lead when it came to his critique of science and reason, and the limits that Kant enforced, but none of them were particularly happy with the nature of the faith he left them with. Kant may have made room for faith, but it was not a faith they recognized. They all aspired to a faith that would mean more and say more than Kant would allow. For they all wanted a faith that would go beyond the veil of appearances and touch the thing in itself. To look at a number of the ingenious theological proposals to circumvent the limits Kant put on the nature of faith, from his own day up to and including the twentieth-century theologian Karl Barth, takes us to the heart of modern theology.

## Beyond the Veil

Many theologians after Kant were more than happy with Kant's claim that science only has an indirect relationship with reality (and in that sense has limits). What they were not happy with were the limitations Kant then applied to theology, to any knowledge of God. They were more than happy to see Kant clip the wings of scientific materialism, but they had major reservations when Kant suggested the same needed to happen with theology. That secular reason was not allowed access to the holy of holies (the thing in itself), only getting as far as the veil of appearances, was to the theologian perfectly understandable. But, for the theologian, that such limitations must also apply to religious belief was wholly unacceptable.

According to Kant, the reason for these restrictions, as we have seen, is that to know anything we cannot but work within the limited categories of human understanding. This consequently implies some severe limitations when it comes to any knowledge of God. But the theological dissatisfaction with the conclusions of Kant's philosophy for theology did not, as you might have expected, lead to the abandonment of Kant's philosophical revolution, for Kant's strictures on scientific rationality were too valuable for that. Rather it led to some ingenious theologies. Creative strategies in a religious effort to get beyond the veil of appearances to the holy of holies. Something

6. Chapman, *Ernst Troeltsch and Liberal Theology*, 85.

it was claimed only religion could achieve. Something that lay beyond the limitations Kant had given to scientific rationality. We see this wholehearted acceptance of Kant's critique of reason, but with this special exception given to faith, being pursued by theologians and philosophers soon after Kant's critique appeared. But as we will see, this theme continued to be explored throughout the nineteenth century into the twentieth and up to the present day. The theologian Bruce McCormack explains the situation: "It was above all, Kant's limitation of theoretical knowing to the intuitable which made knowledge of God so deeply problematic to modern theologians. For if God is a transcendent, wholly spiritual being as the Christian tradition maintained, then God is unintuitable and—if Kant's restriction hold—cannot be known . . . the question of whether and how God is known stood at the heart of theological reflection in the modern period."[7]

## Below the Radar

One of the things that always ruined a holiday in the British countryside was the sound of jet fighters. Now you might think that is the last place you would hear a jet. But it was quite common when sitting in a Welsh or Scottish valley to hear a sound of a jet flying remarkably low along that valley. The reason why these holidays were regularly disturbed by jet fighters became fairly obvious. One of the few ways (before we had stealth fighters) to avoid being picked up by radar was to fly as low as possible, particularly up a valley. This might have avoided the jets being detected but it scared the living daylights out of my children and ended with many a dropped ice cream.

For Immanuel Kant, any claim to knowledge was going to be detected. It was going to get picked up and processed as we have seen by Kant's universal categories of understanding. The thing in itself could never get to you without going through that processing. So, as we have seen, any claim to a knowledge of God was going to have to go through that same conditioning. But at the end of this process what we had was an indirect, distant, and distorted understanding. The question was, is there a way of flying below the radar? Could we have some awareness of God that would not be picked up and conditioned in that way?

7. McCormack, *Orthodox and Modern*, 24.

## The Nature of Religious Faith

In the centuries following Kant the two most significant attempts to get under the radar were also unparalleled in terms of significance. Both defined the nature of religious faith for their generation and beyond. These were Schleiermacher's *Religion and Its Cultured Despisers* (1799) and *The Idea of the Holy* (1917) by Rudolf Otto. There is no doubt that both books were working with Kant's *Critique of Reason*. When, as a student, I first encountered these texts it was only through some understanding of Kant's philosophy that I began to make some headway with them. I often wondered what sense could be made of these books without some familiarity with Kant's Copernican revolution.

## Schleiermacher: A Theology of Stealth and Touch

When last year I was in hospital and facing a time of crisis, like any husband and father I particularly valued the visits by my wife and daughters. It was not always what they had to say that I valued, sometimes it was the fact that they just held my hand. It was this reassuring contact that meant so much to me, whether it was accompanied by words or not. In fact, I think I would find it difficult to put into words what it meant. So my awareness of that person and all they meant to me was being communicated by touch and by what was felt. In some sense this seemed to be bypassing the normal processes of understanding and even more fundamental than them.

The theologian Schleiermacher, in line with his Romantic contemporaries and building on his upbringing within a spiritual renewal movement (known as Pietism), saw an experience like this as a way to understanding the nature of religious faith. Namely, that in religious faith we gain an awareness that is more fundamental and primordial than could be detected or processed by any cognitive faculty. In this way, faith was operating at a level well below Kant's critical radar. This, for Schleiermacher, was to be located at the level of feeling resembling the analogy of touch. Something that is experienced before any mental processing takes place.

As the theologian Bruce McCormack explains, "Schleiermacher's response to . . . [Kant's] challenge, as is well known, was to assign the origins of religion to a region of human being and existence which he called 'feeling'; . . . the Source of this feeling does not belong to the series of 'objects' known and acted upon by the human subject but is to be fundamentally distinguished from them."[8]

8. McCormack, *Orthodox and Modern*, 24.

This was a way to escape the restrictions that Kant had put on any knowledge of God, to become aware of what is beyond any cognitive processing. It was a religious faith that did not fall foul of Kant's critique. As the theologian Bruce McCormack concludes, "It is clear what Schleiermacher has gained from this move. Kant had made theoretical knowledge of God an impossibility. Schleiermacher has located a point of access to God—or, more accurately, a point in human consciousness of God's access to us—which overcomes the restrictions Kant placed on theoretical knowledge. . . . The knowledge of God is a special kind of knowledge which is distinguished from all other form of knowing by the fact that here a purely receptive moment is involved."[9]

Schleiermacher in this way believed that he was getting beyond the veil of appearances and touching the holy of holies; or, rather, what was holy was touching him. This primordial feeling for Schleiermacher captured the essence of religious piety or perhaps, in our context, what we might call the essence of spirituality. Schleiermacher expressed this in terms of a sense of dependence, the feeling of being finite in the midst of the infinite. As Schleiermacher explains, "The self-identical essence of piety, is this: the consciousness of being absolutely dependent, or, which is the same thing, of being in relation with God."[10]

Where for Kant, we are continually involved as active subjects in constituting the objects of our experience, for Schleiermacher with God we experience a feeling of total dependence that does not involve that cognitive processing. This feeling comes from beyond, as something we are dependent on and do not contribute to.

In Bruce McCormack's words, "That humans are conscious of being absolutely dependent upon the Other for the whole of their receptive and active lives sets that Other apart from all other objects of our experience. . . . To put it another way, humans stand in a relationship of reciprocity with respect to the 'world.' Not so with respect to God. God, as the Whence of our feeling of absolute dependence, is not given directly to us as intuitable objects and persons are given. . . . In sum, feeling is to be located at a different level of human being and existence than knowing and doing and is prior to both."[11]

Now, because this awareness of the infinite is not something that can be captured in objective terms, it is therefore not something that the scientist can examine in a test tube or the philosopher so easily deny. In this way

9. McCormack, *Orthodox and Modern*, 24.

10. Schleiermacher, *Christian Faith*, 12.

11. McCormack, *Orthodox and Modern*, 24.

religion could have an independence from other disciplines because it dealt with something unique, having this distinct nature. In this way, Schleiermacher suggested a way forward for modern theology in the light of Kant's restrictions on religious faith.

As theologian Westerholm explains the situation

> It is this account of the independence of religion that proved decisive for the development of modern theology more generally. A host of experientially oriented theologies in the nineteenth and twentieth centuries followed Schleiermacher in sheltering religion from the "storms of Enlightenment and Idealist [Kantian] critiques" in the "safe haven" of religious feeling. Philosophical and scientific critique may establish the need for the revision of religious claims that encroach on the terrain of philosophy or science but claims of this kind are finally a second-order aspect of religion. The true essence of religion is a first-order experience that the philosopher and scientist cannot call into question.[12]

## Otto and Fries

If Schleiermacher, who set the character of much nineteenth-century theology, got around Kant's restrictions by pursuing a theology of preconceptual awareness and precognitive feeling, possibly the best-known philosopher of religion in the twentieth century, Rudolf Otto (1869–1937), in his landmark publication the *Idea of the Holy*, pursued a similar approach to Schleiermacher when it came to the limits Kant set on our cognitive knowledge. Rudolf Otto's work was inspired by a renewal of interest in the Kantian Philosophy of Jakob Friedrich Fries (1773–1843). At the beginning of the nineteenth century, Fries had continued to defend Kant's philosophy when it had largely fallen from favor, and been eclipsed by that of Hegel. But at the beginning of the twentieth century there was a resurgence of interest in Fries's adaptation of Kant's philosophy, with new editions of his major works being published. As Wilhelm Bousset (a theologian of the time) comments, "It was Fries who 'stood in the midst of a new spiritual spring which was bestowed on Germany'. In short, 'it was a wonderful time when Fries wrote; it was the daybreak of the ascent of national freedom' when a tabula rasa was made of the past."[13]

12. Westerholm, *Ordering of the Christian Mind*, 48.
13. Chapman, *Ernst Troeltsch and Liberal Theology*, 121.

Particularly noteworthy is that, even though as a philosopher Fries was a staunch defender of Kant, when it came to the question of religion, he wanted to say something more. Like Schleiermacher, Fries had a Moravian upbringing and schooling and this meant, as it did for Schleiermacher, a rather eventful introduction to Kant's philosophy, particularly Kant's *Critique of Pure Reason*. "Against regulations, Fries sneaked out of the seminary and walked to a bookdealer in neighbouring Görlitz. There he bought only parts of the book, some printed sheets; he dared not buy a whole bound copy, because this would have attracted the suspicion of the inspectors. When the seminary's doctor visited the bookshop in Görlitz, the bookdealer praised the youth's intellectual curiosity; the doctor raised the alarm, and the inspectors duly confiscated the sheets. . . . It is clear that Kant had become 'forbidden fruit' for students at the seminary."[14]

When it came to religion (as we have seen repeatedly) it is Kant's distinction between noumenal, the realm of things in themselves, and phenomena, things as they appear to us, that was fundamental to Fries's defense of Kant's philosophy. "Kant's [noumenal-phenomenal] dualism provided the essential structure for his philosophy of religion, the basis for his reconciliation of the conflicting claims of reason and faith. For Fries, the Kantian dualisms are the solution."[15]

Fries sees Kant's noumenal-phenomenal dualism doing this in two ways "First, by showing that knowledge has a subjective origin and validity, so that it cannot claim to be any more objective than faith. Second, by demonstrating that knowledge is limited to the sphere of nature alone. . . . He does so by defending and re-interpreting Kant's dualism between appearances and things-in-themselves. It was only by defending this dualism, Fries believed, that he could protect faith and separate it from knowledge."[16]

As for so many philosophers and theologians of the time (this was particularly true of the German Romanticism at the close of the eighteenth century) the thing in itself that resides in Kant's noumenal realm had become synonymous with what is timeless, eternal, infinite, and divine. "The idea . . . of absolute independent being, is for him [Fries], just as it was for . . . Schleiermacher and all the Romantics, the same as that of the divine or eternal. Belief in the existence of the thing-in-itself is then the same as belief in the existence of God itself."[17]

14. Beiser, *Genesis of Neo-Kantianism* 28.
15. Beiser, *Genesis of Neo-Kantianism*, 65.
16. Beiser, *Genesis of Neo-Kantianism*, 65.
17. Beiser, *Genesis of Neo-Kantianism*, 70.

Like Schleiermacher, Fries believed it was essential that faith be an encounter with the thing in itself and not restricted to the world of appearances. But how can Fries pursue this approach to faith and remain true to Kant's noumenal-phenomenal dualism. Fries does this by appealing to the concept of *Ahndung* (there is not an obvious English equivalent to this German word). But Fries defines Ahndung as "a feeling of the recognition of the eternal in the finite."[18] As Frederick C. Beiser goes on to explain,

> The main reason Fries introduces the concept of *Ahndung* is to define the mental state characteristic of religion. Religion, he insists, should not be reduced to metaphysics or ethics. Rather, its distinctive characteristic is a kind of attitude or mental state towards life and existence. This mental state consists not in knowledge, still less in action, but in a kind of feeling, a responsiveness or sensitivity to the world. What is characteristic of religious life is devotion, which involves a feeling or mood.[19]

In a way that is reminiscent of Schleiermacher's theology, Fries also sneaks under, as we have put it, Kant's cognitive radar. In this way, Fries again sees an encounter with the divine (the noumenal) not in our cognitive understanding (precluded in Kant's philosophy) but rather through a sense or feeling of the infinite. As Frederick C. Beiser argues:

> Belief in the existence of the thing-in-itself is then the same as belief in the existence of God itself. Fries then goes a step further in connecting this belief with his philosophy of religion by saying that the existence of the thing-in-itself is an object of *Ahndung* or feeling . . . the essential point to see now is that Fries places belief in the existence of the thing-in-itself in the practical realm. With that manoeuvre he was confident that he had pulled off the apparently impossible: he managed to maintain belief in the existence of the thing-in-itself without having to transcend the limits of knowledge, . . . he did not have to step outside the Kantian system at all. Whatever its merits, it was an ingenious solution to an apparently intractable problem.[20]

It is in this way that Fries, the great defender of Kant's philosophy in the nineteenth century, peers past the veil of appearance to the holy of holies, the thing in itself. Therefore, in similar terms to Schleiermacher's approach (and paralleling the Romanticism that was prevalent at the time),

18. Beiser, *Genesis of Neo-Kantianism*, 70.
19. Beiser, *Genesis of Neo-Kantianism*, 236.
20. Beiser, *Genesis of Neo-Kantianism*, 87.

Fries sees that the transcendent supersensible world of faith shines through the sensory world of appearance. As Frederick C. Beiser concludes:

> Fries' definition of religion resembles no one more than his fellow Moravian, Schleiermacher. . . . Fries' *Ahndung* and Schleiermacher's *Anschauen* [feeling ] both involve the recognition of the infinite in the finite, and both resist conceptual or systematic articulation. Seen as a whole, Fries' . . .[work] was an original synthesis of Kantian and Romantic themes. Its Kantian themes are its dualisms between appearance and thing-in-itself, knowledge and faith; its Romantic themes are its aesthetic attitude towards the world and making feeling characteristic of religion. While faith deals with the infinite, and while knowledge concerns the finite, Ahndung deals with the intersection or connection between these realms, namely, the presence of the infinite in the finite.[21]

## *The Idea of the Holy*

It was this revival of interest in Kant's philosophy and its religious adaptation by Fries that set the scene for Rudolf Otto's philosophy of religion and his *Idea of the Holy* (1917), possibly the most referenced work in the philosophy of religion of the twentieth century. What we first see in Rudolf Otto's work should look very familiar by now. For on the basis of Kant's philosophy as a defence of the faith we witness yet another valiant attempt to hold back the tide of scientific reductionism and determinism with its "ceaseless clockwork." As Mark Chapman concludes, "In the first years of the twentieth century it was Rudolf Otto more than anybody else who sought to defend the religious dimension of human life from the onslaught of naturalism and materialism."[22]

In terms similar to Fries, Rudolf Otto's interpretation of Kant's philosophy is clearly reminiscent of Schleiermacher's theology. Mark Chapman explains this in his fascinating study of the interaction between theology and the German intellectual culture of the time.

> From as early as 1899, in the preface to the centenary edition of Schleiermacher's *Speeches*, he [Otto] recognized the need to respond to the threats to religion posed by *"l' homme machine"* [*Man a Machine*] of the French Enlightenment; despite the great

21. Beiser, *Genesis of Neo-Kantianism*, 70.

22. Chapman, *Ernst Troeltsch and Liberal Theology*, 120.

> advances in science during the eighteenth century, he claimed, there was one dimension which had been neglected; namely, human piety. Schleiermacher's contemporary relevance thus rested in his delineation of religion as its "own free arena of human being" . . . Otto pointed to [Schleiermacher's] originality in relocating "piety" at the centre of human life.[23]

Following Kant's now familiar lead, science and faith had their own separate domains, one not impinging on the other. But as for Kant, ultimate reality was not something that the scientists could adequately represent or fully capture in their cognitive categories. As Mark Chapman points out,

> This reassertion of the religious dimension of human life did not deny science but grounded it in an "unshakable certainty of the priority of the absolute value of the Spiritual in the world, the conviction that . . . the totality of all being and happening, was neither ceaseless clockwork nor a meaningless collection of . . . chance and purposeless coexistence."[24]

In her outstanding study entitled *Religion as the Province of Meaning: The Kantian Foundations of Modern Theology*, the theologian and philosopher Adina Davidovich argues that you can only properly understand Otto's philosophy of religion and his *Idea of the Holy* in the light of this dimension of Kant's philosophy.[25]

> It is therefore one of my goals . . . to establish that in his striving to secure the veracity of religious convictions, Otto turned to Kant, in whose critiques of Reason and its domains he found methodological anchorage. . . . Readers of Otto's most popular book, *The Idea of the Holy*, who were unaware of this Kantian background, systematically misunderstood Otto's theory of religion. What is most important, namely, his notion of feeling, was totally misinterpreted. This is due partly to the fact that in the *Idea of the Holy* Otto assumed the Kantian background; . . . he did not undertake to restate, to explain, and to justify it, although he did do so in previous works to which he constantly refers. Accordingly Otto's place in the Kantian tradition has not been duly appreciated. It is . . . [my] task . . . in part, to reappraise Otto's theory of religion in its true Kantian context.[26]

23. Chapman, *Ernst Troeltsch and Liberal Theology*, 120.
24. Chapman, *Ernst Troeltsch and Liberal Theology*, 120.
25. Davidovich, *Religion as a Province of Meaning*, 161.
26. Davidovich, *Religion as a Province of Meaning*, 161.

As Adina Davidovich's study of the importance of Kant's basic philosophical distinctions for understanding Otto's philosophy of religion[27] is a perfect example of what we have been surveying, we will follow her argument in some detail. Davidovich begins by making it clear that the important distinction we have concentrated on in Kant's philosophy (that between things as they appear to us [*phenomenal*] and things in themselves [*noumenal*]) is, for Otto, Kant's greatest contribution to understanding the true nature of religion. Therefore, for Otto, Kant is on a par with the father of Protestantism. "Otto accepted the sharp Kantian dualism of nature and freedom that corresponds to a distinction between phenomenal and noumenal being—a distinction he considered an essential religious insight, and on account of which he regarded Kant as an important successor to Luther."[28]

When it comes to Otto's analysis of the essence of religion, Otto again sees in some sense a "bridging . . . [of] the abyss between the finite and the infinite"[29] as essential. So, as Mark Chapman goes on to explain, in the Spirit of Fries and Schleiermacher's philosophy of religion:

> Otto . . . was not content to remain merely with . . . appearances, since for "the religious person, this is no matter of indifference." Religion seemed to require an epistemology which allowed for direct access to things-in-themselves. According to Otto, it was Fries "improvement" to Kant's philosophy that allowed for this direct apprehension of things-in-themselves.[30]

27. She also more briefly looks at the work of the twentieth-century theologian Paul Tillich in these Kantian terms.

28. Davidovich, *Religion as a Province of Meaning*, 161.

29. Davidovich, *Religion as a Province of Meaning*, 161.

30. Chapman, *Ernst Troeltsch and Liberal Theology*, 125.

# 14

# KANT'S SUGGESTIVE POSSIBILITY

SOME NEO-KANTIANS FELT THAT attempts like Schleiermacher's and Fries's to bridge Kant's noumenal-phenomenal dualism (followed as we will see by Otto) betrayed the fundamentals of Kant's philosophy. For example, Mark Chapman quotes one angry reviewer of any attempt at "bridging the abyss between the finite and the infinite" to reach the thing-in-itself as having "smashed idealism in the face" and "has failed to understand Kant and does not have the right to dress . . . up with this name."[1]

Adina Davidovich in her *Religion as a Province of Meaning* develops throughout her book a convincing argument to the contrary. That the attempt to bridge the Kantian abyss of the finite/infinite divide can be seen as directly inspired by developments in Kant's own philosophy. She argues that this can be seen particularly in the final critique Kant wrote, the *Critique of Judgment*. For we have seen that Kant began his philosophical revolution with *Critique of Pure Reason*. Kant then progresses to write *Critique of Practical Reason* and then finally produced *Critique of Judgment*.

In his final critique (of judgement) Kant explores experiences that are clearly not based on his categories of pure reason. We have this kind of experience Kant argues, when for example we get a sense of the whole of what we might encounter, rather than just discrete parts. For Kant, the perfect example of this is in our appreciation of what is beautiful. When we make an aesthetic judgement, we do not analytically dismember what we are admiring, but rather get an overwhelming sense and feel for how it works together as a whole. So, Kant sees in our appreciation of beauty, an engagement with our environment that works at a different level from the analytical approach of (scientific or reductionist) pure reason. Therefore, as

1. Chapman, *Ernst Troeltsch and Liberal Theology*, 133.

Davidovich explains, "Focus on the effect the beautiful object has on our . . . faculties provides Kant with a means for distinguishing judgments of taste from scientific . . . judgments."[2]

Most importantly for Kant, in these judgments the divide between the phenomenal and noumenal, between the appearance and the thing in itself is breached. The two worlds that distinguished Kant's philosophy are for a moment brought together, the infinite in the finite. The problem is that much of Kant's thought at this point is suggestive rather than conclusive. There are lots of tantalizing lose ends that Kant has not tied up but that others have been keen to resolve. "Kant hedges when discussing the problem of unity in the Third Critique. His solution is therefore never quite conclusive and straightforward. Nevertheless, from his various partial attempts to address the issue it is possible to recognize the solution he never refined."[3]

Rudolf Otto wanted to develop what Kant says about our experience of beauty and apply it to our religious consciousness of the world. He does this again in his *The Idea of the Holy*. "Building upon Kant's analysis of aesthetic judgment, Rudolf Otto offers a theory of religion as an ability to perceive the meaning of crucial moments of human experience—or, in his technical terminology, to perceive the infinite in the finite—in a form of judgment . . . like Kant's aesthetic feeling."[4]

When trying to communicate what is distinctive about our experience of what is holy and the Other, Rudolf Otto often uses the example of aesthetic experience. It has understandably been argued that Otto's use of this example of aesthetic experience has come straight from Immanuel Kant's third critique.

## No Accounting for Taste

Kant, in his final critique, *Critique of Judgement*, repeatedly makes the point that what we perceive as beautiful is not something that we can conceptualise objectively in cognitive terms. This is something that you immediately experience, or you don't. No one can persuade you on the basis of pure reason that what you are looking at is beautiful or not.

Now for me there is no question that the music of heaven will be that of Johann Sebastian Bach. But even though for me that is an indisputable fact (as for anybody with any taste) you would never be able to persuade the theologian Karl Barth. Because for him the divine was always the music of

2. Davidovich, *Religion as a Province of Meaning*, 72.
3. Davidovich, *Religion as a Province of Meaning*, 55.
4. Davidovich, *Religion as a Province of Meaning*, 152.

Mozart. But it would be no good trying to persuade him of my case conceptually or logically (for example, that Mozart's music is far too ornate to pass through the Pearly Gates), it's something he either gets or he does not. You cannot correct a lack of musical taste in cognitive terms. I am also deeply worried about people who don't like jazz. But I can't make up for their lack of imagination and love of life in terms of well-constructed argument. They either get what's so energetic, cool, and exciting about such a sublime art form or they don't. For as we say, there's no accounting for taste. As Kant explains:

> If we judge objects merely according to concepts, then all representation of beauty is lost. Thus, there can be no rule according to which anyone is to be forced to recognise anything as beautiful. We cannot press up on others by the aid of any reasons or fundamental propositions or judgments that a coat a house, or flower is beautiful. We wish to submit the object to our own eyes, as if the satisfaction in it depends on sensation, and yet if we then call the object beautiful, we believe that we speak with a universal voice, and we claim the ascent of everyone, although on the contrary all private sensation can only decide for the observer himself and his satisfaction.[5]

As Kant says succinctly. "[This] is as much to say that the determining ground of a judgment of taste may indeed be objective, but that it cannot be reduced to definitive concepts and that consequently about the judgment itself nothing can be decided by proofs, although much may rightly be contested."[6]

In a similar way, Otto argues that in religion what is described as "holy" is not something we can sufficiently explain in other categories but needs to be experienced in order to be appreciated.

> "Holiness"—"the holy"—is a category of interpretation and valuation peculiar to the sphere of religion. . . . While it is complex, it contains a quite specific element or "moment," which sets it apart from "the Rational" . . . and which remains inexpressible . . . in the sense that it completely eludes apprehension in terms of concepts. The same thing is true . . . of the category of the beautiful.[7]

5. Kant, *Critique of the Power of Judgment*, 8.5.216.
6. Kant, *Critique of the Power of Judgment*, 69.5.385.
7. Davidovich, *Religion as a Province of Meaning*, 171.

## An Experiential Study

In line with Kant's analysis of our sense of what is beautiful, Otto does not try to argue his case in terms of the validity of any religious experience. As with our sense of the beautiful, there is no conceptual proof to be demonstrated, no logical argument to be made. In contrast, Otto, at the beginning of his book *The Idea of the Holy*, gets the reader to recall their own experience, to remember what they in the past must have themselves been conscious of. He then leads the reader on a reflective journey examining something he expects the reader will have some familiarity with. As Davidovich explains:

> Otto undertakes to guide his readers in a sympathetic process of anamnesis, or remembrance, to evoke in them the religious feeling and the trust in its noeticity [noetic is related to noesis, . . . the action of perceiving or knowing]. Here too, it seems to me, Otto follows Kant's insight regarding the nature of the beautiful. In his discussion of aesthetic taste Kant argues that in order to judge an object beautiful one must perform the judgment oneself; one must feel the unique aesthetic feeling which alone discloses the harmony in the beautiful object. One can be guided in this experience by exposure to examples, but one cannot be taught rules of inference, as the aesthetic judgment is not founded on [a] . . . concept. The aesthetic judgment, according to Kant, is a matter of personal and immediate experience.[8]

Therefore, as Davidovich concludes, "Armed with his understanding of the Critical method Otto sets out to show that religion is a distinct realm of meaning which must be understood and evaluated in its own terms."[9]

Otto begins, *The Idea of the Holy* with a meditation on what the reader should be familiar with. If they don't share the experience they might as well close the book. "The reader is invited to direct his mind to a moment of deeply-felt religious experience, as little as possible qualified by other forms of consciousness. Whoever cannot do this, whoever knows no such moments in his experience, is requested to read no further; for it is not easy to discuss questions of religious psychology with one who can recollect emotions of his adolescence, the discomforts of indigestion, or, say, social feelings, but cannot recall any intrinsically religious feelings."[10]

On this reflective journey it becomes clear that for Otto the essence of religion cannot be reduced to a set of particular doctrines or prescribed

8. Davidovich, *Religion as a Province of Meaning*, 62.
9. Davidovich, *Religion as a Province of Meaning*, 62.
10. Otto, *Idea of the Holy*, 8.

actions but is rather a form of experiential awareness. "In Otto's invitation we find expression of the insight that what is essential in religion is neither assent to some propositions, nor the performance of some rituals, but a state of consciousness that he characterizes as "feeling." Otto calls the fundamental religious state of mind a "numinous feeling" which arises in our mind in the presence of an object perceived as qualitatively superior. Perceiving such an object as wholly other, we are both attracted to it and repelled by it. We consequently feel deficient. Otto characterizes this experience of deficiency as the feeling of creatures who are submerged and overwhelmed by their own nothingness in contrast to that which they conceive as supreme above all."[11]

For Otto, the reality of our experience of the holy and our reaction to the wholly other is again, not something you could establish through purely rational argument or define within a list of propositional statements.

> Otto argues that the religious feeling is a primary and unique property of the mind and as such can only be pointed out and discussed, but not strictly expressed or defined. He contends that the religious apprehension of the "wholly other" eludes logical proof and conceptual demonstration. It is rather a matter of inward and spontaneous awareness that issues from deep within our souls.[12]

Davidovich, in her detailed study of the relationship between Otto's and Kant's philosophy, is very well aware of some of the objections that might be raised to this experiential approach. But again, Otto's analogy with our experience of the aesthetically beautiful comes to mind. For Otto can explain that, in the same way that we cannot prove the reality of the aesthetically beautiful but need to experience it, when it comes to religion, we need to approach it in similar terms.

> Claims that something must be directly experienced in order to be understood may be suspected of being a disingenuous attempt at making one's position invulnerable to criticism. While the suspicion may at times be justified, its critical force is rather limited. It seems rather unreasonable to deny that some things must be experienced in order to be understood. . . . We should remember that the model Otto has in mind is Kant's claim that an object must be experienced in order to be judged beautiful.[13]

11. Davidovich, *Religion as a Province of Meaning*, 168.
12. Davidovich, *Religion as a Province of Meaning*, 168.
13. Davidovich, *Religion as a Province of Meaning*, 199.

We have seen that Otto's philosophy of religion developed in the context of a neo-Kantian revival and particularly the resurgence of interest in Fries's philosophy. But Davidovich in her *Religion as a Province of Meaning* demonstrates that this approach to religious experience does not rely on anything peculiar to this neo-Kantian interpretation but goes directly back to Kant and his third critique. "While Otto's work cannot be understood other than in its neo Kantian matrix, the validity of most of what I find important in Otto's work depends directly on Kant's theory of aesthetic judgment. This is true particularly of Otto's phenomenological analysis of the various moments of the religious experience . . . [and] Otto's identification of the essence of religion in an ability to perceive the infinite in the finite."[14]

But there is one major difference between Kant's analysis of aesthetic experience and how Otto presents religion. That is the fact that Kant conceives of the aesthetic experience as a rarefied encounter of the cultured few but in contrast, Otto sees religion as universal. "Unlike Kant, who found disclosure of ultimate meaning only in rare reflective moments that are accessible to an aesthetic and scientific elite, Otto thought that such moments of awareness were possible to all people at all times. . . . He maintained that this category [i.e., the numinous] is . . . constitutive of the . . . essence of religious life."[15]

Therefore Davidovich in this extensive study of Otto's work in relation to Kant's philosophy sees this analysis of feeling as the means to bridge the distinction between the phenomenal and noumenal, the thing as it is for us and the thing in itself. "Throughout the whole of his career Otto characterized the essence of religion as an 'immediate feeling' or the apprehension of the 'numinous' . . . the double-sided character of reality to which Kant gave expression . . . is overcome in the experienced unity of all that exists in the knowledge guaranteed by . . . feeling."[16]

So, Otto sees religion as something that cannot reduced to other categories of understanding but must be seen as a domain of meaning and form of experience in its own right. "Otto did not write his book *The Idea of the Holy* simply to describe the various affective moments that are involved in the religious experience, though such a description was certainly an important part of his project. Otto wrote this book to present religion as a distinct realm of meaning that must be understood and evaluated in its own terms."[17]

14. Davidovich, *Religion as a Province of Meaning*, 156.
15. Davidovich, *Religion as a Province of Meaning*, 155.
16. Davidovich, *Religion as a Province of Meaning*, 128.
17. Davidovich, *Religion as a Province of Meaning*, 171.

## Critical Concerns

When in part three we review the next generation of philosophy after Immanuel Kant's (particularly the philosophy of Hegel) some critical questions will be raised concerning Kant's influence on theology and the philosophy of religion. Hegel, for example, will question whether it is possible to construct an entire theology merely on the basis of feeling and more fundamentally will question whether such a non-cognitive awareness could supply us with anything we could possibly call knowledge. That such a preconceptual awareness may be just too nebulous and indistinct to be significant.

The next philosophical generation after Kant will also witness the collapse of Kant's noumenal-phenomenal dualism and will see Kant's third critique as suggestive in that respect. For if you continue constructing substantial bridges across a divide sooner or later the significance of that divide will disappear. For surely, if a border becomes porous, it will cease in time to function as any kind of divide. So, it will be argued that the bridging of Kant's dualism in his third critique (for example in aesthetic feeling) has the potential to undermine the fundamental noumenal-phenomenal divide in Kant's critical philosophy.

# 15

# KARL BARTH

## *Kant at Every Twist and Turn*

### Theological Shock

WHEN REVIEWING THE RELIGIOUS reliance on Kant's philosophy we can make the remarkable statement that, not only is the most renowned philosopher of religion (Rudolf Otto) reliant on Kant's philosophical analysis, but also the best-known theologian of the twentieth century, Karl Barth. Karl Barth's fame is such that Pope Pius XII called him the greatest theologian since Thomas Aquinas. Barth is alleged to have replied that the Pope's verdict was confirmation of papal infallibility.

As we know, the first half of the twentieth century witnessed a number of catastrophic events, that saw empires collapse, cities wiped off the map, and whole peoples threatened with extermination. These events likewise shifted irrevocably modern theology. This began in the most unlikely of places, in a commentary on the apostle Paul's epistle to the first-century church in Rome, written by a young pastor Karl Barth, from a small industrial town in Switzerland.

It was not the carnage of the Somme, the experience of trench warfare, or a humiliating German defeat that triggered this new theology; rather it was the declaration of war itself. Karl Barth witnessed those who had taught him theology, and with whom he had worked closely, being unreservedly swept along in a fervor of enthusiasm in support of German militarism. Looking back on these events with some simplified hindsight Barth writes:

> One day in early August 1914 stands out in my personal memory as a black day. Ninety-three German intellectuals impressed public opinion by their proclamation in support of the war policy of Wilhelm II and his counselors. Among these intellectuals I discovered to my horror almost all of my theological teachers whom I had greatly venerated. In despair over what this indicated about the signs of the time I suddenly realized that I could not any longer follow either their ethics and dogmatics or their understanding of the Bible and of history. For me at least, 19th-century theology no longer held any future.[1]

*The Manifesto of the Ninety-Three* was in fact published on October 4th, 1914, not in August. At the time, what seems to have shocked Barth most were, rather, a number of editions of a journal he had worked on that supported what he saw as the "German war experience."

The fact that the theology that he had been trained in so quickly caved was a complete indictment of its authenticity. That it had retained so little in terms of critical distance from its cultural context was also profoundly worrying. So the modern theology he had adopted during his theological education was seen as baptizing and sacralizing German militarism. Therefore, Barth became committed to founding a theology that was not susceptible to this failing: a theology that was not dependent on human subjectivity and its historical experience and was deeply distrustful of the cultural expressions of religion. This will be the major theme that we will be exploring in the development of the distinctive nature of Barth's thought. As the theologian Westerholm explains so eloquently:

> How can the truth of God be acknowledged without reducing it to an element within creaturely reality? . . . how may divine truth be acknowledged without transforming it into untruth? This . . . is decisive for his work from the tumultuous days of the First World War. . . . How may human beings speak of God without taking God under their own "management" and transforming the righteousness of God into "the highest of a variety of high ideals"? What becomes of speech about God when human beings begin to ask: "haven't we just measured God with our standards, conceived God with our conceptions, wished for a God according to our wishes?" It is these questions that Barth wishes to bring to the fore. . . . It is, for Barth, this dilemma that presents the basic question of truth to the theologian: how may

1. See Karl Barth's "Evangelical Theology in the Nineteenth Century" in Oakes, *Karl Barth on Theology and Philosophy*, 47.

> the truth of God be acknowledged without being reduced to a creaturely quantity?[2]

But why was it that Barth was not himself swept along on the same wave of German triumphalism as his mentors and theological peers? Why was it that Barth could step back from this "war experience" and see what was theologically catastrophic? Well, part of the reason was that Barth was not in Germany and was not German. Even though Barth would insist that he wanted "to remain totally and unflinchingly in the centre of German theology and the German church," he could also say, "never forget for a moment that I am Swiss."[3] Barth had been born in Basel, Switzerland and his father had also been a Christian pastor and teacher of theology in Switzerland.

Since the time of his confirmation Karl Barth had known he wanted to study theology: "On the eve of the day of my confirmation [March 23rd, 1902] I made the bold resolve to become a theologian: not with preaching and pastoral care and so on in mind, but in the hope that through such a course of study I might reach a proper understanding of the creed in place of the rather hazy ideas that I had at the time."[4]

As a student he wanted to leave his native Switzerland and study in Germany with the celebrated theologians of the day. His father was not convinced, wanting his son to stay in Switzerland and study in the faculty in which he was teaching. So as Barth recalls, "I began to study in Berne, with my father's kind but earnest guidance and advice."[5]

Barth believed that much that he was being taught was irrelevant and hopelessly outdated, yet for his father's sake went through the motions. Looking back on this experience Barth became convinced that his father's caution backfired as Barth explained:

> One of the best remedies against liberal theology and other kinds of bad theology is to take them in bucketsful. On the other hand, all attempts to withhold them by stratagem of force only causes people to fall for them even more strongly, with a kind of persecution complex. . . . Only much, much later did I find my way out of this liberal swamp of my own accord, by quite a different route.[6]

2. Westerholm, *Ordering of the Christian Mind*, 33.
3. Busch, *Karl Barth: His Life*, 217.
4. Busch, *Karl Barth: His Life*, 31.
5. Busch, *Karl Barth: His Life*, 33.
6. Busch, *Karl Barth: His Life*, 43.

## Every Turn

What is most noticeable is that when looking back on the development of Barth's theology, Kant seems to be there at every turn. Eberhard Busch, Barth's biographer, recounts:

> It was [Immanuel Kant's] work which began to stand out for Karl Barth, even in these early Berne days, and to show him a course which he at first pursued with delight. "The first book which really moved me as a student was Kant's *Critique of Practical Reason*." A few years later Barth could even depict this reading of Kant in the tones of a conversion story: "Then came the time when I began to make a great discovery. This was the discovery that the gospel was simple, that the divine truth was not a complicated, difficult construction with hundreds of different propositions and opinions and hypotheses, but a simple clear knowledge, accessible to any child—I still remember vividly how this insight came to me."[7]

So, even at Berne, Barth was working through the theological implications of Kant's philosophy, a theme that will frequently recur during Barth's theological development. As Barth later wrote, "in my Berne semester I was earnestly told, and learnt . . . that all God's ways begin with Kant and, if possible, must also end there."[8] So, following his studies at Berne, as Barth explains: "After the preliminary examination, according to Swiss practice I was ready for study abroad. I wanted to go to Marburg while my father was very anxious that I should go either to Halle or to Greifswald. The consequence was that I went to Berlin, which was supposed to be more neutral."[9]

Marburg, where Barth wanted to study, was at the heart of the revival in Kantian philosophy and where the best-known neo-Kantian Hermann Cohen taught. It was also where the theologian Wilhelm Herrmann (a friend of Cohen) was seen to be developing something of a synthesis between Kant's philosophy and Schleiermacher's theology.

So in compromising with his father he settled for Berlin. Even though what would bring Karl Barth international recognition was his dramatic turn against key aspects of the progressive liberal theology he studied in Germany, there was no sign of that yet. He in fact admits that when he first went to study in Berlin he saw little if anything of the capital, spending most of his time preparing work for the professor of modern theology he most

7. Busch, *Karl Barth: His Life*, 35.

8. Busch, *Karl Barth: His Life*, 34.

9. Busch, *Karl Barth: His Life*, 38.

admired, Adolf Von Harnack. "My admiration reached such a pitch that because of the work which I had to do for his seminars and with which I was occupied virtually night and day for months, I almost completely neglected . . . the . . . Berlin sights." Among landmark scholarly works on the development of Christian doctrine, Harnack was to write the best-known popular introduction to the essence of modern liberal Christianity, based on his 1901 lectures, *What Is Christianity?*

Even in Berlin, listening to Harnack, Barth still longed to study at neo-Kantian Marburg with its theology professor William Hermann. As Busch, one of Barth's biographers, explains:

> Karl Barth now began to diverge noticeably from his father's "positive" line. . . . "Alongside Kant, Schleiermacher took a clearer place in my thought than before." Having "worked through Immanuel Kant's *Critique of Practical Reason*, and *Critique of Pure Reason* (which I read then for the first time, but equally intensively)," he moved on to Schleiermacher, and from the time of the Berlin semester onwards, Schleiermacher was for years the leading light in his thought. "In Berlin . . . along with Wilhelm Herrmann's *Ethics*, I bought myself a copy of Schleiermacher's *Speeches on Religion, to its Cultured Despisers*, in R. Otto's edition, which I still use. Eureka! I had evidently been looking for 'The Immediate,' and had now found it . . . with Schleiermacher. . . . I was inclined to believe him blindly all along the line."[10]

We have heard a good deal from Rudolf Otto's forward to Schleiermacher's *Speeches on Religion, to its Cultured Despisers*, the edition that Barth purchased in Berlin and read as a student and continued to use. Overall his time in Berlin just intensified Barth's desire to go to Marburg:

> Just as he turned to Schleiermacher, something else happened to Karl in this Berlin semester which his father had sought to prevent by forbidding him to study in Marburg. In Berlin Karl became a committed pupil and follower of Wilhelm Herrmann (1846–1922): "I can remember the day when I . . . first read his Ethics as though it were yesterday. . . . I think that my own personal interest in theology began on that day." Thus the semester in Berlin had no way distracted Barth from wanting to study in Marburg; indeed it strengthened his resolve.[11]

10. Busch, *Karl Barth: His Life*, 40.

11. Busch, *Karl Barth: His Life*, 41.

Eventually his father relented and Karl got to study at "his Zion" with the theologian who had most inspired him and was to greatly influence Barth's own development. In his book *The Barthian Revolution* Gary Dorrien explains what this move meant: "At Marburg, Barth found the greatest contentment and inspiration of his student career. 'Herrmann was the theological teacher of my student years,' he later recalled, adding elsewhere, 'I absorbed Herrmann through every pore.'"[12]

As Barth explains:

> On the one hand Herrmann was a Kantian . . . and on the other a pupil of the younger Schleiermacher. . . . The first four of the speeches were so important to Herrmann that he told us in his seminar that they were the most important pieces of writing to have appeared before the public since the closing of the canon of the New Testament. I did not accept that from him without question.[13]

Even though Barth did not follow Herrmann blindly, he treated what he had to say

> with great respect. . . . Especially since I myself had worked through the whole of Kant before I made my pilgrimage to Marburg. That is really where I came from: . . . I studied Kant's *Critique of Practical Reason*, and then I went twice through the *Critique of Pure Reason* almost with a toothcomb. At that time we thought that it was the way one had to begin theology—and after Kant, I then hit upon Schleiermacher.[14]

## Karl Barth's Inheritance

Wilhelm Herrmann of Marburg, the principal theological inspiration for Karl Barth as a student, was also to considerably reinforce Barth's belief in the vital importance of Kant's philosophy for any modern theology. In a subsection of his book entitled "Kantian" dualism in Wilhelm Herrmann's "theology and philosophy" the theologian Mark Chapman reminds us of what we noted earlier: "The threat to Protestantism . . . became more and more pressing in the face of the dominant all-embracing world-view of Herrmann's time. Vulgar materialism and monism . . . threatened to destroy

12. Dorrien, *Barthian Revolt in Modern Theology*, 15.
13. Busch, *Karl Barth: His Life*, 44.
14. Busch, *Karl Barth: His Life*, 45.

the reality of faith and ethics altogether. This meant [the] . . . justification of Christianity over and against the all-pervasive materialism of popular culture appeared to be more important than anything else."[15]

Directly inspired by Kant and in the context of the neo-Kantian revival at Marburg, the now familiar strategy of Kant's critique of reason was adopted by Barth's teacher. "Instead of seeing the materialistic view of science as the 'true' reality"[16] it was seen as only able to supply us with knowledge of a limited sphere of understanding and because of these limitations could not threaten the things of faith.

> In his attempts to counter this threat, Herrmann made use of . . . [Kant's] distinctive epistemology, with its dualistic methodology. Instead of seeing the materialistic view of science as the "true" reality, he insisted that the scientific and the faithful world-views were to be pursued "alongside one another, without disturbing or destroying one another." In this way Christianity was removed from the sphere of theoretical understanding altogether and given its own different and special mode of inner perception. This was quite distinct from that of science, since "science involves facts as they are interrelated," as they are ordered by laws, not as "they affect our individual lives."[17]

As with the other theologians and philosophers of religion we have surveyed Kant's dualism was welcomed as the best way to maintain the distinct and self-sufficient autonomy of both science and faith, and as the way to prevent one from encroaching on the other's territory.

> Herrmann maintained that it was Kant himself who was originally responsible for the differentiation of science and religion, a distinction for which "Christianity and Protestantism should be most grateful." Indeed, Kant had "freed that faith in which the human heart finds peace from an unworthy dependence on science." The Kantian conception of science, Herrmann maintained, could never achieve an understanding of religious experience as scientific, since "a science of supernatural reality . . . just does not exist." Science, concerned as it was purely with the explanation of the natural and human world, would find the notions of eternity of the supernatural soul quite meaningless.

15. Chapman, *Ernst Troeltsch and Liberal Theology*, 92.
16. Chapman, *Ernst Troeltsch and Liberal Theology*, 92.
17. Chapman, *Ernst Troeltsch and Liberal Theology*, 92.

> Indeed, according to Herrmann even "faith in God was quite untenable for science."[18]

Herrmann believed that theology had to pursue its own distinctive way of knowing, different from the reasoning of any science. This is because its object lies beyond the world that the sciences have mastered. So, as the theologian Bruce McCormack explains when looking at the major influences behind Karl Barth's theology:

> Herrmann's theology can best be set forth by focusing upon its central theme: the "way to religion." The fundamental concern reflected in this theme was to show that religious knowing—the knowledge of faith—is a special kind of knowing which is independent of all other forms of cognition and therefore cannot be reduced to any branch of scientific knowledge that was acknowledged by the neo-Kantians. The reason for this lies first of all in the fact that the reality known by faith (i.e. God) lies beyond the reality to which science has access. God, for Herrmann, was a unique, transcendent, supramundane being, not to be confused with the world which science knows.[19]

As Mark Chapman concludes: "Thus, on the one hand, there was that mode of being expressed by a natural or scientific reality which could only help to sustain life, but which could never reveal anything of true life, since everything it touched was 'dead'; on the other hand, there was the reality of faith, of 'life', which made manifest a higher realm of absolute or 'authentic' being."[20]

## Direct Experience

Herrmann looked to an experience of God as the basis of any theology. An experience that was not seen in any knowledge of the world but was accessible only to the inner life.

> For Herrmann, although it was impossible to prove the reality of God, his reality could nevertheless be *asserted* on the basis of a direct experience of a higher reality. In such an experience the normal canons of scientific proof did not apply. Thus, although it might appear that religion was in competition with science, "in truth it was quite the opposite," since, according to

18. Chapman, *Ernst Troeltsch and Liberal Theology*, 92.
19. McCormack, *Karl Barth's Critically Realistic Dialectical Theology*, 54.
20. Chapman, *Ernst Troeltsch and Liberal Theology*, 92.

> Herrmann, religion was never concerned "with the world, neither with the world as a whole or with particulars in the past or the future, but only with the inner vitality of the individual human being." Indeed, he claimed, religion was real "only in the inner composure in which we differentiate ourselves from the law-governed . . . world of experience."[21]

As Mark Chapman concludes, "Religious Knowledge thus seemed to Herrmann to require a move to a different mode of perception which could reach an immediate awareness of God. Only such . . . could provide a certain knowledge which could overcome the merely human activity of Kantian reason."[22] Consequently we cannot come to God by the application of a scientific rationality in terms of a speculative metaphysics. Rather God has to be revealed, to come to us in the act of redemption, a theme that will become very familiar in Barth's own theology. As Herrmann himself puts it:

> For me, the elimination of metaphysics from theology signifies the clear insight that the methodical knowing of the real in science absolutely does not reach to the reality of our God. It lays hold of nature and the eternal ground of nature, the natural law, . . . but it does not hold for the supranatural God Himself. We therefore eliminate metaphysics from the theological presentation of faith, we confess thereby that we can only come to God because He has come to us in history.[23]

As far as faith is concerned, science only really has one purpose, as Mark Chapman sums it up: "Science can achieve only one thing in the study of theology: it can show that in the sphere of knowledge which is established through faith, there is not even the slightest trace [of science] to be found."[24] As McCormack concluded:

> Given that science has no access to God, Herrmann had nothing but contempt for those philosophies of religion which sought support for faith in some kind of scientific demonstration. God's reality lies beyond all of that which science can prove. If we understand that, then our faith will not be weakened thereby but will rather be reminded of the hidden element which is its strength. On the other hand, this understanding will overthrow that lame science which lives from the prejudice that it is

21. Chapman, *Ernst Troeltsch and Liberal Theology*, 93.
22. Chapman, *Ernst Troeltsch and Liberal Theology*, 92.
23. McCormack, *Karl Barth's Critically Realistic Dialectical Theology*, 55.
24. Chapman, *Ernst Troeltsch and Liberal Theology*, 96.

> necessary for the protection of faith. When this science . . . dies, faith will be made to stand on its own feet.[25]

## The Concern

When reflecting on the parameters of Herrmann's theology McCormack voices some concern that when it comes to religious faith Herrmann shows a disregard for all forms of purely human knowing and understanding: "It is a mistake to want to banish all that can properly be called 'knowledge' from the sphere of religion as Herrmann seemed bent on doing."[26] Chapman's conclusion to his analysis of Herrmann's theology is remarkably similar:

> Although Herrmann's system provides an elegant attempt to circumvent Kantian epistemology, without denying its truth, from the scientific sphere, it nevertheless gives rise to more questions than answers. . . . In the face of the massive scientific and technological edifice of modern society, there seemed to Herrmann to be no place left for religion other than in the corner. Religion, in Herrmann, appears to have retreated into its own sphere: it may be the "true" sphere, but it is hard to know how it is connected with the remainder of human life.[27]

So, Chapman concludes that in this way: "Theology, in pushing religion beyond the limits of communicability, appears to have rendered Itself scientifically irrelevant and apologetically useless."[28]

The words of Bonhoeffer that serve as the epigraph for chapter 10 no doubt spring to mind: "God is being increasingly pushed out of a world that has come of age, out of the spheres of our knowledge and life, and that since Kant he has been relegated to a realm beyond the world of experience."[29]

25. McCormack, *Karl Barth's Critically Realistic Dialectical Theology*, 55.

26. McCormack, *Orthodox and Modern*, 27.

27. Chapman, *Ernst Troeltsch and Liberal Theology*, 110, 109.

28. Chapman, *Ernst Troeltsch and Liberal Theology*, 110.

29. Bonhoeffer, *Letters and Papers from Prison*, 341.

# 16

# KARL BARTH'S MODERN THEOLOGY

*With such a man [Kant] a conversation . . . is possible*

—KARL BARTH

THEOLOGIAN KARL BARTH, WHO in the twentieth century towered above all others in significance, published in 1946 an extensive series of lectures on the history of modern theology. This included a lengthy discussion of a number of modern philosophers, and it is fascinating to note Karl Barth's assessment of Kant.

Barth spends the beginning of the lecture on Kant, as we have done, assessing Kant's critique of reason. In terms of what Kant is wanting to achieve, Barth has nothing but praise. As a critic of reason, Kant, for Barth, is nothing less than a modern-day "prophet." What Barth fundamentally approves of are those now-familiar limits that Kant's philosophy puts on reason in making room for faith. In fact, in the first four pages of Barth's introduction, we get the theme of "limit" or "confine" some dozen times, making it abundantly clear what Barth approves of in Kant's philosophy.

As Barth begins this chapter

> It was in the year . . . 1781, that Kant's *Critique of Pure Reason* appeared. What was the significance of this man and of this work? In connexion with our observations in this book our answer must simply be that it was in this man and in this work that the eighteenth century saw, understood and affirmed itself in its own limitations. Itself—in its limitations! . . . With Kant only this one simple thing happened and for this reason he stands, in

> effect, much more basically, much more comprehensively and more radically, and, in historical terms, much more interestingly and more significantly at the turning-point of his age.[1]

So, our ongoing theme that Kant limited the pretensions of Enlightenment reason to make room for faith, is what Barth overwhelmingly approved of. So as Barth observes, the Enlightenment has been humbled, has "found humility": "In Him . . . it has quite simply come to terms with itself; it therefore knows where it stands, and it has thus acquired humility."[2]

Barth in fact waxes biblical; Kant is a philosophical John the Baptist, a modern-day "prophet," heralding the dawning of a new age. But like John, Barth does not belong to the old or the new, but stands betwixt the two. "The singularity of Kant's position can be seen already by the fact that, comprehensive and typical in both directions as it is, it is a solitary one . . . an incomparable figure. . . . He stands by himself, . . . a stumbling-block and rock of offence also in the new age, someone determinedly pursuing his own course, more feared than loved, a prophet."[3]

This is not the height of his approval, Barth goes beyond these biblical illusions, for he then compares Kant's philosophy with the music of his beloved Mozart. For Barth, a lifelong admirer of Mozart's genius, there was no greater compliment. "In Kant's philosophy, as in the music of Mozart, there is something of the calm and majesty of death which seems suddenly to loom up from afar to oppose the eighteenth-century spirit. That is why in Kant, thrown completely back upon humility, it shines forth once again in its full splendor. That is why it here commands our respect."[4]

## The Confusion of Both Worlds

Kant, for Barth, also stands alone in another way. A way that is worth reflecting on, as this also met with Barth's wholehearted approval. As Barth explains, "The confusion of both worlds, which is more or less likely to lead one astray with everybody else, is almost impossible with Kant."[5] In the context, it seems we have Barth making the now-familiar point, that Kant keeps strictly separate the supersensible world from the world of our common-sense experience. The world of sensory appearances is not to be

1. Barth, *Protestant Theology in the Nineteenth Century*, 266.
2. Barth, *Protestant Theology in the Nineteenth Century*, 268.
3. Barth, *Protestant Theology in the Nineteenth Century*, 266.
4. Barth, *Protestant Theology in the Nineteenth Century*, 269.
5. Barth, *Protestant Theology in the Nineteenth Century*, 267.

confused with the ultimate reality of things in themselves. So what Barth approves of in Kant's fundamental philosophy is the keeping of reason confined to the island of truth and not straying into the sea of faith. Where religious rationalism before Kant confused these two worlds (and we will see philosophers doing so after Kant, most notoriously in Hegel's philosophy) Kant did not get led astray. Notice Barth's final words, that the confusion of these two worlds became "almost impossible with Kant." It was this, as we have seen, that made a cognitive knowledge of God so questionable. Yet the fact that Kant makes a philosophical knowledge of God so difficult is not for Barth a problem but will be seen as a theological blessing in disguise. So after all this approval it is not surprising that Barth concluded "with such a man a conversation . . . is possible."[6]

Barth's primary concern in forging his own distinctive theology is with this "confusion of both worlds."[7] This confusion between the divine and the human was to be avoided at all cost. It was precisely this that had bedevilled the theology of his teachers and predecessors. But whatever it took, Barth believed theology needed liberating from this "confusion of . . . worlds."

## Karl Barth's Philosophical Inspiration

There is little doubt that Kant was the philosophical inspiration for Barth's first attempt at his own distinctive theology. This became known as "dialectical theology" where we will see Barth holding together, in a back and forth (dialectical) tension, fundamentally contrasting accounts of God in his revelation to us, without any sign of final resolution. This "dialectical theology" was communicated by Barth in terms of his own distinctive interpretation of particular biblical texts.

With regard to the importance of Kant's philosophy for Barth's biblical interpretation and for this "dialectical theology," we have his own word for it: "the dialectical movement in which alone the texts gain vitality for us we may show that we are disciples of the thought of the thought of Plato and Kant."[8]

The story that is so often told is that Barth in his more mature theology moved beyond his early adherence to Kant's critical philosophy. But what does not square with this suggestion is the fact that the lecture that was given by Barth on Kant, which we discussed above, is not from his early days

6. Barth, *Protestant Theology in the Nineteenth Century*, 267.

7. Barth, *Protestant Theology in the Nineteenth Century*, 267.

8. Barth, *Gottingen Dogmatics*, 259.

of theological development. This high regard for Kant comes from a time when Barth is meant to have left such philosophical inspiration behind.

## An Introductory Text

When I was tasked with teaching students about Barth's theology, I searched for a helpful introductory text for them to read, but the most engaging text I could find was a five-hundred-page tome! This tremendous work was Bruce McCormack's *Karl Barth's Critically Realistic Dialectical Theology* and he has written a good deal on Barth theology beyond that book, some of which has been collected in his *Orthodox and Modern Studies in the Theology of Karl Barth*. His work is particularly helpful in assessing the importance of Kant for understanding Barth's distinctive approach.

## The Major Breakthrough

McCormack's work questioned the way I had been taught to understand Karl Barth's theology as a student. It was common, after the commencement of the First World War, to see Karl Barth's reaction to the theology of his teachers as a root and branch rejection of modern liberal theology (that we saw beginning in Schleiermacher) with its philosophical origins in Kant. In this way, Barth's theology was presented as a theology that in rejecting modern theology and philosophy went back to premodern Christian classical orthodoxy. So, rather than being inspired by Kant or Schleiermacher, one needed to look back to the Reformation, the Middle Ages, or the early church (patristic theologians) to understand the true nature of Karl Barth's theology. So as one writer argued:

> [Barth] wants to be "orthodox," to adhere to the line which theology followed until the dawn of the "Enlightenment," of "Rationalism." On this line, he wants to insert into theology that which the Reformed and Lutheran orthodox did not allow to come into its own with respect to Bible, confession and dogma. Therefore, "medieval" and "patristic" elements, so far as a Luther and a Calvin continued them, should remain and be reappropriated.[9]

This interpretation of Barth's theology was reinforced by the way Karl Barth's approach was presented in a widely read text of twentieth-century

9. Kattenbusch in McCormack, *Karl Barth's Critically Realistic Dialectical Theology*, 25.

theology and then contrasted to that of the author's own outlook. That text was a *Systematic Theology* by another famous name in twentieth-century German theology, Paul Tillich. As McCormack explains:

> Tillich saw in Barth the spectre of a "kerygmatic theologian" who wanted to derive the contents of his theology solely from the Bible (and perhaps the confessions) without regard for the "situation." To the extent that the "situation" was not systematically integrated into Barth's method it became a "neo-orthodox" method which served the cause of repristination.[10]

McCormack's work critiques this suggestion, that Barth's theology is merely the restoration of orthodoxy. So as McCormack's book title suggests, Barth is to be seen as "orthodox and modern." It is, in fact, at this very point that Kant becomes all-important for understanding the story. For according to McCormack, one of the main reasons why Barth's theology is to be seen as fundamentally modern is the fact that it is working with Kant's modern philosophy.

So it is fair to say that Barth does not end up with a "*neo*-orthodoxy" but rather with a "*critical* orthodoxy" (what McCormack calls a "critical realism"). The critical part coming largely from Kant's philosophy. So, one of the distinguishing features about McCormack's approach to Barth's theological development is the important part Kant plays in this story. McCormack demonstrates in detail that Barth is not only working closely with Kant's philosophy when under the influence of his teachers at Marburg but *also* when he begins to break away from this into what is described as Barth's "dialectical theology." In fact, according to McCormack, some basic Kantian presuppositions remain throughout Barth's theological development. He states:

> My own contribution to the European discussion of Barth's relation to modernity was to demonstrate the extent to which Kant and the later Marburg neo-Kantianism influenced not only his earliest "liberal" theology (prior to 1915) but also decisively stamped his dialectical theology. From Kant, Barth took the view that human knowing is the consequence of the synthesizing activities of the mind (the combination of intuited sense data with the categories of the understanding). Barth would never see any serious reason to question this basic epistemological commitment later.[11]

10. McCormack, *Karl Barth's Critically Realistic Dialectical Theology*, 26.

11. McCormack, *Orthodox and Modern*, 12.

Kant's philosophy often lies on the very surface of Barth's text, so what Barth writes can be difficult to comprehend without a knowledge of Kant's philosophy.

## That "Thing-in-itself" Again

Barth's first published book was a biblical commentary on Paul's New Testament epistle to the church in Rome. Here Barth integrates Kantian terms into his commentary. So, when he begins to discuss chapter three of Paul's epistle to the church in Rome, he discusses the contrast between the "thing-in-itself" and what Barth calls the "unknown God." He writes: "As such, He [God] is precisely no 'thing-in itself'"[12] and "we make of the eternal and ultimate presupposition of the Creator a 'thing-in itself.'"[13]

Outside of a knowledge of Kant's philosophy it is difficult to know what this rather strange term "thing-in itself" could mean. For this idea of a "thing-in-itself," as we have seen, lies at the core of Kant's distinction between phenomena and noumena. But if you were not aware of Kant's revolutionary suggestion that all our knowledge is thoroughly processed and conditioned and that we can never encounter or know the "thing-in-itself" beyond our categories of understanding, how would you have any idea to what this phrase might be referring? It is not a common phrase or idea beyond the technicalities of Kant's thought. Yet Barth believes that such a philosophical distinction can be made. If, for example, he was a common-sense realist or Hegelian, he would deny that such a distinction could be made. But, in contemplating this distinction, is he not following the main premise of Kant's Copernican revolution in philosophy and all that it implies? Barth does not suggest it is not a legitimate distinction to make; he just states that the "thing in itself" is not synonymous with what he refers to as "the unknown God."

And how can a reader not versed in Kant be expected to follow all this? Without such knowledge it surely means that the reader would have to pass over whole passages of Barth's seminal work without any means of comprehension.

12. Barth, *Epistle to the Romans*, 77.

13. Barth, *Epistle to the Romans*, 77.

## Kant in a Barthian Nutshell

Barth also talks about a "transcendental pre-supposition" in this biblical commentary, "Only by . . . upsetting the transcendental pre-supposition can they bring about a change."[14] And elsewhere in the commentary we get Barth's account of how transcendental presuppositions work (not something I have come across before in any biblical commentary). For when discussing the apostle Paul's words "I speak according to human logic," Barth comments:

> The words—according to human logic—suggest, however, that a quite different conclusion lies near at hand and must be substituted for a deduction which, though it appears inevitable is nevertheless wholly uncritical, far too straightforward, and, when applied to God, simply the result of a wild and illegitimate method of thought.
>
> In spite of innumerable warnings, human logic always tends to arrange its propositions in a series and to leave out of account what is not pro-posed, which is in fact the pre-supposition of all pro-positions. In speaking of God, human logic characteristically ignores both His nature and the fact that, when the reference is to Him, the, argument from operation to cause is inapplicable, since He is not a known thing in a series of things.[15]

Barth carries on in this vein for another paragraph or so. So, firstly, here in the passage above we have the transcendental consideration that we need to take into account that "human logic always tends to arrange its propositions in a series and to leave out of account what is not pro-posed, which is in fact the pre-supposition of all pro-positions."[16] Barth then argues that when such "presuppositions" are applied to God in natural theology the "argument from operation to cause is inapplicable . . . and become simply "the result of a wild and illegitimate method of thought," as Kant warned us about many times. Here we have Kant's transcendental argument from his *Critique of Pure Reason* against the speculations of natural theology in a few paragraphs. As theologian Trevor Hart explains:

> God does not belong to the world of objects with which human apprehension and speech ordinarily have to do and to which they are fitted to pertain. God's reality transcends this realm in such a way that human knowing could never aspire to lay hold

14. Barth, *Epistle to the Romans*, 175.

15. Barth, *Epistle to the Romans*, 82.

16. Barth, *Epistle to the Romans*, 82.

> of it and render it into an object. God is beyond human classification, understanding and description. At this point Barth is at one with his Kantian heritage in its refusal to treat God as if he were just another phenomenon within the world of human experience.[17]

Even though Barth distanced himself at several points from the theology he received from Herrmann and his other teachers, there is little sign that Barth was leaving Kant's *Critique of Pure Reason* behind.

What will be argued below is not only the importance of this transcendental philosophy for understanding Barth's seminal work, but also its importance for the systematic theology Barth began writing after he left his pastorate and had taken up an academic post. As the theologian George Hendry writes:

> It was pointed out by some critics in the 1920s that what Barth presented in his Romans, in the guise of a biblical theology, was really a philosophy of religion. . . . But this was disregarded at the time, and later disregarded as anachronistic, as the pattern of Barth's thought changed. The changed pattern was, however, deceptive; for the underlying structure remained, largely unchanged.[18]

## Karl Barth's Philosophy of Scripture

It is now common to argue that in fairness to Barth we should primarily focus on his exposition of the biblical text and in this way to put to one side any underlying philosophical assumptions Barth might have as of minor importance. But when discussing the interpretation of Scripture, Barth sees the significance of inquiring into the philosophy that inspires and often informs exegesis, including his own, and he is somewhat concerned about the naivety of those who would ignore this:

> None of us has any right to boast that we do not intermingle the New Testament with our own worldview but simply let the thoughts of scripture speak for themselves. . . . In letting the text speak, they cannot avoid betraying the fact that they have a specific epistemology, a specific logic and ethics, specific ideas about the relations of God and the world and humanity, specific ideals—in short, a specific philosophy. . . . Naturally, few readers

17. Hart, "Revelation," 42.

18. Hendry, "Transcendental Method in the Theology of Karl Barth," 218–19.

> of the Bible or biblical scholars are philosophers by profession. But there are simple, popular, dilettante philosophies as well as academic philosophies. Even the old peasant has some philosophy—and perhaps not the worst. . . .
>
> I set myself wholly in the same group. I do not pretend to be any better than the rest. . . . Of none of us is it true that we do not mix the gospel with philosophy, Luther and Calvin had their philosophy. So far as I can see they were both Platonists, although of different schools. And to none of us in our understanding of scripture is it a matter of indifference where we come from in this sense or what presuppositions we bring with us. In one sense this is decisive, in our fixing of the thoughts of scripture, of what is meant, or supposed to be said, with what is said in the text. Some people think that mystical feelings are the true content of the Bible, . . . others a cosmic drama embracing heaven and earth.[19]

What is fascinating is that Barth then tells us explicitly what his philosophical presuppositions are when interpreting the Word of God and from all we have seen they should come as no surprise:

> in the cosily pragmatic and unreflecting way in which we work we may show that we are naïve followers of Aristotle, or by the manner in which we stay aloof from the content of the text and merely study it we may give evidence that we are modern agnostics, or by the dialectical movement in which alone the texts gain vitality for us we may show that we are disciples of the thought of Plato and Kant.[20]

As the theologian and interpreter of Barth's development Kenneth Oakes comments in his fascinating study, *Karl Barth on Theology and Philosophy*: "Everyone engages in 'allegorical exegesis' and Barth's own preferences are for Plato and Kant. As for shedding or jettisoning a philosophy or background and approaching the texts without any presuppositions, Barth responds, none of us can do this."[21]

So Barth is clear that his interpretation of Scripture is influenced by Plato and Kant and he presents this as something positive "in which alone the texts gain vitality." He contrasts this with other philosophical approaches which he sees as "naïve" or "agnostic" and appears to claim that no other philosophy will assist in making the message of Scripture come alive today.

19. Barth, *Gottingen Dogmatics*, 258–59.

20. Barth, *Gottingen Dogmatics*, 259.

21. Oakes, *Karl Barth on Theology and Philosophy*, 109.

This does not seem to be the reluctant acknowledgment of the fact that we do not approach any interpretation with an empty head with the neutrality of "a view from nowhere" but always from limited cultural and historical horizons weighed down with a host of inherited presuppositions in serious need of correction. He seems to recommend his Platonic Kantianism in contrast to other philosophical perspectives that are open to us.

So it seems that not only is a knowledge of Kant's philosophy necessary for an understanding of Barth's theological development but even necessary to fully appreciate his interpretation of the Scriptures. As Barth says above, this is not a matter of "indifference" but "in one sense this is decisive." Barth would not recommend that when reading his seminal commentaries, we should put his philosophical concerns to one side and primarily focus on what he is telling us about the Pauline passage in question. Not if we want to the texts to "gain vitality."

## Heidegger and Bonhoeffer

The reaction of Barth's contemporaries, both in philosophy and theology, is also illuminating. Take, for example, Martin Heidegger's reaction—the most influential continental philosopher of the twentieth century. When first introduced to Barth's theology, through Barth's close friend and fellow traveller Eduard Thurneysen, Heidegger voiced concern about Barth's continued Kantianism. Heidegger believed Barth should have broken free from this, in the same way he believed that at the Reformation Luther had broken free from Aristotle's philosophy, that many believed had set the agenda for the theology of the high Middle Ages.[22]

The twentieth-century Christian martyr Bonhoeffer, who Barth would visit when in jail, was also struck by the neo-Kantian presentation of Barth's new theology. While full of praise for the theology, he added, "in spite of all the Neo-Kantian egg-shells."[23]

22. As Kenneth Oakes explains, "the next day Thurneysen wrote to Barth detailing . . . how Thurneysen's lecture had gone, and who was present, adding, 'the philosopher Heidegger—very approving, methodologically everything was in order, no limits overstepped, but with questions regarding our relationship to Kant, whom he counts among Aristotle, from whom the young Luther broke away" (Oakes, *Karl Barth on Theology and Philosophy*, 86).

23. Bonhoeffer, *Letters and Papers*, 328.

## What's New Then?

We noted in the previous section that a groundbreaking study of Karl Barth's theological development by McCormack made much of the continuity in the evolution of Karl Barth's thought with his Kantian teachers. Yet McCormack highlights at least three major differences between the theology Barth was now developing and what he had inherited from his teacher, Hermann of Marburg. These three major differences can be seen most clearly when understood in the light of Kant's strictures on any claim to a knowledge of God.

## Real Knowledge of God

In the theological response to Kant's philosophy we have surveyed so far, we have seen a distinct pattern emerge, a particular way to get under what we have called Kant's cognitive radar. Because Kant had made direct knowledge of things in themselves impossible and had seen all cognitive knowledge as a product of our mental processing, faith needed to find a way around this. So, starting with Schleiermacher, we have seen an appeal to something that is precognitive, an awareness of God in religious feeling, for example, a precognitive awareness that does not fall foul of Kant's critique of reason. A sense and feeling of the reality of God need not be objectified in cognitive and conceptual categories, thus circumventing Kant's critique. As McCormack explained: "Schleiermacher's response to . . . [Kant's] challenge, as is well-known, was to assign the origins of religion to a region of human being and existence which he called 'feeling.' . . . It is clear what Schleiermacher has gained from this move. Kant had made theoretical knowledge of God an impossibility. Schleiermacher has located a point of access to God . . . which overcomes the restrictions Kant placed on theoretical knowledge."[24] As the theologian Trevor Hart explains further,

> For Kant the "phenomena" which constitute the proper objects of human knowledge are constructed in a synergistic transaction between the mind and what is given to it from beyond itself. The mind (appealing to universal categories) imposes form on the particular content perceived by our senses. Insisting that the category of knowledge is confined to things which we know in this manner, Kant concluded that God is not a legitimate object of human knowledge "at all" but rather corresponds to "faith." . . . From this there followed a widespread tendency in

24. McCormack, *Orthodox and Modern*, 24.

> nineteenth-century theology to insist that real religion was essentially a matter of the heart.[25]

As McCormack succinctly puts it, "the assumption widespread among liberals that God is experienced but not known."[26]

It is precisely at this point where Barth is going to disagree with the liberal theology that had inspired him as a student, particularly the theology of Schleiermacher and Herrmann. Going against what he had learnt at Marburg, Barth wants to insist that in revelation God must become for us "intuitable"; that in revelation we are not just given some awareness, feeling, or sense of the almighty but rather we are given a true knowledge of God. As the theologian Westerholm explains, according to this interpretation: "the problem that Barth seeks to address is not, in the first instance, the subjectivism of the modern tradition, but rather the philosophical critique of the knowledge of God that gave rise to this subjectivism in the first place."[27] Barth does not take this move in ignorance of Kant's embargo on any such knowledge, but rather in the light of reading Kant and in dialogue with the Kantian philosophy of the day.

## Every Twist and Turn

In the wake of his growing disillusionment with the liberal theology of his day Barth decides, with a close friend Eduard Thurneysen, to make a fresh start. And what does Karl Barth begin reading before he turns to the Scriptures? As McCormack tells the story:

"At the beginning of June 1916, Barth and his good friend, Eduard Thurneysen, decided that the time had come to rethink the foundations of the theology they had inherited from their teachers in a more systematic fashion than heretofore. Barth devoted himself initially to an intensive reconsideration of the writings of Kant."[28] Therefore Barth can write to Thurneysen, on June 26th, 1916, while he was working on the first edition of his commentary on Romans.

> Our deliberations of two weeks ago about renewed study of philosophy and theology are still in my mind and grow ever more important to me as I look at them from all sides. . . . A position as bold as we would like to take must simply for the sake of

25. Hart, "Revelation," 38.
26. McCormack, *Orthodox and Modern*, 160.
27. Westerholm, *Ordering of the Christian Mind*, 36.
28. McCormack, *Karl Barth's Critically Realistic Dialectical Theology*, 136.

> order have a solid substructure, and that is something that does come about with an occasional little bit of metaphysical construction. . . . The matter itself demands a more comprehensive treatment than is possible to a thirty year old pastor in his working situation. I am already at work making excerpts from Kant (meanwhile the *Prolegomena* and *The Fundamental Principles of the Metaphysics of Ethics*, next it will be *The Critique of Pure Reason*—Oh!), as if I had to take another exam; this clearing up and revision of old studies is refreshing me very much.[29]

I wonder how many biblical scholars, who have written commentaries on the apostle Paul's letters, have in preparation studied Kant's *Critique of Pure Reason* and other philosophical works by Kant. I must ask my colleagues who teach biblical studies whether this is commonplace!

Not only does Barth have the Kant of the past to consider; he also had the Kant of the present. For in the early days of the development of his new theology, he was in close dialogue with a modern Kantian scholar, in the shape of his own younger brother who, like him, had also studied at Marburg with the neo-Kantians. As his brother Henrik Barth states: "I received my foundational academic instruction in the years before the First World War in the so-called 'Marburg school'. This school, in which the transcendental idealism of Kant was renewed."[30]

Again, it was in terms of a knowledge of God witnessed to in divine revelation, where Barth differed from his brother's interpretation of Kant's philosophy. When discussing Barth setting forth his "positive theological vision" and what McCormack comes to refer to as Barth's new "critically realistic theology" McCormack then contrasts the difference in the developing philosophy of the two brothers.

> Both Kantian, but his brother more Neo-Kantian than Karl was becoming. For Barth not only wanted to stress that the "Unintuitable" (i.e. God, revelation, the resurrection) must become "intuitable" but that this also means that we must be talking about having "intuitions of objectively real empirical data. In other words that the "thing in itself" is all important and cannot be ignored.[31]

Finally, a most crucial difference between Karl Barth's critical theology and Heinrich Barth's critical philosophy lay here:

29. See Barth's *Theologische Fragen und Antworten Gebundenes Buch* in Hendry, "Transcendental Method in the Theology of Karl Barth," 214.

30. McCormack, *Karl Barth's Critically Realistic Dialectical Theology*, 136.

31. McCormack, *Karl Barth's Critically Realistic Dialectical Theology*, 226.

> Barth would make much in his doctrine of revelation of the idea that the "Unintuitable" (i.e. God, revelation, the resurrection) must become "intuitable" if it is to be known by human beings. And that could only occur where human beings have intuitions of objectively real empirical data. Such a view constituted a movement away from the thoroughgoing constructivist epistemology of the neo-Kantians. . . . Without the element of intuition . . . a critically realistic theology in the form Barth was now developing would have been impossible.[32]

As Kevin Diller in his illuminating study of Barth's theological epistemology states, "No doubt [Barth] thinking about cognition is shaped by Kant, but for Barth a cognitive human knowledge of the noumenal God is a real possibility thanks to God."[33]

## The Central Problem

This contrast between Barth and the liberal tradition in theology, a tradition stretching back to Schleiermacher, came to a head in the first book that Barth published, the commentary on the apostle Paul's New Testament letter to the Romans, especially in the second edition of that work. As McCormack explains:

> the central problem addressed by the famous second edition of Barth's *Romerbrief* [Romans commentary] is that of the knowledge of God. It was not just a problem for him, however; the question of whether and how God is known stood at the heart of theological reflection in the modern period. . . . It was, above all, Kant's limitation of theoretical knowing to the intuitable which made knowledge of God so deeply problematic to modern theologians. . . . Briefly put . . . [Barth's] solution now read: if the unintuitable God is truly to be known, God must make Godself intuitable. Whereas Kant and Schleiermacher had left God unintuitable, Barth wanted a conception of a God who could make Godself intuitable. For in that case alone would God be truly knowable in the theoretical sense.[34]

Therefore "He did . . . affirm (on Kantian grounds) that if genuine knowledge of God (rather than a mere experience of God) were to be possible,

32. McCormack, *Karl Barth's Critically Realistic Dialectical Theology*, 226.

33. Diller, *Theology's Epistemological Dilemma*, 201.

34. McCormack, *Orthodox and Modern*, 23–24, 28.

then God must enter into the realm of intuitability. God must make himself to be phenomenal."[35]

In Karl Barth's multivolume work of Christian doctrine, the *Church Dogmatics*, which he begins to write in 1932, Barth makes an interesting comparison between what we have seen in Rudolf Otto, concerning a possible knowledge of God and Barth's own approach. Where Barth sees revelation in terms of a word from God that can be cognitively understood, he sees in Rudolf Otto's philosophy of religion just a vague and irrational awareness of the numinous which he believes will be inadequate for any Christian theology. "Whatever 'the holy' of Rudolf Otto may be, it certainly cannot be understood as the Word of God. For it is the numinous, and the numinous is the irrational, and the irrational can no longer be differentiated from an absolutized natural force. But everything depends on this differentiation if we are to understand the concept of the Word of God."[36]

In contrast, Barth argues that when considering revelation: "we must certainly not leave the level of . . . concepts of speaking, hearing, understanding and obeying if we are not to set ourselves at some other place than where God's Word is heard."[37] There is clearly in Barth's new theology, an insistence that God's revelation to us will be in the form of a word to be understood and not a noncognitive numinous awareness or feeling. In a very helpful chapter on Barth's approach to revelation, theologian Trevor Hart explains that following Kant, "knowledge of God is an impossibility for humans. Barth's conclusion, however, is not that God can thus never be 'known' and may be encountered only in some essentially non-cognitive relation. To move in this direction could be entirely false to the logic of God's actual revelatory engagement with us and would thereby let go of the proper objectivity of theological statements."[38]

## The Philosophical Idol

Following Kant, Barth's approach, as we have seen, is in one very important respect emphatically anti-metaphysical. In other words, he has no time for the kind of natural theology that starts with our reflection on a common human experience and then moves up from that to postulate a designer or first cause of all there is. So, in the second edition of his Romans commentary,

35. McCormack, *Orthodox and Modern*, 125.
36. Barth, *Church Dogmatics* 1.1.135.
37. Barth, *Church Dogmatics* 1.1.135.
38. Hart, *Revelation*, 42–43.

he makes it abundantly clear that such a natural theology produces an idol of our own metaphysical making. As McCormack says:

> Barth's theological epistemology in Romans II stands everywhere in the long shadow cast by Immanuel Kant. As we have already indicated, he took for granted the validity of Kant's epistemology as set forth in the First Critique, as well as the success of his attack on metaphysics. . . . "Metaphysics," as Barth understood it, refers to the classical attempt to provide an account for the order which a human subject observes in the world about her. Extrapolating from observed phenomena, she posits the existence of a First Cause or a First Principle. It is the rejection of this order of knowing which is in view when we speak of Barth as "anti-metaphysical."[39]

## The Well-worked Metaphor

In this light, Barth's theology has understandably been described as a complete rejection of any theology from below. A theology from below starts with human experience and reflection and then, on the basis of that, speaks of God. In contrast, it is argued that Barth is only interested in a theology from above, purely on the basis of God's revelation. This has perhaps been an overused metaphor in characterizing Barth's theology for, as we will see, things will become more complex than this metaphor perhaps suggests. But it is a metaphor that Barth was happy to use in the second edition of his Romans commentary. "The word . . . heard by faith . . . cuts down vertically from above"[40] and the "prime factor is provided by the illusion that it is possible for men to hold communication with God . . . without a miracle—vertical from above."[41]

## Having the Kantian Cake, Eating It Too

I believe one can only see how original, and frankly astonishing, Barth's groundbreaking new theology is when one understands it in terms of this debate we have looked at surrounding Kant's philosophical embargo on knowledge of God (or in Kantian terms of things in themselves). For in

39. McCormack, *Karl Barth's Critically Realistic Dialectical Theology*, 246.

40. Barth, *Epistle to the Romans*, 39.

41. Barth, *Epistle to the Romans*, 136.

Kantian terms, in this break with the theology of his teachers, Barth is trying to achieve the impossible. A fact that we will see Barth recognizes.

Barth in his Romans commentary, particularly the second edition, wants to make claims about revelation giving us a cognitive and conceptual knowledge of God, yet without relinquishing Kant's dualism between phenomena and noumena. In other words, Barth seem to remain philosophically committed to what, in Kant's philosophy, would call into question any cognitive knowledge of God but, at the same time, claims that his new theology can give such knowledge. So, Barth seems to want to have his philosophical cake but theologically eat it too; a very clever trick indeed!

As far as his continued commitment to Kant's dualism is concerned, Barth makes this clear in the preface to the second edition of *Romans*. For when he lists the differences between the first and second editions he can say that one of the contrasts is a "closer acquaintance with Plato and Kant. The writings of my brother Heinrich Barth have led me to recognize the importance of these philosophers."[42] With regard to his brother's Kantian influence he could also write in the 1920s: "My philosopher brother, Heinrich, took care that I should once again seriously confront the wisdom of Plato as well. And Father Kant, who had provided the initial spark for me once before, also spoke in a remarkably new and direct way to me in those years."[43] So, it is understandably that McCormack concludes "Barth's theological epistemology in Romans ii stands everywhere in the long shadow cast by Immanuel Kant"[44] and "no exposition of Barth's earliest theology can afford to overlook the impact of Marburg neo-Kantianism."[45]

## Before Dogmatics

The dilemma, for anyone who wants to give an account of a knowledge of God while still wanting to hold to a Kantian dualism, can be seen in the question Barth was debating with his contemporaries before starting the first volume of his *Church Dogmatics* in 1932. Martin Westerholm takes a fresh look at a study that Barth was writing on the theology of the medieval theologian Anselm in 1931, seeing in this study Barth addressing our Kantian question. We have seen that nineteenth-century liberal theology wrestled with this same question—how to claim any knowledge of God after the *Critique of Pure Reason*?

42. Barth, *Epistle to the Romans*, 4.
43. Oakes, *Karl Barth on Theology and Philosophy*, 74.
44. McCormack, *Karl Barth's Critically Realistic Dialectical Theology*, 226.
45. McCormack, *Karl Barth's Critically Realistic Dialectical Theology*, 42.

Before Barth wrote his book on Anselm, Westerholm sees a debate surrounding our question ignited by Barth's penultimate attempt to start a survey of Christian doctrine. This

> debate . . . in Germany in the late 1920s concerned the mode in which the object of faith may be presumed to be present to the believer. . . . A range of thinkers fixed on this engagement as an important moment in Barth's text; these thinkers shared Barth's recognition that the question of the understanding of faith was important in the wake of the breakdown of neo-Protestantism [the liberal theology of Barth's teacher's and their predecessors since Kant], but they disputed the value of the alternative to which Barth sought to point.[46]

One important response to Barth's work argued that even though this was a difficult question before Kant's philosophy, Kant made it particularly difficult

> to separate the presence of faith from the presence of the object of faith. Barth's "Kant-trained thought" is equipped with a "critical reservation" through which the object of faith is kept apart from the reality of faith itself. Faith appears in the phenomenal sphere, but the object of faith shares in the . . . hiddenness of the noumenal. The possibility of understanding this object is thus not given in and with faith itself.[47]

In the light of this question Westerholm concludes that

> What is required, on Barth's telling, is a new conception of theological understanding that comes out from under the constraints of the Kantian critique and allows the Word of God to be acknowledged as a reality that is genuinely grounded in the activity of God. . . . [F]or the neo-Protestant [liberal Post Kantian] conception makes the possibilities and activities of consciousness principal for understanding, and thus precludes the acknowledgement of realities that are grounded in divine activity.[48]

And, as we have seen, this was Barth's question from the very beginning: "the question of how the truth of God may be acknowledged without being reduced to a creaturely quantity; . . . that Barth's work is marked by the view that the decisive theological question of truth is the question of

46. Westerholm, *Ordering of the Christian Mind*, 196, 172.

47. Westerholm, *Ordering of the Christian Mind*, 172.

48. Westerholm, *Ordering of the Christian Mind*, 172, 180.

acknowledging the truth of God without converting it into a creaturely quantity."[49]

Before we look in more detail at how Barth's newfound theology addresses this dilemma, it may help to lay out more systematically what is at stake.

## Kant's Problem with Revelation

In the light of Barth's Kantian inheritance, what explicitly was the problem that Barth faced in wanting to claim cognitive knowledge of God? This, let us be reminded, was a dilemma that, for good reason, none of his theological predecessors believed they could solve in cognitive terms. We will look at this particularly with regard to Barth's interest in a special revelation "from above" which Barth will rely on for knowledge of God in contrast to any theology "from below" based on human experience. In other words, a theology of divine grace rather than nature.

## The Deterministic Nature of Phenomena

Kant saw that the world that the sciences were discovering in the eighteenth century was not a world that could sustain religious belief, as it was a heartless, deterministic machine. In fact, it was not a world that was even suitable for affirming our human freedom and dignity. Now, as we know very well, Kant's solution was to make a division. The deterministic world is just a world of appearance and the world of free spirits lies behind it, as a solution, Kant made the world of phenomena (appearance), the machine and the world behind it, free from that determinism.

But for us to have any knowledge of God, would not God's self-revelation have to enter the world of phenomena—a world, as we have seen, totally unsuitable in its mechanistic terms for such a revelation to happen? For the word of God to appear, would it not have to become part of the world of phenomena, part of the machine, one of the deterministic cogs? All of this, in other words, would have to happen in a realm of time and space, cause and effect, and all the other things that determine our material existence. If these are the conditions of the world of phenomena, it will be a very strange kind of revelation that could conform to that environment. It would, of course, be difficult to conceive of any of this as a personal revelation of the living God.

49. Westerholm, *Ordering of the Christian Mind*, 192.

Westerholm sees this as one of the major concerns Barth had with the liberal theology influenced by Kant that he had embraced as a student: "Barth responds that what is required is a new account of understanding, for the neo-Protestant (Liberal) conception makes the possibilities and activities of consciousness principal for understanding, and thus precludes the acknowledgement of realities that are grounded in divine activity alone."[50]

## God on Production Line

How did Kant ensure that the laws of nature are universal and necessary? Well, when it comes to the world of appearance, he said that the world of appearance is just a product of our minds' work. In order to make this point we used the example of raw material being processed. Kant then insisted that this processing is the necessary condition for us to have knowledge of anything. So on Kant's model of human knowing, for us to have any knowledge of God, that knowledge would also have to go through the same conditioning. So, with Kant we are faced with the strange idea that the Almighty would have to be put on the conveyor belt and be processed by the knowledge factory. But then, as we have asked repeatedly, after the radical conditioning had happened, could we still see what came out at the end as a self-revelation of God?

That Barth sees God entering our world of human conceptuality is clearly stated in the lectures he gives in his first teaching post at Gottingham. As Barth states quite plainly,

> Revelation is God's entry into the world of conceptuality. . . . For theologians faith means seeing in the "only" that would forbid us concepts a temptation of the devil, who wants to suppress God's Word. Hence, they should not evade the appropriate defining, describing, and thinking. . . . By Silence, by indefinite, weak and generalized talk about God, by religious poetry, we neither come ourselves to the place where God himself gives us his Word, nor do we lead others there.[51]

In doing this Barth turns his back on the obfuscation of many of his predecessors in modern theology. Theologians who, as we have seen, wanted to get under the radar of Kant's critique of reason by suggesting that we could have an awareness of God in what is not conceptual. "For theologians who know what they are about, the concept of God is not something

50. Westerholm, *Ordering of the Christian Mind*, 180.

51. Barth, *Gottingen Dogmatics*, 359–60.

shameful or contemptible or even laughable. The idea that it is better to keep silence about God's nature than to speak about it, that it is better to represent it in music or song or poetry, leads finally to mystical knowledge and to its juggling away of the relation of revelation."[52] So Barth says again in conclusion, "The inconceivable God has come into the world of human conceptuality."[53]

However, if Barth insists that the Word of God must enter the world of human conceptuality, how will he get over the problem we have highlighted, that the Word of God would be transformed into a human construct, the product of our mental processing? As Westerholm explains: "Were God's activity to be considered in light of the activities of consciousness, it would be transformed into something other than itself."[54] And Westerholm believes that this is the problem that Barth saw with what he calls the " Neo-Protestant" theology of his liberal predecessors: "How can the believer apprehend the truth of God without converting it into something other than itself? We can see now that it is concern for this question that grounds Barth's rejection of the neo-Protestant conception of understanding, for this latter conception precludes the acknowledgement of the truth of God by transforming it into something that is conditioned by human-activity."[55] This concern is also underlined by McCormack:

> If God were, so to speak, simply transformed into a creature, God would have placed Godself wholly and without reserve at the mercy of the constructive activities of the human knower. God would have become an object like any other constructed by human epistemic activity and, as such, the clear possession of the human knower. Such a conclusion would not entail any real advance over a starting point in religious experience. It too would be subject to ideological manipulation.[56]

## Agnosticism: Entirely Unknown to Us

This is the point we have looked at repeatedly. We saw that Kant, has to make the contrast between the raw material and the end product so great that, on the basis of the end product, you would not be able to say anything about

52. Barth, *Gottingen Dogmatics*, 359.
53. Barth, *Gottingen Dogmatics*, 360.
54. Westerholm, *Ordering of the Christian Mind*, 167.
55. Westerholm, *Ordering of the Christian Mind*, 168.
56. McCormack, *Orthodox and Modern*, 28.

the nature of the raw material (he needed to do this for his dualism between phenomena and nouemena to work). So, as we saw at the very beginning, Kant would then end up saying that on the basis of our knowledge of phenomena we could say next to nothing about the "thing in itself." He says repeatedly, "What may be the case with objects in themselves and abstracted from all this receptivity of our sensibility remains entirely unknown to us. We are acquainted with nothing except our way of perceiving them, which is peculiar to us."[57] So, even though the "thing in itself" maybe the cause of what appears to us, again in the words of Kant it remains "worlds apart from the appearances we experience." For "The representation . . . contains nothing at all that could pertain to an object in itself, but merely the appearance of something and the way in which we are affected by it; and this receptivity . . . remains worlds apart from the cognition of the object in itself even if one might see through to the very bottom of it (the appearance)."[58]

If for Barth in revelation the "thing in itself" appears in cognitive terms, such knowledge "remains worlds apart from the cognition of the object in itself" so that the "[thing-in-itself] remains entirely unknown to us."[59] It was precisely this that led to our philosophers of religion to say "that world is entirely inaccessible to us."[60] So if a self-revelation of God enters the phenomenal realm (God gets processed by the factory) of human knowledge, in Barth's words "God's entry into the world of conceptuality," the "thing in itself" (in this case God) is still according to Plantinga "entirely inaccessible to us."

McCormack recognizes that this is very much the Kantian dilemma that faced modern theology. "It was, above all, Kant's limitation of theoretical knowing to the intuitable which made knowledge of God so deeply problematic to modern theologians. For if God is a transcendent, wholly spiritual being as the Christian tradition maintained, then God is unintuitable and—if Kant's restriction holds—cannot be known."[61]

But this is also a dilemma that is central to Barth's own theological development: "the central problem addressed by the famous second edition of Barth's *Romerbrief* [*Romans*] is that of the knowledge of God. It was not just a problem for him, however; the question of whether and how God is known stood at the heart of theological reflection in the modern period."[62]

57. Kant, *Critique of Pure Reason*, Doctrine of Elements Part 1, A42.
58. Kant, *Critique of Pure Reason*, Doctrine of Elements Part 1, A44.
59. Kant, *Critique of Pure Reason*, Doctrine of Elements Part 1, A44.
60. Plantinga, *Knowledge and Christian Belief*, 2.
61. McCormack, *Orthodox and Modern*, 24.
62. McCormack, *Orthodox and Modern*, 12.

## Kant's Embargo on Natural Revelation and Special Revelation

Those who want to stress revelation as the means of knowing God, in contrast to natural theology, are more than happy with Kant's critique of the proofs of God. But the more I think about this the more I am struck by the fact that the reasoning that Kant used in his attack on natural revelation will also apply to special revelation. What is new in terms of Kant's argument against the proofs of God, in his First Critique, is the point that on Kant's logic it is not legitimate to reason back from phenomena to nouemena. You cannot say that something in the world of phenomena is to be explained in terms of something beyond in, for example, the realm of nouemena. You cannot say that something you have experienced in the world of phenomena is caused by what is outside that world. But this is not only something we do in constructing a natural theology. We also must surely do this when coming to recognize what we see as a special revelation from God. For in this recognition, are we not saying, that something in the world of phenomena (in terms of a revelation) was by God who is outside that world of phenomena? But, as with the proofs of God, Kant's philosophy does not allow for that form of reasoning. For in both instances, we are using an argument from cause to effect, beyond the realm in which this form of reasoning applies. We are saying that a particular phenomenon is caused by something beyond that realm or that a particular phenomenon exists because of the activity of something that is itself not in that world of phenomena. So if a theologian is happy with the logic of Kant's critic of natural theology it will also prove problematic for belief in special divine revelation.

## Hold Your Philosophical Horses

Is not the very basis of Kant's philosophy the idea that what we experience in the phenomenal realm is an effect of the noumenal realm; that what we experience in one, is caused by the other? But since *Critique of Pure Reason* was written, one of the most frequently repeated concerns has been that Kant is not being true to his own philosophical reasoning at this point. In saying that the phenomenal realm is explained or caused by the noumenal he is undermined by his own logic, the logic that you cannot reason from one to the other in terms of saying, one is caused, or explained, by the other. In fact, it seems as if this was one of the main reasons why the majority of neo-Kantians gave up postulating the "thing in itself" at all, as they could not do so on the basis of Kant's own logic.

This is the logic that we have seen Kant explore so explicitly in his critique of natural theology, that the idea of cause and effect cannot be extrapolated beyond the world of phenomena into the world of noumena. I am suggesting that this logic would also apply to the idea of special revelation, which argues that something that has appeared in the realm of phenomena is a revelation caused by what is in the world of noumena (God).[63]

## Work, Not Grace

There is another concern. If all our knowledge of the world is based on the preexisting categories that we bring to whatever we experience, will not our knowledge of God be just a product of our human nature and not a gift of grace? This is of particular concern to a writer like Karl Barth. For Barth, coming from a reformed Protestant tradition, believed that anything to do with divine revelation or salvation must be all of God's doing and not of our doing. So Karl Barth, in his *Church Dogmatics*, explicitly sees Kant's approach to a knowledge of God as problematic, in that it might be seen as a work of man and not solely as a gift of God's grace:

> The question is whether this event [revelation of the word of God] ranks with the other events that might enter man's reality in such a way that to be able to enter it actually requires on man's part a potentiality which is brought by man as such, which consists in a disposition native to him as man, in an organ, in a positive or even a negative property that can be reached and discovered by self-reflection, by anthropological analysis of his existence, in short, in what philosophy of the Kantian type calls a faculty.[64]

This means for Barth that a revelation of the word of God to us is not to be seen as a necessary feature of our human makeup; or, in Kantian terms, a preexisting category in our human understanding. It must be seen as a free choice and a free decision on God's part.

We understand the

> Word of God very badly in isolation from the unconditional freedom in which it is spoken, but we also understand it very badly if we regard it as a mere possibility rather than freedom exercised, a decision made, a choice taking place. A choice

63. That Kant objected to special revelation as well as natural revelation can be seen in his book *Dreams of a Spirit-seer*.

64. Barth, *Church Dogmatics* 1,1.193.

> taking place: In the humanity of Christ, in the Bible and in proclamation of the Word of God . . . it is by choice that the word of God is identical with the humanity of Christ, holy scripture, and proclamation.[65]

## Plato's Shadowlands

One of the problems that historic Christianity had with Platonism is that the Platonism it often encountered so prioritized the transcendent realm of the eternal and timeless, that the world of our sensory experience had little if any significance. So this world became nothing more than a fleeting show of transient shadows. This made Christian orthodoxy's belief in the Word becoming flesh and dwelling among us, or the historical drama of revelation and redemption presented in the Christian Scriptures, difficult to sustain.

On a Platonic reading of things, why would the transcendent want to be involved in a realm of mere shadowy appearances? Is this not the very condition that Platonists want to escape from? So Plato writes of the prisoner escaping from the Platonic cave and then encouraging others to do likewise.

But it may seem as if Kant has raised this problem again. For to undermine Andreas, our materialist, and his preoccupation with sensory experience, Kant suggested that "this life is nothing but a mere appearance, sensible representation of the purely spiritual life, and the entire world of the senses is a mere image, which hovers before our present kind of cognition and, like a dream, have no objective reality in itself."[66]

In presupposing Kant's epistemology, it seems as if Barth came to a similar conclusion.

As McCormack explains: "Barth everywhere presupposed . . . the validity of Kant's epistemology (where it touched upon knowledge of empirical reality). . . . That the 'real' for Barth was not the world known empirically. The truly 'real' is the wholly otherness of . . . God in comparison with whom the empirical world is mere shadow and appearance."[67]

Theologian Graham Ward in a chapter entitled "Barth, Modernity and Postmodernity" argues that "Barth, following Kant, accepts that we cannot know 'things in themselves'. We work with the mediated representations of

65. Barth, *Church Dogmatics* 1.1.157.

66. Kant, *Critique of Pure Reason*, 664.

67. McCormack, *Karl Barth's Critically Realistic Dialectical Theology*, 130.

these things and, on this basis, we live in the world as if we had immediate awareness."[68] So Barth can write:

> Consciousness of ourselves and the world, i.e., our awareness and conception of our ego, and of people and things existing outside ourselves, might well be a matter of mere supposition, of pure appearance, a form of nothingness, and our step from consciousness to being a hollow fiction. It is not true that we have an immediate awareness of our own or any other reality. It is only true that we immediately suppose that we have such an awareness.[69]

As we have argued repeatedly, Ward also sees Barth's use of what he calls Kant's "nonrealism," as a response to the materialistic realism of the Enlightenment.

> Philosophical non-realism developed as a critique of realism as realism came to be understood in modernity. . . .These are forms of realism covering Hobbesian materialism, Lockian and Humean empiricism . . . and positivism . . . .
>
> Fundamentally the realist bases knowledge on experience or sense data—for these present the realist with the world as it objectively stands outside of any subject—and trusts that language more or less accurately mirrors that experience of the world. Space is filled with numerous bodies, each of which has an autonomous, discrete existence. Each body is made up of its substance and its predicates. Each body can be identified, named and catalogued and the world, as such, stripped of mystery and miracle. . . . [A]ll things appear full and manifestly as they are. Realism endorses, then, presence and the self-validating experience.[70]

Graham Ward then argues (as we have) that Barth uses what he calls provocatively Kant's "non-Realism" as a philosophical strategy to combat this threat of scientific materialistic realism

> working within a neo-Kantian framework . . . Barth understands . . . that human consciousness of the world and what the world is in and of itself are distinct. . . . Only God sees things as they are. . . . [T]he world . . . is always and only mediated to us. . . . This position is reiterated and developed . . . with respect to countering

68. Ward, "Barth, Modernity, and Postmodernity," 285.

69. Barth, *Church Dogmatics* 3.1.345.

70. Ward, "Barth, Modernity, and Postmodernity," 285.

> naturalism emphasizing the unreality of human constructions of creation (which are, after Kant, "world-views").[71]

But if following Kant, the "empirical world is mere shadowy . . . appearance" are we not faced with the same problem that Christian theology had with Plato, for how, as we have seen, can you uphold incarnation or the history of revelation/salvation in a world of mere shadow and appearance?

71. Ward, "Barth, Modernity, and Postmodernity," 285. See Barth, *Church Dogmatics* 3.1.345.

# 17

# KARL BARTH'S SOLUTION

WHEN CONSIDERING THE CONCERNS this adoption of Kant's philosophy raises for theology, we have considered the following:

1. That a self-revelation of God would have to be humanly processed to be known, that in this processing the revelation would also become part of the realm of deterministic phenomena, and finally that in this process it would, of course, also have become a humanly achieved work and not just a God-given act of grace.
2. That after that conditioning the thing as it is in itself (God's self-revelation) would remain "entirely unknown to us."
3. That in coming to know that a special revelation had happened, the challenge that Kant raised for natural revelation would also apply to special revelation.
4. And that ultimately all this ends up happening in a world of shadow and mere appearance.

What is Barth's response? Is Barth's response to back down and admit (with Schleiermacher and much of the liberal theology that followed him) that, given these challenges, we cannot on Kant's terms, have cognitive knowledge of God, but only perhaps an indistinct awareness or feeling? As we have seen, in no sense is Barth willing to do this. As a reminder: "Revelation is God's entry into the world of conceptuality."[1] McCormack notes, "Whereas Kant and Schleiermacher had left God unintuitable, Barth

1. Barth, *Gottingen Dogmatics*, 359.

wanted a conception of a God who could make Godself intuitable. For in that case alone would God be truly knowable in the theoretical sense."[2]

Therefore, will Barth reject Kant's critique of reason? This being the very thing that, as we have seen, structures the whole of Kant's philosophy. What is so striking is that Barth does the opposite of this. For example, rather than distancing himself from the limitations Kant puts on our human knowing, Barth wants to outdo Kant in terms of that boundary. So, in the second edition of his commentary on Romans, Barth's first published book, Barth in fact talks about outdoing Kant in tightening up the limits of what we think we can know: "So to outstrip even Kant in the careful preservation of the boundaries of humanity."[3]

From a Kantian perspective it's looking as if Barth is wanting it both ways, the best of both worlds, to have his Kantian dualistic cake and to receive cognitive revelation too. But is it really reasonable to want to have it both ways? Can he appreciate the benefits of Kant's dualism that limits human knowing in combating scientific materialism—something he highly values in his discussion of Kant in his history of nineteenth-century thought—but also have knowledge of "the thing in itself" in terms of a cognitive knowledge of God? How on earth, you might ask, does Barth pull this off? How does he square the Kantian circle?

## Impossibility

It is clear that Barth sees what he is wanting here as impossible. One of the most common ways Barth describes the possibility of any knowledge of God is that it is impossible. In his Romans commentary, when commenting on the apostle Paul's discussion of Abraham's faith and comparing it with ours, Barth writes: "To us, as to him, knowledge is impossible, resurrection impossible, the union of 'here' and 'there', which is established only by God and can be awaited only from Him, is likewise impossible."[4]

Barth carries on piling up the impossibilities: "Here is the impossibility of knowing, the impossibility of resurrection, the impossibility of God, Creator and Redeemer, in whom 'here' and' there' are both One. Abraham is brought within the scope of the impossibility by faith itself the . . . impossible factor."[5] Then, when commenting on chapter 3, that discusses how

2. McCormack, *Orthodox and Modern*, 28.
3. Barth, *Epistle to the Romans*, 367.
4. Barth, *Epistle to the Romans*, 148.
5. Barth, *Epistle to the Romans*, 141.

the Jewish people have been entrusted with the oracles of God, Barth talks about the "impossible possibility," a phrase that he repeats often:

> They [the Jewish people] direct their attention to the possibility that the unknown can as such become an object of knowledge. By their recollection of the impossible they are themselves the proof that God stands within the realm of possibility, not as one possibility among others, but—and this is precisely what is made clear in their case—as the impossible possibility. The oracles of God, of which they are the possessors and guardians, are the comprehensible signs of the incomprehensible truth.[6]

Then Barth carries on to argue, "When the 'Jew' realizes this peculiar possibility, when he recognizes that he has been set at the barrier between two worlds, he is able to rejoice in his peculiarity. Such realization and perception lie beyond the possibility of our knowledge and are the becoming possible of that which is impossible."[7] So Barth recognized that knowledge of God is an impossibility, but he also believes that through faith it can become a possible impossibility (if that makes sense)! "For all faith is both simple and difficult; for all alike it is a scandal, a hazard . . . to all it presents the same embarrassment and the same promise; for all it is a leap into the void. And it is possible for all, only because for all it is equally impossible."[8]

One might ask, is this impossibility of a knowledge of God that Barth is talking about necessarily the philosophical restriction Kant puts on human knowing that Barth has in mind? Now that might not be the whole story, but as Barth comments below concerning Kant's philosophy, "Naturally it is this too: . . . We must not get the wrong impression that the statement that God is incomprehensible is merely the broken confession of the human spirit as it becomes aware of the abyss of its own ignorance and despairs of itself, that it is merely the sum of Kant's critique of reason. Naturally it is this too."[9] This reflection came from the first opportunity Barth had to teach systematically on these questions when moving from his pastorate in Safenwil to teach in Göttingen. At the end of the passage quoted above Barth refers us to a further discussion later in the book: "All this is no evidence of the hopeless philosophical naivete with which our forefathers are often charged today. Even without Kant they knew something of the distance that we must keep here, of the dialectic that is at work here. Nevertheless, one has to admit that among our predecessors a certain sharpness in posing the problem is

6. Barth, *Epistle to the Romans*, 78.
7. Barth, *Epistle to the Romans*, 91.
8. Barth, *Epistle to the Romans*, 99.
9. Barth, *Gottingen Dogmatics*, 356.

regrettably absent."[10] This sharpness, we have seen, comes with Kant's distinction between phenomena and noumena.

So how is the impossible possible? How can he talk about a knowledge of God that from a Kantian philosophical perspective he recognizes is impossible (let alone from other perspectives)?

## It's a Miracle!

Well Barth's predominant answer to this question is to say, "It's a miracle!" In fact, he gives the title "Faith Is Miracle" to his comments on the fourth chapter of Romans. He says,

> We are incompetent to see what is invisible and to comprehend what is incomprehensible. We have no sensible organ wherewith to perceive the miracle. Human experience and human perception end where God begins. In so far as there is human comprehension and affirmation of God, in so far as spiritual experience is directed towards God, receives its impress from him, and possesses the form of faith, there has occurred what is impossible, the paradox and the miracle. . . . Faith is a vacuum and a limitation encompassed by miracle and by paradoxical impossibility.[11]

As McCormack explains,

> how can the God who is described as Unknown and unknowable become known? That Barth was convinced that an affirmation and understanding of God can and does come about is clear. But how is this possible? The short answer is that God can only be known through God—Knowledge of God is possible only as a divine possibility (miracle!) and never as a human possibility—The human who possesses no organ for the miracle, no capacity in herself for the knowledge of God, must somehow be made a participant in God's knowledge of Himself. This is what Barth calls "the impossible possibility of a possibility whose source lies in God alone." But is this really a solution or only a refined statement of the problem?[12]

And the miraculous nature of our knowledge of God continues to be recognized in his more mature theology:

10. Barth, *Gottingen Dogmatics*, 345.
11. Barth, *Epistle to the Romans*, 120–21.
12. McCormack, *Karl Barth's Critically Realistic Dialectical Theology*, 248.

> It is the miracle of revelation and faith . . . when proclamation is for us not just human willing and doing characterized in some way but also and primarily and decisively God's own act, when human talk about God is for us not just that, but also and primarily and decisively God's own speech. It is this miracle that [is the] innermost circle of our deliberations we have not so much to explain as rather to evaluate as this specific miracle.[13]

## Tinkering with the Machinery

McCormack sees in this possible impossibility, in the miracle of revelation, and its accompanying faith that:

1. Barth is trying to keep Kant's basic dualism, that works with the idea that all our knowledge is conditioned by pre-given mental categories.
2. Barth also wants to suggest that with this miracle of divine revelation leading to our knowledge of God, God must also be mastering those Kantian cognitive categories, making them conform to their object, the object of revelation.

So, in the light of the restrictions to the world of phenomena that Kant puts on all knowledge, Barth comes up with one of his most radical suggestions. This is the idea that rather than God as the object of knowledge being made to conform to the Kantian structures of all possible knowing, the reverse of this is suggested. The knowing apparatus that Kant saw as necessary for the possibility of all cognitive knowing, can be made to conform rather to God's self-revelation and not the other way around.

McCormack puts Barth's suggestions concerning the redirecting of the Kantian categories of knowing, in the historical context of Barth's move away from Herrmann's Marburg theology:

> After his "break" with Herrmann, the problem continued to be shaped by the challenge originally posed by Kant. But his new solution represented an attempt to relocate the problem and thereby to transcend Kant's restrictions in what Barth believed to be a way less prone to ideological manipulation and distortion. . . . Revelation, Barth now wanted to say, occurs within the realm of theoretical knowing. If it nevertheless remains a "special" kind of knowing (distinguished from all other acts of theoretical knowing), it is because it has its source in an act of God

13. Barth, *Church Dogmatics* 1.1.59.

> by means of which the human knowing apparatus described by Kant is "commandeered" (laid hold of, grasped) by God from without and made to conform to God as its object.[14]

McCormack at a number of other points in his discussion of Barth's new theology makes this important point concerning Barth's response to Kant's philosophy. "Such communication: is said to be 'immediate' because it is direct; i.e. it is not mediated by the "objects" known through the neo-Kantian constructivist epistemology. God is present to the human knower immediately and creatively, laying hold of the knowing apparatus and re-directing it."[15] He further comments, "What occurs in revelation is that the divine Subject lays hold of or grasps the human knowing apparatus through the phenomena from the other side. In this way, the limitations placed on human knowing by the Kantian subject-object split are overcome by a transcendent, divine act."[16]

It is difficult to know what sense Kant could have made of this most radical of suggestions. For as we have understood it, this is the very reversal of Kant's approach. For Kant, as we have seen, our mental factory was set up and orientated in such a way as to put the raw material of experience within a space-time continuum and within the matrix of cause and effect. To set it up so it doesn't do this (as Kant understands things) would not produce anything we could understand as a form of knowledge.

From a Kantian perspective, it would be very difficult to see how what Barth is suggesting could produce knowledge of any kind, for the way the categories work is necessary for the possibility of any form of knowledge at all. They are not the kind of things that can be changed. Putting what is to be known in the space-time continuum and in a relationship of cause and effect to other things—which are some of the fundamental things Kant's categories do—is fairly fundamental and it is difficult to see how these relationships could be altered.

To reverse this process and say that these categories of knowing conform to the objects to be known is the very opposite of what Kant intended. I worry that Kant would see this as undermining the dualism between things in themselves and things as they appear to us and therefore in the process undermine all that he hopes to achieve through sustaining that dualism. What was so central to Kant's philosophy (and something that Barth appreciated) could be seen to be put in question by Barth's radical move. In this way I am not sure if Barth would be able to have his Kantian epistemological

14. McCormack, *Orthodox and Modern*, 27.

15. McCormack, *Karl Barth's Critically Realistic Dialectical Theology*, 161.

16. McCormack, *Orthodox and Modern*, 111.

cake (the dualism) and eat it too (in redirecting the categories to conform to the object of knowing).

The theologian Martin Westerholm also sees something of a reversal of Kant's approach to knowledge taking place in Barth's theology. He sees this in Barth's response to the challenge that Kant's philosophy posed to any acknowledgement of the truth of God.

> This act of assent brings with it a shift in the believer's noetic standpoint, for the believer lives in light of realities that cannot be comprehended from the standpoint of the empirical or transcendental subject . . . .
>
> It speaks of knowledge where the freedom of the mind is reordered by the reality that is known. . . . It does not turn to its own possibilities and activities in order to apprehend the content of its knowledge; instead, it allows itself to be brought into conformity with the reality of God. It recognizes that . . . the thought of God's existence is more fundamental than the realities of its own self-reflection, and it orders its possibilities accordingly. . . .
>
> It involves the reality that is known "bending" the knower's thought and bringing it "into conformity with itself" by virtue of the obedience of the knower.[17]

Westerholm sees the beginnings of this idea of a radical reordering of thought as to what is beyond the world of phenomena, in the commentaries on Paul's epistles that Barth first wrote when turning away from the liberal neo-Protestantism of his teacher. This reordering is based not in what has been given in terms of known phenomena but in terms of what Westerholm sees as the origin and eschatological end of all existence in God:

> Barth sets himself apart from important elements within neo-Protestantism by claiming that a critical reason that confines attention to the phenomenal enslaves human beings to nature, and history. In place of the critical thinker's account of the limits of reason, Barth commends an eschatologically conditioned ordering of thought in which the phenomenal is understood in terms of an origin and end that is not itself given. This conception gives Barth space to respond to the hopelessness that he sees as the result of the self-enclosed world-view of the critical thinker.[18]

17. Westerholm, *Ordering of the Christian Mind*, 205, 215.
18. Westerholm, *Ordering of the Christian Mind*, 91.

Westerholm also realizes, as we have, that the critical thinker following Kant would quite likely be bemused by the unusual nature of this response to our post-Kantian dilemma:

> Yet Barth recognizes that the critical thinker could respond that Barth's conception of an eschatological ordering of thought is reduced to incoherence because it oversteps the limits of human knowledge. The critical thinker might wonder what exactly it means to consider the phenomenal in relation to an origin and end that are not given. Does this suggestion amount to any more than empty gesturing that violates a basic understanding of the limits of human knowledge?[19]

## A Dialectical Theology

The theology that Barth developed starting with his commentary on Romans has often been described as a dialectical theology. One needs to make clear that what Barth has in mind here in talking about a dialectical approach in theology is the very opposite of what will come to mind for most students of modern philosophy. The most famous example of a dialectical approach to any issue at hand is overwhelmingly associated with the philosopher Hegel and then, following him, Karl Marx.

Here the dialectical is the thought of two opposing ideas in fundamental contradiction to each other coming together to create a higher truth. In this process the two opposing ideas are not denied but taken up and incorporated in what finally resolves the tension between them. But for Barth there is no final resolution where the conflict is resolved. For Barth, the stark opposition remains. Any human resolution will not do justice to the contradictory realities that Barth's theology witnesses to. The truth that Barth wants to express lies in the tension between them, as McCormack makes clear with the contrast to Hegel in mind: "A method which calls for every theological statement to be placed over against a counter-statement, without allowing the dialectical tension between the two to be resolved in a higher synthesis."[20]

For Barth, as we have seen, God in terms of revelation cannot become synonymous with the world of phenomena or any part of it. The freedom and sovereignty of God is not to be compromised or jeopardized in this way. There can be no coming together of God and the world that denies

19. Westerholm, *Ordering of the Christian Mind*, 91.

20. McCormack, *Karl Barth's Critically Realistic Dialectical Theology*, 11.

the difference. The contradiction between God and the world must remain; there can be no ultimate synthesis:

> And yet, if the "wholly otherness" of God were not to be sacrificed in the process, then God must never become directly identical with any one medium of his self-revelation. He must take up the medium in such a way that the ontological difference between God's being and the being of the creaturely medium is not for a moment set aside. No "divinization" of the creaturely occurs in this process; God remains God and world remains world.[21]

So "If the unintuitable God is truly to be known, God must make Godself intuitable. But God must do so in such a way that the unintuitability proper to God is not set aside."[22]

## At a Tangent

Therefore one of the key metaphors that appears at the beginning of his Romans commentary, and Barth spends some time exploring, is to illustrate the way in which the two worlds might touch each other but still be kept apart. He in fact picks up on a geometrical idea, that of the tangential touching of a line and a circle. Even though the line forming a circle and the straight line are fundamentally different, they can geometrically touch each other but without extension across either line. This is how, for Barth, time and eternity manage to touch in Jesus Christ.

In Jesus' name,

> two worlds meet and go apart, two planes intersect, the one known and the other unknown. The known plane is God's creation, fallen out of its union with Him, and therefore the world of the "flesh" needing redemption, the world of men, and of time, and of things—our world. This known plane is intersected by another plane that is unknown. The world of the Father, of the Primal Creation, and of the final Redemption. . . . The point on the line of intersection at which the relation becomes observable and observed is Jesus, Jesus of Nazareth, the historical Jesus—born of the seed of David according to the flesh. The

21. McCormack, *Orthodox and Modern*, 125.

22. McCormack, *Orthodox and Modern*, 28.

> name Jesus defines an historical occurrence and marks the point where the unknown world cuts the known world.[23]

But for Barth, as for Kant, these two worlds must still be kept apart. So, in the touching, one world is not drawn into the other or merged with the other. In this tangential touching there is no deifying of humanity and history. But also, in the opposite direction, neither is there any capturing of divinity within human historical categories. "This does not mean that, at this point, time and things and men are in themselves exalted above other times and other things and other men, but that they are exalted in as much as they serve to define the neighborhood of the point at which the hidden line, intersecting time and eternity, concrete occurrence and primal origin, men and God, becomes visible."[24]

Even at its most pronounced in Christ's resurrection there is no synthesis between the divine and human:

> In the Resurrection the new world of the Holy Spirit touches the old world of the flesh, but touches it as a tangent touches a circle, that is, without touching it. . . . There is here no merging or fusion of God and man, no exaltation of humanity to divinity, no overflowing of God into human nature. What touches us—and yet does not touch us—in Jesus the Christ, is the Kingdom of God who is both Creator and Redeemer.[25]

The key point of this illustration is that even though in one sense the two contrasting lines clearly touch, it can also be said that they barely meet.

> The point on the line of intersection is no more extended onto the known plane than is the unknown plane of which it proclaims the existence. The effulgence, or, rather, the crater made at the percussion point of an exploding shell, the void by which the point on the line of intersection makes itself known in the concrete world of history, is not—even though it be named the Life of Jesus—that other world which touches our world in Him. In so far as our world is touched in Jesus by the other world, it ceases to be capable of direct observation as history, time, or thing.
>
> As Christ, Jesus is the plane which lies beyond our comprehension. The plane which is known to us, He intersects vertically, from above. Within history, Jesus as the Christ, . . . He brings the world of the Father. But we who stand in this concrete

23. Barth, *Epistle to the Romans*, 29.

24. Barth, *Epistle to the Romans*, 29.

25. Barth, *Epistle to the Romans*, 29–30.

> world know nothing, and are incapable of knowing anything, of that other world.[26]

## Lightning Strikes, Bomb Craters, and Flood

Barth also uses a number of dynamic metaphors to illustrate how different the act of divine revelation is from the way it has registered in the world of phenomena. For example, that of a crater that a bomb makes, as he writes: "The astonishing bomb-craters and depressions by means of which [Divine Revelation] makes itself noticeable within the realm of historical intuitability . . . insofar as this, our world, is touched in Jesus by another world."[27] That of a lightning strike: "In Christ the krisis breaks forth. . . . the roots of their being are lit up, as by a flash of lightning, at the eternal 'moment' of revelation."[28] And he also talks of divine revelation in terms of a flash flood that leaves behind it a dried up river bed or "empty canal of revelation."[29]

Not only are all of these metaphors illustrating the fact that revelation is not in continuity with the world (they are not, for example, metaphors of growth from within the world) but they break in, in devastating terms. Barth has gone out of his way to think of examples where there is clearly no inherent similarity or intrinsic analogy between the impression left in the world and the act that has left it. The blasted tree whose "roots . . . are lit up" by the lightning strike does not resemble the lightning in any way. The dark bomb crater is not in any sense similar to the blinding explosion that made it and the dried-up river bed could not be more different from the life-giving water that once coursed through it. Barth could hardly think of more dramatic examples of how the mark made in the world of phenomena could be more different to what made the impression. For as the theologian George Hendry argues: "From Kant he took the emphasis that the other . . . world is beyond the reach of our knowledge in this world, that it registers in this world only negatively. A vacuum, a crater, a shell-hole, or, punctually like a tangent touching a circle or a vertical line intersecting a horizontal. . . . The new possibility, which is the revelation of God in Christ, is not a direct incursion of the divine into the human sphere, the eternal into the temporal, the transcendent into the immanent, the absolute into the relative."[30] For as

26. Barth, *Epistle to the Romans*, 29–30.
27. Barth, *Epistle to the Romans*, 5–6.
28. Barth, *Epistle to the Romans*, 345.
29. Barth, *Epistle to the Romans*, 66.
30. Hendry, "Transcendental Method in the Theology of Karl Barth," 217.

McCormack reminds us: "One of Barth's central concerns . . . was to show how these two realities could be brought into relation with one another while maintaining and properly safeguarding the absolute fundamental difference between them."[31]

## The Light of the Knowledge of the Glory of God

Even more shocking than bombs and lightning bolts (pun unintended) is the suggestion that, in the one who the early church saw as the "image of the invisible God, the Unintuitable is still hidden and veiled:

> Barth's favorite way of describing this in Romans II—drawing upon the term employed in Kant's epistemology—is to say, the Unintuitable (God) must become intuitable; Yet in such a way that no change in the Unintuitable is involved. So, in order that God remain distinct from the medium of revelation, He veils Himself in the medium. He hides Himself and remains hidden in the medium of revelation. . . . Where does He do this? What is the medium? A provisional answer is: in Jesus Christ (God reveals Himself relentlessly as the hidden, only indirectly to be known God).[32]

In a very helpful discussion of Barth's approach to divine revelation, theologian Trevor Hart sees this theme of God remaining veiled in the humanity of Christ, as a point that Barth continues to stress as he develops a more systematic theology. As Trevor Hart explains,

> in apprehending the man Jesus, we do not as such and without further ado lay hold of God. We are, after all, beholding his humanity which serves as a created veil for the divinity as well as a door which, at God's own behest, may open for us. . . . In order for this same human to become transparent with respect to God's own being, the event of revelation must come to completion . . . .
>
> Even though Jesus, life, death and resurrection constitute the primary objective locus or site of God's self-revealing . . . these pertain precisely to the human nature of the incarnate one; they are wholly other than God as such, and Barth is adamant that we should not confuse 'revelation' with anything we know or believe at this level.[33]

31. McCormack, *Karl Barth Critically Realistic*, 141.
32. McCormack, *Karl Barth Critically Realistic*, 249.
33. Hart, *Revelation*, 52, 54.

As the philosophical theologian John Macquarie observes in a survey of modern Christology, for Barth "Any revelation of God must be a veiled revelation, for God cannot be revealed directly in a finite medium. Therefore . . . a measure of ambiguity attends even the revelation in Christ."[34] In fact, for "the light of the knowledge of the glory of God"[35] to shine though the veil, it still needs an act of God, and without this act God still remains hidden in Jesus. For Barth is continually concerned that the phenomena of revelation must remain distinct from the thing itself: "this objective human form is in itself merely the vehicle through which God encounters and lays hold of us. Knowledge of Jesus is not revelation as such. Faith must be called into being, faith which travels through and transcends the veil of the flesh . . . not in and of itself, but as God takes it up into dynamic revealing activity."[36]

McCormack explains how this works in Kantian terms:

> God establishes human knowing by giving to the recipient of revelation the knowledge of something he or she would never possess in the case of any other "object"—that is, a knowledge of the "noumenal" reality that God is. True knowledge of the God-human entails not only a knowledge of the "phenomenon" that we call Jesus of Nazareth but also a Spirit-given knowledge of the "hidden" subject of this life.[37]

By seeing the importance of this modern philosophy for the development of this distinctive theology McCormack concluded, "My own view is this: what Barth was doing, in the end, was seeking to understand what it means to be orthodox under the conditions of modernity: . . . This is why he was willing to think for long stretches with the help of Kant's epistemology."[38]

## An Obvious Irony

Given his experience, Barth understandably was very wary of a theology looking to anything within human nature, whether that be in terms of experience, rationality, or religiosity to resource it. So it cannot but seem ironic that Barth's agenda concerning the possibility of a knowledge of God was set

34. Macquarrie, *Jesus Christ in Modern Thought*, 282.
35. 2 Cor 4:6 (ESV).
36. Hart, "Revelation," 53.
37. McCormack, *Orthodox and Modern*, 159.
38. McCormack, *Orthodox and Modern*, 12.

(in large part) by a modern philosophy and his analysis of such knowledge conducted in its terms.

## Conclusion[39]

As we have seen it is difficult to fully comprehend the challenge that Barth's theology was addressing and the form it took without some knowledge of the philosophical context in which it was forged.

But what should we make of it? I have suggested in philosophical terms that it is difficult to know what Kant would have made of what Barth was suggesting; I fear he might have dismissed it as special pleading. But perhaps McCormack is right in his conclusion that what Barth is arguing for, in terms of a knowledge of God, needs ultimately to be assessed in theological terms:

> To conclude this discussion with a critical question: has Kant really been overcome by means of Kant? God has become intuitable . . . without becoming intuitable. Is this even a coherent notion? The answer, it seems to me, cannot be decided by philosophers as such; it must be resolved theologically. . . . If the idea that the work of the Holy Spirit completely reorients our thought without altering our rationality is theologically defensible, then it will not be incoherent to say that God "commandeers" the human knowing apparatus described by Kant without altering it. . . . Of course, it is true that Kant is no longer Kant by the time Barth has finished with him. Barth's solution is not Kantian, my contention is simply that the problem being addressed is described in Kantian terms. For a solution, Barth has had to look . . . to . . . divine causality.[40]

39. Some readers of the material on Kant and Barth got the impression that I was suggesting that any modern theology needed to fully embrace Kant's Copernican revolution. I believe the nature of modern theology cannot be understood without a knowledge of that philosophical revolution and its implications. But I largely agree with Martin Westerholm's critique of Kant's philosophy for doing theology. See Westerholm, "Kant's Critique and Contemporary Theological Inquiry."

40. McCormack, *Orthodox and Modern*, 34.

# 18

# KANT'S MORAL FAITH

## "Dad, It's Not Fair"

WITH THE ARRIVAL OF my first daughter I often wondered what my wife had given birth to. At first, she seemed like any normal baby and then any adventurous toddler, but in no time at all I found out that she was in reality a fully fledged and passionate civil-rights lawyer!

If her younger sister got into trouble, she would immediately come to her defence, claiming that as parents we were not being fair. Any moral or ethical decision my wife or I would make she would scrutinise and cross-examine first.

When watching the TV, she would often, in a loud voice, tell the characters off for misbehaving, and defend those who were being put upon—something she still unconsciously comes out with as an adult.

She seemed to have been born with an unerring moral compass and a fearless sense of justice. It was difficult to know where she had got this from. I don't think it was from us as parents, as we would often be in the dock, as the accused

## "The World's Not Fair, Dear"

As a father I could deal with all this, as it is what makes her the great personality she is. What I found most difficult to deal with was seeing her discover that the world was not fair and seeing that sense of justice and fairness and those high moral ideals coming to terms with what is so often tragic and unjust. I can still remember her anguish when her favorite TV character came to a tragic end.

Kant may not have seen this in children (not having any) but he was aware of this seemingly natural desire for justice that many possess. As Kant puts it, "It is as if they heard an inner voice that said: This is not how it should be."[1]

But Kant also saw the tragic side of this, that such high moral ideals and a desire for justice appear to be little more than whistling in the dark. He puts this in graphic terms in his third critique.

> As concerns the . . . righteous people . . . : no matter how worthy of happiness they may be, nature, which pays no attention, will still subject them to all the evils of deprivation, disease, and untimely death, just like all the other animals on the earth. And they will stay subjected to these evils always until one vast tomb engulfs them one and all (honest or not, that makes no difference here) and hurls them, who managed to believe they were the final purpose of creation, back into the abyss of the purposeless chaos of matter from which they were taken.[2]

As the philosopher John Hare comments, "The despair here is about whether the universe makes moral sense."[3]

## Moral Faith

So Kant in his second critic of what he calls "Practical Reason" faces this dilemma head-on. The just world my daughter instinctively desired is summed up by Kant as the "Highest Good." The highest good is where the world is bought in line with our moral convictions and the cry for justice. The highest good for Kant is where the world becomes fair and the good ultimately triumphs. As the philosopher Ronald Green explains,

> at the centre of Kant's argument in the *Critique* and almost at the centre of the book itself is the concept of the "Highest Good." Kant defines this as an idea involving the exact "unity," or "connection" of virtue and happiness such that each moral agent is to be conceived as necessarily being happy in direct proportion to his moral worth. Kant further insists ". . .it is the state of affairs which the reason concerned with conduct (practical reason)

1. Kant, *Critique of the Power of Judgment*, 87.5.458.
2. Kant, *Critique of the Power of Judgment*, 87.5.452.
3. Hare, "Kant and the Instability of Atheism," 67.

> must, in its 'pure' (or moral) employment, hold as the complete end which it must bring into existence."[4]

This is the just and fair world that every moral ideal and every moral idealist looks for and works towards. A hope that can be seen as rooted in the Hebrew Scriptures and of all importance for the Christian tradition.

> Crucial to his conception of the highest good is a powerful moral intuition, one central to the Judeo-Christian tradition. This is the ancient lament of Job [and the Psalmists]: Life is unfair, and we live in an unjust world where the vicious prosper and the virtuous suffer. We think that there ought to be a connection between virtue and happiness, vice and misery; in life there is nothing like it; indeed, almost the very opposite seems to be the case.[5]

But the corollary that Kant draws from this analysis is, that this highest good, this just world where virtue and happiness meet, is in fact impossible.

But since from a human perspective that seems to be the case (as the wicked so often prosper), will this not necessarily undermine human morality and any striving for what is just or what is good?

> If, therefore, the highest good is impossible according to practical rules, then the moral law which commands that it be furthered must be fantastic, directed to empty imaginary ends, and consequently inherently false. . . . Since, now, the furthering of the highest good . . . is . . . a . . . necessary object of our will and is inseparably related to the moral law, the impossibility of the highest good must prove the falsity of the moral law also.[6]

As Hare explains, "Significantly, after describing the evils . . . any good person will recognize in the world, Kant says: 'And so, this well-meaning person would indeed have to give up as impossible . . . the purpose that the moral laws obligated him to have before his eyes.'"[7] As Ronald Green sums it up: "striving for any end becomes pointless if the end is hopelessly beyond our reach."[8] Or as the philosopher Charles Wood states: "morally disposed people are involved in a kind of practical irrationality unless they believe in a future life and a providential and gracious Deity."[9]

4. Green, *Religious Reason*, 55.
5. Beiser, "Moral Faith and the Highest Good," 597.
6. Kant, *Critique of Practical Reason*, 1.5.113.
7. Green, *Religious Reason*, 63.
8. Green, *Religious Reason*, 58.
9. Wood, "Rational Theology, Moral Faith and Religion," 403–4.

For Kant, his bleak analysis of the prospects for morality leads him to advocate what Beiser calls Kant's "moral faith." Not only is this moral faith the theme of his Second Critique, *The Critique of Practical Reason*, it also appears at the end of the First Critique in a brief form. Beiser in fact claims: "This doctrine is the very heart and soul of Kant's mature philosophy of religion. Its exposition and defence were a central concern of Kant's in the late 1780s and early 1790s. The doctrine played a pivotal role in Kant's final sketches for a system of philosophy."[10]

## The Kingdom of God

One way to see how this became central to Kant's philosophy of religion is to understand that for Kant the highest good became synonymous with the Christian hope for a kingdom of God.

> Assuming that the highest good consists in both virtue and happiness, how are we to connect these distinct elements? Kant joins them according to a principle of distributive justice: Happiness should be in direct proportion to merit. The highest good is therefore that ideal where everyone receives happiness in proportion to virtue. . . . This is the ideal of "the moral world." . . . Not surprisingly, Kant explicitly and frequently describes this ideal in religious terms: it is "the Kingdom of God." . . . In "Religion" [Kant's book *Religion within the Bounds of Reason*] he identifies it with "a universal republic based on the laws of virtue, an ethical community whose single lawgiver is God alone (698–9). In the first Critique, Kant betrays the immediate source of this ideal : It is the . . . "City of God," a republic ruled by God himself, and governs all souls according to love and the strictest principle of justice (B 840). The ultimate provenance for this view was, of course, Augustine. Kant knew this perfectly well; in . . . 1785 . . . he explicitly identifies his highest good with what Augustine . . . called . . . the kingdom of grace.[11]

Now there is some debate whether Kant had in mind a heavenly or an earthly kingdom, or perhaps he began by thinking in transcendent terms, but as time went on his concept of the kingdom of God and the highest good began to be understood as human historical realities.

10. Beiser, "Moral Faith and the Highest Good," 588.

11. Beiser, "Moral Faith and the Highest Good," 597.

## Ignorance of Christian tradition

But I think Beiser is right in pointing out that if Kant is drawing from the Christian tradition we need not see any dichotomy here. As Beiser explains:

> Before we proceed, . . . it is important to clarify one point that has been the source of much confusion about Kant's concept of the highest good. Scholars have debated the ontological status of Kant's . . . highest good, asking whether it is noumenal or phenomenal, transcendent or natural, other-worldly or this-worldly; . . . this entire discussion proceeds from a false premise, one that betrays ignorance of the Christian tradition. The false premise is the common assumption that these realms are exclusive. It is an assumption that would have aroused the indignation of the Bishop of Hippo, and that would have perplexed the sage of Konigsberg himself. For it is central to Augustine's theory that the City of God does not exist in heaven, in some supernatural realm beyond the earth; rather, it exists on the Earth and in this World; but on the Earth and in this World insofar as it is completely transformed by the second coming of Christ. We should view Kant's ideal of the highest good in a similar light. It always meant for him, as he described it in "Religion," "the Kingdom of God on Earth." But this did not imply, as modern scholars believe, that the Earth will remain natural; it means rather that the Divine will come down to the Earth, which will be completely transformed. Once we realize this simple point, we have no reason to think Kant is inconsistent, or that he changed his views . . . Kant's views were consistent and persistent. They were those of the Augustinian tradition."[12]

So for Kant this highest good, which is needed to make any sense of human morality, is something that God ultimately must bring into being. For only God can bring about his kingdom. And it is only then that the righteous are vindicated and virtue triumphs over vice. As Ronald Green concluded in his book *Religious Reason*: "Because of this, as rational agents we have reason to believe that our sufferings in the name of morality may not be the final condition we experience, that a perfectly moral power somehow supreme over all causation and for which the constraints of time and space pose no obstacle can in some way ensure that unhappiness, even death, prove only minor facets of our total experience."[13] As Beiser made clear:

12. Beiser, "Moral Faith and the Highest Good," 599.
13. Green, *Religious Reason*, 65.

What Kant is looking for is not rewards for moral intentions and actions, but the motivation to persist in moral action at all. His ultimate worry is (for lack of a better word) existential: the despair that comes from believing that all our moral efforts and strivings in the world are in vain. If we believe that all our actions will have no effect on the world—that all our efforts will come to nothing—then we will have no motivation to act at all.[14]

## Practical Reason

So for Kant, belief in God becomes a moral obligation, a moral duty. Not something that can be established on the basis of pure speculative reason, but only on moral or ethical grounds on the basis of "practical reason," as Kant calls it:

So, in the end, the highest good is indeed a goal of human striving; but the problem is that it cannot be approached, still less achieved, through human effort alone. What we also need, Kant believes, is that fundamental Christian virtue: hope, or faith in divine . . . providence. We can believe that all our efforts to create a better world will come to something, Kant argues, only if we also assume that there is a divine providence that has so organized nature and history that finite human efforts constantly progress toward their ultimate ideal.[15]

So for Kant there is a logic to faith in God—a moral logic:

Put at its simplest and most schematic, Kant's argument in the second Critique takes the following form. (1) We have a duty to promote the highest good. (2) We must assume the conditions for the possibility of this good. (3) God is a condition of the possibility of the highest good. Therefore, we have a duty to assume the existence of God . . . .

According to the second *Critique*, we have the right, indeed the duty, to believe in the existence of God and the immortality of the soul. Although we cannot prove their existence through theoretical reason, we have the right to believe in their existence through practical reason. Moral faith means, therefore, that God and immortality are legitimate objects of belief . . . .

14. Beiser, "Moral Faith and the Highest Good," 617.

15. Beiser, "Moral Faith and the Highest Good," 604.

> In other words, we cannot demonstrate through reason the fundamental truths of . . . religion, namely, the existence of God, providence, and immortality; rather, the only possible justification for these beliefs has to be moral.[16]

In Kant's first *Critique* he made it clear that it had been his aim to argue this case all along: "At some future time we shall show that the moral laws do not merely presuppose the existence of a supreme being, but also, as themselves . . . absolutely necessarily, justify us in postulating it, though, indeed, only from a practical point of view."[17]

Without this moral faith it can appear as if one's worldview and one's morality are in unresolvable opposition, with a view of the world that can appear tragic and pessimistic and inhospitable to a morality of any kind. For moving backwards is as good as moving forwards when there's no light at the end of the tunnel.

## Kant Was Rejected

If this moral faith is so crucial to Kant's philosophy of religion, why have we not mentioned it earlier? Should we not have mentioned it before we surveyed Kant's influence on modern theology? There is however an obvious reason why it was not discussed and that is the simple fact that the modern theologians we looked at were not impressed. The father of liberal theology, Schleiermacher was critical of what he saw as Kant's total reduction of religion to morality. This rejection of Kant's moral faith was even more pronounced in the father of twentieth-century theology, Karl Barth. So where Kant's dualism between phenomena and noumena set the philosophical agenda for much modern theology, Kant's moral faith was largely rejected as wholly inadequate theology. To have discussed it earlier, I believe, would have confused an introduction that was complex enough already.

## Unresolved Tensions

To conclude, there is something particularly curious about Kant's moral faith. Let me put it like this; if we were surveying a history of ethical thought, in another important regard Kant would stand out as one of the first philosophers who insists on not basing ethics in a theology. For interestingly, in Kant's study of the metaphysics of morality, at no point does Kant say that

16. Beiser, "Moral Faith and the Highest Good," 604, 618, 591.
17. Kant, *Critique of Pure Reason*, 2.2.2.3.7 A634/B662.

an ethical principle of any kind should have its basis in divine command or on God's authority or be grounded in God's being. But is that not the exact reverse of what we have seen Kant argue above, and the basis of Kant's moral faith, that ethics will make no sense without God?

To illustrate this fact, in Schneewind's history of moral philosophy entitled *The Invention of Autonomy* the history culminates in Kant. This is because it is Kant's moral philosophy that epitomizes the modern invention of our autonomy in ethics over and against an ethics based on any God-given authority. In fact, the study begins with the words "Kant invented the conception of morality as autonomy."[18] As Schneewind explains:

> It was only from about the early eighteenth century that the effort to create a theory of morality as self-governance became self-conscious. Moral and political concerns led increasing numbers of philosophers to think that the inherited conceptions of morality did not allow for a proper appreciation of human dignity; and therefore, did not properly allow even for the moral teachings of the Christianity that many still accepted.[19]

For Schneewind, it is Kant who is the best example of this distinctly modern turn in moral theory:

> Kant's explanation of this belief was fuller and more radical than any other. He alone was proposing a truly revolutionary rethinking of morality. He held that we are self-governing because we are autonomous. By this he meant that we ourselves legislate the moral law. It is only because of the legislative action of our own will that we are under moral law; and the same action is what always enables everyone to be law-abiding. Kant was the first to argue for autonomy in this strong sense.[20]

In fact, Schneewind then concludes: "His [Kant's] theory is, of course, of more than historical interest. It is more fully involved in current philosophical ethics than is the work of any other early modern thinker."[21] Therefore:

> Kant invented a new way of understanding morality and ourselves as moral agents. . . . At the centre of Kant's ethical theory is the claim that normal adults are capable of being fully self-governing in moral matters. In Kant's terminology, we are

18. Schneewind, *Invention of Autonomy*, 3.
19. Schneewind, *Invention of Autonomy*, 5.
20. Schneewind, *Invention of Autonomy*, 6.
21. Schneewind, *Invention of Autonomy*, 6.

> "autonomous." Autonomy involves . . . that no authority external to ourselves is needed to constitute or inform us of the demands of morality. We can each know without being told what we ought to do because moral requirements are requirements we impose on ourselves.[22]

For Kant this is an explicit rejection of a theory of morality based on a divine command imposed externally on a moral agent. The only way an ethic can be seen as divinely ordained is by demonstrating its intrinsic rationality and worth: "We . . . will believe ourselves to be in conformity with the divine will only insofar as we hold as holy the moral law that reason teaches us from the nature of actions themselves, believing ourselves to serve this divine will only through furthering what is best for the world in ourselves and others. Moral theology is therefore only of immanent use. . . . We will not hold actions to be obligatory because they are God's commands, but will rather regard them as divine commands because we are internally obligated to them."[23]

Thankfully this is not a book on ethical theory, so we don't have to explore the mechanics of how Kant attempts to construct a self-governing morality. But I do want to notice the curious relationship between Kant's fully self-legislating ethical theory and the equally important idea that for Kant (that we have seen in some detail above) religious faith is also necessary in making sense of any morality. Kant expressed the relationship between his two convictions in these terms:

> Natural morality must be so constituted that it can be thought independently of any concept of God, and obtain zealous reverence from us solely on account of its own inner dignity and excellence. But further it serves for this if, after we have taken an interest in morals itself, to take an interest also in the existence of God, a being who can reward our good conduct; and then we obtain strong incentives which determine us to observe.[24]

As the philosopher of religion John Hare comments: "So we have here two components, and the proper order of them is crucial—There is the belief in a supreme intelligence governing the world, and there is the commitment to obey the moral law for its own sake. Kant is insistent that the commitment to obey the moral law for its own sake has to come first."[25]

22. Schneewind, "Autonomy, Obligation, and Virtue," 309.

23. Kant, *Critique of Pure Reason*, 2.2.2.2.3 A819/B847.

24. Kant, "Lectures on the Philosophical Doctrine of Religion, 349.

25. Hare, "Kant and the Instability of Atheism," 72.

Kant was not the first to try balancing these two convictions between, on the one hand, the importance of preserving human autonomy together with, on the other hand, a strong moral faith in the providence of divine vindication. As Schneewind argues:

> Briefly, the claim that the main effort of the moral philosophy of the eighteenth century was to secularize morality simply does not stand up to even the most cursory inspection. Indeed, if I were forced to identify something or other as "the Enlightenment project" for morality, I should say that it was the effort to limit God's control over earthly life while keeping him essential to morality. Naturally this effort took different forms, depending on how the relation between God and morality were conceived.[26]

As the philosopher Gordon Michalson states: "The self-referential feature signals on Kant part . . . a broad 18th century effort to breakaway from dominant conceptions of morality as a form of obedience and reconceptualize morality as a form of self-governance."[27]

Because a self-legislating ethic is more developed in Kant's philosophy than any other to date, and because religion for Kant is founded entirely on his so-called moral faith, the dilemma of balancing these two contrasting convictions has become for Kant more pronounced and exposed to the charge of instability than any previous attempt. As Michalson points out in his book *Kant and the Problem of God*: "In a manner suggestive of the challenges facing the wider culture, the problem for Kant gradually becomes that of somehow fitting God into a process that, by definition, is governed by human freedom."[28] Since, for Kant, reason replaces God as legislator for both nature and morality: "Kant promotes the unhooking of the rational will from all external constraints, reconceiving it as a capacity to generate its own constraints. Something such as this image of self-invention is what is central to Kant's definition of autonomy as the will's capacity to legislate laws to itself."[29]

This has made Kant's philosophy particularly vulnerable to the criticism that it is inherently conflicted. In fact, Michalson, in the long run, cannot see how these two aspects of Kant's philosophy could be brought together. As he says bluntly: "Kant's theory of autonomy turns this difficulty into a virtual impossibility."[30] He claims this is a virtual impossibility

26. Schneewind, *Invention of Autonomy*, 8.
27. Michalson, *Kant and the Problem of God*, 63.
28. Michalson, *Kant and the Problem of God*, 58.
29. Michalson, *Kant and the Problem of God*, 22.
30. Michalson, *Kant and the Problem of God*, 58.

because: "God's will is inextricably entangled with the dictates of the highest good which, in turn, have been rationally generated rather than divinely ordained."[31] So Kant's

> moral argument [for God] may be designed to recover the positive . . . relationship with God jeopardized by the *Critique of Pure Reason*, but the result is the subordination of the divine will to the dictates of reason's conception of, and interest in, the highest good. . . .
>
> While Kant insists that it is "morally necessary to assume the existence of God" it is necessary only to complete or round off a train of thought that has its point of departure in an autonomous rationality.[32]

So Michalson cynically sees the relationship between Kant's first two critiques (the first on pure reason and the second on practical reason) in these terms: "We might conclude, crudely but not misleadingly, that in the first Critique God is shown the way out by the front door, for all to see. In the *Critique of Practical Reason*, however, God returns almost furtively by the back door, just before day's end, after all the truly important matters concerning the integrity of the moral life have been addressed."[33] So Michalson concludes his critique of Kant in these terms: "Kant's philosophy demands autonomy, but it only accommodates theism. Such would appear to be the clear moral of the preceding investigation, which has traced the way . . . reason devises its own ends, generates its own momentum, and presses towards its self-designed goal."[34]

In the next section we will see how Hegel addressed the same concerns but tries to resolve them in a different way to Kant's philosophy.[35]

31. Michalson, *Kant and the Problem of God*, 48.

32. Michalson, *Kant and the Problem of God*, 21, 49.

33. Michalson, *Kant and the Problem of God*, 47.

34. Michalson, *Kant and the Problem of God*, 123.

35. In a groundbreaking study of Kant's theological context (*The Intolerable God: Kant's Theological Journey*) Christopher Insole also sees Kant wrestling with the fundamentally theological concerns of human freedom and divine transcendence.

# Part 3

## HEALING THE DIVIDE

*Reconciling Freedom—Human and Divine:*
*From Hegel to Pannenberg via Schleiermacher, Marx,*
*Feuerbach, and Moltmann*

# 19

# HEGEL

## *The Spirit of Music*

### A Musical Overture

On particularly long car journeys, my family sometimes played a guessing game. Before the name of the composer being played on the radio was announced, we would try to name them. The first thing I would try and do was to work out which period the piece might be from. If what I was hearing was very orderly, tightly structured and regular, weaving together an almost mathematical pattern of notes, that would give me a clue. If, when I had heard the start of the piece, I knew it was going to be pretty much that same tempo and volume throughout, that there would be no great crescendos or diminuendos, no dramatic or sudden changes, that would also help me. If it was not taking me on some heart-wrenching emotional journey and there were no cannons being set off at the end, all of that put together would give a pretty good idea of the era. From these immediate observations I might guess that the music was likely to be a Baroque or early classical composition.

Music from this time does not necessarily reveal much about the composer's life or character, let alone their inner life and soul; you don't hear much in this period in the way of existential angst or personal tragedy. In fact, it is possible to imagine that a contented person and a tortured soul from that era might write similar music. So, from all this you might place the music in the late seventeenth or early eighteenth century.

If, in contrast, the music on the radio was broad and expansive with epic, meandering themes, great highs and lows, torturous tension and then resolution, then at times it was very quiet and mournful, then building to a seismic crescendo (music like this never really works on a car radio), and if by the end of this piece it felt as if the composer had bared their soul on a journey of self-discovery or self-realization, I then know for certain this was not Baroque. This was nineteenth-century music, a product of Romanticism, perhaps late Beethoven.

The contrast between the two musical compositions, between the Baroque and the Romantic, illustrates the ways the relationship between God and the world was often conceived of in those two periods. The most well-known example of the second approach is the philosophy of Hegel. As a contemporary of Beethoven, Hegel wrote his epic works of philosophy when the Romantic composers were writing their great symphonies.

Hegel sees the relationship between God and creation in the way a Romantic composer was likely to see the relationship between himself and his composition. For in Hegel's philosophy, creation is a great work of Romantic self-expression, self-revelation, even self-realization. With Hegel we are entering, as the great analyst of the modern mind Charles Taylor says, an age of "self-expression," but I would suggest that that is not just in terms of how people see themselves (as Taylor argues) but also how they see God and the world. In this process the creator does not just affect his creation; his creation has an affect on him. With any great work there is an element of self-discovery, self-fulfilment, even vulnerability.

## From Static to Dynamic

The Baroque or Classical divinity, like the seventeenth-century composer, is all about establishing an order and regularity, giving a stable nature to the world. You can see the work of God in the mathematical regularity of the creation (as Newton did), as you can see the artistry of the maestro in his masterpiece.

For the Romantic, what is created is never static, it is not about establishing a regular order in things. Rather, things are always changing, always developing towards the next movement of the cosmic composition. Like the Romantic epic there are real tensions that need resolving, tragedies that need to be overcome. The natural world, society, humanity, and even human consciousness changes in this unfolding drama. You cannot step out of this process to find truth or peace in what is above or beneath. The swirling changing music is all there is.

This new world of constant change is the one that Hegel inhabits, but not reluctantly or fearfully. He celebrates it, embraces it, and enthusiastically invites us to enter, he sees it as full of promise for every area of life, including religion.

## No Exaggeration

There are few philosophers other than Hegel for whom you can express their all-pervasive influence without any exaggeration or need for qualification. For example:

> "The greatest philosopher of the modern experience, G. W. F. Hegel . . . inspires nearly every great philosophical idea and movement of the past two centuries."[1]

> "So extensive has been the influence of Hegelian ideas, that, if one is to understand the major intellectual developments of the nineteenth and twentieth centuries, one has to come to grips with Hegel."[2]

> "It is a remarkable fact that virtually every major philosophical movement of the twentieth century—existentialism, Marxism, pragmatism, phenomenology and analytic philosophy—grew out of reaction against Hegel. The concepts, arguments and problems of these movements will remain forever alien . . . to us until we understand what they grew out of and what they reacted against. So here we have at least one good reason to read Hegel: to understand the roots of our culture."[3]

> "Hegel has . . . had an unparalleled impact on the modern world. Marx's conception of historical dialectic and his analysis of capitalism are heavily indebted to Hegel; Kierkegaard's existentialism was developed in response to Hegelian philosophy; . . . indeed the whole modern interest in historical understanding have all been deeply influenced by Hegel. . . . Given the extraordinary way in which Hegel's thinking pervades modern intellectual life, it seems to be undeniably true that 'no one today who seriously seeks to understand the shape of the modern world can avoid coming to terms with Hegel.'[4]

1. Dorrien, *Kantian Reason and Hegelian Spirit*, 159.
2. Houlgate, *Hegel Reader*, 2.
3. Beiser, *Hegel*, 2.
4. Houlgate, *Introduction to Hegel*, 2.

Is it possible to beat that? I doubt it.

## Upsetting Them, Left and Right

My aim in this introduction to Hegel is to annoy as many people as possible. Because I want to suggest that Hegel was a deeply religious thinker, in fact a committed Christian and possibly a great theologian. That has the potential to upset both the radical left and the conservative right.

The left has never liked the suggestion that Hegel was really a Christian theologian. For after Hegel's death the many students of his thought fundamentally disagreed on how to interpret their master. There was a radical split in his followers between what were imaginatively known as right and left Hegelians. The left included a little-known philosopher called Karl Marx. (Marx acknowledged his debt to Hegel throughout his life, calling himself long after Hegel's death a "pupil of that mighty thinker.") The students on the left were determined to read their master's thought in purely humanistic and secular terms. In fact, some believed that Hegel was fundamentally against religion and opposed to Christianity.

In fact, the prolific essayist and critic of the time Heinrich Heine (1797–1856) could write in his confessions in these terms about the effect of first encountering Hegel's philosophy: "I was young and proud, and it was good for my arrogance when I heard from Hegel that not, as my grandmother thought, God Almighty, who lives in heaven, was God Almighty, but rather I myself living here on earth."[5] He concludes "that Hegelian philosophy gave the most formidable support to all . . . forms of atheism."[6]

Even today some highly regarded scholars of Hegel's thought are still convinced that the left best understood his philosophy.

The problem is that their master had a tendency of saying things like this.

> God is the beginning of all things and the end of all things; [everything] starts from God and returns to God. God is the one and only object of philosophy. [Its concern is] to occupy its self with God, to apprehend everything in God, to lead everything back to God, as well as to derive everything particular from God and to justify everything only insofar as it stems from God, and is sustained through its relationship with God, live by God's radiance and has [within itself] the mind of God . Thus,

5. Heine, "Confessions," 207.
6. Heine, "Confessions," 207.

> philosophy is theology, and [one's] occupation with philosophy . . . is of itself the service of God.[7]

To make things even more problematic Hegel begins his philosophical logic with these words.

> The objects of philosophy, it is true, are upon the whole the same as those of religion. In both the object is Truth, in that supreme sense in which God and God only is the Truth. Both in like manner go on to treat of the finite worlds of nature and the human mind, with their relation to each other and to their truth in God.[8]

The left would not take their master at his word. All of this they insisted was just his public face; in private he would never have said such things. The problem is we now have a good deal of Hegel's private correspondence and it sounds pretty similar to what he said in public, proving that it is not just religious believers who try to deny the undeniable.

Hegel's earlier work is commonly called his theological writings, and understandably so for in them is his *Life of Jesus* and a number of works discussing the nature of Christianity. Those who want a secular Hegel will also tell you that these early theological writings are really not what they seem, that they are really opposing religion and faith. But more of that later.

Why would taking Hegel at his word and seeing him in terms of a philosophical theologian upset the religious conservatives as well? Surely it would greatly please them to know that the most influential intellectual in the modern world was a committed Christian? Should they not be celebrating this fact? The most famous theologian of the twentieth century, Karl Barth, once asked in astonishment (probably with his tongue firmly in his cheek): "Why did Hegel not become for the Protestant world something similar to what Thomas Aquinas was for Roman Catholicism?"[9]

But no, the conservative would be just as unhappy with seeing Hegel as a Christian theologian as the Marxist would. This I believe is because Hegel represents a Christian tradition that has largely disappeared, or if it is still there it is rarely noticed. If you look at Hegel's ideas from the perspective of the Christian tradition that now largely dominates the church, Hegel's form of Christianity would hardly be recognized, and he would definitely not be considered a Christian thinker. As we will see, this is a very strange state of affairs because Hegel believed in all the things that Christians are

7. Hegel, *Lectures on the Philosophy of Religion*, 1:84.

8. Hegel, *Hegel's Logic*, 263.

9. Barth, *Protestant Theology*, 384.

meant to believe and that the rest of the world think are unbelievable. For example, he believed in the Holy Trinity (three divine persons in one divine substance), the incarnation (God becoming human), divine providence, etc. Some of the students I have trained for the priesthood probably believe less Christian doctrine than Hegel did, but for some reason many, as we will see, have doubts about his genuine faith.

So, the approach I am going to adopt will take Hegel at his word as a religious thinker and will upset I am sure all and sundry. One unusual conclusion we can therefore draw from all this is that the most influential thinker in the modern world was a Christian theologian. I am not alone in this conclusion, as the most exhaustive study of Hegel's intellectual development to date concludes that "we should remember that although Hegel is known primarily as a philosopher, he was basically a theologian manqué."[10]

The one thing that makes Hegel's thought pretty well unique, and something we will examine later, is the fact that not only did his philosophy indirectly spawn the most antireligious regimes of the twentieth century, but it is also largely responsible for a renaissance in Christian doctrine over the last fifty years. How can this one author be such a constructive influence in modern theology and also the root of Marxism, Leninism, and Maoism?

## The Genius Trinity

Can you recognize genius when it is young and undeveloped? If so, I would imagine you might be somewhat overwhelmed when entering Hegel's college room at Tübingen. On one side of the room there would be Hegel lying on his bed reading the works of Lessing, an author he loved, on the next bed deep in thought a student who would become one of Germany's most famous lyric poets, Friedrich Hölderlin. Pacing the room, younger than the others, would be a boy wonder, Schelling, who by his early twenties would be a well-recognized, published philosopher and then soon after the professor at a leading university. What one would give to be a fly on the wall in that intellectual cauldron!

What drew them together at the time and what would have been frequently discussed in their shared accommodation was their adolescent enthusiasm for what was happening across the Rhine. For in the revolution sweeping France in the 1790s they saw the beginnings of a new world order. They sang the Marseillaise, read newspapers which they managed to get from France, and started a club to discuss revolutionary ideas. Little did

10. Dickey, *Hegel: Religion*, 6.

they know that their own philosophies would one day be as revolutionary as those they were hearing from Paris.

But what were all these promising intellectuals studying? You might expect philosophy or literature or science, but this room they shared was in a church seminary for training Protestant ministers, so the main focus of their studies was undoubtedly theology. It is worth noticing that this is the only higher education that Hegel ever received.

We know a good deal about the theology the three friends studied at Tübingen because there was a well-known controversy that was dividing the faculty. The issue was how theology could cope with the philosophical challenges of the day. The philosopher who had just upset everything was Kant (who we looked at in the previous chapter). One of Hegel's teachers was convinced, much to the students' surprise, that Kant's thought would allow belief in the most conservative Christian orthodoxy. Another of Hegel's tutors took the opposite approach, arguing that Kant's philosophy radically challenged traditional beliefs. The over-enthusiastic Schelling embraced the radical interpretation of Kant, but Hegel was not so sure. This is a characteristic of Hegel with which we will become familiar. Yes, he shared with Schelling the rejection of unquestioning orthodoxy that he observed in the conservative lecturer, but he would not be radicalized. He was, as we will see, always keen to find some middle way, some synthesis of the two.

Hegel's nickname when he was at school had been "the old man." He was never one for pulling up every intellectual root and starting from scratch. He had a great love for the past, particularly classical culture. Schelling would remind Hegel later in life that when they were roommates at college, Hegel was not that interested in discussing the philosophy of the day but looked to the past. It was his other roommate, Holderlin, and he who were part of the radical student group studying Kant's new ideas.

There is no doubt, as others have observed, that Schelling was the hare. After a flurry of books Schelling would burn out, and Hegel the tortoise would eclipse him after Schelling's youthful star had fallen.

Hegel did not get ordained after his time at seminary, but the question of the nature and role of religion in society remained a central concern of his. When first leaving Tübingen Hegel's ambition was to become a man of letters who would educate society and reform the church, much like the Enlightenment thinkers he admired. Hegel was inspired by the fact that Lessing, Rousseau, and Voltaire had not had university posts (universities being places associated with old learning) but had still successfully fought injustice and oppression with a sharpened quill. So initially he was not interested in a university post.

It is often suggested that Hegel's development into the philosopher he eventually became was a direct consequence of the intervention of his two old roommates from his Tübingen days. In 1796, when he moved to Frankfurt to be with Holderlin the direction of Hegel's interests begin to change. Before that time, when writing on religion, Hegel's concerns had largely mirrored that of the Enlightenment. But with Holderlin, who was involved in the first stirrings of German Romanticism, Hegel became sympathetic to Romantic interests. He began to present faith as something mystical and beyond rational comprehension.

Hegel's next move was to Jena in 1801, where he was close to Schelling, who was by then a published and well-recognized philosopher. It was while engaging with Schelling's work that Hegel decided to write philosophy himself, his seminal work being *The Phenomenology of Spirit* and the basis for his mature philosophy. But before he got the academic job he was hoping for in philosophy, he held a variety of different posts, even for a time being a newspaper editor and a headmaster. His academic dreams eventually materialized when he became chair of philosophy at the newly established University of Berlin.

In moving to Berlin, Hegel knew there would probably be conflict to contend with, as well as fulfilment to enjoy. For at the center of Berlin's salon society was Friedrich Schleiermacher who in time put all nineteenth-century Germany in his theological shadow, and also became Hegel's nemesis. Hegel was well aware that their approach to religion (and most else come to that) was poles apart. So, when he reached Berlin, he feared the worst and his fears were not unfounded. But more of their rivalry later.

## Two Metaphors

We are going to explore Hegel's mature philosophy with the help of two metaphors, the first taken from human culture and the second from the natural world. We will push each metaphor as far as it can go in order to illustrate the shape of Hegel's philosophy. They will give us something of an overview of what Hegel wanted to achieve and how ambitious he was before looking at his philosophy in more detail. The metaphors will also help us in a cursory examination of strengths and weaknesses.

## Developing the Overture

What would Bach have made of Beethoven? If all you had known was Baroque music, listening to the music of a mature Beethoven might at the very least have been somewhat disorienting. Where is the familiar regularity and symmetrical structure that we talked about at the beginning of the chapter? Everything seems in flux all familiar things have gone. This composition is revelling in the dark and disordered and then soaring to new heights of the sublime. At first the Baroque composer is unlikely to know what to make of it.

Encountering nineteenth-century thought can be equally baffling if you are used to the order of the eighteenth. The philosophy we will encounter is not trying to find the underlying structure in things or the regularity of nature. All that has gone. For when reading the masters of nineteenth-century thought—like Hegel, Schopenhauer, or Marx—there is no interest in stable forms or everlasting structures. The turbulence of history and fluid cultural change is at the center of their thought.

Having written the first draft of this chapter and extensively developing the musical analogy it was interesting to come across this, in a fascinating study of the relevance of Hegel's philosophy for contemporary theology by the theologian Nicholas Adams:

> Reading Hegel is more like listening to Beethoven. There is a wildness, a genuine and self-conscious history. . . . For one's foremost question to be, "what is Hegel's conclusion?" is as crass as to press fast forward on the remote during a Beethoven symphony. The length, and the manner of composition, are not ephemera. They are central to the kind of thing they are, and need to be attended to. . . . Hegel's works are long for the same reason that Beethoven's are: there is just a lot of development in them.[11]

## A Little Plato Detour

This initial shock is not surprising, as the desire for structure, regularity, and order runs deep in the Western mind. It is there in religion, philosophy, morality, and much else. It seems natural to want to find something that is lasting and dependable, for surely finding what is changeless is what religion should be all about? The one who is the same yesterday, today, and forever. Surely finding God is finding the solid rock on which we stand in all the changing scenes of life, the foundation on which to build. The changing and developing world is the problem, the threat to our stability.

11. Adams, *Eclipse*, 14.

This is not only a religious inclination but also an ethical or moral one, searching for universal norms and principles that do not alter from one culture to the next. If we cannot unearth these universals we can feel at sea, disoriented.

It is therefore no surprise that Plato, the most influential philosopher in the West, was interested in timeless truth. For Plato the things of this world were insubstantial, fleeting shadows that had no permanence and could not be depended on. However, he believed it was possible to mentally rise above the material world we inhabit and get a glimpse of its blueprint, a universal and heavenly blueprint that dictates the nature and structure of all we experience.

To illustrate the contrast between what we perceive in this world and its eternal blueprint Plato talked about the difference between drawing something like a triangle and the geometric equation it is modelled on. Our drawings are just an illustration or approximation of the geometrical equation that is the essence of a triangle. Our drawings can change, be deleted, fade away, but that does not alter the equation our triangle represents, that does not change over time. It cannot be deleted or destroyed as it is the eternal blueprint, the everlasting equation. So, for Plato this was the nature of the world's eternal pattern and form that people could glimpse with their mind's eye. Those who were wise were engaged in the contemplation of these transcendent forms and ideals. No wonder that for much of Western history it has been difficult to distinguish religion from philosophy.

It takes time to fully realize the impact of Hegel and his contemporaries in leaving this classical outlook behind and basing their philosophy on historical development rather than the changeless nature of things. Therefore, like someone only familiar with baroque music hearing the music of Romanticism for the first time, it is all a little disorienting.

Some writers have gone so far as to suggest that Hegel was the first philosopher in the West to take history and the historical nature of all our experience seriously. Before his time thought and reasoning sought to find a viewpoint above history or some solid ground under it.

Because of this, Hegel is considered the first advocate of what is called historicism, the belief that all human institutions, ideas, and activities can be understood, explained, and accounted for historically. In an article on Hegel and historicism Frederick C. Beiser, who spent his academic career studying German philosophy in the nineteenth century, explains. "Some scholars have even seen historicism as Hegel's central contribution to philosophy. Supposedly, it was Hegel who first historicized reason and who introduced the idea of development into philosophy itself."[12] As the philosopher Stephen Houlgate explains,

> for philosophers such as Marx, Heidegger and Gadamer, Hegel's most important contribution to modern thought is to have demonstrated that human life is irreducibly historical. After Hegel, so these thinkers argue, we must not only be acutely aware of our own historical position when examining a given phenomena, but any understanding of such a phenomenon—of society, philosophy or art—must always conceive of it as itself developing historically.[13]

Thus, Hegel's philosophy is in stark contrast to the dominant philosophical tradition in the West that followed Plato's lead. "In making this point, Hegel was taking issue with the Platonic tradition of philosophy, which had been responsible for so much of the a-historicism . . . of philosophy. According to the Platonic tradition, the object of thought is an eternal form, and the reflection upon it is an eternal contemplation a . . . timeless perception."[14] So "Hegel's historicism amounted to nothing less than a revolution in the history of philosophy."[15] In fact, Hegel was not the first philosopher to focus on history. It's just that for Hegel history becomes central to his approach. "With Hegel, historicism becomes the self-conscious and general method of philosophy, the weapon to be wielded against its own pretensions and illusions."[16]

## Not the Whole Story

Romantic music may seem rather chaotic to the baroque mind, it may seem to have little order or structure. This could not be further from the truth. Such music is normally a masterpiece of intricate development. It has a different structure than seventeenth-century music, but it has a clear end in sight; there is a linear structure, a storyline. The different themes will eventually be brought together and there is normally a grand finale and resolution at the end. What initially seemed disorienting and even disturbing all eventually place in the larger whole.

12. Beiser, *Hegel*, 261.
13. Houlgate, *Hegel Reader*, 2.
14. Beiser, *Hegel's Historicism*, 272.
15. Beiser, *Hegel's Historicism*, 270.
16. Beiser, *Hegel's Historicism*, 272.

Although not all historicism was that optimistic, Hegel clearly believed that history had an overall purpose, a greater meaning. You might not be able to see its structure in the middle, but it would eventually reach a satisfying conclusion.

The parallels at this point are important. You don't find your happy ending by leaving the music, there is no peace to be found outside it, no nonmusical truth to be found beyond the complex score. It is only at the end, after all has been played out, that you can get a sense of what it was all about.

## Spirit of the Music

The composer does not get up from the audience and walk up on the stage and intervene in order the bring things to a harmonious end. Rather, the development to the ultimate conclusion is intrinsic to the music; the ending naturally follows from within the music. Its harmonious end is in the logic of the composition; it is naturally evolving in that way, there is an inner rationality to it all, and it has been set up to reach that conclusion.

Hegel therefore does not believe in a composer who is wholly detached from the performance, who could interrupt it or bring it to an end. Hegel believes in the spirit of the music (which is probably also the name of some pretentious prog rock classic), that the spirit is more than the sum of the musical parts, the notes on the page or the sound waves in the air. However, being the spirit of the music, it cannot be separate from the music itself, it does not properly exist apart from it. The spirit of the music is revealed in the music and finds its fulfilment there. It gives the music its shape, its direction, its rationale, it is the music's logos.

One of the most frequent words used by Hegel and certainly one of the most debated, is the German term *geist*, which is normally translated as "spirit" or "mind." On hearing this term "spirit," Hegel is aware that we may interpret it as an ethereal, ghostly, or incorporeal substance, transcending all that is physical, but this is not Hegel's intention. What Hegel has in mind is more like an animating principle or dynamic process, in the way you might be true to the spirit of the law rather than the letter of it, or again just woodenly reproducing notes from a score and not entering into the spirit of the music. As Hegel explains

> [*Geist*] is not an inert being but, on the contrary, absolutely restless being, pure activity, the negating . . . of every fixed category; . . . not an essence that is already finished and complete before its manifestation, keeping itself aloof behind its host of

> appearances, but an essence which is truly actual only through the specific forms of its necessary self-manifestation; and it is not . . . a soul-thing only externally connected with the body, but is inwardly bound to the latter.[17]

Hegel also makes this point in his *Lectures on the Philosophy of World History:*

> When the spirit strives . . ., it strives to perfect its own freedom; and this striving is fundamental to its nature. To say that spirit exists would at first seem to imply that it is a completed entity. On the contrary, it is by nature active, and activity is its essence; it is its own product and is therefore its own beginning and its own end. Its freedom does not consist in static being, but in a constant negation of all that threatens to destroy freedom.[18]

Of course, Hegel would be very aware that the Christian God is described and defined as Spirit in the New Testament Scriptures. "God is spirit, and those who worship him must worship in spirit and truth."[19]

Hegel also understood by this term a means of drawing human action and divine action into relationship. As theologian Nick Adams explains, "in Christian theology, talk of the Spirit is a way of talking of the relation and the bond between divine and human action. . . . 'Spirit' may not be substitutable for 'Holy Spirit' . . . in any direct way but it may well be a way of drawing attention to the way in which human action participates in something other than itself . . . that divine and human action are bound up with each other."[20] As Hegel states "It was Christianity, by its doctrine of the Incarnation and of the presence of the Holy Spirit in the community of believers, that first gave to human consciousness . . . comprehensive knowledge of 'Geist' in its absolute infinitude."[21]

## Modern Providence

Anyone who has studied theology often sees at this point in Hegel's work the development of another familiar theme. We clearly have here a particular take on divine providence. Traditional views of divine providence are normally seen in terms of God's governance of events leading to his preordained

17. Hegel, *Encyclopaedia*, 285.
18. Hegel, *Lectures on the Philosophy of World History*, 48.
19. John 4:24 (KJV).
20. Adams, *Eclipse*, 46.
21. Hegel, *Encyclopaedia*, 285.

conclusion. In the apostle Paul's words, "all things work together for good."[22] Hegel would be very happy with that and these words might easily sum up his philosophy at this point. The only difference is that Hegel has a rather immanent (and one might say rational) take on divine providence.

For Hegel it is an evolutionary providence working itself out in human progress and on the basis of rationality. So, when he talks about what it is that is working all things out together for good, he calls it the "cunning of reason." His is a doctrine of providence for an age of reason. Yet human progress is more than just a human endeavor, it is also the advance and development of spirit what Hegel can call "spiritual reason":

> I have made my position clear on this issue from the beginning, . . . that reason rules the world, and consequently its History, and continues to do so. . . . This universal reason exists as an immanent principle within history in which and through which it fulfils itself. . . . But in the actual process of world history seen as something as yet incomplete, we find, that the subjective element or consciousness is yet in a position to know the true nature of the ultimate end of history the concept of the Spirit.[23]

For many this does not sound much like traditional Christian theology. It sounds far too humanistic, rationalistic, or one might say optimistic. Where have all the "pessimistic" doctrines normally associated with Christian theology gone? What has happened to humanity's original sin and total depravity? Is not the world supposed to be a dark, evil, and wretched place that sinners need saving from? In the Christian view, surely, the only thing history is moving towards is God's judgment, a final judgment and then hell and damnation, unless you are divinely chosen and your soul has been mercifully saved, in which case at the last you will be taken to a better place. From this perspective it seems totally implausible to see Hegel as fundamentally a theologian, he seems more likely to be fundamentally a heretic.

In objecting to that conclusion, in the most thorough study of Hegel's theological background and development, Laurence Dickey spends almost five hundred pages arguing that this negative theological assessment of Hegel's thought is completely mistaken. Dickey's point is that this argument compares Hegel with the wrong Christian tradition. If you compare Hegel with a particular form of Augustinianism that developed in the West, which the description above was caricaturing, then no wonder Hegel looks like a complete heretic, but that is not the only tradition there is, and it is not the one that Hegel was part of, had been nurtured in, or wanted to develop.

22. Rom 8:28 (ESV).

23. Hegel, *Lectures on the Philosophy of World History*, 74.

## Miles Davis

Here is a trivial example of this logic, yet again in terms of musical styles. I worked for some time with a woman who on most weekends went to hear jazz. I was very keen to play her the jazz loved. When she heard it (I think it was something inspired by Miles Davis) she repeatedly assured me I was mistaken. What I listened to was not jazz and she definitely did not like it, and she would rather I did not play it all the time. But she was comparing what I listened to a very different tradition, she had only ever heard trad jazz, the kind associated with New Orleans. No wonder she said that Miles Davis was not playing jazz. But if you were to compare Davis to a different jazz tradition the result would be very different. If you compared him, say, to American hard bop, jazz that is associated with New York, then Davis would be positively acknowledged for introducing an inspired take on that tradition. That is exactly Laurence Dickey's point, scholars who don't see Hegel as a Christian thinker or theologian are comparing him with the wrong tradition, so understandably he does not fare that well.

If you were able to speak to Hegel about this, he would insist on going back before Augustine and his ubiquitous influence on the West to an earlier Christian tradition, to the Alexandrian fathers of the church in the East. This tradition, he would argue, has a far more optimistic view of humanity, of human rationality and human history than Augustine. Dickey calls this tradition one that is centred on "evolutionary eschatology."[24] (Eschatology being the theology of death and the final judgment . . . never mind if you don't understand eschatology, it's not the end of the world!) One way in which Augustine influenced eschatology is in terms of the world going downhill and people needing saving from it. This Eastern tradition is about history travelling *uphill* until the kingdom of God has been established. This evolutionary eschatology can be seen in the great historian of the early church, Eusebius of Caesarea, a view that was then explicitly rejected by Augustine of Hippo. This optimistic eschatology came back in to favor in the twelfth century with Joachim of Fiore. If it were Joachim's Christian eschatology that was compared with Hegel's thought, not Augustine's, then Hegel is not that heterodox.

> This claim about the coming of a new age in history, then, involved a "new kind of exegesis," and at the heart of that exegesis was an evolutionary eschatology. . . . Specifically, Joachim offered an exegesis of Scripture that held that mankind's spiritual evolution was not meant—as Augustine had claimed—to cease

24. Dickey, *Hegel: Religion, Economics, and the Politics of Spirit*, 45.

> with the Incarnation, with the foundation of the Apostolic church, or with the subsequent development of the sacraments. Furthermore, Joachim made it clear that this evolutionary process had not been meant to cease with the end of Christ's life.[25]

If Paul's words "all things work together for good" sum up Hegel's view of providence, then the prayer that Jesus instructed his followers to repeat captures something of Hegel's eschatology. For Jesus told them to pray "may God's kingdom come, may God's will be done on Earth as it is in heaven."[26] For Hegel this suggests that faith is not about going to heaven, it is about heaven coming to earth.

To Hegel, this included political engagement and what he would call a civil or social piety.

> The modern association of Protestantism, Lutheranism, and Pietism with "inwardness," "individualism," and "subjectivism," on the one hand, and with submission to outer political authority on the other, overlooks the fact that there was a strong, anti-authoritarian, civil impulse within the Lutheran religious tradition itself [the tradition Hegel belong to]. The failure to appreciate the impulse toward "Protestant civil piety" in the culture . . . lies behind much of the confusion over the religious and political aspects of Hegel's thought. . . .
>
> Religious reform entailed engaging the world, not retreating from it. . . .
>
> That was a reformist conception of the world that Hegel ascribed to for most of his life.[27]

All of this was set in the context of an evolutionary eschatology. "That, of course, was because evolutionary eschatology offered its proponents no opportunity for other-worldly escapism. For the other world was the future of this world, and it was their responsibility to cooperate with God in making the future actual in the present. The tension itself, however, was nicely balanced in that despair about the present was motivation to anticipate and prepare for the promise of the future."[28]

So, was Hegel just the Miles Davis of a particular Christian tradition we are no longer familiar with? Hopefully by the end of this chapter you will be able to make up your own mind.

25. Dickey, *Hegel: Religion*, 53.

26. See Matt 6:10.

27. Dickey, *Hegel: Religion*, 9, 11, 12.

28. Dickey, *Hegel: Religion*, 44.

## The Dark Side

To return to our ever-expanding metaphor, you might say this is all very inspiring, Hegel, but all I ever get to play in this evolving masterwork of history are the parts in a minor key, which can be pretty bleak. I never get to play the triumphant and joyful melodies. In fact, you might say that much of history does not look anything like a great musical work of art leading to a happy resolution. Much of history seems more random than the wildest composition, much more pointless and for most people life is nasty, brutish and short. But Hegel will not back down, he still believes that the "cunning of reason" will bring all things around eventually. You may, like Ivan Fyodorovich in Dostoevsky's *The Brothers Karamazov*, want to return your violin and bow and not be part of this symphony anymore, but Hegel insists that you stay to the very end and see how it all works out.

At this point many have found Hegel's philosophy a little cold-hearted, to say the least. Few people with any sense of history have been convinced by Hegel's cosmic optimism, but you don't even have to have a historical perspective to have trouble with providence. A colleague of mine recently went to a funeral of a man, a father, who had committed suicide. The text with the famous words "all things work together for good" was read at the service. My colleague said that she could not have read those words in front of that grieving family.

# 20

# ORGANIC SPIRIT

## The Second Metaphor: Organic Life

I HAVE NO IDEA whether in his many publications Hegel ever explored the metaphor of musical composition but, as we have noted, other people apart from me have made the connection."Perhaps it is not too fanciful to suggest that Hegel became the Beethoven of philosophy, and Beethoven the Hegel of music; for they both sought pattern, harmony, and redemption in and through a world of conflict, disharmony and suffering."[1]

There is another metaphor that Hegel definitely approved of, and that is the metaphor of organic growth. In the introduction to his most famous book *The Phenomenology of Spirit* Hegel explores four or five metaphors and most of them are organic. One of these metaphors captures the developmental nature of Hegel's thought in a nutshell (to use another organic metaphor) and it is worth reading in full. We should see

> philosophical systems as the progressive evolution of truth . . . rather [than see] . . . contradiction in the variety. The bud disappears when the blossom breaks though, and we might say that the former is refuted by the latter; in the same way when the fruit comes, the blossom may be explained to be a false form of the plant's existence, for the fruit appears as its true nature in place of the blossom. . . . But this ceaseless activity of their own inherent nature makes them at the same time a moment of organic unity, where they do not merely contradict one another, but where one is as necessary as the other; and this equal necessity of all moments constitutes alone and thereby the life of the whole.[2]

1. Hodgson, *Hegel and Christian Theology*, 3.
2. Hegel, *Phenomenology*, 4.

This metaphor of organic growth also appears repeatedly in Hegel's history of philosophy.

When giving an example of the all-important "dialectical" way (modelled on human dialogue) in which he believed philosophical thought progresses, Hegel gives the example of the growth of a tree, where very different phenomena (in philosophy seemingly opposing ideas, or in a tree or plant different forms of growth) are incorporated into its overall development, where what first appears seems to be refuted by what then develops (by losing the tree's flowers or blossoms so the fruit might develop) but is in fact essential to its overall growth.

> Refutation of this kind occurs in every development e.g. the growth of a tree from its seed. The flower is a refutation of the leaves. It seems to be the highest and true existence of the tree. But the flower is refuted by the fruit. The fruit which comes last contains everything which preceded, all the forces developed earlier. It cannot become actual without the prior emergence of all the earlier stages. . . . In the Spirit this succession occurs too. . . . The latest, and most modern, philosophy must therefore contain in itself the principles of all the previous philosophies and consequently it is the highest one.[3]

What is particularly significant is that when working through Hegel's first major philosophical work, *The Phenomenology of Spirit*, I could find no mechanistic metaphors, even though, as we have seen, that was an image and model that had dominated the eighteenth century. There is much from the eighteenth-century Enlightenment that Hegel admired, but like Kant before him, Hegel saw the scientific revolution and its mechanistic model of explanation as not only a step towards human progress but also a challenge to it.

## The Clock at Strasburg

The analogy most frequently employed by eighteenth-century philosophy and science was taken from human artefacts and human invention. The most impressive human creations at the time were the great clocks and intricate watches seen as the modern marvels of their day. So, a metaphor in terms of intricate mechanics was ready to hand and often used for the workings of the world. For example, in John Locke's *Essay Concerning Human Understanding* Locke famously uses the example of the great clock at

3. Houlgate, *Hegel Reader*, B.2.41.

Strasburg and its "springs and wheels and other contrivances within" as an analogy for the intricate workings of nature.[4] David Hume is also happy to use this analogy.

> Look round the world: Contemplate the whole and every part of it: You will find it to be nothing but one great machine, subdivided into an infinite number of lesser machines, which again admit of subdivisions to a degree beyond what human senses and faculties can trace and explain. All these various machines, and even their most minute parts, are adjusted to each other with an accuracy which ravishes into admiration all men who have ever contemplated them.[5]

But if the world is analogous to clockwork where do we fit in, are we just part of the one great machine? The most impressive clocks of the time were often found on town halls across Europe. For the onlooker's amusement they would incorporate miniature human figures that would appear on the hour and were sometimes made to look as if they were striking the chimes. If the mechanistic metaphor is pressed, are we not reduced to this, nothing more than novel automata, particularly clever parts of the machine? Ironically, this was also an age of human emancipation, rights, self-expression and individualism, and the beginning of democracy, yet the new science that was also seen as a principle of human achievement had incarcerated people in a prison of cogs and pulleys.

But was this not as soul-destroying as any tyranny of the past. Rather than the tyranny of the divine despot on earth or in the heavens they were now subject to the iron laws of cause and effect and had no more liberty than the cogs of the machine. If this were true, what sense could be made of our human cultural values; in Plato's words, the true, the good, and the beautiful? What sense could be made of moral responsibility, aesthetics, love, spirituality—could they survive such an inhuman environment as this universal mechanism?

I wonder why we laugh so much when Basil Fawlty gives his little car a thrashing.[6] It's surely because he has made a major category error, for you cannot expect a machine to be morally responsible. After the scientific revolution punishing any one of us automata would be just as ridiculous.

4. Locke, *Essay Concerning Human Understanding*, 3.5.14.

5. Hume, *Dialogues*, 15.

6 In the classic BBC comedy series *Fawlty Towers* (1975–79).

## Change Metaphor

We have looked at Kant's most radical of responses to this dilemma. One popular suggestion among Hegel's Romantic contemporaries to the same dilemma was to change metaphors. Rather than seeing the world as nothing more than a system of cogs, pulleys, levers, and weights, a better analogy might be taken from organic life. Hegel was no exception. "One of the first impressions Hegel's writing make on any reader is their ubiquitous organic metaphors. This is indeed one of the most important clues for a proper understanding of Hegel's entire philosophy. For all Hegel's thinking essentially proceeds from an organic vision of the world. A view of the universe as a single vast living organism."[7]

Frederick C. Beiser, in his study of Hegel's philosophy, suggests then that the analogy we should be investigating to understand Hegel's mature philosophy is an organic one. We will be pushing this a little further than Beiser does.

There are of course a number of key differences between the mechanistic metaphor and the organic. Firstly, a machine will always remain the same unless it is changed by some external intervention. In contrast, organisms like plants and animals have a life of their own; they can grow and develop without the need for external intervention.

Added to that, the explanation for that development is not just the simple logic of cause and effect that is basic to a mechanism. An organism's development can be described as holistic, in the sense that the whole organism often has an effect on the development of its parts. It is not just the parts affecting the whole as with mechanisms.

One of the crucial things about an organic conception of life is that it is non-reductive though still quite naturalistic. It does not reduce everything down to its constituent parts by saying it is nothing but molecules and atoms, the whole is just as significant as the parts. But it is still naturalistic, it is doing all this itself without recourse to any supernatural agent. It also probably goes without saying but for some reason being a shiny emerald leaf on the great tree of life is a little more bearable than being a lifeless cog in a dark industrial mill.

## Reconciling Opposites

Another major theme in seeking to understand Hegel's mature thought is the reconciliation of opposites. He is always wanting to resolve tensions and

7. Beiser, *Hegel*, 80.

reconcile what is seemingly contradictory. Given the chance, he would love to convince you that, seen in the right light, black is really white. He sees that one of the greatest problems in the cultural aftermath of the Enlightenment is that it is riven with damaging oppositions and dualisms that were not there before. The individual against society, science against faith, matter against spirit, body against soul, reason against theology, philosophy against culture, even God against the world. Hegel modestly "claimed that his system provides the only viable middle path between every . . . antithesis."[8] For Hegel, the organic analogy is the great example of seeing unity in diversity. For within an organism the parts have to be valued for the sake of the whole and are not independent of it. (I am sure someone in the first century said something about this [1 Cor 12:12–31].)

There is a tendency in works about Hegel to examine how his philosophical speculations develop (with for example the use of organic metaphors) and then conclude that in order to be seen as culturally acceptable to his Christian audience Hegel tries his utmost to persuade them that his new philosophy can become happily married to Christian theology. Or, in the eyes of his critics, Hegel shoehorns a Christian theology into his philosophy with disastrous effect. But any idea that philosophical and theological concerns have been kept wholly apart in Hegel's work, then to be clumsily reunited, does not work as an interpretation of any text by Hegel I am familiar with. As theologian Nick Adams writes in his analysis of Hegel's theological logic, "The problem is that there is no easy division between the 'philosophical' and 'theological' in Hegel: it is all philosophical, and it is all concerned with God in various ways. There is no 'religious dimension' in Hegel, . . . the work is saturated and permeated with religious concerns."[9]

To illustrate the distinctive nature of Hegel's philosophy, we could have as easily used theological themes and ideas, as the organic or musical ones we have employed. So Hegel could use organic metaphors to explain how there could still be clear distinctions made within what was ultimately united and working together. For example, in the parts of a body or the development of a plant, basic ideas that structure so much of his thought. But according to the theologian Nicholas Adams, Hegel would have happily made a similar point using theological motifs. In Christian doctrines such as the Trinity, we see unity and diversity, persons that can be seen as distinct but together; in the terminology of the creed, three persons in one substance. To put too much emphasis on the three at the expense of the one or to reduce the distinctiveness of the three to the one, became seen as heretical. Both diversity

8. Beiser, *Hegel and the Problem of Metaphysics*, 1.

9. Adams, *Eclipse*, xviii.

and unity had to be equally affirmed. So as Adams explains, "Hegel derived logical forms from Christian doctrines, especially the doctrine of the Trinity. . . . [H]is work reflects on prior theological practices and draws attention to the rules that govern them, to the systems of classification in play, and to the categories in which they cast their descriptions of God and the world."[10]

## Two Natures in One Person

Adams not only sees this in Hegel's use of the doctrine of the Trinity, but also in the way the church defined the person of Christ at the fifth-century Council of Chalcedon. Here the incarnation is seen in terms of two natures in one person. That according to the council of Chalcedon and its creedal definition the human and divine natures are kept distinct yet united, without confusion but without separation.

> The key thing to notice, for our purposes, is that in Hegel's logic, as in the Charlestonian formula, we are dealing not with opposites that are separate, but with differences that are in relation. Hegel notices that modern philosophy very often deals with opposites that are separate, which then need to be brought back together again: individual and community, thinking and being, idea and thing, freedom and determinacy, mind and body, . . . theology and philosophy, reason and revelation, faith and reason, and so on. Hegel generally diagnoses these as false oppositions and attempts to find an alternative logic in which they are different rather than opposed in relation rather than separated. That means that the primary task is not to bring two separate things back together, but to refuse their primordial separation.[11]

So

> Hegel is guided by a "Chalcedonian" logic. By this I mean that his tendency is to describe certain terms as distinct but in relation, rather than as utterly opposed to each other (or as identical to each other). Hegel is a modern philosopher, and he is greatly interested in forms of thought, which he inherits, in which terms are falsely or one-sidedly opposed to each other. . . . Hegel thinks in a recognizably orthodox way, in one sense, not because he holds one doctrinal view rather than another, but because he is often repairing errant logics which produce false oppositions.[12]

10. Adams, *Eclipse*, 11.
11. Adams, *Eclipse*, 11–12.
12. Adams, *Eclipse*, 20, 7.

To use a fairly straightforward example, but one that demonstrates distinction in unity.

> To speak of individuals is to speak of those who are related not only to other individuals, but to the community in which all are related. To speak of community is to speak neither of an aggregate of individuals, nor of a single entity that absorbs all individuality into itself, but of a unity in which distinctions between individuals are retained, but in a way such that to do justice to an individual requires doing justice to relations to other individuals and to the community.[13]

When exploring this aspect of Hegel's philosophy further, Adams refers to this as a logic of participation.

> The logic that guides this claim is emphatically Chalcedonian or Trinitarian: it preserves distinctions and at the same time expresses unity. For a logic of opposition . . . one must choose unity or distinctions. For a logic of participation (a Chalcedonian logic) . . . unity in inseparable relation. . . .
>
> Again this is not because Hegel has an idea about logical form, and then by happy accident alights on poetic language from Christian doctrine which can add some color to his account. On the contrary Hegel discerns in the Christian tradition a kind of logic which relates God and humanity in a certain way, and this logic can be put to work governing all sorts of relations . . . I have referred to this . . . as "Chalcedonian logic" or a "logic of participation."[14]

## Resolving Another Clash

Like many of his time Hegel turned his back on mechanistic metaphors that had dominated the eighteenth century and developed other ways of understanding the world. But, unlike his contemporaries, Hegel can be seen to take this to a new level. In the wake of the scientific revolution many people puzzled over the question of how we could make sense of our human agenda in a natural world that does not seemed to share it. How can we affirm our human values when they seem so absent from the world that the natural sciences have revealed? For, this picture could not be more different to our human agenda. We look for purpose, meaning, spirituality, morality

13. Adams, *Eclipse*, 31.
14. Adams, *Eclipse*, 62.

and freedom of self-expression, but the natural world as conceived by the eighteenth-century scientist sees none of these things in nature. It reveals a cold, merciless, deterministic cosmos, without meaning or purpose. As scientist Richard Dawkins put it,

> In a universe of electrons and selfish genes, blind physical forces and genetic replication, some people are going to get hurt, other people are going to get lucky, and you won't find any rhyme or reason in it, nor any justice. The universe that we observe has precisely the properties we should expect if there is, at bottom, no design, no purpose, no evil, no good, nothing but pitiless indifference.[15]

The first wave of German Romanticism, which Hegel was very familiar with, adopted a different idea. They wanted to argue that the natural sciences could not tell us the whole story; in fact, they suggested that there was more to the world than met the eye. They believed that at the very heart of things there was something far more in tune with our human concerns, that at the very core of all human knowing there was something that could give meaning and purpose, that could offer spiritual fulfilment. In other words, we do not strive alone for what we value and treasure, our voice is in harmony with something far greater, in the sense that our human spirit is part of a cosmic spirit and this greater spirit resonates with our striving for what is true, beautiful and good. As the philosopher, sociologist, and Hegel scholar Charles Taylor explains, "So for Hegel and his Romantic colleagues underlying natural reality is a spiritual principle striving to realize itself."[16]

Some years ago, when I was not well, I remember seeing a fascinating program on Van Gogh. As I heard about his story, I realized that I was possibly suffering from a mild version of what he had gone through (thankfully for me alleviated by a good deal of medication). But as the documentary talked about works, he probably painted when he was suffering the pictures made sense to me in a way they had not before. Even the most challenging and dark painting seemed to make some sense. This realization occurred because I could relate a little to the human experience behind the art. In the same way, Hegel and the first advocates of Romanticism experienced that engagement with what they believe was at natures heart. They believed that their spirit could make some connection with its spirit. In nature they were not dealing with something that was fundamentally alien, but with what also flowed through them. As Charles Taylor explains,

15. Dawkins, *River Out of Eden*, 133.

16. Taylor, *Hegel*, 39.

> If the highest spiritual side of man, his moral freedom, is to come to more than passing and accidental harmony with his natural being, then nature itself has to tend to the Spiritual. . . . Then the requirement of unity is that nature in this sense come to be seen as having a bent to realize spiritual goals. . . . If I am to remain a spiritual being and yet not be opposed to nature in my interchange with it, then this interchange must be a communion in which I enter into relation with some spiritual being or force.[17]

The connection between the individual and the cosmic is even greater than this for Hegel. It's not just the loose connection between them of both wanting to realize a similar goal. The primordial spirit is involved in human history. It is not only revealed in human history, it comes to fulfilment through that history. The spirit comes to its full realization in that process of development. We of course saw something of this when we talked about the composers or artists of Romanticism. The music is not something distinctly different to the artist, it is a work of self-expression and the art they create realizes their own potential. What had been subjective to them in the great idea they had for the composition has become objective in its production and performance. In this the artist will understandably talk about a feeling of self-discovery.

Hegel says that the same thing happens for the world spirit through creation and through human history. Moreover, what humanity achieves in its cultural development can be seen as milestones towards the Spirit's own fulfilment. So, as the history of human development moves towards a greater freedom and higher morality, this is a work of the spirit but also the spirit's own fulfilment.

This demonstrates why the organic metaphor can only be a metaphor, as most organisms in the natural world do not reach this kind of self-consciousness or become self-determining. As Allen Wood explains.

> Perhaps the best way to bring out the inadequacy of the living organism to serve as a model . . . is to contrast a living thing with a self-consciousness: . . . A plant or animal organism, once it has grown to maturity, has a single, stable organic structure. Its whole life consists in the struggle to impose this structure on its matter. . . . A self-conscious personality is therefore like an organism whose structure . . . is consciously self-imposed. Therefore, a self-consciousness is like an organism which can survive radical changes in its organic structure, and can even

17. Taylor, *Hegel*, 39.

> initiate these changes. . . . Thus a self-conscious being is like an organism whose final tendencies are not limited to the . . . self-maintenance of its structure, but include systematic tendencies to overthrow and transform its structure through consciousness. . . . As the personality strives to fulfil its goals, it learns more about itself and about what goals it should be striving for. Its conception of itself and of its goals therefore changes, sometimes passing through stages of crisis and deep spiritual conflict. Hegel sees this pattern of organic development as fundamental to all change which expresses the nature of spirit.
>
> The whole nature of a spiritual being (a human personality, a historical people, a philosophical vision) thus consists not in a single organic structure or idea, but in a definite series of such structures, the determinate stages of its inner organic development.[18]

So Allen Wood concludes, "Spirit in its true form is like a living organism which is wholly master of the material in which it is embodied and finds nothing recalcitrant to its life-principle."[19]

## The Two Metaphors

We have now explored our two introductory metaphors, seeing Hegel's philosophical vision in terms of a complex composition reaching a final resolution and in terms of his organic metaphor. We have also seen in the process how these two metaphors give expression to a philosophy more hospitable and affirmative to human dignity and value than the mechanical picture given to us by the scientific revolution. By using these two images, hopefully we are beginning to see the structure and shape of Hegel's thought.

## A Higher Synthesis

Hegel would never totally reject a previous philosophy that differs from his own. Rather, he tried to incorporate what had gone before into what he saw as a broader perspective. He did this with theology as much as he did with science and philosophy. His aspirations were nothing if not ambitious (and possibly pretentious to postmodern sensibilities), as what he clearly wanted to attain, was a synthesis between Enlightenment ideals and Christian

18. Wood, *Marx*, 204.
19. Wood, *Marx*, 202.

theology. In the process both were critiqued and somewhat transformed but Hegel believed that what was kept was true to the original.

A perfect example of this is Hegel's imaginative synthesis of the eighteenth-century ideal of human independence, self-expression, and fulfilment with traditional theological beliefs about God and the world. Two beliefs that understandably could be seen as opposed to one another.

In order to see the point clearly one needs to acknowledge the fact that most monotheistic religions tend to think of God as all powerful, all knowing and omnipresent. The problem is that if you perceive God as so great and so dominant there may seem to be little space left for anything else. So, the logic goes that the more the concept of God is inflated the less room there is for the life of anything other than God. This is particularly true of course for humanity.

But for Hegel, interestingly, there is not the competition for space and the crowding of each other out, because there is an interdependence between God and humanity. They are in fact fulfilling each other's agenda. They need each other to reach their own goal. It is a three-legged race: you cannot get to the finish line without the other. For Hegel the historical search for human freedom and human self-realization is the way in which the cosmic spirit's own potential is fulfilled. So, Hegel "finds fault with the idea that God and man are separate and distinct, in which God is infinitely superior and we are mere 'slaves.'"[20] "Thus, man does more than reflect a nature complete in itself, rather he is the vehicle whereby the cosmic spirit is bought to completion and self-expression."[21]

Hegel clearly wanted to pull off on a cosmic scale what we find it difficult enough to achieve between ourselves. It may be counterintuitive but bad managers are those who have worked everything out in advance, because there is no space for those taking part to participate in the planning or give anything of themselves to the execution. They don't feel as if what they have to bring to the project has been valued and their opinions have not been heard. When they face the manager with this complaint, she points out that if they were left to themselves, they might never get the work done properly, and of course she is right. It is difficult to achieve a goal and allow for creative freedom. The genius of a great supervisor is to manage this.

Hegel wants to manage this on a cosmic scale; he wants the spirit to reach its goal but to do so through human freedom. Hegel realizes that this goal can only be reached with humanity's involvement. "A conception of cosmic spirit of this kind . . . is the only one which can square the circle, as

20. Solomon, "Hegel's Phenomenology of Spirit," 186.

21. Taylor, *Hegel*, 44.

it were, that is, which can provide the basis of a union between finite and cosmic spirit which meets the requirement that man be united to the whole and yet not sacrifice his own self-consciousness and autonomous will."[22]

In doing this, Hegel, in one imaginative leap, has brought together the human emancipation of the Enlightenment and the fundamentals of religious belief.

The most advanced example of this interdependence for Hegel comes from the way in which spirit achieves self-awareness. According to Hegel, there is only one way it can find this, and that is through humanity. As human self-consciousness emerges throughout history, that is also the cosmic spit achieving self-awareness. The synergy could not be greater here, for Hegel argues that spirit cannot become self-conscious without us. As Hegel explains in his normal paradoxical prose, "Spirit is when finite selves become conscious of themselves as infinite; and then the infinite becomes self-conscious through finite selves."[23] As Charles Taylor explains, "On this view, the cosmic spirit which unfolds in nature is striving to complete itself in conscious self-knowledge. . . . But at the same time Geist is not reducible to man, he is not identical with the human spirit, since he is also the Spiritual reality underlying the universe."[24]

## Opposites Attract

What can appear particularly strange is the fact that Hegel will often talk of the spirit going out of itself to find itself. If this sounds reminiscent of some of Jesus' teaching ("For whoever wants to save his life will lose it, but whoever loses his life for my sake and for the gospel will save it" [Mark 8:35]) this is not a coincidence. It may reflect the fact that he first wrote about this when considering the teaching of Jesus and the place of love within the Christian faith in an essay entitled "The Spirit of Christianity and Its Fate."

At the start of many great love stories the situation hardly seems promising. The pair seem to have little time for each other and are sometimes even antagonistic, but amazingly by the end of the story they are together and discussing their preferred names for a boy or a girl. To see this happen is of course what is so entertaining. For this to properly work they have to start off as strong independent characters. When thinking about examples it is difficult not to think of *Pride and Prejudice* but any good rom-com will do (I am not sure it was the kind of thing Hegel read, academics miss

22. Taylor, *Hegel*, 44.
23. Beiser, *Hegel*, 116.
24. Taylor, *Hegel*, 44.

out on all the fun, but Hegel probably knew *Much Ado About Nothing* and he refers to Juliet's lines in Romeo and Juliet, "The more I give to the thee more I have"). In *Pride and Prejudice* Elizabeth Bennet has to be as strong a character as Darcy for the resolution to be so satisfying. In Hegel's terms, these very different subjects end up finding themselves in something quite other than themselves. All the time their independence is important, one never subsumes the other or dominates the other: that would not be love, it would be something far less fulfilling, profound, or paradoxical. In fact, the saying "opposites attract" sums up a great deal of Hegel's thought.

> Love is the paradoxical process whereby the self both loses itself (as an individual) and finds or gains itself (as a part of a wider whole). Love contains therefore the moments of self-surrender and also of self-discovery. There is a moment of self-surrender in love because in love the self also finds itself in and through the other; it sees that it is no longer something opposed to the other but the unity of itself with the other. . . .
>
> Hegel calls what both produces and results from love, the whole process of self-surrender and self-discover, of externalization and internalization, spirit (Geist). . . .Whatever the original context of Hegel's use of the term, its introduction would later prove decisive for his philosophy as a whole. When Hegel later writes of spirit it always had the structure of development that he once gave to the experience of love.[25]

## Divine Romance

Sorry to break up this romance, but the contemporary critic of Hegel's philosophy William Desmond perceptively points out that Hegel seem to be "under the bewitchment of . . . erotic sovereignty." Hegel seems to forget that when the apostle Paul writes in his hymn to love he does not have erotic love in mind but *agape* (as most couples who have 1 Corinthians 13 read in their wedding service seem not to have noticed). This is not primarily a love that finds its fulfilment in the other, you cannot say of *agape* as Juliet says to Romeo "the more I give to thee the more I have"; there is no circle of reaffirmation or self-realization with *agape*. In the New Testament, *agape* is given without the promise of getting anything back. We are told that God is love it is not erotic love but *agape*, but when Hegel uses the logic of love to talk about the divine, he seems to have *eros* in mind, not *agape*. Desmond concludes that "I am convinced that Hegel's God is an . . . Erotic absolute. . . .

25. Beiser, *Hegel*, 114–15.

He is under the bewitchment of . . . erotic sovereignty."[26] For the Christian preacher this is a schoolboy error that Hegel has fallen into, one that every student of the New Testament is aware of.

It is all very well Hegel's critics getting on their theological high horse about this and saying that Hegel's concept of love is not that of Christian love, but a love that finds its fulfilment in the other is hardly in opposition to Christian virtue.

26. Desmond, *Hegel's God*, 40, 41.

# 21

# REASON TO SPIRIT

It's about time we asked Hegel an obvious question. If reason has led so many Enlightenment philosophers in the eighteenth century to such a heartless materialistic atheism how did you get to your belief in a cosmic spirituality? In other words, Hegel, how can you justify all your speculations about the nature of this creative cosmic spirit when so many Enlightenment thinkers before you believed in nothing of the kind and would have ridiculed such metaphysical flights of fancy?

This is where Hegel gets really creative. He has to do some very imaginative thinking for at least two important reasons. Firstly, he is only too aware that the Enlightenment produced a lot of skepticism about anything beyond the material world. For example, thinkers who modelled their philosophy on the natural sciences were insisting that we can only believe what we can confirm with the experience of our senses (See Kant and Hume). We can only believe what we can examine in our test tubes. Clearly, on this criterion, religious beliefs are out of the question.

We still hear this argument repeatedly today. As the well-known atheist and chemist Peter Atkins states, "In short, I stand by my claim that the scientific method is the only means of discovering the nature of reality, and . . . will forever survive as the only way of acquiring reliable knowledge."[1] And even when it comes to considering religious belief Richard Dawkins confirms this view. "The presence or absence of a creative superintelligence is unequivocally a scientific question. . . . The methods we should use to settle the matter . . . would be purely and entirely scientific methods."[2]

1. Atkins, *On Being*, 109.

2. Dawkins, *God Delusion*, 58–59.

In these statements you can clearly hear an echo of David Hume's maxim we considered earlier. "If we take in our hand any volume; of divinity or school metaphysics, for instance; let us ask, does it contain any abstract reasoning concerning quantity or number? No. Does it contain any experimental reasoning concerning matter of fact and existence? No. Commit it then to the flames: for it can contain nothing but sophistry and illusion."[3]

Using this logic even Hegel's modest talk of cosmic spirit appears as groundless speculation. Yet in contrast to many philosophers and theologians of his day, Hegel is going to take up the challenge. He is going to defend his belief in cosmic spirit against the most radical skepticism. And what is more, at no point will he cheat and say, "Sorry folks at this point a leap of faith is required." He will get you to God by reason alone without the aid of faith, a very clever trick if he can pull it off. In fact, like the confident escapologist who put some extra chains around his straitjacket just to impress, Hegel starts where his hope of success appears least promising, with the most basic of human experience, our sensory awareness of the world.

## The Hegelian Rope Ladder

Hegel does this, I believe, by demonstrating that there are not just solid ladders that stand on the ground, there are also rope ladders that are lowered from above. Most arguments used by Enlightenment philosophers tended to be a form of foundationalism. The name says it all, as foundationalists argued that in order to establish any form of knowledge we need to start with a firm foundation that everyone accepts as indisputable and then build up from that. If we then accept this foundation as given, then it follows that we will accept what is built on it until we eventually reach the point that the argument is wanting to establish. This form of demonstration clearly resembles a ladder that sits on the ground and is supported from below.

Hegel would not object to the ladder illustration, but I think he would prefer us to think of a different kind of ladder. His thought more resembles a rope ladder (I am not suggesting that Hegel ever mentions rope ladders, but I do not think he would object too much to the metaphor). In contrast to normal ladders, rope ladders are used when there is no ground below to rest on. They are let down from the side of a boat or a cliff and are consequently held up by what is above them.

In *The Phenomenology of Spirit*, Hegel constructs a pretty impressive philosophical rope ladder. He starts with something we all experience and

3. Hume, *Enquiry Concerning Human Understanding*, 12.3.

then says if this experience is to have any stability and not to collapse under critical examination it will need something higher to support it.

Now in constructing this argument Hegel starts with the most basic experience we have: what Hegel calls sense certainty. This is the very thing that philosophers who were keen to emulate the natural sciences started with, and I am sure that is no coincidence. The empiricists, as they were known, always suggested that we needed to start with the very fundamentals of experience and be guided by that sense experience, in the way they believed the natural sciences always were. And these empiricists then argued, as the philosopher Robert Solomon explains, "that errors in human knowledge, when they arise, must arise after this level. For on this level, our knowledge is certain and becomes fallible only when we attempt to conceptualise or to understand our experiences."[4]

So this is where Hegel begins, at this most unpromising point as far as theology is concerned, with sense certainty. Remember, his plan is to get to metaphysical belief about a cosmic spirit from here. He is starting in enemy territory with sense experience, the very thing that has been used against metaphysical speculation, the very thing that has been used to cut religion down to size.

Hegel (following Kant) argues that this approach to knowledge based on sense certainty is often astonishingly naive. He suggests that a great deal of mental processing needs to be applied to any sense experience before we can recognize it as knowledge. This is as true for the natural sciences as it is for any other form of thought. If you were to look down a telescope and see something interesting and when asked what you saw, if you were to say "I witnessed an event," or if you were doing some interesting work in a lab and when asked what you had found you say "we experienced something," that would explain next to nothing. That experiencing or witnessing of an event is not of any interest unless you can name the experience and therefore give some meaning to the event.

It needs to be an experience of something, but when we start to describe it, we bring into play a host of ideas and concepts that were not given directly in the experience. In other words, the world does not come to us with labels attached saying "I am an atom," "I am a molecule"; all of that comes from our mental processing and conceptualizing of the experience. So, the first rung of the rope ladder sense experience is dependent on the second rung, our conceptual processing, in order to become knowledge of any kind at all.

4. Solomon, "Hegel's Phenomenology of Spirit," 196.

## The Naive Builder

When Hegel examines sense certainty, he begins to show how impoverished this kind of experience is. He argues that to express what is experienced in sense certainty we need access to a number of categories that are not supplied by the senses.

It's like asking a builder what he might use to build a house and for him to answer that all he will need is a good local clay, that is all he needs! But will he not also need something to shape the clay into bricks, and then something in which to bake them solid, then of course some cement to stick them together. Hegel is arguing that to construct anything from sense experience you also need a lot more than experience can ever give you. You need some basic ideas to describe and name the experience to give it some meaningful identity; you then need a conceptual framework in which to understand and to connect it with other things. In fact, the reason why sense experience can seem so certain and indisputable is that in its raw and preconceptual form it may not be saying much at all.

As Robert Solomon explains,

> At the beginning is the common-sense notion which Hegel calls "sense-certainty," that we simply know, prior to any verbal description or conceptual understanding. Hegel points out that . . . such a conception of knowledge is woefully inadequate. . . .
>
> This is the pure data of the senses which so many philosophers, of this century as well as the past, have taken to be the indubitable, secure foundation of human knowledge. . . . Thus, Hegel concludes that there can be no knowledge without concepts, and the supposed certainty of sense certainty seems certain only because it is not knowledge at all. It is, at best, mere presence. The infallibility of sense-certainty, of pure experience, lies in its failure to assert any claim to knowledge which might be shown to be wrong. This knowledge which "is called the unutterable, is nothing else than the untrue, the irrational."[5]

## Straight from Kant

Hegel develops this argument (against naive empiricism) in a way that is very reminiscent of Kant, arguing that in describing what has been experienced you will have to say when and where it happened, the time and the place. But the immediacy of sense certainty, Hegel says, cannot supply

5. Solomon, "Hegel's Phenomenology of Spirit," 196.

the needed concepts of time and space. It is even questionable that sense certainty can give us the distinction between a subject who is the knower and the object that is known, which seems essential for the formation of any knowledge.

Without these categories, not supplied by the senses, an appeal to sense certainty is not going to get us very far. In order to make something of what we receive from the senses we need another level of understanding, bringing into play the categories of time and space, subject and object, theories and concepts and everything else you need to say anything about anything. Hegel calls this kind of reasoning speculative reasoning, an unfortunate name as speculative often today means suspect. He also calls this dialectical reasoning, for as he goes through the different levels of our consciousness, he often sees tensions or contradictions at a lower level that can only be resolved by moving to the next rung up.

"The dialectic is rather a complex interplay of conceptions, some of which are simply improvements on others, some of which are indeed opposites demanding synthetic resolution, but others simply represent conceptual dead ends."[6]

## The Broadest Context

Hegel, starting with sense certainty, moves from that lowest level of experience and moves up rung by rung, each time to a richer, more complex level of understanding. These levels are not only to do with what we know but are also to do with the context in which we know: the personal context, interpersonal setting, then the social context. Eventually Hegel argues that all of this only makes sense when seen in terms of a unifying spirit, which brings him finally to religion. As Robert Solomon concludes, "The purpose of this ordering is to demonstrate how each level corrects inadequacies of the previous conceptual level and how it is possible to correct all these inadequacies once we adopt an all-encompassing vision of the whole rather than limit ourselves to . . . this or that."[7]

Hegel has done what was promised, he has constructed his rope ladder from the lowest rung of our sense experience up to the heavens. This rope ladder of human understanding can only be properly supported, he claims, if it is lowered down from above, if it has its anchor in the almighty, in the infinite.

6. Solomon, "Hegel's Phenomenology of Spirit," 200.
7. Solomon, "Hegel's Phenomenology of Spirit," 194.

To follow every line of Hegel's reasoning over hundreds of pages is quite a feat in itself, but even if the logic is at times torturous and the conclusions at times stretch credulity until it squeals, Hegel's dialectical approach is so intriguing, insightful, and stimulating it has inspired many great minds over a whole array of disciplines. As Frederick C. Beiser sums up, "The aim of the Phenomenology was to show the possibility, indeed the necessity, of a strictly immanent metaphysics based upon experience alone. Of course, it was one thing for Hegel to sketch the plan for his dialectic and another for him to execute it. Surely, the Hegelian dialectic makes demands of a tall order, which perhaps can never be fulfilled. Yet there can be no doubt that the dialectic presented a legitimate metaphysic. . . . Even if Hegel's dialectic fails, we cannot accuse him of an uncritical indulgence."[8] To capture what Hegel is trying to do in *The Phenomenology of Spirit* in less than one paragraph takes some doing but one very brave soul has tried it. Here is Timothy Bradshaw's summary:

> [Hegel argues that] it must be possible for our reason to move from the lower reaches of our world upwards to the higher level of thinking and mind. . . . If we start with the basic simple dimensions of reality, of atoms, stones and energy, we can see that our minds classify and order these things and produce scientific laws tracking the regularities of natural relationships of things. We can then ponder the fact that our minds can reason in this way to move from objects to their patterns and scientific laws; we can reason about our capacity to reason about the phenomenon of minds and its power to understand the world. This however raises the question of how our minds do reason and raises the issue of mind behind our minds, overarching mind, the absolute mind. Hegel follows this route philosophically to argue for the infinite or the Spirit behind the whole of reality.[9]

## My Boring Calculator

I am of an age when I remember the first portable calculator becoming available (I assure you I was fairly young at the time).

I remember a friend showing me one his father had bought. It looked amazing and it cost a lot of money. I was told it would answer any question in no time at all. I went home insisting that we should get a calculator as well and said, as I was told, it would answer any question in no time at all.

8. Beiser, "Hegel and the Problem of Metaphysics," 20.

9. Bradshaw, *Pannenberg: A Guide for the Perplexed*, 3–4.

I think it was my older brother who then took the wind out of my sails. I think he said: "Tim, since when have you been interested in numbers and mathematics? Yes, it will answer any question you have but only if the question involves numbers. But most of the annoying questions you come up with, Tim, have nothing to do with numbers."

And of course, when I eventually got a calculator the novelty wore off in seconds. My brother was right, I still have no interest in numbers!

If you were to try to get your calculator to process something other than numbers people might question your sanity. This was Kant's point about human reason. Human reason, like the calculator, was developed to process one particular thing, and if you try to use it for something else you may end up with nonsense. Kant's argument was that human reasoning was designed to process what we receive from our senses and that is all. Like the calculator there is no doubt it does the job it was developed to do: look at what the natural sciences have achieved. Beyond that you cannot expect too much from our reason for like the calculator, as impressive as it is it is strictly limited.

According to Kant, this mistake has been made time and time again; human rationality has been asked to work with things it was not developed for. Reason has been asked to settle religious and metaphysical questions that go well beyond the world of sense experience, well beyond anything reason can deal with. Categories such as cause and effect that reason employs and that work so well when understanding the workings of the material world will get us nowhere if we try to apply them to what might lie beyond our world of normal experience. If we try to apply the worldly categories of cause and effect, so central to our everyday reasoning, to religious or metaphysical issues it will not compute. Why should cause and effect mean anything beyond this world? Kant's point is that this is exactly what the classical arguments for the existence of God tried to do.

As already noted, Kant talks of reason trying to fly to a place where there is no air resistance to work with, where the bird's wings might beat but to no effect. "Encouraged by . . . the power of reason, the drive for expansion sees no bounds. The light dove, in free flight cutting through the air the resistance of which it feels, could get the idea that it could do even better in airless space."[10]

The wings of the dove for Kant are of course the elevating powers of rationality and the air that the wings beat against is our sense experience, what we receive from the world around us. Trying to fly beyond this world of

10. Kant, *Critique of Pure Reason*, Introduction, A5/B9.

sense experience, beyond any atmosphere, is the speculation of metaphysics where reason has nothing to work with and beats its wings to no effect.

The big difference between Kant and Hegel is that Hegel thinks he can ask the dove to fly far higher than Kant would ever allow. Hegel seems to have started asking the calculator metaphysical and religious questions again. He looks to the calculator of reason to settle questions about the existence and nature of God.

Why was this? Hegel was concerned that Kant's constraints on what reason could tackle ended up in a sophisticated form of agnosticism. It meant that we could say little if anything about most of the major questions of life, those major questions of life that lay well beyond this world.

Hegel believed that he could use reason to address these big questions, but in a way that would not fall foul of Kant's embargo. In *The Phenomenology of Spirit* Hegel vows that he will not use the arguments for God that Kant had already discredited and will model his work on Kant's approach. In doing this Hegel believes he will be able to decide religious and metaphysical questions on the basis of reason alone. He will not use the classical arguments for God's existence, like the cosmological argument we looked at. Hegel's form of argument is not taking a category we use to understand the world around us and then pushing them almost to breaking point until they reach what is transcendent. It is not a logical argument that moves back step-by-step like links in a chain until it reaches what is beyond this world. Hegel's approach can be seen as more contextual. It is saying that certain phenomena we all experience only fully make sense within a wider context. And that wider context eventually becomes metaphysical.

Hegel's rope ladder did not work from foundations in this world in logical terms to God. Instead, he argued that so much of what we conceive of in our experience needs to be put with in a broader setting in order to properly function and be fully supported, eventually leading to what is spirit.

The other major contrast with Kant's philosophy we have already noted is that Hegel did not see God and the world as mutually exclusive categories, the two for Hegel might be distinct but were not separate. For Hegel, God and the world are intrinsically connected; there is no philosophical abyss to traverse between them. These differences fundamentally challenged the metaphor that Kant used when summing up the relationship between the world we know and what might lie beyond.

## That Island and Sea Again

After Kant, in his critique of pure reason, has given a detailed survey of what reason can establish, he stands back and asks where we have got to. He then discusses what has been accomplished in terms of a metaphor. He says that through the use of pure reason we have established an island of truth, but an island of truth surrounded by a threatening sea of the unknown.

That island of truth and knowledge is the way our minds process the sensory world around us and the categories it uses to make sense of it. We are very familiar with these and we can rely on their predictability. But what lies beyond this island is a turbulent sea of doubt. As the theologian Peter Hodgson sums it up, "Kant's . . . position led to an agnosticism with respect . . . to non-empirical realities, such as the soul, freedom, and God."[11]

Hegel complains that "The doctrine that we can know nothing of God, that we cannot cognitively apprehend him, has become in our time a universally acknowledged truth, a settled thing, a kind of prejudice. . . . It is the distinction of our age, by contrast, to know each and everything, indeed, to know an infinite mass of objects, but only of God we know nothing."[12] As the theologian Gary Dorrien sums up the situation: "The so-called 'wisdom' of Kantian modernity turned God into 'an infinite phantom, far removed from our consciousness.'"[13]

If Kant's metaphor was of a small island of scientific certainties surrounded by a forbidding ocean of the unknown, how would that metaphor need to be changed in order to express in what way Hegel's approach was different to Kant's? It would I suggest be a very different picture. In Hegel's philosophy it would be difficult to know where the island ends, and the ocean begins. This is true in a number of ways. If, for Kant, the land of truth is where reason reigns and the sea is the metaphysical beyond where reason becomes impotent, at this point Hegel's philosophy could not be more different. Firstly, for Hegel reason is not limited to what the natural sciences can establish; reason can establish so much more than that. It is through reasoning that we come to accept that history is the outworking of spirit. It is through reasoning that we come to establish and understand major Christian doctrines. So, for Hegel, there is no uncharted foggy sea beyond rationality. All can be encompassed to some degree by speculative reason.

But there is probably another major contrast at work here. A great ocean brings with it a sense of the unknown, the unpredictable, of the

11. Hodgson, *Hegel and Christian Theology*, 84.

12. Hegel, *Lectures on the Philosophy of Religion*, 1:86.

13. Dorrien, *Kantian Reason*, 211.

mysterious doubts, frightening powers, something that cannot be tied down or tamed. But because Hegel has established the things of God through reason and shown through reason how God needs the world in order to become self-conscious, and reason has told us how everything will end, the critic might ask has not the mighty ocean been drained, transcendence been tied down and tamed, and the mysterious depths charted?

Kant's agnosticism, for Hegel, has overcome but, in the process, have we travelled too far in the opposite theological direction and domesticated the almighty within the bounds of human reason? Before, we consider this question further we need to look at another major difference in Kant and Hegel's philosophy.

## Galileo's Telescope

When Galileo first started using a newfangled device to look at the heavens (he did not invent the telescope as some have suggested) he found it difficult to get what he saw taken seriously. Why was this? Was it because people objected to his findings? Well that may have been part of it, but there was another reason, one that we might find difficult to understand. They did not know how accurate it was, in other words they did not know whether it was distorting, coloring, and affecting what was seen when looking through it.

That probably would not cross our minds today, but at the time, how could Galileo assure them that his telescope was not distorting the images? Well it may sound a little extreme but possibly the only surefire way that Galileo could have establish the accuracy of his telescope was through space travel. If he were to transport the doubters to the crater of the moon that they had been looking at through the telescope, that would probably have done the job. Galileo may have been ahead of his time, but I don't think even he was up to that.

The historian of philosophy and Hegel scholar Robert Solomon suggests that this was the problem that philosophy had been struggling with before Hegel. One of the key metaphors for knowledge that had been used had been "the metaphor of knowledge as a medium through which the 'light of truth' must pass." As he points out, this can easily lead to the skepticism we have been talking about. For as with the example of the first telescope, how can we distinguish between what the telescope is pointed at and the potentially distorted image we get of it? Kant had made much of this distinction, arguing that we can obviously only have access to the world as it appears to us through the medium of our knowing and never to the world independent of it. In other words, "there can be no escape from the conclusion that we can know only the world as it is for us."[14] This meant that "Kant . . . abandons the search for absolute reality and simply investigates the tool by which we come to know reality."[15]

Hegel was not content with this. In fact, he rejected Kant's distinction and the metaphors that supported it. This distinction suggested that the world we are investigating is something alien, something that has a radically different nature to the knowing subject. Hegel's whole philosophy questioned that supposition. What we are investigating in the world, for Hegel, is a manifestation of spirit, a spirit that is coming to its ultimate fulfilment in us. Examining the world is therefore much more like a meeting of minds, rather than grappling with something unknown, it is a matter of like knowing like. Therefore, there is not the division between the subject and the object that the subject is investigating. As Hegel concludes, "the true objectivity of thinking consists in this: that thoughts are not merely our thoughts, but at the same time the in-itself of things and of whatever else is objective."[16]

## Theology's Greatest Concern

You don't have to have read any theology to want to ask questions at this point about what all this implies for the relationship between God and the world; in this meeting of minds, in this like knowing like and "that thoughts are not merely our thoughts, but at the same time the In-itself of things."[17] For the other mind we meet in nature that resembles our mind is surely the mind of God.

Now the theologian Nicholas Adams at this point has a question for us rather than for Hegel. He wants to warn us about what kind of logic we're using in raising this question.

When discussing the God-world relationship in Hegel theologians have a tendency to be reductionist. We want to know in strict logical terms what exactly is going on. Is humanity, the world, and its history being swallowed up into the life of God and therefore denied any autonomy or contingent reality? That is one theological accusation commonly levelled at Hegel. Or perhaps it's the reverse, that God has been reduced to nothing more than a epiphenomenon of human history and human consciousness. And consequently, divine transcendence, freedom, or even independent existence is

14. Solomon, "Hegel's Phenomenology of Spirit," 192.

15. Solomon, "Hegel's Phenomenology of Spirit," 192.

16. Hegel, *Encyclopaedia* 84, 13.

17. Hegel, *Encyclopaedia* 84, 13.

put into question. As Nicholas Adams puts it, "many commentators think they must interpret Hegel either as divinizing humanity or humanizing God."[18]

But Nick Adam's interesting point is that, in this way we are using the very reductionist (Enlightenment) logic that Hegel spent every effort striving to combat. In logically wanted to boil down what Hegel is saying and being so reductionist by saying: "Hegel it has to be logically either one or the other." He is concerned that in Hegel's terms we are completely missing the spirit of Hegel's philosophy and the very logic he was wanting to question. "We cannot say that Hegel 'reduces' everything to human thinking, or that Hegel 'absorbs' everything into divine being. To say these things is to reinstate the false opposition between thinking and being. This is, of course, what many commentators do when they criticize Hegel. But they completely miss the point of the whole exercise in so doing."[19]

In contrast, Nicholas Adams suggests that if we use Hegel's alternative logic inspired by trinitarian belief and Chalcedonian Christological thought we might get a different answer. "When one's speech about God is governed by a logic of distinction in inseparable relation, the opposition between subject and object, between self and God, is cast in a quite different light. Speech about God becomes a display of the distinction-in-relation, not one-sidedly either of the distinction or of the relation."[20]

> What, then, of the difference between divine and human action? Has Hegel abolished it or not? The answer to this question turns on whether the reader adopts Hegel's Chalcedonian logic of participation or an alternative . . . logic of opposition. If one's reading is governed by opposition, then the question is: unity or distinction? Is God's action the same or different from human action? In the face of such a question, Hegel's philosophy seems overwhelmingly to assert unity and sameness. His is in the end a denial of transcendence. If one's reading is governed by participation, the question is: what kind of unity in distinction? In what ways are Gods action and human action distinct in inseparable relation?[21]

18. Adams, *Eclipse*, 46.
19. Adams, *Eclipse*, 14.
20. Adams, *Eclipse*, 15.
21. Adams, *Eclipse*, 53.

We will revisit this question at the end when we see how the modern theologian Wolfhart Pannenberg interprets Hegel's philosophy and distinguishes his own Hegelian theology from it.

# 22

# FAITH WITHOUT BELIEF

For many years I have taught Christian doctrine to men and women training to be priests. When we study the doctrine of the Holy Trinity or the incarnation or something like that, they sometimes look shocked, and then ask whether in order to get ordained as priests they have to believe all this. I am equally as surprised, and feel like saying, "It is the Christian church you will be ministering in; you did know that? And all of these have been Christian doctrines for quite some time now. In fact, in every liturgy you have recited there is a part where you say the creed and affirm what the church believes. What have you been thinking all these years? Have you just been playing with your phone or thinking about what's for lunch? Have you not noticed any of the beliefs you have been affirming?"

But in most cases, it is not that they have been ignoring the creeds that talk about the Holy Trinity and the incarnation, it is rather that they don't think that is what a real living faith is all about. When you inquire, they explain that for them a living faith is about something deeper than just a list of doctrine, it is about what is far more personal, heartfelt and experiential. It is about the experience of love, grace, forgiveness, fellowship, and peace, things that they explain cannot be captured in any written creed and that cannot be defined by a church council.

They might in fact go on to argue that the only way for you to fully understand what is important to them in terms of faith is for you to have the experience yourself. They are often kind enough to say that they will pray for you (a good way to put your college tutor in their place).

So, if this is your idea of faith why would you be interested in complex doctrines like the Trinity or the incarnation, they are not going to help with your personal walk with the Lord, they just appear to complicate or detract from a simple living faith based on heartfelt experience.

In this respect things have not changed that much since the time of Hegel. Many in his day would recognize this distinction between heartfelt religion and a list of high-and-dry doctrinal statements from the church. Understandably, those who were primarily interested in personal piety were called Pietists. This interest sometimes came at the expense of doctrine. Some have traced this interest in personal piety over and against the creeds and counsels of the church back to the Reformation. The first Lutheran theologian, Philip Melanchthon, famously claimed that "knowledge of Christ consists in knowing his benefits to us. . . . Any philosophical reflection on the nature of Christ and the . . . incarnation would be subjects better left to the corrupt hallucinations of the Roman Catholic scholastic theology."[1] The first edition of his introduction to the faith, covering "the principal topics of Christian teaching," notably did not discuss the Trinity and how that might be of benefit to the Christian life.

The same emphasis can be seen in the eighteenth-century leader of German Pietism, the Moravian Count Zinzendorf. Rather than looking to doctrine or belief as the main focus of faith, Zinzendorf prioritized the development of the spiritual relationship between the believer and their savior.

This distinction was to be used against Hegel, for when Hegel eventually got his post in the new university of Berlin, he found that Pietists objected to his philosophical theology. Even though Hegel was a firm believer in Christian doctrines like the Holy Trinity this did not satisfy his pious critics, as the theologian and philosopher Gary Dorrien explains:

> August Gottreu Tholuck, recently transferred from the University of Berlin to the University of Halle, . . . fervently pious, learned, . . . worried that people with dubious Christian credentials were being treated as leading Christian thinkers. Hegel was example A. Hegel's robust Trinitarianism did not impress Tholuck, as Tholuck regarded the Trinity as an unfortunate Nicene pick-up from Aristotelian and Neo-Platonist philosophy. Pietists of Tholuck's type were comfortable with rationalist criticism on this topic. . . . Tholuck suggested that Hegel covered his lack of pious feeling with a doctrine of dubiously Christian merit.[2]

1. Powell, *Trinity in German Thought*, 17.
2. Dorrien, *Kantian Reason*, 222.

## Schleiermacher

The most influential theologian in the Lutheran Church of Berlin when Hegel arrived was Friedrich Schleiermacher, whose spiritual roots were also in Pietism.

Schleiermacher had grown up in a Pietistic community of Moravians and it has been argued that something of his Pietistic background never left him. When first in Berlin, as a hospital chaplain, Schleiermacher was introduced to the salon life of the city where the intellectual issues of the day were debated. Here he came across some of the leading figures in the first wave of German Romanticism. However, he soon realized that those he got to know from these fashionable salons were not that interested in the church and its teachings.

Schleiermacher believed that his new friends had not understood the essence of Christianity and were rejecting it without fully appreciating it. It was not that their lack of interest in Christian religion meant that they had rejected belief in the transcendent or what was spiritual. As burgeoning Romantics, they were not content with purely the finite, often seeing something of the infinite shining through in the natural world. What was true of this cultural elite at the beginning of the eighteenth century is true of many people today, who don't want to be seen as religious but still want to be recognized as spiritual.

This was not totally foreign to Schleiermacher, as the faith he had been nurtured in made a not dissimilar distinction. As Pietists found it difficult to get excited by books on doctrine or lists of church dogma, if that was all faith was about, they too would have dismissed it.

Schleiermacher was keen to explain to his contemporaries that they had made a mistake, what they were rejecting was not the essence of Christianity at all. In his seminal work *On Religion: Address in Response to its Cultured Despisers* Schleiermacher appeals to the Romanticism of his age when he writes:

> I want to lead you into the innermost depths from which every religiously oriented experience and interpretation takes form. I want to show you from what disposition of humanity religion proceeds and how religion interlocks with what you yourself most highly value. I want to take you up to the heights of the temple, so that you may survey that whole sanctuary of religion and discover its innermost secrets.[3]

Such modest aspirations!

3. Schleiermacher, *On Religion*, 51.

He continues:

> You have no doubt reviewed the various structures of religious doctrine, from the nonsensical fables of uncivilized peoples . . . to those ill-assembled fragments of metaphysics. . . . And you have probably pronounced them all "without rhyme or reason." . . . But this consummation of doctrines and systems, I will have to reply, is often anything but the consummation of religion. Indeed, these doctrines and systems very often move forwards without having anything at all in common with religion. Personally, I cannot even speak of this without feeling revulsion. . . . Now surely—if I may appeal to your own feeling for a moment—surely it is not the character of religion! If, therefore, you have paid attention only to these religious dogmas and opinions, you do not yet know religion at all, and religion is not what you are objecting to. Why haven't you gone deeper to find the kernel lying inside these outer layers? . . . Why don't you look at the religious life itself? Look especially at these extraordinary moments when a person's spirit is so caught up in the highest reaches of piety that all others activities know to you are restrained, almost supplanted by it—moments in which one's feeling is wholly absorbed in an immediate sense of the infinite and eternal and of its fellowship with the soul. . . . Your task is . . . to transport yourself into the interior depths of a pious soul, so as to try to understand its inspiration.[4]

This passage could be read (with very few qualifications) as a manifesto for the Moravian Pietism that Schleiermacher had been nurtured in, yet it was being written to appeal to the cultured elite of Berlin. Both Pietism and Romanticism had little time for scholastic theologies full of abstract reasoning and both wanted something that engaged more than just the mind.

If at times Schleiermacher can sound like an advocate of the simple piety his Moravian father would have been proud of, at other times he can give any Romantic poet a run for their money. So when describing the experiential origins of religion he can write:

> If I might at least compare, since I cannot directly describe it, I would say that it is fleeting and transparent like the vapor dew breathes upon fruits and blossoms, modest and tender like a maiden's kiss, sacred and fruitful like a bride's embrace. In fact, it is all these things. For it is the first encounter of universal life with an individual, though it fills no span of time and fashions nothing palpable. It is the holy wedlock of the universe

4. Schleiermacher, *On Religion*, 56, 58.

> with incarnate reason, direct, suspending all error and misunderstanding, consummated in a creative embrace. When this happens to you, you lie, as it were, on the bosom of the infinite world, in that instant you are its soul. . . . Out of such a beginning . . . arises every religious stirring.[5]

I am sure it sounds better in the German. But I think it is clear that the holy wedlock we really have here is that between Miss Truly Romantic and Mister Moravian Piety.

## A Higher Order

When Schleiermacher returned to his Moravian seminary in 1802 he famously claimed that "I have become a Herrnhuter [Moravian] again, only of a higher order."[6] In fact, Schleiermacher could testify how the personal piety that he had embraced in his youth had helped him to keep his faith through all the critical questioning he had encountered in his studies.

Schleiermacher's father had sent him to Moravian schools and colleges where Schleiermacher had been somewhat shielded from the Enlightenment philosophy that had swept much of Europe. But Schleiermacher and a number of his classmates refused to be cloistered in this way and would secretly read philosophers of the Enlightenment together and meet to discuss these new ideas. When this group was discovered by the college authorities one of Schleiermacher's friends was expelled and Schleiermacher's father was distraught that his son was embracing these new ideas.

What was it that so concerned the college authorities and so disturbed Schleiermacher's father? Well the works that Schleiermacher and his friends had been clandestinely reading were suggesting that in principle everything should be open to critical questioning, that nothing was sacrosanct, and this included long-cherished religious beliefs.

There had been a number of religious responses to this. One key response was to argue that there was something about the nature of faith that is beyond the reach of critical enquiry.

Schleiermacher, drawing on his Moravian upbringing and marrying it with the new Romanticism of his day, could argue along these lines. That the essence of faith was an experiential immediacy that could not be fathomed by intellectual enquiry. That religion was not primarily about intellectual ascent to a list of propositional creedal statements nor was it there just to

5. Schleiermacher, *On Religion*, 87.

6. Schleiermacher to Georg Reimer, April 30, 1802.

bolster social morality but was concerned with something that engaged the very ground of our being. That the faith could not be put in a test tube and critically examined in a science lab. This is the kind of thing that engages the heart as much as the head. One way to put it is to say that it is primordial or precognitive, even noncognitive, something that we engage with at a deeper level than our cognitive faculties could ever fathom.

## Personal Experience

When tutoring students in their initial years of theological training I would often get a response that was in some respects a variation of this, even if it was not articulated in quite these terms. The student would experience some critical analysis of their beliefs and would come to me as their personal tutor somewhat perplexed. They would recount to me how uncomfortable they found all this critical thinking and how it led them to question the tenets of their faith. They would often conclude, though, by saying that even though so much of what they believed had been questioned no one could question their own experience, their personal experience of God, often in terms of forgiveness, reconciliation, renewal, etc.

Interestingly when these students in class heard about Schleiermacher's Pietistic upbringing and his subsequent appeal to the experiential and to the depth of religious feeling their eyes would light up in a way they never had before in the lecture course. Whether they found a kindred spirit in Schleiermacher is somewhat questionable, but the deeply experiential nature of his theology they found understandably appealing.

In contrast it was exactly this aspect of Schleiermacher's theology that Hegel found most troubling, and that led to them clashing when Hegel arrived in Berlin.

Hegel believed that Schleiermacher's approach was at best playing down or at worst giving up on the intrinsic structure of the Christian faith. Hegel wanted to argue that within the faith, behind its pictorial narratives, were philosophical truths that were of critical importance. Fundamental truths that could give direction and purpose to society and culture. That the Christian faith could not be reduced to something experiential that offered nothing in the way of cognitive content. That in fact Schleiermacher, according to Hegel, was filleting and gutting the faith, leaving it spineless, without structure. It was becoming an amorphous mass of religious feeling with nothing of substance to say about the issues of the day.

In his critique Hegel initially makes a fairly obvious point that feeling is not discerning and can be used to support anything you like to imagine, however bizarre. Religious experience could be used to advocate what Orthodoxy might consider blatant heresy or the downright dangerous. "Feeling is . . . nothing justificatory, for everything possible is capable of being in feeling. If what is in feeling were true for that reason, then everything would have to be true: Egyptian veneration of [the sacred bull] Apis, Hindu veneration of the cow, and so on."[7]

He then carries on seeing how dangerous this might be:"If feeling is the justifying element, then the distinction between good and evil comes to naught, for evil with all its shading and qualifications is in feeling just as much as the good. Everything evil, all crimes, base passions, hatred and wrath, it all has its root in feeling."[8]

## A Double Bind

Those sympathetic to Schleiermacher might argue that Hegel has not really understood Schleiermacher's theology or that he is taking cheap shots. For it might be argued that Schleiermacher is not talking about any old feelings but has in mind something far more fundamental, "a feeling of absolute dependence," as Schleiermacher put it, a preconceptual and noncognitive awareness. Something, you might say, that is felt even prior to the subject-object relationship that is so characteristic of all knowledge.

The problem is that in appealing to something experiential, however deep, primordial, or profound you can easily be caught in a double bind. If for Schleiermacher the experiential essence of religion is sufficiently deep that it can escape rational scrutiny, what real *content* can such experience have? Will not such an experience become so vague and formless that it ends up saying next to nothing at all? If in order to escape critical reasoning you say that what is experienced is preconceptual and precognitive there is the danger of it becoming so nebulous it would become difficult to isolate and identify.

But if in order to avoid this problem religious experience is brought to the surface so it can be clearly and conceptually identified, and if now it has some content and is saying something, are we not back to the beginning and have we not then achieved nothing? For what has content and conceptual form is open to debate and criticism and the appeal to experience has gained us very little. Put succinctly, *if it has no content it has nothing to say and if it has content then what it says can be questioned.* As Frederick C. Beiser argues, "We can identify the object of our intuition only by applying

7. Hegel, *Lectures on the Philosophy of Religion*, 1:403.

8. Hegel, *Lectures on the Philosophy of Religion*, 1:394.

concepts to it, for it is only through concepts that we can determine what a thing is."[9] But without this "an . . . intuition will be at best ineffable at worst empty."[10]

As Richard Crouter explains in a study of Schleiermacher's intellectual context:

> Hegel's point is that reason cannot be systematically excluded from the deepest and holiest moments of our experience. . . . The price paid for immunising religion to the attack of its cultured despisers is too high. Theology that seems to be invulnerable can be so only at the cost of its own intelligibility. . . . The very act of pointing to immediacy requires us to say how immediacy is mediated. . . . The alternative is to remain mute in the face of one's private experience.[11]

## Essential Mediation

Hegel, in his lectures on the philosophy of religion, makes this point in terms of mediation. Mediation is for Hegel the concepts, content, the cognitive element in all we know.

As Hegel says,

> It is a very widespread view or tenet that knowledge of God is found only in an immediate mode; . . . Mediated knowledge is ruled out; it corrupts the certainty and security of faith, . . . the assertion is that cognition is the very evil that has to be kept at a distance. . . . But even though we empirically relate ourselves [to the world] . . . there is still nothing at all that is immediate. There is nothing to which only the determination of immediacy is applicable to the exclusion of mediation. . . . [I]t is more specifically the case in regard to religious knowledge; . . . first, I am the knower, and second, there is an object, which is God. My knowing God is in general a relationship, and therefore is something mediated. I am a knower and a religious believer only through the mediation of this content. . . . We cannot point to anything at all that does not contain mediation within itself.[12]

9. Beiser, *Hegel and the Problem Metaphysics*, 18.

10. Beiser, *Hegel and the Problem Metaphysics*, 18.

11. Crouter, *Schleiermacher: Between Enlightenment and Romanticism*, 93, 96.

12. Hegel, *Lectures on the Philosophy of Religion*, 1:407, 409, 306–7.

Mediation becomes Hegel's constant theme and his questioning of immediacy in a religious context bears a striking resemblance to his questioning of sense certainty. As Solomon explains: "Accordingly, sense-certainty also includes the claims of many mystics and intuitive philosophers . . . who have claimed that the knowledge of the Absolute is not conceptual or rational but strictly intuitive, a pure experience, undistorted by human concepts and categories."[13]

The modern theologian Pannenberg gives a brief summary of what we have observed in regard to theology's response to the Enlightenment a response that Hegel bemoaned. "Philosophy . . . contains in itself . . . the substantial content of religion, its truth, which Hegel considered the theology of his time was abandoning under the pressure of the intellectual criticism of the Enlightenment, theology had withdrawn into the subjectivity of emotion, and had abandoned all content to the critics."[14] Pannenberg therefore concludes,

> One might suppose that Christian theology would have had sufficient reason to welcome Hegel's philosophy as a means of rescuing itself from its difficult situation, as a liberation from the attacks of rationalist criticism upon the substance of Christian faith and from the pressure to seek refuge from these attacks in an inward piety without content. Hardly any of the great thinkers of the modern age have done as much as Hegel to set Christian religion back upon the throne from which the Enlightenment had removed it. . . . It is quite clear that one of Hegel's greatest disappointments was that with some exceptions theologians did not take the opportunity offered by his thought, but regarded the refuge of an inward piety, to which they had fled from the attacks of the Enlightenment, as the Promised Land itself.[15]

13. Solomon, "Hegel's Phenomenology of Spirit," 196.

14. Pannenberg, *Basic Questions*, 3:156.

15. Pannenberg, *Basic Questions*, 3:159.

# 23

# TRINITY AND INCARNATION

## A Holy Trinity of a Passion

PART OF THIS POTENTIAL is that Hegel, like no other, breathed new life into largely neglected doctrines of the church. Doctrines that had fallen on hard times in the eighteenth century.

Here again Hegel's thought is full of surprises. Who would think a major intellectual writing at the beginning of the nineteenth century would see the doctrine of the Trinity and the incarnation as central to their thought? (The only other philosopher who was doing anything like this at the time was Hegel's old roommate Schelling.) And I think Hegel would be surprised and pleased to find that his work on the Trinity has inspired a great revival in trinitarian theology at the end of the twentieth century and into the twenty-first century.

In the eighteenth century such doctrines of the church had been at best neglected and at worse ridiculed by both ends of the theological spectrum. Philosophers at the beginning of the Enlightenment like John Locke and Isaac Newton who were keen to defend the faith in their philosophy and science had little time for beliefs like the Trinity. Not only had the more radical side of the Reformation made it clear that such a doctrine as the Holy Trinity cannot be found explicitly taught in the Christian Scriptures, but also, for those who wanted to construct a rational faith in tune with the Enlightenment, belief in the Holy Trinity was something of an illogical embarrassment.

At the other theological extreme, for the Pietist, the doctrine of the Trinity had never seemed that relevant for nurturing the faith or developing the inner life. Even in Schleiermacher's exposition of the faith a discussion of the Holy Trinity comes in the appendices. Why this is is open to debate, but for Schleiermacher it is clearly difficult to see how a doctrine about the inner life of God can be constructed on the basis of religious feeling as Schleiermacher hoped all doctrine would be. For the Trinity as traditionally conceived talks about God's eternal nature and not just about God's work of salvation in us.

## Trinitarian Jazz

What I love about jazz is the improvisation. I have played guitar for many years and would love to play jazz but one of the things I have always struggled with is improvisation. The jazz I would love to emulate is the kind that starts with an enchanting theme over some haunting chords and then, as the soloist takes up the tune, develops it in ways you would have never expected (it's at that point I seize up and give my guitar to someone who can play proper jazz).

Improvising is not simply playing the main tune, that is just boring. But if you did something that bore no relation to what went before, if you developed a new tune with new chords, that would also not be improvisation, that is playing a different piece of music entirely. Improvisation is somewhere between those two extremes and when done well is an art. In doing this you are taking the musical or harmonic structure that has already been established and exploring its every aspect.

This is of course an analogy that Hegel could never have used, but if he had lived in the jazz age, I would like to think he would have been happy to play with the metaphor. It might not strike you as obvious, but I think this can be an analogy for Hegel's approach to the Trinity. As we have seen, if you were developing a philosophy for the modern age, Enlightenment criticism and Pietistic disdain would make the doctrine of the Holy Trinity an unlikely idea to put at the center of your thought. All this was about to change as Hegel was to argue that this largely discredited doctrine encapsulated the essence of his philosophy.

In his outstanding study of the Trinity in German theology, Samuel Powell concludes, "The doctrine of the Trinity . . . is not ancillary to Hegel's purposes, but is in fact the apex of the system, for only here is there a final reconciliation of thought and being."[1]

1. Powell, *Trinity in German Thought*, 115.

## Structured Improvisation

What has all of this got to do with jazz though? Well you can see the Trinity in Hegel's philosophy as the main theme, the theme that is going to give structure to the coming improvisation.

He argues, to start with, that in the trinitarian distance between Father and Son we see in embryo the distance between God and creation. Hegel also sees this in the distance between the crucified Christ and his Father God that Jesus cries out to in his death. (My God, my God, why have you forsaken me.)

You have the theme of difference in relationship, plurality in unity, in God the Trinity and the variations or improvisations on that theme in creation and salvation finding its highest manifestation and tension at the cross. You could also use one of Hegel's favorite metaphors and say that in the eternal Trinity you have the whole of salvation history in embryo or in bud, then in creation and human history you see the Trinity fully developed, in full flower.

Hegel's concept of a trinitarian God appears in contrast to classical themes in theology (reminiscent of Platonism), which put the divine realm above division, separation, and difference, and have prioritized the indivisible oneness of God as a divine simplicity. But Hegel sees the trinitarian relations as defining the being of God. There is no one before the three. The self and the other, the I and the thou are there from the beginning.

Hegel argues that in the relationship between Father and Son something other than the father, something that is different from the Father, is there from the beginning. This distinction in the Godhead becomes the root of the distinction between God and creation, for the Son constitutes what is other, what is separate from the Father. As Hegel says, "It is in the Son, in the determinacy of distinction, that the advance to further distinction occurs, that distinction comes in to its own as [true] diversity. . . . This is the second element—the creation of the world. The first element . . . is only the relationship of the Father to the Son."[2]

This movement becomes most pronounced in incarnation and crucifixion. Here we have the Son taking on what is traditionally thought of as most alien to God. However, this distinction is not wholly new as it is rooted in the trinitarian relationship between Father and Son yet made explicit in the drama of salvation. In Jesus we do not just see the Son going into a far country, we also see the bringing of what became estranged home. In Jesus

2. Hegel, *Lectures on the Philosophy of Religion*, 1:435.

we see creation and God coming together as one, what was other than God becomes one with God.

But at the time this is only seen in Jesus, so this is where the third member of the Trinity comes into play. This bringing together of God and creation in Jesus is universalized in the Spirit, all can know and share this union with God achieved by the Son in the life of the Spirit.

Hegel considered the different members of the Trinity as intimately related to different aspects of the history of salvation. The Father as the unbegotten, the Son with creation and at his most alienated in death, the Spirit with the reunification of all back to the Father. Hegel's great love of what appears opposed being united is epitomized in this Christian doctrine of the Trinity.

## Death of God

Hegel, in stretching the Trinity to practically breaking point, can talk about the death of God (long before Friedrich Nietzsche) in the experience of the Son. For in the Trinity's involvement in history, particularly in the second person of the Trinity, the Son, human frailty, vulnerability, and death are experienced. As Hegel writes:

> But this humanity in God—and indeed the most . . . ultimate weakness, the utmost fragility—is natural death. "God himself is dead," it says in a Lutheran hymn, expressing the awareness that the human, the finite, the fragile, the weak, the negative are themselves a moment of the divine, that they are within God himself, that finitude, negativity, otherness are not outside of God and do not, as otherness, hinder unity with God. Otherness, the negative, is known to be a moment of the divine nature itself. This involves the highest idea of spirit.[3]

If we think that God's embracing of what is other and alien in Jesus is new to God, Hegel will say, "No, it is just the ultimate example of the difference that was already there from eternity within the trinitarian relations." For in the Trinity we have, according to Hegel, every experience of the subject and object the I, thou, every experience of diversity and pluralism every experience of alienation. We have the contrast between God and creation and the history that follows from it culminating in Christ's cry of degradation and alienation "My God, My God, why have you forsaken me."

3. Hegel, *Lectures on the Philosophy of Religion*, 3:326.

Again, we can see the organic illustration and the musical one. We have already used the organic idea of embryo or bud to suggest that the history of salvation is the flowering of what was there in trinitarian form from eternity. But to do full justice to Hegel's thought we need a less deterministic analogy than the embryonic one. Because in the act of creation and its history Hegel is exploring all the potential, even tragic potential of themes that are already there in trinitarian relationships. So in that respect the jazz metaphor is more helpful for the jazz musician is at one level involved in the development of something new, often in ways you could not predict, and at its best pressing improvisation to its limit, but is also exposing the potential of what was in some sense harmonically there. So when you hear the main theme again it is heard afresh, now enriched by the inventive improvisation. As the interpreter of Hegel's philosophy of religion Peter Hodgson explains, "God does not abandon the world but preserves and saves it, and indeed is enriched and completed by it; but this is an existential not a logical completion. Both truths must be maintained: that God is complete apart from the world, and that God achieves completion through the world."[4] This sounds almost as contradictory and counterintuitive as the Trinity itself, so this writer is probably on to something.

## A Ball of Wool

The Trinity had been something that orthodox Christians knew they should believe in but more often than not were not all together sure why. Hegel drew out of this neglected doctrine an epic dynamic that has fascinated theologians ever since. So, Hegel almost single-handedly puts the Trinity back on the agenda for modern theology (one of his old roommates had already had a go, what a surprise!) and his trinitarian legacy is still very much with us today. Well, can you imagine theologians leaving something as intriguing as Hegel's take on the Trinity alone for long? It's like giving a cat a ball of wool.

It would in fact be difficult to name any significant modern theologian who has a highly developed doctrine of the Trinity who has not been influenced by Hegel. If one were asked to name the four most influential German theologians of the twentieth century, Karl Barth, Ederhard Jüngel, Jürgen Moltmann, and Wolfhart Pannenberg would all probably come to mind, all of whom have theologies of the Trinity largely shaped by Hegel's philosophy. As Samuel Powell explains:

4. Hodgson, *Hegel and Christian Theology*, 144–45.

> the fact that there is any contemporary interest in the doctrine at all owes a great deal to Hegel. . . . [T]he doctrine was on the way to becoming a little used religious ornament at the beginning of the nineteenth century; . . . even at the end of the nineteenth century a great many theologians had simply given up on the doctrine and others were content largely to repeat the traditional doctrine like a litany that has become familiar and tedious. . . . Nevertheless, when it experienced a powerful resuscitation in the theology of Karl Barth, its Hegelian character was unmistakable . . . [and] the impressively Trinitarian theology of Wolfhart Pannenberg is unthinkable apart from Hegel.[5]

But the importance of Hegel's philosophy for trinitarian thought is not just true of Protestant theology, it is also true for a number of Roman Catholic thinkers. It is there in the popular writer Hans Küng's *The Incarnation of God: An Introduction to Hegel's Theological Thought* and in the work of the two giants of twentieth-century Roman Catholic theology, Hans Urs von Balthasar and Karl Rahner. So when Rahner writes, "In fact the whole of Christology [theology about the nature of Christ] could be seen as the unique and most radical realization of the relationship of God to what is other than himself."[6] It is pure Hegel. And the same is the case when reading a summary of Hans Urs von Balthasar's Trinitarian theology.

> Balthasar . . . finds in the . . . life of the Trinity the ground of the world process. . . . The eternal act of the Son's generation by the Father is grasped as "the positing if an absolute, infinite distance" within the Godhead itself, a "distance" that contains and embraces all the other "distances" that are possible within the world. . . . [T]he Holy Spirit maintains "the infinite difference" between the Father and the Son, and he bridges this difference, since he is the Spirit of both. . . . For it is only from within this trinitarian separation, for Balthasar, that other separations can take place; creation, the history of salvation, and even those that are most alienating and painful. . . . The original trinitarian drama . . . constitutes the condition of possibility for the drama that unfolds between God and the world.[7]

If you were to come across this description of trinitarian theology, not knowing who it was describing I think you could be forgiven if you thought it was a condensed description of Hegel's philosophical theology. So, when

5. Powell, *Trinity in German Thought*, 141.

6. Rahner, *Theological Investigations*, 176.

7. Emery, "Immutability of the God of Love," 50.

it comes to developed trinitarian theologies of the twentieth century Hegel is ubiquitous for both Catholic and Protestant theology.

## Incarnation

Hegel saw other related Christian doctrines of key importance to his philosophy. When considering the person of Jesus one major study of Hegel's religious thought has claimed.

> The figure of Jesus acquires in Hegel's work an importance matched by few other philosophers. Many features that distinguished Hegel's Christology in its time are today so much a matter of course. . . . Jesus no longer appears as a teacher or as virtuous human being, as in Enlightenment philosophy or rationalist theology; nor does he appear as an embodiment of a universal idea, as an ideal figure of a humanity well -pleasing to God, as in Kant. . . . But in [Hegel's] philosophy of religion Jesus is the object because his destiny is accessible to religious considerations, and the latter alone is of consequence.[8]

## The Square Circle

There is of course an obvious point we can make concerning Hegel's understanding of the incarnation. I have often made this point when lecturing with a visual example. Imagine that you have two shapes in front of you, a square and a circle. Because they are fundamentally different in character it is difficult to bring these two shapes together, they do not unite easily. When philosophers want to give you an instance of the logically impossible, they will sometimes give the example of a square circle. Some traditional theologies seem to present God and the world in these terms as fundamentally incommensurable. In fact, critics of Christian belief in the incarnation have sometimes used this analogy saying that to believe in the incarnation is like believing in a square circle. This then makes incarnation an example of the logically impossible because being so fundamentally different God cannot be one with the world. So, incarnation cannot be seen as in any way natural it has to be seen as something supernatural, something totally miraculous, an alien intrusion into nature.

But because Hegel sees the relationship between God and the world differently, we do not get this problem when it comes to incarnation. We are

8. Jaeschke, *Reason in Religion*, 314.

not faced with two fundamentally different shapes that have to be combined. We are faced with two things that are very much related to each other, shapes that resemble each other. If, for Hegel, the Spirit of the world finds its full realization in becoming incarnate in the world, if it only ever comes to full self-consciousness through history then we end up seeing what Christians believe happened in Jesus in a very different light. From the perspective of Hegel's philosophy incarnation is not any more a supernatural, logically impossible, or miraculous event but could not be more natural, it is what the Spirit of the world naturally does, it becomes incarnate. So "The basis of Hegel's Christology is the idea of the implicit unity of the divine and the human. . . . Hegel uses every new turn of phrase to express the unity of divine and human nature. . . . The divine nature is no other than human nature. . . . What [this unity] posits is that divine and human nature are not intrinsically different."[9]

Will not Hegel now end up with exactly the opposite problem? For if human history is already an incarnation of the divine in the Spirit's act of self-realization, how is Jesus distinctly different from the rest of human history. One response Hegel makes to this question is to argue that something that philosophers like Hegel may know is the case (that spirit is working through everything in history) needs to be made plain to all and seen in objective terms that everyone can recognize. "The implicitly subsisting unity of divine and human nature must be revealed to humanity in an objective way; this is what happened through the incarnation of God."[10]

## Theological Picture Language

If this has not challenged traditional theological convictions sufficiently, Hegel then comes to a conclusion that could make theology redundant. For Hegel suggests that all these Christian doctrines are really just childish pictures or illustrations of philosophical truth. We need this picture language so the uneducated can get some understanding of these truths, but the philosophically educated can go beyond the picture language and perceive the higher truth of the intellect. As Hegel writes,

> in religion, the content of the idea appears in forms accessible to sense experience or understanding, because religion is the truth for everyone. Hence, we have the expression "father" and "son" a designation taken from a sentient aspect of life, from a

9. Jaeschke, *Reason in Religion*, 336.

10. Hegel, *Lectures on the Philosophy of Religion*, 3:314.

> relationship that has its place in life. In religion the truth has been revealed as far as its content is concerned; but it is another matter for this content to be present in the form of the concept, of thinking, of the concept in speculative form.[11]

It is almost as if he is saying that the theologian cannot tell you what the Trinity is really all about, you need the philosopher to do that. For what the Trinity is really expressing is a philosophical truth about the movement from an empty unity to all the diversity of the world back to a higher and richer unity. So as much as theologians have been inspired by Hegel's philosophical Trinity and incarnation few theologians like to be told that the philosopher has a better idea of what they are doing than they have.

> So, when orthodox Trinitarian dogmatics states that the Father eternally begets the Son and that the Spirit proceeds from the Father and the Son, Hegel understands these relations of origin to be pictorial ways of expressing the logical dialectics of differentiation and reconciliation. . . . For these reasons, Hegel believed that the doctrine of the Trinity sets forth the movement of the Spirit in representational form. . . . In the end, we must judge that as Hegel worked out his philosophical convictions in the light of the cultural and religious situation of his day, he came to identify with the main tenets of Christian theology as he understood them, keeping in mind he believed he understood them better than the theologian did.[12]

11. Hegel, *Lectures on the Philosophy of Religion*, 3:283.

12. Powell, *Trinity in German Thought*, 122.

# 24

# EXISTENTIAL IMPLICATIONS

## Master and Slave

IN ORDER TO BECOME fully developed as persons, Hegel argues, we need the recognition of others, something no one is likely to dispute today. For example, we only develop a rich self-consciousness, a clear idea of our identity and who in fact we are as individuals through a relationship with others.

Prior to Hegel, when philosophers envisaged how society had been formed, they imagined a scenario where isolated individuals were making contracts with others to promote the common good. Few today would be that naive, any book you come across on human self-development is likely to make the point that our social relationships shape our identity. It is our engagement with others that make us who we are and the way we see ourselves.

In order to explore the extremes of this insight Hegel uses an illustration. It is an illustration that has become the best-known part of Hegel's work and probably the most influential and definitely the most disputed (there are a number of themes here that Karl Marx will develop). He tells a dehumanizing story of enslavement. Someone is taken under the power of another and on pain of death is enslaved and made to work for them.

## The Slave's Mastery

As ever, Hegel likes to take a situation where we think we know what is happening, and then show us through his dialectical reasoning that there is far more going on than meets the eye. He does this by taking the idea we started with, that in order to be fully developed as a person we need the recognition of others. He then takes that insight and gives a very different spin on this story of mastery.

We might think that the master is in the best situation, he is in a situation of power and has all he needs. But Hegel points out that if you need the recognition of another for self-development the master is not in a good position at all. For he has dehumanised the slave, he has made him little more than an object, so the slave's recognition means very little to the master. As Frederick C. Beiser explains, "The recognition of the slave is therefore of little value. If not worthless, to him. It is not the free recognition of another rational being, but it is only the humbled submission of an animal. Recognition loses all value if it comes from domination or coercion; it is only of value when it derives from the free choice and judgment of another. Since the master despises the slave. He does not get the assurance that he is after"[1]

The only way that the master can get what he needs, is to free the slave. As the master will only value the recognition of another free person. Not only is the master in need of the slave for the fulfilment of his identity, Hegel suggests that the slave is in one respect already experiencing greater fulfilment than the master. For the master is just the consumer whereas the slave can fulfil himself in his work. In his work the slave can fashion and shape the world, and this is a form of self-expression and fulfilment. As Hegel argues, "Through work and labour, however, this consciousness of the bondsman comes to itself. . . . Thus, precisely in labour . . . the bondsman becomes aware . . . of having and being a 'mind of his own.'"[2]

Such dysfunctional relationships will become for Hegel the engine of historical change and will inspire the student of Hegel's philosophy Karl Marx in his theory of economic development.

## An Existential Objection

When a celebrity is asked what the most important piece of advice they can give young people as they are choosing their careers, the answer now has become so predictable it is hardly worth asking any more. The celebrity, in all sincerity, as if you have never heard it before, will say, "As you start out in life the one thing you should always do is follow your heart, be true to yourself, and follow your dreams." But I would suggest that as common as this advice is today it is the kind of popular advice you would not hear at any other time in history and in no other place than in the modern West.

1. Beiser, *Hegel*, 189.
2. Hegel, *Phenomenology of Spirit*, 53–54.

In other cultures, and at other times, the idea that we are to make our own way in the world and that our lives are somehow a form of self-expression would be unheard of. Being the captains of our own souls and the masters of our own identity and destiny is one of the most blatant manifestations of modernity. In the past meaning was found by being part of a preordained structure whether this was a social structure or religious one. Conforming to what had been eternally ordained was the means to fulfilment. Today if the celebrity were to say, "Always remember your place, submit to what is ordained, take up the occupation your parent and grandparents have always pursued," that celebrity would never be asked again. But before the Enlightenment and then the rise of Romanticism that response would have been quite acceptable and following the heart and being true to self incomprehensible.

The structures that gave identity and meaning were not just historical accidents the social construction of a particular time and place, they were God-given. Your place was not just in society but within a divine plan. In all of this you found purpose and meaning in an order not of your own making. I am tempted to say like the individual notes in a composition or musicians in an orchestra, but that might be stretching our compositional analogy to its musical breaking point.

Despite all Hegel's efforts to make religion fit for a modern world he still retains this traditional theme. For finding your place within the greater whole is a pervasive motif. This traditional idea may have been transposed into an evolutionary key, but it is as important as ever. However, in terms of self-expression and individual autonomy is this more liberating than what preceded it? As Frederick C. Beiser points out,

> Although Hegel purged the Christian concept of providence of its traditional, transcendent meaning, he still retained its underlying thesis, that the purpose and meaning of life came from fulfilling my place in the divine order. . . . In his view, no individual had by himself the power to give life meaning, to create the values by which he lived. The purpose of his life had to be made for him by the greater wholes of society, state and history, which give the individual a specific role to perform. . . . We are not existential heroes that give our lives meaning through individual acts of choice, apart from our specific place in society and the state.[3]

It is revealing that in Terry Eagleton's popular book, *Why Marx was Right,* Eagleton looks at major complaints about Marxist philosophy and

3. Beiser, *Hegel*, 276.

one of these is that "Marxism is a form of determinism. It sees man and woman simply as the tools of history, and thus strips them of their freedom and individuality. Marx believed in certain iron laws of history, which work themselves out with inexorable force and which no human action can resist. . . . As such, Marx's theory of history is just a secular version of Providence or Destiny. It is offensive to human freedom and dignity just as Marxist states are."[4]

## Calling Yourself Milly

We know very well by now where Marx got this from and its resemblance to the Christian doctrine of providence is not lost on Eagleton. He even thinks the way some theologians have traditionally addressed this question (of how belief in Gods foreknowledge can be squared with the experience of human freedom) will help Marxists resolve their dilemma.

> There is an analogy here with the Christian interplay between divine providence and human free will. For the Christian I act freely when I strangle the local police chief; but God has foreseen this action from all eternity and included it all along in his plan for humanity. He did not force me to dress up as a parlour maid last Friday and call myself Milly; but being omniscient, he knows I would, and could thus shape his cosmic schemes with the Milly business well in mind. . . . Just as for the Christian human action is free yet part of a preordained plan, so for Marx the disintegration of capitalism will unavoidably lead men and women to sweep it away of their own free will.[5]

What is a problem for Eagleton and his Marxism is that quite a few philosophers of religion are now unconvinced by this way out of the providential dilemma and suggest something more radical than Eagleton has in mind. In other words, that God does not necessarily know in advance you will call yourself Milly; for all he knows you may want to be addressed as Daisy when in drag. In other words, history is not sewn up in advance with God; rather, God takes a genuine risk with creation.

4. Eagleton, *Why Marx Was Right*, 30.
5. Eagleton, *Why Marx Was Right*, 45.

## There's an Evil-looking Fly in your Ointment

We started by reflecting on the great works of Romantic composers and we observed that even if they are not ordered in the measured and mathematical way, we see baroque compositions are, they are still very carefully orchestrated to reach the desired resolution. A great composer will put together a seamless work were one part naturally develops from the next, as if the peace is working with an internal logic of its own.

In a great work there are no unintended abrupt stops and starts, it feels as if the music has its own momentum, its own inherent structure and all the different parts come together to make something whole. As we have seen this is not an order that is imposed from outside; it is rather the natural way things evolve. To change the metaphor, it is in history's DNA to take the forms that it does and there is no stopping it. As we have seen, this is the way Hegel's spirit of the world becomes manifest. So, it is only by performing the music that the spirit takes form and is fully realized.

Hegel, as we have seen, sees this as a variation on the Christian doctrine of providence. The idea that God is somehow orchestrating history to achieve his purposes. "The great assumption that what has taken place in the world has also done so in conformity with reason . . . is nothing else than trust in Providence, only in another form."[6] But amazingly he believes that this view of providence can be established philosophically.

> [Philosophy reveals] . . . that God's will must always prevail in the end, and that world history is nothing more than the plan of providence. The world is governed by God, and world history is the content of his government and the execution of his plans. To comprehend this is the task of the philosophy of world history, and its initial assumption is that the ideal is fulfilled.[7]

So, Hegel argues, as Robert Solomon explains, "to one who 'looks with a rational eye' . . . 'history in turn presents its rational aspect.' The history of humanity, brutal as it has been, nevertheless displays an ineluctable sense of progress and increasing freedom."[8]

The problem is that every time I turn on a TV or go online and get the day's news I don't see any sign of a rational plan. I never come away from hearing about what is happening in the world saying "Oh, it's great to see everything working out so well, it's only a matter of time before everything comes right." In fact, I can never remember hearing the day's news without

6. Hegel, *History of Philosophy*, 35.
7. Hegel, *History of Philosophy*, 67.
8. Solomon, "Hegel's Phenomenology of Spirit," 189.

some feeling of despair, confused about what is going on, and wondering what sense could be made of it all. Surely you would have to do some very radical editing of your newspaper or news feed if you wanted it to fit with Hegel's picture of progress.

But Hegel is not daunted by this fact. Rather Hegel wants to take a step further and argue that his philosophy should be seen overall as a theodicy, theodicy being a defence of Gods ways in the world. As Hegel writes,

> In our knowledge, we aim for the insight that whatever was intended by the Eternal Wisdom has come to fulfilment . . . . To that extent our approach is a theodicy, a justification of the ways of God, . . . so that when once the evil in the world was comprehended in this way, the thinking mind was supposed to be reconciled to it. Nowhere, in fact, is there a greater challenge to such intellectual reconciliation than in world history. This reconciliation can be achieved only through the recognition of that positive aspect, in which the negative disappears as something subordinate and overcome. It is attained (on the one hand) through the awareness of the true end-goal of the world, and (on the other) through the awareness that this end has been actualized in the world and that the evil has not prevailed in it in any ultimate sense.[9]

Hegel is very aware of the daunting magnitude of this task. For Hegel can talk about history as the "slaughter bench" on which many great sacrifices have been made, and is willing to ask the question "to whom, and to what ultimate end . . . have these monstrous sacrifices been made."[10] And his summary of the situation is as chilling as anything you can find.

> Without rhetorical exaggeration, we need only compile an accurate account of the misfortunes which have overtaken the finest manifestations of natural and political life and personal virtue or innocence, to see a most terrifying picture take shape before our eyes. Its effect is to intensify our feeling to an extreme pitch of hopeless sorrow with no redeeming circumstances, to counterbalance it.[11]

9. Hegel, *Introduction to the Philosophy of History*, 17–18.

10. Hegel, *Introduction to the Philosophy of History*, 96.

11. Hegel, *Lectures on the Philosophy of World History*, 96.

The only comfort he can offer is that it is all part of a necessary process. "We can only harden ourselves against it or escape from it by telling ourselves that it was ordained by fate and could not have been otherwise."[12]

The thought that Hegel cannot abide is that "shit" just happens. The only way he can cope with suffering is to show that it is part of a required process that certain higher goods cannot be achieved without these necessary evils. The thought that things just happen for no good reason plunges us into darkness, something he will not accept.

> For Hegel eliminating contingency means showing this world to be necessary after all. It means saying that the world as a whole, and everything within it, is purposive. Purposiveness was defined as the lawfulness of the contingent. To open any door of the world to contingency is to open the whole to Chaos; if law is not universal it isn't really law. To accept that the world we inhabit is not the best is to accept essential unintelligibility that leaves understanding in the dark.[13]

So as Hegel insists, "The sole aim of philosophical enquiry is to eliminate the contingent."[14] For "Philosophy should help us to understand that the actual world is as it ought to be."[15] In fact, in Hegel's *Lectures on the Philosophy of World History*, Hegel insists, "Contingency must be eliminated entirely. This can be done with logic that doesn't stop at guaranteeing the contingent events are simply necessary. Rather, it should show that what is essential is morally necessary. Every 'is' and every 'ought' must be identical."[16]

As we have seen this is not a process imposed from without, it is immanent to the development of history, it is the natural way things evolve. "If history is the history of progress, it would contain its own cure. The overcoming of present evils is slow, but it's imminent. For we need not appeal to another reality in order to do it. Overcoming evils is part of the progress process evident in history itself."[17]

The famous struggle between master and slave is for Hegel not just an isolated instance; it is rather the perfect example of how the greater good can come from the evils of oppression and conflict. For as we have seen this is not just two brutes slugging it out, something far deeper and more profound

12. Hegel, *Lectures on the Philosophy of World History*, 96.
13. Neiman, *Evil in Modern Thought*, 93.
14. Hegel, *Lectures on the Philosophy of World History*, 28.
15. Hegel, *Lectures on the Philosophy of World History*, 66.
16. Neiman, *Evil in Modern Thought*, 92.
17. Neiman, *Evil in Modern Thought*, 93.

is happening. That in fact this historical conflict is a necessary process that has to be gone through in order for humanity to find self-conscious freedom. As the philosopher Susan Neiman explains:

> Using history to reveal the effects of reason . . . requires finding sense inside evil itself. This is why the struggle between slave and master in his phenomenology of spirit is a paradigm of the process he saw in history as a whole. . . . Good theodicy makes everyone feel that his troubles were justified. The master has his 15 minutes in the limelight, then councils himself with the knowledge that his subsequent eclipse results not from a failure of his performance but from the structure of recognition itself. The slave can take pride, and revenge if he wants, in the knowledge that he drives world history. Since increasingly refined work is a higher form of activity and battle, he is closer to the Spirit and power that reflects the creator then the master who subsumed him. The world spirit can be conscious that the design he created was the best means of pushing history forward with the right combination of freedom and necessity where there seemed to be none. . . . For Hegel it was clear that history must have an end. He found it in the progressive unfolding of human freedom.[18]

The poignant moral question is of course to what extent is it justifiable to use this logic of an end justifying the means. Cannot questionable means in time utterly discredit any desired end? For some theologies and indeed philosophies this justification of means to end is not so pronounced. Evil is often then encountered as unfathomable mystery that philosophy can never comprehend.

But for Hegel that would be tantamount to a philosophical lack of nerve and would be scorned as intellectual cowardice. In Hegel's system everything is to be comprehended and incorporated into the overall plan even the most mind numbing of evils. It is of necessity leading to a greater good and this greater good could not be achieved without the suffering. I have no doubt that Hegel has become the philosophical patron saint of ends justifying means (a dubious honor). But as Neiman concludes dryly when discussing Hegel in her remarkable book, *Evil in Modern Thought*, "If you set out to justify suffering, you may find in the end that you've justified suffering."[19]

18. Neiman, *Evil in Modern Thought*, 96–97.

19. Neiman, *Evil in Modern Thought*, 100.

I also wonder what Hegel would have thought of the fact that a Marxist variation of his logic of unrelenting historical development was probably used to justify Stalin's Gulag, Mao's cultural revolution and Pol Pot's Reign of Terror. The Marxist/Hegelian end justifying whatever means necessary.

In the light of Hegel's ambition to create a theodicy suitable for modernity, if Hegel had gone back to the seminary where he had first studied, how many of the students there would have seen Hegel's sophisticated philosophical theodicy as an improvement? I have a feeling some may have thought that Hegel's philosophical approach to faith may be making the question of theodicy more acute.

# 25

# FLIPPING HEGEL

## Karl Marx: Hegel Upside Down

STRANGELY IN ORDER TO see how important Hegel has been for modern theology we need to say something about the importance of Hegel's philosophy for Karl Marx. After Hegel's death at least two recognizable groups were seen to emerge: A conservative group that became known as "the old Hegelians" and interpreted Hegel's philosophy in support of the religious status quo and a more radical group that became known as "the Young Hegelians" which in various ways turned Hegel's critical analysis against religion and theology. As philosopher Robert Nolas explains.

> Largely through lectures delivered at the University of Berlin, Hegel built up a circle of followers, mainly contemporaries or pupils, who were intent on working out aspects of the philosophical system that their master had suggested but left undeveloped. After Hegel's death in 1831 this circle, later dubbed "the Old Hegelians," became the core of a group of philosophers whose task was to put the finishing touches to the Hegelian philosophical edifice. . . . True to its dialectical character, Hegel's philosophy did contain contradictory tendencies which if taken too far would transform the apparent unity of his system into a clash of opposites. When "the Young Hegelians" emerged in the 1830's they exploited in various ways these contradictory tendencies thereby dissolving the unity of Hegel's system and

> bringing about what Marx called "the putrescence (decaying) of the absolute spirit.[1]

Included in this second group (the Young Hegelians), and numbering among them those who had attended Hegel's lectures in Berlin, were the radical biblical scholar David Strauss (1808–74), the humanist philosopher of religion Ludwig Feuerbach (1804–74), and the well-known partnership of Karl Marx (1818–83) and Friedrich Engels (1820–95).

It can be argued that ironically it was following the logic of their teacher's critical philosophy that eventually radicalized these students of Hegel's work and gave them the notoriety that alienated them from the intellectual establishment of their day. As the philosopher Van Harvey picks up the story.

> The young Feuerbach and Marx, like so many other mid-nineteenth century intellectuals . . . were preoccupied with the significance of Hegel, whose shadow so dominated the intellectual horizon of the time. . . . Hegel was a god-like figure whose magnificent philosophical vision had liberated them from provincial political and religious views and taught them to think critically. . . . He taught them that the advance of Spirit into freedom was only made possible by ruthless criticism of everything static and irrational in cultural life. They aspired, like him, to become professors and yet, when they did criticize the religious and political irrationalities of German culture, they were censored by governmental authorities. This censorship radicalized them still more until, within a few months, they were mounting wholesale attacks on the alliance of Christianity and German culture of which Hegel, ironically, was often seen as the legitimating symbol.[2]

As we saw in the introduction, the high esteem in which Marx held Hegel's philosophy remained with him to the end. He could even comment that Hegel's dialectical philosophy was "the last word of all philosophy."

Now in our hunt for useful metaphors Marx very obligingly provides some classics, for he employs two pictures to help us in understanding both the continuity and discontinuity between his philosophy and his philosophical master Hegel. These pictures were clearly going to be the basis of something he was hoping to develop further. So as Allen Wood points out in his book *Karl Marx*: "What is unmistakably clear about Marx's attitude toward the Hegelian dialectic is that he accepts some of it, but not all. Marx

1. Nola, "Young Hegelian Feuerbach, and Marx," 290.
2. Harvey, "Feuerbach and Marx," 292.

acknowledges that Hegel's philosophy (especially his system of logic) is of great service to him in constructing the economic theory of Capital. . . . Marx never fulfilled his intention to 'make accessible to the ordinary human understanding, in two or three printer's sheets, what is rational in the method which Hegel discovered and at the same time mystified'. Instead, he left us with two images or metaphors for what he intended to do."[3]

## The Mystical Shell

One metaphor is the contrast between a kernel of truth but in a shell or a husk that can be discarded, and the other metaphor suggests that poor Hegel has been on his head for too long and needs to be flip the other way up. "Hegel's dialectic is, on the one hand, enclosed or shrouded in 'mysticism'. It must be 'stripped of' this false form, 'to discover the rational kernel in the mystical shell'. On the other hand, with Hegel the dialectic is 'standing on its head'. It must be 'inverted' or 'turned upside down' before it can assume a rational shape."[4]

The first piece of imagery is fairly straightforward. Marx is not disagreeing with what is at the center of Hegel's philosophy. Marx would heartily agree with Hegel's rejection of classical philosophy that from Plato onwards was wanting to find eternal essences, transcendent truths, everlasting principles, behind the contingencies of history. The historical nature, all we know had to be taken seriously, there was nothing ahistorical you could base your philosophy on. But Karl Marx, like Hegel, firmly believed that such historicism did not leave us rudderless and aimless, for like Hegel, Marx believed history was going somewhere. There was a point to it all, a destination.

But again, following Hegel, Marx did not believe that this conclusion was going to be imposed externally. He believed that there was a logic in History and its development from one epoch to the next. So in this fundamental way he is following the philosophy of his master. But here is the big difference, this kernel of Hegel's philosophy may be inspiring for Marx but what is not is the fact that Hegel has presented his revolutionary philosophy in a way that relies on religious beliefs such as spirit and God. It has been wrapped and presented in this overtly theological and mystical package. Every other page is about the movement of the spirit or the development of the divine. It's all been couched in religious regalia and expressed in theological terms. So Marx wants to keep the "rational kernel" (the historical logic

3. Wood, *Marx*, 215.

4. Wood, *Marx*, 215.

of human revolutionary development) but discard the "mystical shell" (the religious speculation and theological themes).

The "rational kernel" of Hegel's dialectic, then, is his vision of reality as structured organically and characterized by inherent tendencies to development. The "mystical shell" is Hegel's logical pantheistic metaphysics, which represents the dialectical structure of reality as a consequence of thinking spirit's creative activity.[5]

## Flipping Hegel

But the more familiar metaphor that Marx uses is the one-off flipping Hegel. It is not so much standing Hegel on his head, it's more the idea that Hegel has been standing on his head and needs to be on his feet.

Here I am afraid we might be hearing a rather reductionist and one-sided interpretation of Hegel from Marx in order for Marx to create some distance from his philosophical mentor. So rather than reality being the logical outworking of a cosmic idea, the objectification and manifestation of an eternal logos or rational principle, Marx wants to reverse this, flip it, turn it on its head. In contrast, Marx suggests that our philosophical ideas don't come first and structure reality, rather the life of the mind is, at best, a reflection of material structures we see behind all historical development.

> For Marx . . . the dialectical structure of the world is a complex empirical fact about the nature of material reality. It is not a vestige of God's creative essence, and it is not to be explained or understood by means of a priori speculative principles. . . . If people think best when they think dialectically, that is because they think best when their thought mirrors the real world. According to Marx, it is this difference from Hegel which makes the Marxian dialectic different from the Hegelian, even its "direct opposite."[6]

As Marx put it, "For Hegel the thought-process . . . is the demiurge of the actual, which forms . . . its external appearance. With me, on the contrary, the ideal is nothing other than the material transposed and translated in the human head."[7]

To be honest, I get the impression that Marx has not just flipped Hegel, it feels as if he has taken his mentor into a hall of mirrors, where what you

5. Wood, *Marx*, 209.
6. Wood, *Marx*, 217.
7. Wood, *Marx*, 217.

see is recognizably Hegel but distorted into some strange shapes and at times, yes, also inverted. The hall of mirrors always reflects the person looking in but in ways that you were not expecting or could not have anticipated. So Marx seems to have constructed a fascinating Hegelian hall of mirrors. So as Alan Wood sums this contrast between Hegel and Marx up:

> As I read Marx, he accepts Hegel's vision of reality but rejects the Hegelian metaphysical underpinnings of this vision. . . . For Marx the world is a system of organically interconnected processes characterized by inherent tendencies to development, and subject periodically to radical changes in organic structure. Because Marx thinks the world is structured in this way, he also believes that the best way to mirror this structure is a dialectical theory, one which views its subject matter organically, and traces . . . the changes in this structure by the developmental tendencies inherent in it . . . .
>
> Because Hegel was the first to champion this vision of reality and to work out the theoretical program which is capable of understanding things in terms of it, Marx credits him with being "the first to present [the dialectic's] general forms of movement in a comprehensive and conscious way." Marx's "inversion" of Hegel consists in viewing the dialectical structure of thought not as a cause or explanation for the dialectical structure of reality, but merely as a consequence of the fact that it is thought's function to mirror a dialectically structured world.[8]

## Feuerbach: Hegel's First Flipper

Marx was not the first person to turn Hegel upside down. One of the other radical young Hegelians (whose work made a great impression on Marx) had already flipped Hegel. But when telling the story of the revolution in philosophy from Hegel to Marx he does not often get much of a mention. But in wanting to put the record straight the philosopher Van Harvey explains:

> Most discussions of the relationship between Karl Marx and Ludwig Feuerbach (1804–72) focus on the brief period between 1841 and 1844 when the young Marx was profoundly influenced by Feuerbach's criticism of Hegel, his theory of religion as the projection of human attributes, and his new humanism. Because Marx was ultimately to emerge as the more influential

8. Wood, *Marx*, 216.

> thinker of the two—although at the time it was Feuerbach who was famous and Marx almost unknown-such discussions tend to interpret Feuerbach as a minor, transitional figure in the larger movement of intellectual history from Hegel to Marx. . . . From the standpoint of religious thought, however, this interpretation underestimates the significance of Feuerbach's life-long attempt to develop what Paul Ricoeur has called a "hermeneutics of suspicion," that is, a systematic interpretation of religion based on atheistic principles.[9]

## Dog Is Dead

The argument that is forever associated with Feuerbach seems to have become part of popular culture and can be heard in the most unlikely of places. After a morning's teaching I would often go into the local park near where I lived and walk around it a dozen or so times (it was on a hill so it gave me plenty of exercise). As I did this on virtually a daily basis I got to know the others frequenting the park, primarily this was people walking their dogs. There was one gentleman who was particularly talkative, and I got to know well.

He once asked me what I did for a living and I said I was a teacher of theology. He then went on to explain his theory about theology and religion. On his theory, religion and theology did not come out looking that good. He explained (as if it was something new and revolutionary) that the reason people have religion and believe in gods is that as human beings we have taken our highest ideals or most basic needs and desires and have correspondingly created gods in order to fulfil or embody them. This is of course commonly seen as a theory of projection. Our human wants and aspirations have been projected on to the heavens as a way of objectifying our values and answering our needs.

Freud would go on and develop this in terms of wish-fulfilment. We wish for security, for guidance, for hope, for reassurance so the gods and the religion we have created oblige. We don't like the idea of being alone in this cold and meaningless cosmos so we create a warm and reassuring religion to comfort us, a celestial comfort blanket you might say for the cold dark night of the soul. At the end of this line of argument one is always told that the religious person needs to grow up and face the stark realities of life without this imaginary cosmic comfort. Being a sensitive soul every time I hear this argument it always gives me pause for thought, even explaining it

9. Harvey, "Feuerbach and Marx," 291.

here in this chapter in these simple terms gets me thinking again about the nature of theology.

So after he had shared his theory with me, my first thought was that Feuerbach was alive and well and walking his dog round my local park. I don't remember what my response was. I have never been particularly good when it comes to a quick response. When I replay things in my head after the encounter I can always think of something to say and it always goes down so well.

I suppose if I'd had my wits about me and the front to do it, I would have asked him if he'd always wanted a dog. It is possible that he had always looked for that kind of companionship that kind of loyalty he finds in his dog. That it is good not to come home to an empty house and to have some company in the evenings. That it is nice to be unconditionally wanted and for the dog always to be excited to see him and to want attention.

I am sure by this point he would have seen were this was going. But let's draw it to a conclusion. Your idea of a dog seems to be fulfilling a lot of your natural desires, it seems to be answering a lot of your needs. If that is the case, on the logic you have been using against religion, it must mean that there's nothing at the end of this lead you're holding onto, that what drags you round the park each day is really just a figment of your imagination. Of course, you can play this game with all kinds of examples parents or partners. Just because something fulfils a lot of desires and answers a lot of needs the desirable objects nonexistence does not logically follow.

## A Promising Theory

Now we could give plenty of other examples of this faulty logic. Let's try one more. You're a research scientist and you have a Eureka moment in the area of your study, you come up with a theory that explains so much that has baffled you and your colleagues. It catches your imagination; you realize that if your theory could be established and confirmed it would make your career. You would become famous in your field. You could see in your mind's eye becoming a professor with a string of eager research students wanting to study with you. Since you started academic study it has always been your dream and desire to make such a breakthrough.

But because such glowing prospects and heartfelt desires hinge on your new theory, will that consequently mean that the theory is wrong or delusional? If that were the case that would mean that every scientific breakthrough must be force, as I'm sure they all have researchers rooting for them and dreaming about their theoretical breakthrough being confirmed.

## Adolescent Rebellion

It never seems to cross the mind of the Feuerbachian that their belief in the nonexistence of any deity might also be a projection, a piece of wish-fulfilment on their part. That they might have just projected their latent adolescent rebellion on to the heavens. That growing up and leaving such stroppy adolescence behind might not always be a bad thing. That the nonexistence of a religious worldview for the secularist is just as much a convenience, a wish fulfilled, as belief is for those who practise religion.

## Under Feuerbach's Skin

But to really get under Feuerbach's skin we need to know our Hegel. Feuerbach is a classic example of where familiarity with philosophers like Hegel is crucial to fully understand what's going on because once we see how Feuerbach had interpreted his master's philosophy, we can see its direct reversal. Feuerbach had clearly interpreted Hegel's philosophy in terms of human history being an objectification or manifestation of spirit. That God comes to fulfilment through the process of historical and human development. That spirit needs the world in terms of self-fulfilment and self-development. So God creates the world to answer his or her needs.

Once we see how Ludwig Feuerbach interprets Hegel, we immediately notice how Feuerbach's theory of religion is such a neat reversal of what he sees in Hegel. Rather than spirit inventing us to fulfil its needs and objectify itself in history, we invent spirit to embody our highest ideals and answer our deepest desires. Feuerbach's theory of religion seems to be a mirror image of his master's philosophy. "If Hegel argues that the world is the self-objectification of the Absolute [spirit], the truth is that the idea of the Absolute is the objectification of the predicates of human nature. In short, the secret of both speculative philosophy and theology is anthropology properly conceived."[10]

So "It is . . . the theory that the idea of God is nothing but the objectification of human attributes with which Feuerbach's name is primarily associated. The central argument is simply an application of the transformative method to Hegel's philosophy of Spirit, and many of its complexities derive from this fact."[11]

> In his most famous work *The Essence of Christianity*, Feuerbach does not deny that religion has a crucial part to play in the story

10. Harvey, "Feuerbach and Marx," 296.
11. Harvey, "Feuerbach and Marx," 296.

> of human development. "Unlike his eighteenth-century atheistic predecessors who simply dismissed religion as primitive superstition, Feuerbach argues that religion is a necessary stage in the development of human consciousness. . . . [T]his view enabled Feuerbach to follow Hegel in holding that Christianity is the highest form of religion and self-consciousness while at the same time claiming that its inner meaning is atheism. . . .
>
> This ingenious inversion of Hegel's philosophy of Spirit enabled Feuerbach to do several important things First it enabled him to adopt a critical stance towards religion; that is, to affirm both its necessity and value while at the same time rejecting its truth claims.[12]

But religion for Feuerbach also has a detrimental effect on human dignity and worth. He argues in his *Essence of Christianity* that the more that humanity elevates God, and God is said to personify humanity's highest ideals, the more humanity impoverishes itself. Taking the words of John the Baptist well out of context, "He must increase, but I must decrease," or, in a different translation, "He must become greater and greater, and I must become less and less."[13] As Feuerbach states succinctly, "To enrich God, man must become poor; that God may be all, man must be nothing."[14] So, as Harvey explains, "It creates a deity that possesses all human perfections and that stands in sharp contrast to mankind's own impoverished condition. More strongly, the projection alienates mankind from its own perfections."[15]

For Marx and Engels, it was Feuerbach's transformative method for interpreting Hegel that inspired them to develop their own reverse image of the master's philosophy. Discarding all the metaphysical trappings, Feuerbach helped Marx and Engels see what was still true at the core of Hegel's philosophy.

> Marx understands Feuerbach's great contribution to be the transformative method that enables one to extract what is valid in Hegel's philosophy of Spirit without becoming entangled in his mystifications. . . . It was Feuerbach who formulated a way (the "transformative method") of interpreting Hegel that enabled the Young Hegelians, Especially Marx, to articulate their intellectual ambivalence toward the great philosopher, to understand why his work was at once so profoundly illuminating and a source of mystification. . . .Engels later reminisced that

12. Harvey, "Feuerbach and Marx," 299, 298.
13. John 3:30 (NLT).
14. Feuerbach, *Essence of Christianity*, loc. 705.
15. Harvey, "Feuerbach and Marx," 298.

> . . . [Feuerbach's interpretation of Hegel] . . . had made all of them Feuerbachians.[16]

## Marx and Feuerbach: The Fundamental Difference

A fundamental difference between Feuerbach and Marx's philosophy can be seen in their approach to religion. Where Feuerbach is happy to begin his analysis of religion by presupposing a universal human nature that appears to transcend time and change and then construct his analysis of religion on the basis of that, Marx in employing Hegel's historicism is deeply suspicious of any such universal and immutable categories (such as human nature). In contrast, Marx sees the human condition as contingent on historical circumstance, to be more precise its economic and material circumstance. Therefore, religion for Marx need not be a universal human phenomenon but just the way that particular people at particular times cope with the economic and material conditions they find themselves in. So according to Marx, if those oppressive conditions are alleviated, then there will be no need for the religious distraction and faith will consequently wither away in a more promising historical and economic environment.

> It is precisely this difference between the two interpretations of religion that is worth exploring . . . because it reflects a more basic disagreement regarding human nature and its relationship to culture. In an oversimplified way we might say that Feuerbach tended, like Freud after him, to see religion rooted in universal psychic structures that underlie all culture, whereas Marx tended to see psychic structures as themselves products of social and economic conditions. When viewed in this light, the contrast between the two thinkers illustrates a basic cleavage that runs through much contemporary scholarship in the discipline of psychology, sociology, history, and philosophy. On the one side of this cleavage are those who like Feuerbach postulate a universal human nature while, on the other, are those who, like Marx, stress the historical and social determinations of human nature.[17]

16. Harvey, "Feuerbach and Marx," 294.
17. Harvey, "Feuerbach and Marx," 294.

As Marx explains, "Life is not determined by consciousness but consciousness by life,"[18] which is, according to Marx, the ultimate inversion of Hegel's philosophy.

18. Harvey, "Feuerbach and Marx," 307.

# 26

# THEOLOGICAL REVOLUTION

IT IS STRANGE TO think that Hegel, a nineteenth-century professor teaching in the new University of Berlin, was to inspire a contemporary revolution in religious thought that has occurred within the last sixty years.

So how did Hegel create such a stir in contemporary theology? At the end of the Third Reich two teenagers (they had not yet finished their schooling) were called up to fight in a desperate attempt to defend the Fatherland. One, Wolfhart Pannenberg, was sent to the Russian front and the other, Jürgen Moltmann, to the Western. Even though these two young men did not have a religious upbringing they were to become two of the most significant theologians in the post-war Protestant church. Pannenberg had read a good deal of philosophy in his youth, particularly the works of Frederick Nietzsche, and was interested in many of the questions that Nietzsche raised. He believed his life was saved by being taken away from the Russian front due to ill health. After the war he and his family settled in East Germany. Having been called up at such a young age Pannenberg had to returned to school to finish his education. The teacher who most impressed him at his new school had been a member of the German confessing church that had fought for some independence from the Nazi regime. He directly challenged the negative model of Christianity that Pannenberg had gained from reading Nietzsche. Spurred on by a transformative personal experience and the influence of his new teacher, Pannenberg was keen after finishing his schooling to study religion and philosophy. Being in East Germany he was encouraged to study the philosophy of Karl Marx. Becoming somewhat disillusioned with his experience of the GDR (German Democratic Republic) he sought a scholarship to study in the West with the theologian Karl Barth.

In the meantime, his contemporary Jürgen Moltmann who had been sent to the Western front became separated from his company and was trying his best to hide behind enemy lines.

> While I was looking for a hiding place in a more densely wooded part of the forest, an English soldier suddenly jumped out in front of me. "I surrender," I called, as clearly as I could, but he thought I was one of his mates who was playing the fool, and he called some of the others. They came, we talked. They didn't shoot me, and more than that the next morning a lieutenant gave me a mess tin of baked beans. It was the first food I had tasted for days, and I've loved baked beans ever since.[1]

Moltmann was held together with other German captives: "We had escaped the inferno, but now we were sitting behind barbed wire and had lost all our hope, some people became cynical, others fell ill, Many people were face with nothing."[2] Moltmann in fact describes some of his fellow servicemen as fading away for lack of hope.

Moltmann eventually found himself in a prisoner-of-war camp in Scotland where many in the local community were antagonistic, particularly after Nazi atrocities had come to light. Shortly after, Moltmann met some local Christians who were quite different and offered him hospitality. It was this and his reading of a Bible for the first time that made all the difference in his outlook.

> For me two experiences raised me from depression to a new hope in life, the friendly encounter with those Scottish working men and their families, and the Bible.
>
> One day a well-meaning army chaplain came to our camp and after a brief address distributed Bibles. Some of us would certainly rather have had a few cigarettes. I read the book in the evening without much understanding until I came upon the psalms of lament in the Old Testament. Psalms 39 caught my attention
>
> I am dumb I must eat up my suffering with him myself
> My life is as nothing before thee
> Hear my pray, O Lord, and give ear to my cry . . .
>
> It was an echo from my own soul, and it called that soul to God. I didn't experience any sudden illumination, but I came back to these words every evening. Then I read Mark's Gospel as a whole and came to the story of the Passion, when I heard Jesus'

1. Moltmann, *Broad Place*, 25.
2. Moltmann, *Broad Place*, 30.

> death cry, "My God, My God, why have you forsaken me?" I felt growing with in me the conviction that this is someone who understands you completely, who is with you in your cry to God and has felt the same forsakenness you are living in now. I began to understand the assailed, forsaken Christ because I knew that he understood me. I summoned up the courage to live again, and I was slowly but surely seized by the great hope of the resurrection into God's "wide space." This perception of Christ did not come all of a sudden overnight, either, *but* it became more and more important to me as I read the story of the passion again and again.[3]

Moltmann originally thought of training as a teacher but quickly realized that his future was in studying theology. When returning to Germany the theology that most influenced him was also that of Karl Barth.

## Basic Orientation/Center of Gravity

What constituted the revolution these two young men initiated, was not the pursuit of a particular idea, or the development of a particular doctrine, but rather a change in basic orientation, a change in what may be called theology's center of gravity.

When you change your center of gravity or basic orientation it does not just affect one or two things—everything gets realigned and reoriented. For example, when planning a house if the architect decides halfway through the design of the home that he will change the home's basic orientation everything of course gets effected. The view from every window, the light in every room, it will not just affect one or two things, it will change everything. I want to suggest that to fully understand this major change of orientation we need to see it as a shift from the influence of Immanuel Kant to that of Hegel.

It may in fact be the case that after the dominant influence of Kant's philosophy we tend to see just a few basic orientations in Protestant theology—under a variety of names but still variations on a few basic orientations. The choice more often than not has been between the two Berlin rivals Friedrich Schleiermacher or Hegel. So I want to argue that what we have seen over the last sixty years has not just been Hegel's philosophical influence on this or that doctrine but rather a resurgence of Hegel's basic theological orientation, an adoption of his religious center of gravity.

3. Moltmann, *Broad Place*, 30.

## Individual Interior to Historical Hope

To fully understand the nature of Jürgen Moltmann and Wolfhart Pannenberg's religious revolution we need to get an idea of what it was replacing and its origins. And this is where our study of Hegel and his historical context is so important. For in the light of what we have learnt about Hegel and the controversy of his day the challenges that face Wolfhart Pannenberg and Jürgen Moltmann will appear very familiar.

The main rival to Hegel's theology/philosophy was a religious faith that was orientated around the inner life. As we will see when this is made the center of gravity for Christian faith everything is made to revolve around it and judged in relationship to it. For example, Christian doctrine will be judged in terms of how helpful it is for nourishing the inner life. The question will be, is it edifying in terms of my particular spirituality? If not it will be condemned as unnecessarily speculative. If one's central concern is the Spiritual life of the individual, other concerns may be seen as of little importance or even dangerous distractions.

In his study of Hegel's religious context, Laurence Dickey describes these brethren who were preoccupied with a devotional inner life as religious separatists. Their focus on the individual interior even eclipsed the study of Scripture.

> Since the Reformation then . . . a mode of separatism had expressed itself in . . . an extreme "religious individualism." . . .
>
> The feeling was that religious sincerity, not knowledge of Scripture, was the only condition necessary for apprehension of the Divine Word. All that was required to understand the Bible, the separatists asserted, was the "inner light" of Faith, and that was a gift every Christian, regardless of his learning or social standing, could acquire.[4]

Basic to this form of Protestantism "is the emphasis laid on pure subjectivity. It finds its expression in the longing to rise above this world. A necessary complement to this pure inwardness is pure externality: the world sinks into indifference for the subject that in longing only rises above the world and does not find where it can be reconciled to it."[5]

The fellowship of a community was of course important to them but it was a community of like-minded brethren who aided you in your personal walk with the Lord.

4. Dickey, *Hegel: Religion*, 94.

5. Jaeschke, *Reason in Religion*, 163.

As we have seen Hegel's religious center of gravity could hardly be more different. His religious faith was not centred on the individual or on a community of brethren or on the inner life, but on a universal historical hope. Controversially Hegel saw this religious Pietism at the root of the sophisticated theologies of feeling so influential in Berlin at the time and surfacing in his conflict with Schleiermacher.

So, when we look at Hegel's importance for understanding contemporary theology, it can be perceived as the conflict between Hegel and Schleiermacher repeated. Not just in one or two different beliefs being affirmed or denied but a complete resetting of one's overall orientation or center of gravity.

By looking at theology in these terms something else also becomes apparent. For Christian orthodoxy Hegel often appears, if not heterodox, to be a classic example of a thinker who has become too carried away with philosophical speculation and only loosely connected to the Christian tradition. However, when you see things in terms of basic orientation those who adopt Hegel's perspective may be more biblical than the Pietist.

## Three Big Themes

To see this in some detail we will explore three big themes: revelation, salvation, and Trinity. These themes I suggest work particularly well with the theologians we have introduced. For example, Pannenberg in his first published works began with a controversial proposal about the nature of divine revelation and Moltmann began with a book that challenged traditional views of salvation and then finally they both produced highly developed trinitarian theologies.

## Revelation as History

*Revelation as History* is the title of Pannenberg's first published work. You don't even have to open the book to hear Hegel's influence. Hegel would have happily used that phrase as a title for his own work!

## Self-revelation

You don't need to know a great deal about the Christian religion to know where God's revelation to humanity is to be found. However, Pannenberg points out that in the eighteenth century the idea of the Bible as a library of inerrant truth inscribed by God was put into question. With the rise of critical historical analysis and new philosophies inspired by the scientific method viewing the Bible as a depository of divinely revealed truth became less and less plausible to the enlightened mind.

Pannenberg points out that within modern theology the traditional view of biblical revelation was replaced by the belief that the Scriptures bore witness to something more profound than divine dictation. That within and through Scripture we can encounter a self-revelation of God. The Bible is not therefore the word of God in its verse by verse detail but rather testifies to the Word as God's self-revelation. As Pannenberg explains:

> The Enlightenment destroyed the old concept of revelation that belonged to seventeenth-century orthodox dogmatics, namely, the identification of revelation and the inspiration of Holy Scripture, the understanding of revelation as the transmission of supernatural and hidden truths. The assertion of such a revelation was suspected of fostering an obscurantism that would avoid the light of scientific reason. From the beginning of the nineteenth century, there was the suspicion that supernaturalism is superstition, and the concept of revelation could only be rescued by means of reducing its content to God's self-revelation.[6]

Pannenberg argues that the most important recent example of this can be seen in the theology of Karl Barth. "Contemporary protestant theology has been quick to characterize itself as a pure theology of revelation. This is especially evident in Karl Barth and in his wider sphere of influence. Revelation is not God's making known a certain set of arcane truths, but—as Karl Barth put it—the self-disclosure of God."[7] Pannenberg recognizes that in one sense the idea of Gods revelation being seen as primarily a self-revelation is first seen in a by now a familiar strand of philosophy.

> The new stress in the exclusive use of the concept "revelation" to mean the self-disclosure of God, without any imparting of supernatural truth . . . can be classed as a legacy of German idealism.
>
> The strictly defined concept of revelation as the self-revelation of the absolute appears to have been first introduced by Hegel. Hegel expressly reserved the designation "a revealed and revealing religion" for Christianity, not because it contains truths that have been transmitted by supernatural means, but

6. Pannenberg, *Revelation as History*, 4.

7. Pannenberg, *Revelation as History*, 3–4.

> because, in distinction from all other religions, it rests on full disclosure of the nature of the absolute as spirit.[8]

Even at the beginning of his first published theology, however, we can hear where Pannenberg's sympathies will lie, as he then comments, "We should also remember that to locate a theological thought in German idealism is not automatically to condemn it."[9]

## Past Event to Present Encounter

What concerns Pannenberg is not so much the idea that God's revelation is now seen as primarily self-revelation rather than a divinely dictated text. What concerns him is that the focus of revelation has changed direction.

- *Past Event:* One way to see this is that before the Reformation God's revelation to humanity could be seen primarily as past event and not as present encounter.
- *Mediate:* Being a past event revelation had to be mediated by history, through Scripture, and through the church and its traditions.
- *Corporate:* This was not focused on the individual, for revelation was something that the church possessed.
- *External and Public:* The revelation that the church bore witness to was not some internal or subjective illumination but something as the Creed says happened in history at the time of Pontius Pilate.

### *The Transition*

Interestingly, after the Reformation through into the Enlightenment and then into modern theology the focus starts to shift, the pendulum moves in the opposite direction. Not of course entirely but significantly and I think Pannenberg would say worryingly. It is now:

- *More Present, Less Past:* Revelation becomes seen in modern theology less in terms of something located in the past and more as a present event or encounter.

8. Pannenberg, *Revelation as History*, 4.
9. Pannenberg, *Revelation as History*, 5.

- *More Direct, Less Mediated:* Revelation is then seen less in terms of something mediated through history or Scripture or tradition and rather as something direct and immediate.
- *More Individual, Less Corporate:* In these terms, revelation is seen less as a property of the church and more as the experience of the individual.
- *More Internal, Less External:* Revelation is less seen as something that happens outside of us that could be objectively observed and more in terms of the experiential internal apprehension of truth.

We have seen this in the popular religion of Hegel's day in the sense that Pietism stressed the present, immediate experience of the individual. Hegel believed it was also there in a more sophisticated form in his theological adversary at Berlin, Schleiermacher. However, we can also see this in twentieth-century theology. For example, this change of direction from past to present can be found in what Pannenberg refers to as "theologies of the Word." When talking about "theologies of the Word" you might think this is referring to theology based on Scripture but, as we have seen above, modern theology had loosened or even severed this connection. The Bible might still be a means of encountering the Word of God as the Bible bears witness to it but the Bible and the word of God, for these theologians, are not synonymous anymore.

The theologies of the word that Pannenberg has in mind represent the most influential theologies of his day. They are particularly the theologies of Karl Barth and Emil Brunner and those influenced by them and to a lesser extent that of Rudolf Bultmann who had originally shared Barth's concerns.

In all these cases we see the pendulum has swung towards the present, away from the past in terms of a contemporary encounter with revelation. In all these cases we see an emphasis on the direct self-revelation of God and less in terms of what mediated it. And typical of Protestant theology in general we see an emphasis on the individual rather than the church.

## The Problem

Pannenberg's first published work points to a major difficulty here. With the help of Old Testament and New Testament scholars (who also contribute to the book) he shows that this way of talking about God's word as a direct and present encounter is not in fact the primary way in which God's revelation is thought of in Christian Scripture.

For the serious-minded neo-Orthodox follower of Barth, this is a little embarrassing as they normally to this day want to be seen as taking the Bible very seriously. Pannenberg does not stop there but adds insult to injury by suggesting that the only place he can find the word referred to as a direct encounter with God is in heretical gnostic literature. Not something a good Orthodox Barthian would want to be associated with.

> As Pannenberg explains, "The modern personalistic theology of the Word, . . . where Word is primarily the direct engagement of a person, . . . has its closest parallel not in the specifically biblical context, but rather in the Gnostic understanding of the Word. . . . Only in gnostic thought does Word appear as the bearer of a direct divine self-revelation. . . .
>
> Likewise, in the history of the biblical tradition, "the Word of God" does not have . . . the meaning that modern personalistic theology invests in it. . . . It never had God as its content in any unmediated way.[10]

The closest example Pannenberg can find in Scripture is in Exodus 3 where God shares his name with Moses, but even this according to Pannenberg is not a clear example of a present and direct self-revelation of God.

> God's announcement of his name has been thought of by some to be a direct self-revelation. Thus Karl Barth (Ch.Dog I/I, pp. 363ff). . . . This interpretation seems plausible, because to ancient man the name is nothing purely outward, and the essence itself lives in the name of the person or thing. . . . But the significance of the name-given in Exodus 3 is not that henceforth the essence of God will be fully known to the Israelites. . . . In this respect, it is noteworthy that Jahweh's answer to Moses' concern about his name did, in effect, dodge the question . . . and [in Exod 6 the giving of the name] . . . is immediately followed by a reference to knowledge of Yahweh only to be had in the future (6:7). The giving of the name in such a passage can hardly be classed as an example of full self-revelation.[11]

In this context, Israel will know who God is through what God does in terms of Israel's exodus from Egypt. In fact, one quickly loses count of how many times in the Hebrew Scriptures God is defined as the one who rescues his people from Egypt. This is particularly evident in the Old Testament Psalms: Psalm 66:5–7; Psalm 135:8; and Psalm 136:10–22.

10. Pannenberg, *Revelation as History*, 12, 10.

11. Pannenberg, *Basic Questions in Theology*, 13.

It is in examples like this that Pannenberg sees the essence of biblical revelation and a view of revelation that he wants to develop.

> Instead of a direct self-revelation of God, the facts at this point indicate a conception of indirect self-revelation as a reflex of his activity in history. The totality of his speech and activity, the history brought about by God, shows who he is in an indirect way. . . .
>
> Every activity and act of God can indirectly express something about God. It can say that God is the one who does this or that. . . .
>
> As acts of God, these acts cast light back on God himself, communicating something indirectly about God himself.[12]

## Universal History

As Pannenberg explains, however, these historical events of revelation cannot be isolated from history as a whole, they find their place and significance in the overall historical process, in what Pannenberg likes to call "universal history" a history that embraces all. These events of revelation are therefore like the significant parts of an overall story. But it is only in the context of the surrounding story that the meaning of any event in the story can be fully understood. This historical revelation that Scripture witnessed to will ultimately need to include the whole of the historical process, that being universal history.

As I am sure you have realized (and this is a point not lost on Pannenberg) in examining the nature of biblical revelation and seeing it as an indirect self-revelation of God, we are getting closer and closer to Hegel's philosophy. As Pannenberg explains, "when the totality of reality in its temporal development is thought of as history and as the self-communication of God, then we find ourselves on the road which German idealism has taken . . . for . . . Hegel gave systematic formulation to the conception of universal history as an indirect revelation of God."[13]

## Biblical Theologian

When I first read about Hegel he was always presented as a thinker who let himself get carried away with philosophical speculation and was the last

12. Pannenberg, *Basic Questions in Theology*, 13, 16.

13. Pannenberg, *Basic Questions in Theology*, 16.

person you would have thought of as in any sense biblical. But Pannenberg would fundamentally disagree. What we have found in Scripture in terms of God's indirect revelation in history is what we have found being developed in Hegel's philosophy. Pannenberg explains when discussing Hegel's idea of Gods revelation in history (a view also shared by his old roommate Shelling) "They all wished to use this conception as validation of the biblical tradition and its way of thinking."[14]

The revolutionary significance of this approach to revelation can only be fully grasped when we remember how it contrasts with the opposite tendency in so much modern theology.

## Contrast to Modern Theology

In post-Reformation Protestant theology there has been a move to emphasize the present over and against the past, the direct rather than the indirect and mediated, the individual rather than the corporate, the internal (subjective) rather than the external (objective and public). Pannenberg, with the help of biblical scholarship and the philosophy of Hegel, has developed a theology of revelation that has clearly moved in the opposite direction in contrast to most other modern theology.

In fact, one theme that we have seen running through all of Hegel's thought is the importance of mediation, the indirect nature of all we know. Indeed, this was the major point Hegel was making against the philosophies of his day, that they had not recognized that our knowledge is always indirect and mediated. Later we saw Hegel making the same point against the theologies of experience that he encountered whether that be in Pietism or in the theology of Schleiermacher. That knowledge of God must also be seen as something indirect and mediated; this is also what is most distinctive about Pannenberg's approach to revelation.

If we see in Pannenberg the beginnings of this move from the individual interior to historical hope it becomes even clearer when we turn to his friend and onetime colleague Moltmann.

14. Pannenberg, *Basic Questions in Theology*, 17.

# 27

# BIBLICAL MARXISM

## Eschatological Salvation

IN ORDER TO BEGIN to understand any idea, it is vital to keep it within its rightful context. A simple phrase like "a star is born" taken out of context can radically change its meaning. If originally used by an astronomer seeing a new light in the night sky it clearly refers to heavenly bodies. If taken out of that context and used in show business, it can mean something completely different.

It can be argued that this has happen when talking about the Christian belief in salvation. For the original context in which the doctrine of salvation developed is an eschatological one. Yet over time it has been taken out of that context and can be seen to have changed its meaning.

To see this point, we need note that the Judaism that Christianity emerged from was shaped by eschatological expectations. In this context the term "eschatology" means much more than what you might find in dictionary definitions of the word.

The eschatology that characterized the first-century Judaism that Jesus and the first apostles were familiar with was primarily a theology of hope. In the words of the Lord's Prayer it was the hope that "one day God's will would be done on earth as it is in heaven." That a world that had departed from God's will would be bought back into harmony with his will and purpose again. That the evil that had torn apart God's creation would be vanquished, and God would renew his creation. In the words of the New Testament apocalypse (a term closely related to eschatology) that there would be a new firmament (heaven or sky) and a new earth where God would dwell with his creation.[1]

## Resurrection Kingdom

Two of the key ideas in the New Testament that express this eschatological hope, inherited from Judaism, are the coming of a kingdom of God and the resurrection of the dead.

Kingdom of God is a phrase used over a hundred times in the first three Gospels and most commonly on the lips of Jesus. It is defined by Jesus in the words we have already used from the Lord's Prayer that when the kingdom of God comes God's will will be done on earth as it is done in heaven (where God is). That God's justice and righteousness will one day reign in this world. Just to note here in passing there is nothing in this theme about a spiritual part of us going somewhere else beyond this world. The kingdom of God in that sense is not otherworldly.

The other belief that was central to the New Testament and had also come from the Judaism that Jesus and his followers had be nurtured in was belief in a bodily resurrection of the dead at the end of time. This is the belief that to be part of a renewed world when the kingdom came, we would need to be bodily renewed or recreated to be part of that new creation.

Notice again that resurrection is not focused on the spirit or soul but on the *body*. God's kingdom and resurrection are both ways in which the world and those who live in it are to be renewed.

It is within this context that the Christian idea of salvation is born. Salvation is ultimately achieved, for this form of Judaism and for the first Christians, when these eschatological things happen. Salvation is when the kingdom comes and when God's will is done in the new creation. From the very beginning, salvation had this future orientation. It is eschatological, it is eschatology. As the New Testament scholar Tom Wright says, "'Salvation' encapsulates the entire future Hope. For first-century Jews it could only mean the inauguration of the age to come."[2] And as the New Testament scholar Greg Beale puts it, "Every aspect of their salvation was to be conceived of as eschatological in nature."[3] So, for the apostle Paul it is quite natural to see salvation as fundamentally a future reality, for as he comments to the church in Rome, "For salvation is nearer to us now than when

1. Rev 21.
2. Wright, *New Testament and the People of God*, 300.
3. Beale, *The Eschatological Conception of New Testament Theology*, 18.

we became believers."[4] As the New Testament scholar James D. G. Dunn concludes, "it becomes clear beyond question, if it was not already so, that Salvation for Paul is something future, essentially an eschatological good, something still awaited, it's wholeness belongs to the not yet."[5] In fact, in some Gospel passages salvation and entry into the eschatological kingdom are synonymous. In the story of the conversation between Jesus and the rich young man, the phrases "to inherit eternal life," "to enter the kingdom of God" and "to be saved" appear to be used with reference to the same thing.[6] From this perspective all that is known of salvation now is just a small taste of what is to come.[7]

## Back in Context

This original eschatological context has so often been forgotten about or overlooked. Central New Testament themes like the kingdom of God, resurrection, and salvation have been removed from their original setting and made to mean something very different, therefore shifting Christianity towards a different orientation. For example, the first Christians would not know what to make of the Spiritual that says "This world is not my home, I'm just a passing through / My treasures are laid up somewhere beyond the blue / The angels beckon me from heaven's open door / and I can't feel at home in this world any more." For they believed this world was their home and they were not just passing through, and heaven was not some other place beyond the blue but rather a world made new.

As I read Moltmann's work I get the impression that on almost every other page he is trying to reorientate us back to that way of thinking. He is trying to change the direction that Christian faith has been facing and get it back to its original outlook. He is wanting to put the major doctrines of the faith, like salvation, back into their original context. Having done that, he is wanting to think through the implication of this for the church and the faith. He is moving, like Pannenberg, away from an individual interior faith back to a historical hope.

4. Rom 13:1 (NRSVA).

5. Dunn, *Theology of Paul the Apostle*, 471.

6. Luke 18:24–26 (NRSVA).

7. Rom 8:24; 1:4; 9:28; 1 Pet 1:5, 9 (NRSVA).

## Mountains Passed Me By

In doing this, he comes across a form of Hegel's philosophy in Western Marxism that resonates with eschatology. In fact, it may be Moltmann's dialogue with Marxism that gets him reexamining the roots of his faith and rediscovering eschatology in the first place. What he comes across is the thought of the East German Marxist philosopher Ernst Bloch and his three-volume work *The Principle of Hope*. As he writes,

> I read it [*The Principle of Hope*] in 1960 while I was on holiday. . . . [T]he beauty of the Swiss mountains passed me by unnoticed. . . . The whole book is shot through and through by "the eschatological conscience that came into the World through the Bible." (German ed 240). Bloch is the only German philosopher for centuries who quotes the Bible extensively and knowledgeably, and in his own way proves himself to be a good theologian of what he calls 'the religion of the Exodus and the kingdom." Talking about the forward-thrusting hope, he writes, "All Christians know it in their own way from the Exodus and the messianic part of the Bible, be it with a sleeping conscience or profoundly touched" (German ed 17). In 1960 I by no means had the impression that we are aware of this biblical message or that this forward hope is something in which we can find ourselves. So I set out to search for this theology of hope.[8]

But why was it that Ernst Block could bring together so naturally aspects of Marxist thought and biblical eschatology? The obvious answer is that Marxism had inherited this biblical orientation from Hegel. So deep-rooted within Marxism was the historical hope of early Christianity. It was Hegel, inspired by his Christian faith, who saw (almost for the first time in the West) the priority of history over against the otherworldliness of Platonism and with it the importance of historical change and development. Without this revolutionary philosophical insight, the birth of Marxism is virtually inconceivable. The philosophical theologian William Carry sees the torso of Western culture as standing on two legs: one leg rooted in Athens, the other in Jerusalem. Much Western thought, up until Hegel, had been leaning heavily on the Athenian leg. With Hegel the other leg takes the lead, the one rooted in Jerusalem and its biblical hope.

8. Moltmann, *Broad Place*, 79.

## Theology of Hope

In Moltmann's search for this *Theology of Hope* he insists on the eschatological character of the biblical faith and the hope of the first Christians. As he writes, "My intention with the *Theology of Hope* was to give back to Christianity its authentic hope for the World." He sums up what he finds in Scripture when he says, "The promissory history of the Old Testament and the gospel history of the new point beyond themselves to the coming Kingdom of God, and belong together in the common reference to the future in which 'the Scriptures are fulfilled.'"[9]

But this is of course revolutionary because:

> hope for an alternative future brings us into contradiction with the existing present and the people who cling to it. The contradiction to existing reality into which the Christian hope brings believers is nothing other than the contradiction out of which this hope itself was born: The contradiction between the world of the resurrection and the world in the shadow of the cross. If we had before our eyes only what we see, then we should come to terms with things as they simply are, either cheerfully or unwillingly. The fact that we don't come to terms with them is the unquenchable spark of hope for the fullness of life, for righteousness and justice on the new Earth, and for the Kingdom of God? That keeps us unreconciled, restless and open for God's great day.[10]

What is central to this hope in the New Testament is the resurrection of Jesus. "Without the coming Kingdom of God's glory and the eternal life of the future world, God's raising of Jesus has no significance, but without his raising, the hope of Christians has no Christian foundation either."[11]

## Pannenberg and Moltmann Converge

Even though Pannenberg was far more politically conservative than Moltmann their eschatological reconfiguring of theology was very similar. As Pannenberg remarked, "Moltmann's renewal of the eschatological theme converges very largely with my ideas."[12] They were even colleagues for a time. Moltmann explains, "Pannenberg was my colleague at the Wuppertal

9. Moltmann, *Broad Place*, 81.

10. Moltmann, *Broad Place*, 103.

11. Moltmann, *Broad Place*, 102.

12. Moltmann, *Broad Place*, 106.

Seminary from 1959 to 1961. . . . We were not unknown to each other, and we had exchanged theological ideas. Consequently, in periodicals and newspapers we were later often made jointly responsible for the new eschatological orientation of Protestantism. . . . We both, each in his own way, tried to do theology in the light of *Christ's resurrection*."[13]

13. Moltmann, *Broad Place*, 106.

# 28

# FROM EXISTENTIALISM TO HOPE

## *The Philosophical Revolution*

In Moltmann and Pannenberg we are not only seeing two late-twentieth-century theologians who, in contrast to their predecessors, were claiming that their theology was based directly on biblical studies, we are also witnessing a major intellectual paradigm shift.

This major shift from the intellectual dominance of existentialism to the dominance of Hegel and Marx was a change that was to be of great significance for theology. For example, the theologies of the Word in their different forms had not only overtly flirted with existentialism but had, in some cases, become fully engaged and been off enjoying their honeymoon! It has been common to suggest that this was true only of Karl Barth's early dialectical theology in the 1920s when Barth was particularly influenced by Danish philosopher and proto-existentialist Kierkegaard. However, as we saw this clear distinction between Barth's early work and his mature *Dogmatics* has for some time been called into question.

To recap: Like so much in post-Kantian continental philosophy, existentialism grew out of the crisis thrown up by the Enlightenment. Particularly the way in which a new scientific outlook threatened human freedom and self-determination.

In James Livingston's crystal-clear two-volume survey of modern historical theology he proposes that since the Enlightenment existentialism has fundamentally been a "critique of rational objectivity." Straightaway we recognize a very familiar theme. As Livingston explains,

> what is wrong with a narrowly objective approach to life (that we have seen as paramount to the 18th century age of reason)

> is that it denies freedom of choice and self-determination. From the scientific point of view everything can be explained deterministically within the cause-effect nexus—But when a person no longer considers her or himself to be self-determining in some important respects, that person comes to view her or himself as a mere product of the environment and loses any sense of individuality; the person becomes other-directed and inauthentic. But deep in the human spirit is a consciousness that one is self-determining and responsible. We know that we do make ourselves by our own free choices. No matter how hard we try to escape, we know that we must live with this awful burden of freedom.[1]

This is the same prioritizing of human freedom we have seen in Kant against the objectifying tendencies of eighteenth-century Enlightenment science.

> What the existentialists distrust about so-called objective reflection is, in the words of Kierkegaard, that it "makes the subject accidental and thereby transforms his Existence into something impersonal, and this impersonal character is precisely its objective validity." But all significant knowledge must, in the existentialist's view, pose the question "What does this knowledge mean for me?" . . .
>
> For . . . there are many questions (and existentially the most significant) that belie logical or empirical resolution and demand the risk of personal decision. What is more, it is not enough that one knows the objective truth but that it be made existentially one's own.[2]

Kierkegaard applied this particularly to Christian faith as Livingston concludes, "A person can believe Christianity is the truth and yet remain personally aloof from it. 'Truth,' as Kierkegaard said, 'consists precisely in inwardness.' . . . Is it not true that we can only know what it means to love, trust, and die by actually loving and trusting and dying? 'One becomes a theologian,' remarked Luther, 'by living, dying, and by being damned—not by understanding, reading, and speculating.'"[3]

The influence of Kierkegaard is particularly relevant since not only were Kierkegaard's writings seminal for twentieth-century religious existentialism but Kierkegaard developed his Christian philosophy in reaction

1. Livingston, *Modern Christian Thought*, 135.
2. Livingston, *Modern Christian Thought*, 135.
3. Livingston, *Modern Christian Thought*, 135.

to Hegel's all-encompassing, and for Kierkegaard, suffocating system of thought.

## Existentialist Theology

Barth also had important associates in his early dialectical days. One was a leading New Testament scholar who would become a theologian of some note in his own right. Rudolf Bultmann started out in the company of Barth but over time their differences became more and more apparent. For Bultmann it was not so much Kierkegaard who was his philosophical inspiration but rather Bultmann's friend and colleague Martin Heidegger. Bultmann's liaison with existentialism was fully acknowledged. As he writes, "the work of existential philosophy, which I came to know through my discussions with Martin Heidegger, became of decisive significance for me. I found here the concepts through which it became possible to speak adequately of human existence and therefore also of the existence of the believer."[4]

## Too Private and Personal

Pannenberg and Moltmann, who had been students when the influence of existentialism on theology was at its peak, became increasingly disillusioned. Moltmann, who had been initially interested in existentialism, came to believe that it had little, if anything, to say to the pressing social and political concerns of his day. In their eye's existentialism was over—prioritizing the individual's faith and that faith had become of purely private and personal concern not dissimilar to certain forms of Pietism. As Moltmann comments,

> In 1951 I heard Rudolf Bultmann give his lecture . . . ["Forms of Human Community"] . . . in which he rejected social legislation because it deprived the rich of the virtue of giving and the poor the virtue of gratitude. That put an end to my interest in his existential theology. . . . In 1957 [we] . . . tried to gain Bultmann's support for our campaign "Fight Atomic Death." Bultmann refused, because for him faith was "a private matter" and could have nothing to do with politics.[5]

4. Bultmann, in Kegley, *Theology of Rudolf Bultmann*, 24.

5. Moltmann, *Broad Place*, 50.

## Existentialism Crumbles . . . Revolution Ignites!

Some observers found this radical shift from Heidegger and existentialism to Hegel and Marx breathtaking. Joseph Ratzinger (who was to become Pope Benedict XVI) writing about teaching theology at the university of Tübingen (where Hegel and his friends had once studied theology and where Moltmann was professor of systematic theology from 1967 until his retirement in 1994) gives this account:

> Almost at a stroke, the philosophical "paradigm" on which students and some of their teachers based their thinking changed. Whereas up to then Bultmann's theology and Heidegger's philosophy had determined the framework of thinking, now the existentialist pattern broke down almost overnight, and was replaced by the Marxist one. Ernst Bloch [the Marxist Philosopher who had inspired Moltmann] was now teaching in Tübingen and belittled Heidegger as a petty bourgeois. In the Protestant theological faculty, Jürgen Moltmann was invited to a chair, almost at the same time I came to Tübingen myself. In his fascinating book *Theology of Hope* he had conceived of theology afresh and completely, in the light of Bloch. Existentialism crumbled away and in the whole university the Marxist revolution took fire and shook it to its foundations. Years before, one could have expected that the theological faculties would be a bulwark against the Marxist temptation. Now the opposite was the case: they became the real ideological centre.[6]

Moltmann's *Theology of Hope* became a major influence on Latin American liberation theology, to the point where the first book of liberation theology by Gustavo Gutiérrez, *A Theology of Liberation: History, Politics, and Salvation,* has numerous references to Moltmann's theology of hope throughout the text.

## Marxist Ideology?

Some readers of *Theology of Hope* complained that it is more Marxist than Christian: "Moltmann precedes in the most scandalous way from Marxist -Leninist ideas, which he 'presses into service for the Christian model of the future.'"[7]

6. Moltmann, *Broad Place*, 162.
7. Moltmann, *Broad Place*, 111.

However, I wonder if this complaint is just missing the point. If Christianity is fundamentally a revolutionary hope for a coming new age, then there is surely going to be some overlap with Marxism. If this is the case it will be virtually impossible to disentangle the roots of one from the other. It may be that when people complain that Moltmann's theology is too Marxist ironically, they may in fact simply be complaining that Moltmann's theology was too influenced by the revolutionary hope of biblical eschatology.

Moltmann and Pannenberg were also in agreement in their concern that this eschatological orientation to Jesus' preaching and the gospel message was, over the centuries, either ignored or more often reinterpreted to fit a philosophy of very different orientation. This change may be seen when the present and future world witnessed to in the New Testament are rapidly replaced by a corrupt material world below, and a perfect spiritual realm above, seen in Christian forms of Platonism. Moltmann believed this disingenuous reinterpretation was not just a thing of the past but was something he was witnessing in his teachers' and colleagues' theology.

## Kant Still Dominating Debate

In Moltmann's first book, *Theology of Hope,* Moltmann looks critically at how the great theologians of his day treat eschatology. He first notes how their approach to God's revelation ignores any eschatological dimension. Taking as an example Barth and Bultmann, Moltmann comments, "Revelation does not . . . open the future in terms of promise, not does it have any future that would be greater than itself, but the revelation of God is then the coming of the eternal to Man or the coming of Man to himself."[8] Intriguingly he traces this dominant interpretation back to Kant. (If you didn't know Kant's philosophy, this lengthy and important discussion of contemporary theology in Moltmann's first book would be a closed book.) "The classical philosophical form of . . . eschatology is found in Immanuel Kant. Its basic features recur wherever Kantian thinking is found in the revelation theology of modern times."[9]

In Kant's view, the things of God (in fact all metaphysics) are beyond our objective and conceptual knowledge. Objective knowledge is restricted to what we can receive from sense experience. Consequently, any talk of eschatology will also be out of bounds and so will any eschatologically orientated theology. "If the . . . [eschatological events] . . . are supra-sensible and as such beyond all possibility of knowledge, then eschatological

8. Moltmann, *Theology of Hope*, 45.

9. Moltmann, *Theology of Hope*, 46.

perspectives are in turn also completely irrelevant for the knowledge of the world of experience."[10]

Kant questioned, as he did with all the things of God, whether we could have any real knowledge of eschatology. "There can be no such thing as an intellectual knowledge of the 'last things', since these 'objects' . . . lie wholly beyond our field of vision. 'It is therefore idle to 'brood over what they are in themselves and in essence'. Taken as particular objects accessible to the intellect, they are 'wholly void'. No provable and convincing knowledge of them can be attained."[11]

However, this did not mean that Kant had nothing to say about eschatology. It just meant that, for Kant, these things could not be spoken about in the same way we talk about objects in the natural world. Yet for Kant the mechanistic world of the natural sciences is not the whole story, there is a reality beyond our sense experience that the sciences, for example, cannot capture or objectify. Within Kantian thought we need to realize that we encounter that other world in a wholly different way. We can only talk about it as a consequence of our convictions about what is right and wrong, of justice and injustice, what Kant calls practical reason, in contrast to the pure reason of the natural sciences. As Moltmann comments when explaining Kant's approach "In moral action man gets 'beyond the mechanism of blindly working causes' 'into an order of things totally other than that of a mechanism of nature."[12] "He attains to the non-objective, not-objectifiable realm of freedom and of ability to be a self."[13] It is in these terms that eschatology has some meaning for Immanuel Kant. "So, Eschatology is not . . . to be considered 'void' in every respect. For what the intellect finds itself certainly bound to dismiss as null and void, acquires through the practical reason a significance of its own that is highly existential, namely moral."[14]

## Barth and Bultmann

Moltmann argues that, rather than challenging Immanuel Kant's interpretation of eschatology, the theologians of his day had largely accepted Kant's approach. As Moltmann explains: "Karl Barth gave one of the reasons for the complete recasting of his commentary on Romans in the second edition of 1921 as the fact that he was indebted to his brother Heninrich Barth

10. Moltmann, *Theology of Hope*, 46.
11. See Kant's *Das Ende aller Dinge* in Moltmann, *Theology of Hope*, 46.
12. Moltmann, *Theology of Hope*, 46.
13. Moltmann, *Theology of Hope*, 48.
14. Moltmann, *Theology of Hope*, 48.

for "better acquaintance with the real orientation of the ideas of Plato and Kant" . . .

> It will be owing to this influence [of Kant] that the eschatology which in the first edition of 1919 was not unfriendly towards dynamic and cosmic perspectives retreated from now on into the background of Barth's thinking, and that early dialectical theology set to work in terms of the dialectic of time and eternity and came under the bane of the . . . eschatology of Kant.[15]

The dialectical theology that Karl Barth first became famous for does not perceive eschatology in terms of any historical process or incident. Rather it is seen as a paradoxical non-objective meeting of time and eternity, an event or moment in the present that cannot be captured. As Moltmann explains for Barth the "eschaton became the transcendental boundary of time and eternity. Being the transcendent meaning of all moments, the eternal 'Moment' it can be compared with no moment in time."[16]

A good example of this eschatological reinterpretation is when Barth comes to comment on the already-visited Romans 18:12: "the hour is nearer now than when we first believed." The idea that Paul is talking about something happening in the future, on Karl Barth's interpretation disappeared. "Of the real end of history, it may be said is any time; The end is near!"[17]

When later Barth comes to writing his church dogmatics he realizes that he has not taken the future sense of this verse seriously, so when writing about this bible verse again he says, "It showed that although I was confident to treat the beyondness of the coming Kingdom with absolute seriousness, I had no such confidence in relation to its coming as such."[18] Moltmann points out that even though Karl Barth recognized that he had not understood the force of this Bible verse correctly, this did not affect Karl Barth's a-temporal approach to revelation. "Can the impression then be allowed to stand that the self-revelation of God means the 'pure presence of God' an 'eternal presence of God in time,' 'present without any future.'"[19]

15. Moltmann, *Theology of Hope*, 46, 50.
16. Moltmann, *Theology of Hope*, 51.
17. Moltmann, *Theology of Hope*, 51.
18. Moltmann, *Theology of Hope*, 57.
19. Moltmann, *Theology of Hope*, 57.

## Bultmann

Moltmann in his *Theology of Hope* then turns to another major voice in theology of the time that being the existentialist theologian Bultmann.

Moltmann argues that, like Barth, Bultmann has also accepted Kant's philosophical approach and has likewise structured his theology in the light of Kant's philosophy. Further he argues that in doing this you can follow the direct influences of Barth and Bultmann's teacher the neo-Kantian theologian Wilhelm Herrmann. As Herrmann explains,

> Revelation is not instruction. . . . Revelation of God cannot be objectively explained, but it can certainly be experienced in man's own self. Namely, in the non-objectifiable subjectivity of the dark, defenceless depths in which we live the moment of involvement. The revealing of God in his working upon ourselves is therefore as unfathomable, as non-derivable, as much grounded in itself as the living of life, which no one can explain, but everyone can experience.[20]

As Moltmann argues, "his Kantian heritage had taken it to be self-evident that revelation cannot be objectively grounded, proved to the theoretic reason. The non-unjustifiability of God and the non-unjustifiability of each peculiar existence or each peculiar 'self' constituted one and the same mystery for him."[21]

Moltmann sees in Bultmann's thought an existential variation on this theme. "Of Herrmann's basic principles, the most outstanding in the theology of Bultmann is the exclusive relation to existence, or self, of all statements about God and his action."[22] Bultmann did not deny the eschatological character of the New Testament. He fully recognized it. What he objected to was the idea that we could accept such a primitive apocalyptic outlook in the modern world. In his terms it needed to be demythologized. The experience that the New Testament testifies to is to be taken seriously but not the end time worldview that accompanies it. The eschatological crisis and transformation that the New Testament talks about should be applied to the individual but not to the cosmos as a whole. It was therefore not an objective transformation of history but rather a subjective transformation for the self. "Eschatology has wholly lost its sense as goal of history and is in fact understood as the goal of the individual human being, it is therefore

20. Moltmann, *Theology of Hope*, 52.
21. Moltmann, *Theology of Hope*, 53.
22. Moltmann, *Theology of Hope*, 59.

just as impossible for Bultmann as for Kant that eschatology should provide a doctrine of the last things in the world process."[23]

Moltmann believes that this also structures Bultmann's approach to revelation "The . . . framework of [Kant's] . . . subjectivity also dominates Bultmann's understanding of revelation, the revelation of God is accordingly a matter of man's coming to himself, truly understanding yourself. Revelation means that opening of what is hidden which is absolutely necessary or decisive for man if he is to achieve 'salvation' or 'authenticity.'"[24]

In this Bultmann also exemplifies what we have talked about in terms of the pendulum moving from the past to the present in modern theology's understanding of the nature of God's revelation.

> Revelation in this sense is the event of preaching and faith. The preaching is itself revelation and does not merely speak about it. It is only in faith that the object of faith is disclosed, therefore faith itself belongs to revelation. Not in what the word of proclamation says or in what it points to, but in the fact that it "happened," addressing, accosting, appealing lies the event of revelation. What is then revealed nothing at all so far as the quest for revelation is a quest for doctrines, but everything, so far is man has his eyes open regarding himself and can understand himself again.[25]

The dualism that Immanuel Kant set up between an objective scientific world of cause and effect and a hidden world of human subjective freedom which cannot be objectified, seems to structure the whole approach.

> Statements of scripture arrived out of existence and that are addressed to existence have not to be justified themselves at the forum of an objectifying science of nature and history since the later does not even set eyes on the non-objectifiable existence of man . . .
>
> Both God and the human self-belong to the characteristic of non-objectifiableability. The closed system of cause and effect in the discernible, explicable, objectively demonstrable world of things is there for set aside. "In faith the closed web presented or produced by objective observation is transcended . . . when it [faith] speaks of the activity of God.[26]

23. Moltmann, *Theology of Hope*, 62.
24. Moltmann, *Theology of Hope*, 65.
25. Moltmann, *Theology of Hope*, 66.
26. Moltmann, *Theology of Hope*, 60–61.

So the strict limits that Kant put on any knowledge of the things of God have been accepted, and with it the implications for any eschatology. Any talk of eschatology now must be based on what cannot be objectified.

Jürgen Moltmann also traces this distinction between the objective and subjective back to its origins in the Enlightenment. In the face of an increasingly secularized cosmos with its burgeoning mechanistic science, religion had turned away from the objective world into the subjective self:

> Ever since the scientific and historical Enlightenment, what theology says, thinks and proclaims about the action of God has been directed evermore strongly to that subjectivity of man which was given a free rein precisely by the secularization of the world affected by the Enlightenment. . . .
>
> Inasmuch as this subjectivity understands itself as the incomprehensible immediacy of our existence, it is attained by distinguishing itself from the non-self, from the world of observable, calculable and disposable things and of our own objectifications.[27]

## Hegel to the Rescue

When writing this section on Hegel, I planned to discuss Pannenberg and Moltmann at the end, knowing that Hegel had some influence on them, but I was surprised by how much of an influence that was. In rereading Moltmann's *Theology of Hope* I was taken aback by the fact that when Moltmann responds to the twentieth-century theologians who in Moltmann's opinion have been captivated by Kant (for example Karl Barth and Bultmann) Moltmann seems to be doing a remarkable impression of Hegel! It is a response that could have been taken straight out of the *Phenomenology of Spirit*. In fact, you sense that the debate you're getting between these twentieth-century theologians is really an ongoing debate taking place between Immanuel Kant and Frederick Hegel.

For example, the view of the self as distinct from the world that Moltmann believes these twentieth-century theological existentialist are working with is on Hegel's account philosophically naive. Hegel argues repeatedly that we can only get a clear understanding of ourselves and our own subjectivity through our engagement with the world and with others, a key insight which Hegel gave to modern anthropology.

27. Moltmann, *Theology of Hope*, 63, 64.

This same insight is exactly what we get from Moltmann when critiquing his Kantian theological forebears. It is hard to believe that these words are Moltmann's not Hegel's:

> Only in his out going towards the World does man experience himself. Without objectification no experience of oneself is possible. Always man's self-understanding is socially, materially and historically mediated. An immediate self-consciousness and a non-Dialectical identity with himself is not possible to man. . . .
>
> Thus, he does not find himself in the air, between God and the World, but he finds himself along with the World in the process to which the way is open by the eschatological promise of Christ.[28]

Well, thank you Moltmann for such a neatly expressed summary of Hegel's philosophy of the self! In fact, if you put Moltmann's words in a Google search you will open up articles about Hegel's philosophy and the Marxist approach to anthropology. I will say no more!

Following this Moltmann gives a word-perfect example of Hegel's philosophy of history, including all the main themes of dialectic, synthesis, the Spirit working through its historical forms and the priority of history as a universal category.

> A new concept of the cosmos in terms of natural science obscures reality as history; while on the other hand human existence pales to an ineffable, solitary subjectivity, which must flee all contact with reality and all concessions towards it in order to abide by itself.
>
> This cleavage into objectification and subjectivity is not to be escaped nor can theology escape it in bringing the gospel to the modern world-by declaring one side of this kind of thinking to be vain, deficient, corrupt and decadent. . . . Rather, theology will have to take the hardened antitheses and make them fluid once more, to mediate in the contraction between them and reconcile them. That, however, is only possible when the *category of history*, which drops out in this dualism, is rediscovered in such a way that it does not deny the antithesis in question but spans it and understands it as an element in an advancing process. The revelation of God can neither be presented within the framework of the reflective philosophy of transcendental subjectivity, for which history is reduced to the "mechanism" of a closed system of causes and effects. . . .

28. Moltmann, *Theology of Hope*, 69, 50.

> Rather, the essential thing will be to make these abstract products of the modern denial of history fluid once more, and to understand them as forms assumed in history by the Spirit in the course of an eschatological process which is kept in hope and in motion by the promise grounded in the cross and resurrection of Christ.
>
> The condition of possible experience which were understood by Kant in a transcendental sense must be understood instead as historically flowing conditions. It is not that time at a standstill is the category of history, but the history which is experienced from the eschatological future of the truth is the category of time.[29]

Moltmann clearly believes that without this Hegelian revival of historical consciousness in opposition to Kant's philosophy of the self it is inconceivable, in the modern world, to think eschatologically.

> It is not possible to speak of believing existence in hope and in radical openness, and at the same time consider the world to be a mechanism or self-contained system of cause and effect in objective antithesis to man. Hope then fades away to the hope of the solitary soul in the prison of a petrified world and becomes an expression of gnostic longing for redemption. . . .
>
> Without cosmic eschatology there can be no assertion of an eschatological existence of man. Christian eschatology therefore cannot reconcile itself with a Kantian concept of science and reality.[30]

Not only is the resurrection of Jesus central to Moltmann's theology, equally important it seems is the resurrection of Hegel!

If Pannenberg and Moltmann mirror Hegel in the priority they give to history, they do the same when it comes to Hegel's philosophy of religion. Just as history is the key category for Hegel's philosophy, Trinity is central for Hegel's philosophy of religion.

29. Moltmann, *Theology of Hope*, 50.

30. Moltmann, *Theology of Hope*, 69.

# 29

# TRINITARIAN THINKING

IF THERE IS ONE feature that has distinguished theology since the 1970s it is a revival in trinitarian theology. This is not only a general revival in trinitarian thought it is also a revival of a particular form of trinitarian thinking. That of Hegel's trinitarian philosophy.

This is immediately apparent in its central thesis, whereas a classical approach to trinitarian theology defined the trinitarian relationships from above, as it were, in terms of eternal origins. Or to put it another way the Father being unbegotten, the son being begotten of the Father, and the Spirit being sent from the Father and Son. Pannenberg and Moltmann, in contrast, begin trinitarian theology from below. The approach to the Trinity, from above and from eternity, being known as the immanent Trinity, in contrast to the economic Trinity that studies the trinitarian persons role in creation and history.

As the theologian Christian Mostert explains, "The immanent Trinity is the essential deity of God, the God who does not need a cosmos in order to be more fully God. The economic Trinity is God working as the trinitarian Persons in the economy of salvation, with a view to incorporating the cosmos into the glory of God, granting it eternal life, and establishing the rule of God in it through the overcoming of all evil and suffering."[1]

For Hegel and this recent trinitarian revival, the trinitarian relations are established from below in terms of the trinitarian persons' role in creation, revelation, salvation and new creation. In this move we see the prioritizing of the economic Trinity over the immanent Trinity.

> The influence of German idealism (Hegel) on his approach to the doctrine of God is undeniable and is readily admitted by

1. Mostert, *Pannenberg's Eschatological Doctrine of God*, 224.

> Pannenberg himself. He lauds Hegel for re-establishing the centrality of the doctrine of the Trinity to Christian theology. In the classical view, God's historical relations to the world, including the incarnation, appear external to the eternal life of God, making the trinitarian God the God of history only in a secondary sense. By building on Hegel's insight, Pannenberg seeks to provide a corrective to this tendency.[2]

The relationship between God and world then define the Trinity and not the eternal relationship between the trinitarian persons. What happens, for example, in the incarnation, cross, and resurrection come to constitute God's trinitarian life.

## Creation in Embryo

The other side of this story for Hegel was that God's relationship to the world was seen in embryo in the trinitarian relations, a theme that Pannenberg also develops. This is true of creation in the sense that the relationship between Father and Son becomes the pattern for the relationship between God and creation. As Pannenberg explains, "Hegel's thesis is that in the Trinity the Son is the principle of otherness, the starting point for the emergence all of the finite as that which is absolutely other than deity. . . . We find here a productive principle behind the emergence of every new distinction and therefore of every new and different form of finite existence."[3]

When Pannenberg then goes on to explain this trinitarian approach to creation the connection to Hegel could not be more obvious.

> The one God in relation to the World is not wholly different from the action in his trinitarian life. In his actions in relation to the World the trinitarian life turns outward, moves out of itself and becomes the deterministic basis of the relation between the creator and the creatures. . . .
>
> In the son is the origin of all that differs from the Father, and therefore of the creature's independents vis-a-vis the Father. . . .
>
> In this sense we may view the Son's mediation in creation not only as a structural model . . . of the determination of all creaturely being for fellowship with God but by acceptance of its distinction from him, but also as the origin of the existence of creaturely reality.[4]

2. Grenz, *Reason for Hope*, 93.
3. Pannenberg, *Systematic Theology*, 2:28.
4. Pannenberg, *Systematic Theology*, 2:25, 22.

## Salvation in Embryo

This approach, as we also noted in Hegel's work, extends to the whole drama of salvation.

"The developed structure of Gods outward action embraces not only the creation of the world but also the theme of reconciliation, redemption, consummation, that are usually differentiated from creation."[5] As one writer on Pannenberg explains, "the life of the one God is constituted by the complementary but different activity of the three Persons. In the space between the work of the Father and that of the Son and the Spirit the world has its history of glory and misery. The creation is on the way to its full communion with God but also experiences its alienation from God and from its vocation."[6]

Following Hegel's logic this will also include the experience of human suffering.

"In his extreme humiliation in his acceptance of death, Jesus took upon himself the ultimate consequence of his self-distinction from the father and precisely in so doing showed himself to be the son of the father. Nor can the father be thought of as unaffected by the passion of his son if it is true that God is love."[7] "In the tension between the creator's power and powerlessness, in the death of his son and with glorification of both through the Spirit, the triune God takes upon himself the suffering of his creation. In this way God is the God of history and its truth."[8]

## Hegelian Thinking

Pannenberg was not alone in pursuing afresh this central theme of Hegel's philosophy for at pretty much the same time it was being explored by Moltmann, Eberhard Jungle, and Robert Jensen. Therefore after surveying Hegel's philosophy when we hear Moltmann summarizing his trinitarian turn in theology it all sounds very familiar. Talking of the 1980s Moltmann writes:

> I begin this new theological series with a social doctrine of the Trinity. My concern here was to perceive the relationship of sociality in God and to practise a new 'Trinitarian thinking.' By that I meant thinking in relationship to communities, and in

5. Pannenberg, *Systematic Theology*, 2:22.
6. Mostert, *Pannenberg's Eschatological Doctrine of God*, 203.
7. Pannenberg, *Systematic Theology*, 1:314.
8. Mostert, *Pannenberg's Eschatological Doctrine of God*, 203.

> transitions. I wanted to put to an end the old thinking in terms of substances and determining subjects a method which cannot work without dividing and isolating its object. . . .
>
> In Trinitarian thinking, however, substances and relations are equally primary. . . . There are no fixable facts and circumstances; there are only fluid states. All fixations are abstractions from these temporal processes. . . . We do not stand over and against the world in a transcendent relationship to it. But are ourselves a part of the World and belong within its developing processes. . . . I called this generally Trinitarian thinking.[9]

I call it a clear case of Hegelian thinking.

## Parting Company with Hegel

I find it fascinating that even though Pannenberg is the modern theologian most influenced by Hegel's thought he is also one of his most penetrating critics.

There are two highly significant ways in which Pannenberg distances himself from Hegel's conception of the Trinity and consequently from Hegel's thought in general.

One of the most distinctive features of Pannenberg's theology is his insistence that methodologically we need to start theology from below. In contrast to his teacher Barth, Pannenberg became famous for establishing a Christology from below in his most influential book *Jesus: God and Man*. Pannenberg very much follows through on this approach particularly when it comes to formulating his doctrine of the Trinity. Rather than speculating from the perspective of eternity about God's nature and how of necessity it might be triune, and then defining the persons of the Trinity on the basis of these calculations, Pannenberg begins from below with the drama of salvation, particularly Jesus' relationship with his Heavenly Father seen in the Gospel accounts. Therefore, like so much recent trinitarian thought, he insists on starting with the economic Trinity rather than the eternal immanent Trinity.

Pannenberg then points out, at this crucial point, that he is not just following Hegel, for he believes that Hegel does not primarily establish the doctrine of the Trinity by reflecting on how God is revealed in Jesus. Instead Hegel, according to Pannenberg, bases his understanding of the Trinity on a piece of philosophical analysis. Pannenberg believes that this kind of speculative argument for the Trinity first appears in the work of the

9. Moltmann, *Broad Place*, 287.

philosopher Gotthold Lessing (1729–81) and then is developed by Hegel. Hegel, in expanding this theme, argues that for human development into self-consciousness we need something other than ourselves to relate to. Hegel argues that spirit needs something other than itself for it to achieve self-consciousness, it is then this analysis that becomes the basis of Hegel's trinitarian theology. Therefore, according to Pannenberg, this is a trinitarian theology born out of philosophical speculation about a necessary process of development. In these terms Hegel's approached to the Trinity is still starting very much from above and not beginning from the below, from Gods involvement with creation and history in the Spirit and the Son.

> Lessing was the thinker who rediscovered and reasserted the grounding of the Trinity in the concept of spirit as an expression of the self-understanding of God in self-awareness. The doctrine of God which was developed in German idealism on the basis of a philosophy of self-consciousness adopted the thoughts of Lessing and impressively expanded them. In Hegel's philosophy of the absolute Spirit the renewal of the doctrine of the Trinity in terms of self-conscious Spirit took classical form. Hegel was aware that in contrast to contemporary theology he was giving new life to the central dogma of Christianity.[10]

In contrast, Pannenberg argues, "To find a basis for the doctrine of the Trinity we must begin with the way in which Father, Son, and Spirit come on the scene and relate to one another in the event of revelation. Here lies the material justification for the demand that the doctrine of the Trinity must be based on the biblical witness to revelation or on the economy of salvation."[11]

## Bid for Freedom

Finally, we must look at the fundamental way in which Pannenberg distances himself from Hegel's philosophy and theology, this divergence having major implications for his understanding of how the Trinity is conceived.

Here again we see Pannenberg, who is so influenced by Hegel's philosophy, offering an important critique. He argues that not only does Hegel's system constrain and even deny human freedom, a common complaint which we have already observed, but, according to Pannenberg, Hegel's philosophy also puts into question God's own sovereign freedom, in the act

10. Pannenberg, *Systematic Theology*, 1:292.
11. Pannenberg, *Systematic Theology*, 1:304.

of creation and revelation. For Pannenberg sees the relationship between God and the world in Hegel's thought as a relationship that God does not choose. For the bringing into being of the created order for Hegel's God is not a free act of the will but something that happens of necessity. It happens as part of the self-realization of spirit and like the growth of a plant it happens as part of its nature and not as the decision of a will. Therefore, as Pannenberg points out, not only in Hegel's system is human freedom threatened the same problem is mirrored in regard to divine freedom. "The . . . charge that can rightly be made against Hegel . . . is that he derives the coming into being of the World with the logical necessity from the inner life of the divine Trinity. . . . [T]he freedom of the divine act of creation is not taken into account in Hegel."[12] So for Hegel "the World was conceived of as a necessary factor in the self-realization of God."[13]

In contrast, Pannenberg argues, "It is essential for the Christian understanding of God's freedom in his activity as creator that he did not have to create the world out of some inner necessity of his own nature. If he did, he would be dependent in his very essence on the existence of the world. This would be true even if we merely thought of the world as a tiny aspect of is divine self-realization."[14]

As Pannenberg concludes, "The idea that God necessarily brings the World into being . . . did not become the main stumbling block for Christian theology without a most serious reason. But it seems to underlie all other theological objections to Hegel's philosophy."[15]

Again this complaint is about both Divine and human freedom. "Thus, from Hegel's assertion of the logical necessity of the creation of the World . . . it is possible to do justice neither to the divine personality or freedom of man. For both fall victim to the logical necessity with which the divine idea passes over into the world process."[16] So for Pannenberg, "A summary of the criticism to be applied to Hegel's thought might be that the experience of freedom must be thought out much more deeply than it has been in Hegel."[17]

12. Pannenberg, *Systematic Theology*, 1:164.
13. Pannenberg, *Systematic Theology*, 1:168.
14. Pannenberg, *Systematic Theology*, 1:19.
15. Pannenberg, *Basic Questions in Theology*, 3:168.
16. Pannenberg, *Basic Questions in Theology*, 3:168.
17. Pannenberg, *Basic Questions in Theology*, 3:177.

## A Balancing Act

In order to try and achieve this Pannenberg employs an intriguing strategy. He suggests that prior to creation our conception of God should not resemble that of Hegel's. As Pannenberg has made clear, creation is not to be seen as something necessary to God's being. It is not the natural overflowing or development of God's nature, as Hegel would have it. God does not need for any reason to create, for there is perfect fulfilment in the life of the Trinity. So, in a sense, Pannenberg protects God's freedom and does not follow Hegel in restricting God in these terms.

But once there is a creation, according to Pannenberg, things must change. Pannenberg's God begins to resemble Hegel's. For now there is creation, creation can question God's sovereignty and in this sense God is vulnerable.

> Without Lordship over his creation, God would not be God. The act of creation is certainly a product of the freedom of God, but once the World of Creation came into existence, lordship over it becomes the condition and proof of his deity. If the Creation were only the author of the existence of the world but could not achieve lordship over it, we could not call him truly God or indeed Creator in the full sense of the word.[18]

This is most clearly seen in the incarnation, since this is God's way of establishing his kingdom while still respecting our freedom.

> The sending of the Son into the world and the fulfilment of his mission by his death is God's way of actualising his rule in the world without oppression and with respect for the independence of creatures, even on the part of God himself. . . .
>
> With the transferring of his power to the Son who is manifested in Jesus, the Father made his deity dependent on the success of the mission of the Son. Not least of all, then the Father suffers with the suffering of the Son. The rejection that the Son experiences puts the kingship of the Father in question too.[19]

Pannenberg goes so far to see the mission of Christ and the work of the Spirit as the self-actualization of the trinitarian God.

> Since we cannot separate God from his royal lordship, it follows that the irruption of the future of this lordship in the World in the son has as its content the absolute reality of God in and for

18. Pannenberg, *Systematic Theology*, 2:175.

19. Pannenberg, *Systematic Theology*, 2:395, 391.

> the world. Because, however, the sending of the son and the Spirit is from the father, in relation to the fulfillment of the mission by the obedience of the son. We thus may speak of a self-actualization of the trinitarian God in the world.[20]

One helpful assessment of Pannenberg's doctrine of God is the suggestion that he is attempting to find a middle way between Hegel's philosophy and Karl Barth's theology. For Karl Barth, in his theological reaction to the liberal theology of his teachers, put great stress on God's sovereign freedom. And Barth, consequently, would have seen Hegel's understanding of God's necessary relationship to the world epitomizing what he railed against. As Christian Mostert argues,

> These options led to one of two views of the relation between God and the cosmos. Either it sees God as completely "other," beyond (even in opposition to) the world (Barth). Or it sees a self-development in God for which the Cosmos is a necessary condition (Hegel). These two views lead to an extreme emphasis respectively on God's transcendence or God's immanence. Pannenberg steers a course between these extremes.[21]

Therefore, Pannenberg "does not want a God who 'develops' in history; nor a God who is untouched by events in time."[22]

Whether Pannenberg manages to achieve this middle way is of course open to debate, but at the very least it does give some clarification with regard to his inheritance from Hegel. What we can say is that for a number of leading theologians over the last fifty years Hegel has been their most fruitful partner in dialogue, Pannenberg and Moltmann being the two most famous examples of this.

20. Pannenberg, *Systematic Theology*, 2:392.

21. Mostert, *Pannenberg's Eschatological Doctrine of God*, 195.

22. Mostert, *Pannenberg's Eschatological Doctrine of God*, 223.

# Conclusion

## PART OF A BIGGER PICTURE

I HOPE THIS BOOK has proved one point conclusively, that trying to understand modern theology without an awareness of its intellectual and philosophical context is like trying to make sense of a tiny fraction of a much larger picture. I have sometimes seen this on quiz shows, where an item is viewed from an unusual angle and out of its surrounding context. What is so amusing to the audience is then the strange ways in which that fragment is perceived. Without some sense of the whole picture, the whole context, no wonder they can make little sense of what they are trying to understand. My contention has of course been that this is exactly the problem in trying to understand modern theology if isolated from its intellectual context.

One student told me that when they had shown an interest in the intellectual context of modern theology their tutor had told them that they were not studying philosophy, they were studying theology, and so need not delve into those wider issues. No wonder students find it so difficult to grasp what's going on in modern theology and understand its theologians, when they are only allowed to see part of the picture.

Not only is modern philosophy the intellectual context in which modern theology has understandably been forged, but the reverse is also the case. Modern philosophy has itself so often been a response to theological concerns or even a substitute for theology. At times the relationship between the two has been so symbiotic that to make a clear distinction is virtually impossible. What the theologian Nick Adams says about Hegel can be said about much of the philosophy we have surveyed. "The problem is that there is no easy division between the 'philosophical' and 'theological', . . . it is all philosophical, and it is all concerned with God in various ways. There is no 'religious dimension', . . . the work is saturated and permeated with religious concerns."[1]

I hope this book has helped in giving some familiarity with possibly the two most influential philosophers of modernity, Kant and Hegel, and the intellectual and theological debate surrounding their thought, and that by following that debate right up to the present day their importance in the formation of modern theology has become clear.

Roughly speaking we have focused on modernity rather than post-modernity (if you can make a clear distinction that is). To develop the story more explicitly into post-modernity would take at the very least another volume, as I know only too well from my doctoral research. But for now, I wish you well with your further explorations.

1. Adams, *Eclipse*, xviii.

# BIBLIOGRAPHY

Adams, Nicholas. *Eclipse of Grace: Divine and Human Action in Hegel.* Chichester: Wiley-Blackwell, 2013.

Allison, Henry. *Kant's Transcendental Idealism.* London: Yale University Press, 2004.

Ariew, Roger. *Descartes and the Last Scholastics.* New York: Cornell University Press, 1999.

Atkins, Peter. *On Being: A Scientist's Exploration of the Great Questions of Existence.* Oxford: Oxford University Press, 2011. Kindle ed.

Augustine. *Augustine: Earlier Writings.* The Library of Christian Classics. Edited by J. H. S. Burleigh. Philadelphia: Westminster John Knox, 1953.

———. *Augustine's Confessions.* Edited by Henry Chadwick. Oxford: Oxford University Press, 1992.

———. *The Confessions, Saint Augustine.* Oxford World's Classics. Translated by Henry Chadwick. Oxford: Oxford University Press, 2008.

———. "The Soliloquies." In *Augustine: Earlier Writings*, edited by J. H. S. Burleigh, 17–23. The Library of Christian Classics. Philadelphia: Westminster John Knox, 1953.

Barth, Karl. *Church Dogmatics.* Translated by G. W. Bromiley. Peabody: Hendrickson, 2010.

———. *The Epistle to the Romans.* Translated by Edwyn Hoskyns, from the 6th ed. Oxford: Oxford University Press, 1968.

———. *The Gottingen Dogmatics: Instruction in the Christian Religion.* English ed. Grand Rapids: Eerdmans, 1991.

———. *Protestant Theology in the Nineteenth Century.* Grand Rapids: Eerdmans, 2009.

Beale, Greg K. "The Eschatological Conception of New Testament Theology." In *Eschatology in Bible & Theology*, edited by Kent E. Brower and Mark W. Elliott, 11–52. Downers Grove, IL: InterVarsity, 1997.

Beck, Lewis White. "From Leibniz to Kant." In *The Age of German Idealism*, edited by Robert Solomon and Kathleen Higgins, 5–39. Routledge History of Philosophy 6. London: Routledge, 1993.

Beiser, Frederick C. *After Hegel: German Philosophy, 1840–1900.* Princeton: Princeton University Press, 2014. Kindle ed.

———. *The Fate of Reason: German Philosophy from Kant to Fichte.* Harvard: Harvard University Press, 1987.

———. *The Genesis of Neo-Kantianism, 1796–1880.* Oxford: Oxford University Press, 2014.

———. *German Idealism: The Struggle against Subjectivism 1781–1801*. Harvard: Harvard University Press, 2002.

———. *Hegel*. The Routledge Philosophers. Abingdon: Routledge, 2005.

———. "Hegel and the Problem of Metaphysics." In *The Cambridge Companion to Hegel*, edited by Frederick Beiser, 1–25. Cambridge: Cambridge University Press, 1993.

———. "Hegel's Historicism." In *The Cambridge Companion to Hegel*, edited by Beiser, Frederick, 270–301. Cambridge: Cambridge University Press, 1993.

———. "Moral Faith and the Highest Good." In *The Cambridge Companion to Kant and Modern Philosophy*, edited by Paul Guyer, 588–630. Cambridge: Cambridge University Press, 2006.

———. *The Sovereignty of Reason*. Princeton: Princeton University Press, 1996.

Beiser, Frederick, ed. *The Cambridge Companion to Hegel*. Cambridge: Cambridge University Press, 1993.

Bonhoeffer, Dietrich. *Letters and Papers from Prison*. Edited by E. B Eberhard Bethge. Enlarged ed. London: SCM, 1997.

Bradshaw, Timothy. *Pannenberg: A Guide for the Perplexed*. London: T. & T. Clark, 2009.

Brown, Peter. *Augustine of Hippo: A Biography*. Berkeley: University of California Press, 2000.

Buckley, Michael, J. *At the Origins of Modern Atheism*. Yale: Yale University, 1987.

Busch, Eberhard. *Karl Barth: His Life from Letters and Autobiographical Texts*. London: SCM, 1975.

Byrne, Peter. *Kant on God*. Ashgate Studies in the History of Philosophical Theology. Aldershot: Ashgate, 2007.

Chadwick, Henry. *Augustine of Hippo: A Life*. Oxford: Oxford University Press, 2009.

Chapman, Mark. *Ernst Troeltsch and Liberal Theology: Religion and Cultural Synthesis in Wilhelmine Germany*. Christian Theology in Context. Oxford: Oxford University Press, 2001.

Cottingham, John. "The Desecularization of Descartes." In *The Persistence of the Sacred in Modern thought*, edited by Chris Firestone and Nathan A. Jacobs, 15–37. Notre Dame: University Notre Dame Press, 2012.

———. *The Rationalists: A History Western Philosophy*. Oxford: Oxford University Press, 1988.

Cottingham, John, ed. *The Cambridge Companion to Descartes*. Cambridge: Cambridge University Press, 1992.

Crouter, Richard. *Schleiermacher: Between Enlightenment and Romanticism*. Cambridge Studies in Religion & Critical Thought. Cambridge: Cambridge University Press, 2005.

Davidovich, Adina. *Religion as a Province of Meaning: The Kantian Foundations of Modern Theology*. Harvard Theological Studies. Minneapolis: Fortess, 1993.

Dawkins, Richard. *The God Delusion*. London: Bantam, 2006.

———. *River Out of Eden: A Darwinian View of Life*. London: Weidenfeld & Nicolson,2014.

De Nys, Martin. *Hegel and Theology*. Philosophy & Theology. London: T. & T. Clark, 2009.

Descartes, René. *Meditations of First Philosophy*. Cambridge Texts in the History of Philosophy. Edited by John Cottingham. 2nd ed. Cambridge: Cambridge University Press, 1986.

———. *The Philosophical Writings of Descartes.* 2 vols. Edited by John Cottingham et al. Cambridge: Cambridge University Press, 1985.

Desmond, William. *Hegel's God: A Counterfeit Double?* Ashgate Studies in the History of Philosophical Theology. Aldershot: Ashbgate, 2003.

Dickey, Laurence. *Hegel: Religion, Economics, and the Politics of Spirit, 1770–1807.* Cambridge: Cambridge University Press, 1989.

Diller, Kevin. *Theology's Epistemological Dilemma: How Karl Barth and Alvin Plantinga Provide a Unified Response.* Downers Grove, IL: IVP Academic, 2014.

Dorrien, Gary. *The Barthian Revolt in Modern Theology: Theology without Weapons.* Louisville: Westminster John Knox, 1999.

———. *Kantian Reason and Hegelian Spirit: The Idealistic Logic of Modern Theology.* Chichester: Wiley & Sons, 2012. Kindle ed.

Dunn, James D. G. *Romans 9–16.* Word Biblical Commentary 38. Nashville: Nelson, 1988.

———. *The Theology of Paul the Apostle.* Grand Rapids: Eerdmans, 2003.

Eagleton, Terry. *Why Marx Was Right.* Yale: Yale University Press, 2018.

Edwards, B. Davis. "That Isaac Newton's Mechanistic Cosmology Eliminated the Need for God." In *Galileo Goes to Jail and Other Myths about Science and Religion,* edited by Ronald Numbers, 115–23. Harvard: Harvard University Press, 2009.

Emery, Giles. "The Immutability of the God of Love and the Problem of Language Concerning the Suffering of God." In *Divine Impassibility and the Mystery of Human Suffering,* edited by James F. Keating and Thomas Joseph White, 27–77. Grand Rapids: Eerdmans, 2009.

Erdozain, Dominic. "A Heavenly Poise: Radical Religion and the Making of the Enlightenment." In *Narratives of Secularization,* edited by Peter Harrison, 71–97. Abbington: Routledge, 2018.

———. *The Soul of Doubt.* New York: Oxford University Press, 2016. Kindle ed.

Feuerbach, Ludwig. *The Essence of Christianity.* Chapman's Quarterly Series 6. Oak Grove: N.p., 2019. Kindle ed.

Firestone, Chris L., and Nathan Jacobs. *In Defense of Kant's Religion.* Indiana Series in the Philosophy of Religion. Bloomington: Indiana University Press, 2008.

Firestone, Chris L., and Stephen Palmquist, ed. *Kant and the New Philosophy of Religion.* Bloomington: Indiana University Press, 2006.

Garrett, Don. *Hume.*The Routledge Philosophers. New York: Routledge, 2015.

Gillespie, Michael Allen. *Nihilism before Nietzsche.* Chicago: University of Chicago Press, 1995.

———. *The Theological Origins of Modernity.* Chicago: The University of Chicago Press, 2008.

Green, Ronald. *The Hidden Debt: Kierkegaard and Kant.* New York: State University of New York Press, 1992.

———. *Religious Reason: The Rational and Moral Basis of Religious Belief.* New York: Oxford University Press, 1978.

Greer, Thomas. *A Brief History of the Western World.* San Diego: Harcourt Brace Jovanovich, 1982.

Gregory, Brad S. *The Unintended Reformation, How Religious Revolution Secularized Society.* Cambridge: Harvard University Press, 2012.

Grenz, Stanley. *Reason for Hope: The Systematic Theology of Wolfhart Pannenberg.* Grand Rapids: Eerdmans, 2005.

Guyer, Paul. *Kant*. New York: Routledge, 2006.

Guyer, Paul, ed. *The Cambridge Companion to Kant*. Cambridge: Cambridge University Press, 1992.

———. *The Cambridge Companion to Kant and Modern Philosophy*. Cambridge: Cambridge University Press, 2006.

Hackett, Stuart. *The Resurrection of Theism: Prolegomena to Christian Apology*. Eugene, OR: Wipf & Stock, 2009.

Hare, John E. "Kant and the Instability of Atheism." In *Kant and the New Philosophy of Religion*, edited by Chris L. Firestone and Stephen R. Palmquist, 62–78. Bloomington: Indiana University Press.

Harrison, Peter. *The Bible, Protestantism, and the Rise of the Natural Science*. Cambridge: Cambridge University Press, 2001.

Harvey, Van. "Ludwig Feuerbach and Karl Marx." In *Nineteenth-Century Religious Thought in the West*, edited by Ninian Smart et al., 291–329. Cambridge: Cambridge University Press, 1988.

Hart, Trevor. "Revelation." In *The Cambridge Companion to Karl Barth*, edited by John Webster, 37–56. Cambridge: Cambridge University Press, 2000.

Hegel, G. W. *The Encyclopaedia of Logic*. In *The Hegel Reader*, edited by Stephen Houlgate, 127–243. Oxford: Blackwell, 1998.

———. *Hegel's Logic: Being, Part One of the Encyclopaedia of the Philosophical Sciences*. N.p.: Digireads, 2013. Kindle ed.

———. *Introduction to the Philosophy of History*. Hackett Classics. Indianapolis: Hackett, 1988. Kindle ed.

———. *Lectures on the History of Philosophy*. Translated by Ruben Alvarado. N.p.: WordBridge, 2011. Kindle ed.

———. *Lectures on the History of Philosophy: Greek Philosophy to Plato*. Lincoln: University of Nebraska Press, 1995.

———. *Lectures on the Philosophy of Religion*. One-volume Edition. Edited by Peter Hodgson. Oxford: Oxford University Press, 2006.

———. *Lectures on the Philosophy of Religion*. Vol. 1, *Introduction and the Concept of Religion*. Edited by Peter Hodgson. Oxford: Oxford University Press, 2008.

———. *Lectures on the Philosophy of Religion*. Vol. 3, *Introduction and the Concept of Religion*. Edited by Peter Hodgson. Oxford: Oxford University Press, 2008.

———. *Lectures on the Philosophy of World History*. Cambridge Studies in the History and Theory of Politics. Cambridge: Cambridge University Press, 1975.

———. *The Phenomenology of Spirit*. Translated by J. B. Baillie. N.p.: Digireads, 2012. Kindle ed.

———. "Philosophy of History." In *The Hegel Reader*, edited by Stephen Houlgate, 319–400. Oxford: Blackwell Publishers, 1998.

Heine, Heinrich. "Confessions." In *On the History of Religion and Philosophy in Germany and Other Writings: Cambridge Texts in the History of Philosophy*, edited by Terry Pinkard, 203–15. Cambridge: Cambridge University Press, 2007.

———. *On the History of Religion and Philosophy in Germany: Cambridge Texts in the History of Philosophy*. Edited by Terry Pinkard. Cambridge: Cambridge University Press, 2007.

Hendry, George. "The Transcendental Method in the Theology of Karl Barth." *The Scottish Journal of Theology* 37 (1984) 213–27.

Higgins, Kathleen, and Rober Solomon, eds. *Routledge History of Philosophy*. Vol. 6, *The Age of German Idealism*. London: Routledge, 1993.

Hodgson, Peter. "Georg Wilhelm Friedrich Hegel." In *Nineteenth-Century Religious Thought in the West*, edited by Ninian Smart et al., 81–123. Cambridge: Cambridge University Press, 1988.

———. *Hegel and Christian Theology: A Reading of the Lectures on the Philosophy of Religion*. Oxford: Oxford University Press, 2008.

Houlgate, Stephen. *Hegel's* Phenomenology of Spirit. Oxford: Bloomsbury Academic, 2012.

———. *An Introduction to Hegel: Freedom, Truth and History*. Oxford: Blackwell, 2005.

Houlgate, Stephen, ed. *The Hegel Reader*. Oxford: Blackwell, 1998.

Houlgate, Stephen, and Michael Baur, eds. *A Companion to Hegel*. Blackwell Companions to Philosophy. Hoboken: Wiley-Blackwell, 2011.

Hume, David. *Dialogues Concerning Natural Religion*. Hackett Classics. Hackett, 1980.

———. *Enquiry Concerning Human Understanding*. Edited by L. A. Selbt-Bigge. Oxford: Oxford University Press, 1963.

———. *The Essential Philosophical Works*. Introduction by Charlotte R. Brown and William Edward Morris. Wordsworth Classics of World Literature. Ware: Woodsworth Editions, 2011. Kindle ed.

———. "A Treatise of Human Nature." In *The Essential Philosophical Works of Hume*, edited by David Hume, 1–533. Wordsworth Classics of World Literature. Ware: Woodsworth Edition, 2011. Kindle ed.

Hyman, Gavin. "Atheism in Modern History." In *The Cambridge Companion to Atheism*, edited by Michael Martin, 27–46. Cambridge Companions to Philosophy, Religion and Culture. Cambridge: Cambridge University Press, 2007.

———. *A Short History of Atheism*. London: Tauris, 2010. Kindle ed.

Insole, Christopher. *The Intolerable God: Kant's Theological Journey*. Grand Rapids: Eerdmans, 2016.

———. *Kant and the Creation of Freedom: A Theological Problem*. Changing Paradigms in Historical and Systematic Theology. Oxford: Oxford University Press, 2016.

Jaeschke, Walter. *Reason in Religion: The Foundations of Hegel's Philosophy of Religion*. Oakland: University of California Press, 1992.

Kant, Immanuel. *Critique of the Power of Judgment*. The Cambridge Edition of the Works of Immanuel Kant. Cambridge: Cambridge University Press, 2002.

———. *Critique of Pure Reason*. The Cambridge Edition of the Works of Immanuel Kant. Edited and translated by Paul Guyer. Cambridge: Cambridge University Press, 1998.

———. *Critique of Practical Reason*. Translated and edited by Mary Gregor. Cambridge: Cambridge University Press, 1997.

———. *Dreams of a Spirit-Seer: Illustrated by Dreams of Metaphysics*. Whitefish, MT: Kessinger, 2010.

———. *Fundamental Principles of the Metaphysics of Morals*. Translated by Thomas Kingsmill Abott. CreateSpace, 2017. Kindle ed.

———. "Lectures on the Philosophical Doctrine of Religion." In *Religion and Rational Theology*, edited by Allen Wood, 341–405. Cambridge: Cambridge University Press, 1996.

———. *The One Possible Basis for a Demonstration of the Existence of God*. Translated and introduction by Treash Gordon. New York: Abaris, 1979.

———. *Prolegomena to Any Future Metaphysics that Will Be Able to Come Forward as Science*. Translated by Paul Carus. 2nd ed. Indianapolis: Hackett, 1977.

Keating, James, and Joseph White Thomas, eds. *Divine Impassibility and the Mystery of Human Suffering*. Grand Rapids: Eerdmans, 2009.

Kegley, Charles. *The Theology of Rudolf Bultmann*. New York: Harper & Row, 1966.

Küng, Hans. *Does God Exist?* Eugene, OR: Wipf & Stock, 2006.

Livingston, James C. *Modern Christian Thought*. Vol. 2, *The Twentieth Century*. Minneapolis: Fortress, 2006.

Locke, John. *An Essay Concerning Human Understanding*. Edited by Roger Woolhouse. London: Penguin, 1997.

Lowe, E. J. *Locke*. New York: Routledge, 2005.

Macquarrie, John. *Jesus Christ in Modern Thought*. London: SCM, 2010.

McCormack, Bruce. *Karl Barth's Critically Realistic Dialectical Theology*. Oxford: Oxford University Press, 1995.

———. *Orthodox and Modern: Studies in the Theology of Karl Barth*. Grand Rapids: Baker Academic, 2008.

McCormack, Bruce, and Clifford Anderson, eds. *Karl Barth and American Evangelicalism*. Grand Rapids: Eerdmans, 2011.

Michalson, Gordon. *Kant and the Problem of God*. Oxford: Wiley-Blackwell, 1999.

Moltmann, Jürgen. *A Broad Place: An Autobiography*. London: SCM, 2012.

———. *Theology of Hope*. London: SCM, 1967.

Mostert, Christian. *Wolfhart Pannenberg's Eschatological Doctrine of God*. Edinburgh: T. & T. Clark, 2002.

Neiman, Susan. *Evil in Modern Thought*. Princeton: Princeton University Press, 2015.

Nola, Robert. "The Young Hegelian Feuerbach, and Marx." In *Routledge History of Philosophy, Vol 6: The Age of German Idealism*, edited by Robert Solomon and Katherine Higgins, 290–330. London: Routledge, 1993.

Numbers, Ronald, ed. *Galileo Goes to Jail and Other Myths about Science and Religion*. Harvard: Harvard University Press, 2009.

Oakes, Kenneth. *Karl Barth on Theology and Philosophy*. London: Blackstone, 2012.

Oppy, Graham, and N. N. Trakakis, eds. *Nineteenth-Century Philosophy of Religion*. The History of Western Philosophy of Religion 4. Durham: Acumen, 2014.

Otto, Rudolf. *The Idea of the Holy*. Translated by John W. Harvey. Oxford: Oxford University Press, 1923.

Pannenberg, Wolfhart. *Basic Questions in Theology*. Vol. 1, *Collected Essays*. Minneapolis: Fortress, 1983.

———. *Basic Questions in Theology*. Vol 3, *Collected Essays*. Minneapolis: Fortress, 1983.

———. *Revelation as History: A Proposal for a More Open, Less Authoritarian View of an Important Theological Concept*. New York: Sheed & Ward, 1969.

———. *Systematic Theology*. 3 vols. Translated by Groffrey Bromiley. Edinburgh: T. & T. Clark, 1988.

Pasnau, Robert. *After Certainty: A History of Our Epistemic Ideals and Illusions*. Oxford: Oxford University Press, 2017.

———. "Divine Illumination." Stanford Encyclopedia of Philosophy. https://plato.stanford.edu/entries/illumination/.

Plantinga, Alvin. *Knowledge and Christian Belief*. Grand Rapids: Eerdmans, 2015. Kindle ed.

———. *Warranted Christian Belief.* Oxford: Oxford University Press, 2000.

Plato. "Republic." In *Plato: Complete Works*, edited by J. M. Cooper, 971–1223. Cambridge: Hackett, 1997.

———. *Plato: Complete Works.* Edited by J. M. Cooper. Cambridge: Hackett, 1997.

Powell, Samuel. *The Trinity in German Thought.* Cambridge: Cambridge University Press, 2009.

Rahner, Karl. *Theological Investigations.* Vol. 1, *God, Christ, Mary and Grace.* London: Helicon, 1961.

Schleiermacher, Friedrich. *The Christian Faith.* London: Bloomsbury T&T Clark, 2016.

———. *On Religion: Speeches to Its Cultured Despisers.* Translated by Terrence N. Tice. Louisville: John Knox, 1969.

Schneewind, J. B. "Autonomy, Obligation, and Virtue: An Overview of Kant's Moral Philosophy." In *The Cambridge Companion to Kant*, edited by Paul Guyer, 309–342. Cambridge: Cambridge University Press, 1992.

———. *The Invention of Autonomy: A History of Modern Moral Philosophy.* Cambridge: Cambridge University Press, 2010.

ShirleyFilms. "FREE WILL—Lawrence Krauss and Richard Dawkins." *YouTube*, Feburary 13, 2012. https://www.youtube.com/watch?v=anBxaOcZnGk.

Smart, Ninian, et al., eds. *Nineteenth-Century Religious Thought in the West.* Cambridge: Cambridge University Press, 1988.

Solomon, Robert. "Hegel's Phenomenology of Spirit." In *The Age of German Idealism: Routledge History of Philosophy*, edited by Kathleen Higgins and Robert Solomon, 6:181–215. London: Routledge, 1993.

Taylor, Charles. *Hegel.* Cambridge: Cambridge University Press, 1977.

Thielicke, Helmut. *Modern Faith and Thought.* Grand Rapids: Eerdmans, 1990.

Ward, Graham. "Barth, Modernity, and Postmodernity." In *The Cambridge Companion to Karl Barth*, edited by John Webster, 274–95. Cambridge: Cambridge University Press, 2000.

Ward, Keith. *The God Conclusion: God and the Western Philosophical Tradition.* London: Darton, Longman & Todd, 2009.

Webster, John. *The Cambridge Companion to Karl Barth.* Cambridge: Cambridge University Press, 2000.

Westerholm, Martin. "Kant's Critique and Contemporary Theological Inquiry." *Modern Theology* 31.3 (2015) 403–27.

———. *The Ordering of the Christian Mind: Karl Barth and Theological Rationality.* Oxford: Oxford University Press, 2015.

Williams, Thomas. *Reason and Faith: Philosophy in Middle Ages.* Course Guidebook. Chantilly: The Teaching Company, 2007.

Wolterstorff, Nicholas. "Is It Possible and Desirable for Theologians to Recover from Kant?" *Modern Theology* 14.1 (2002) 1–18.

———. *John Locke and the Ethics of Belief.* Cambridge Studies in Religion and Critical Thought. Cambridge: Cambridge University Press, 1996.

Wood, Allen W. *Kant.* Blackwell Great Minds 1. Oxford: Blackwell, 2005.

———. *Kant's Moral Religion.* Cornell: Cornell University Press, 1970.

———. *Kant's Rational Theology.* New York: Cornell University Press, 1978.

———. *Karl Marx.* Arguments of the Philosophers. London: Routledge, 2004.

———. “Rational Theology, Moral Faith and Religion.” In *The Cambridge Companion to Kant*, edited by Paul Guyer, 394–416. Cambridge: Cambridge University Press, 1992.

Wright, Tom. *The New Testament and the People of God*. Christian Origins and the Question of God 1. London: SPCK, 2013.

# INDEX OF NAMES

Made in the USA
Middletown, DE
26 May 2022